Effective Supply Management Performance

2nd edition

Linda L. Stanley, Ph.D.

Original Author:
Anna E. Flynn, Ph.D.

This publication is designed to provide accurate and authoritative information in regard to the subject matter covered. It is sold with the understanding that the publisher is not engaged in rendering legal, accounting or other professional service. If legal advice or other expert assistance is required, the services of a competent professional person should be sought.

Published by: Institute for Supply Management®, Inc.

Thomas Derry, Chief Executive Officer

©2014 Institute for Supply Management®, Inc.

2055 E. Centennial Circle, Tempe, AZ 85284

www.instituteforsupplymanagement.org

All rights reserved. No part of this publication may be reproduced, stored in a retrieval system or transmitted, in any form or by any means, electronic, mechanical, photo-copying, recording, or otherwise, without prior written permission of the publisher.

ISBN: 978-0-9960434-2-7

ISM — Your Source for Supply Management Resources

Institute for Supply Management, Inc.® (ISM®) has served the supply management profession since 1915. As the first and largest supply management institute in the world, ISM works with affiliated associations to continually keep its members well informed and trained on the latest trends and developments in the field. ISM's membership base includes more than 45,000 individual supply management professionals. A not-for-profit institute, ISM provides opportunities for the promotion of the profession and the expansion of professional skills and knowledge.

The information available from ISM is extensive. One of the greatest resources is the ISM website, www.ism.ws. In addition to general information, this expansive site features a vast database of supply management information, including a list of general supply management references as well as an extensive article database, listings of available products and seminars, periodicals, contact information for ISM affiliate organizations worldwide and links to other related websites. The *members only* online Career Center is a valuable resource for both individuals seeking jobs and organizations recruiting prospective employees.

The monthly Manufacturing and Non-Manufacturing *Report On Business*®, including the PMI® for the manufacturing survey and the NMI® for the non-manufacturing survey, continues to be one of the key economic indicators available today. ISM members receive this valuable report in the pages of *Inside Supply Management*® magazine. *Inside Supply Management*®, a monthly magazine (available to members only), is the authoritative resource for supply management executives, focusing on leadership strategies and trends.

ISM also publishes the *Journal of Supply Chain Management*, a one-of-a-kind publication for supply management scholars. Authored exclusively by highly recognized scholars in supply chain management, this quarterly subscription publication offers up-to-date research and thought-provoking studies.

Members also enjoy discounts on a wide variety of educational products and services, along with reduced enrollment fees for educational seminars and conferences.

For supply management professionals interested in a professional qualification, ISM administers the Certified Professional in Supply Management® (CPSM®) program. ISM members receive discounts on test preparation materials, study books, and materials and examination fees.

To provide a forum for educational enhancement and networking, ISM sponsors the Annual International Supply Management Conference. The annual conference, which attracts thousands of participants from around the world, provides a unique opportunity for members and nonmembers alike to learn from each other and share success strategies.

To learn more about ISM and the many ways it can help you advance your career, or to join online, visit ISM at www.instituteforsupplymanagement.org. To apply for membership by telephone, call ISM customer service at 800.888.6276 (United States and Canada only) or +1 480.752.6276, option 8.

ISM PROFESSIONAL SERIES

Foundation of Supply Management
Janet Hartley, Ph.D.

Original Authors:
Joseph R. Carter, DBA, CPSM, C.P.M.
Thomas Y. Choi, Ph.D.

Effective Supply Management Performance
Linda L. Stanley, Ph.D.

Original Authors:
Darin L. Matthews, CPPO, C.P.M.
Linda L. Stanley, Ph.D.

Leadership in Supply Management
Lisa M. Ellram, Ph.D., C.P.M., CMA

Original Author:
Anna E. Flynn, Ph.D.

Series Overview

In the past several decades, the supply management profession has matured. No longer looked at as just "purchasing" or "procurement," supply management is viewed today as an integrative process that spans many disciplines and activities, providing both internal and external linkages across the supply chain. Today, ISM defines supply management as:

> *The identification, acquisition, access, positioning and management of resources and related capabilities that an organization needs or potentially needs in the attainment of its strategic objectives.*
>
> *Supply management includes the following components: disposition/investment recovery, distribution, inventory control, logistics, materials management, operations, packaging, procurement/purchasing, product/service development, quality, receiving, strategic sourcing, transportation/traffic/shipping and warehousing/stores.*

This definition cuts across industry sectors, global economies, private and public organizations, and types of purchases. It covers the day-to-day issues faced by supply management professionals, the strategic issues that shape supply management's structure, and its influence in the organization.

In keeping with the spirit of the new, broader definition of supply management, the Institute for Supply Management® broadened the scope of its qualification to fit the latest demands on supply management professionals. This three-book series was designed to specifically address the issues of concern to supply management professionals today. These books help professionals better understand the potential scope and concerns within supply management. These books also are designed to support the updated Certified Professional in Supply Management® (CPSM®) examination and professional credentials.

The three books are organized around the three examinations of the CPSM as follows:

1. **Foundation of Supply Management**
2. **Effective Supply Management Performance**
3. **Leadership in Supply Management.**

These three books all support the strategic supply management concept across various industries, cultures and types of purchases. The strategic supply management concept is illustrated in Figure S-1, below.

On the far left of the figure is the vertical box, "Scope of Supply Management Strategy and Responsibility." This is the way the organization views the scope of supply management, and the way supply management views itself. It embodies the culture of the supply management organization as it works to support the objectives of the larger organization.

Figure S1: Strategic Supply Management Concept

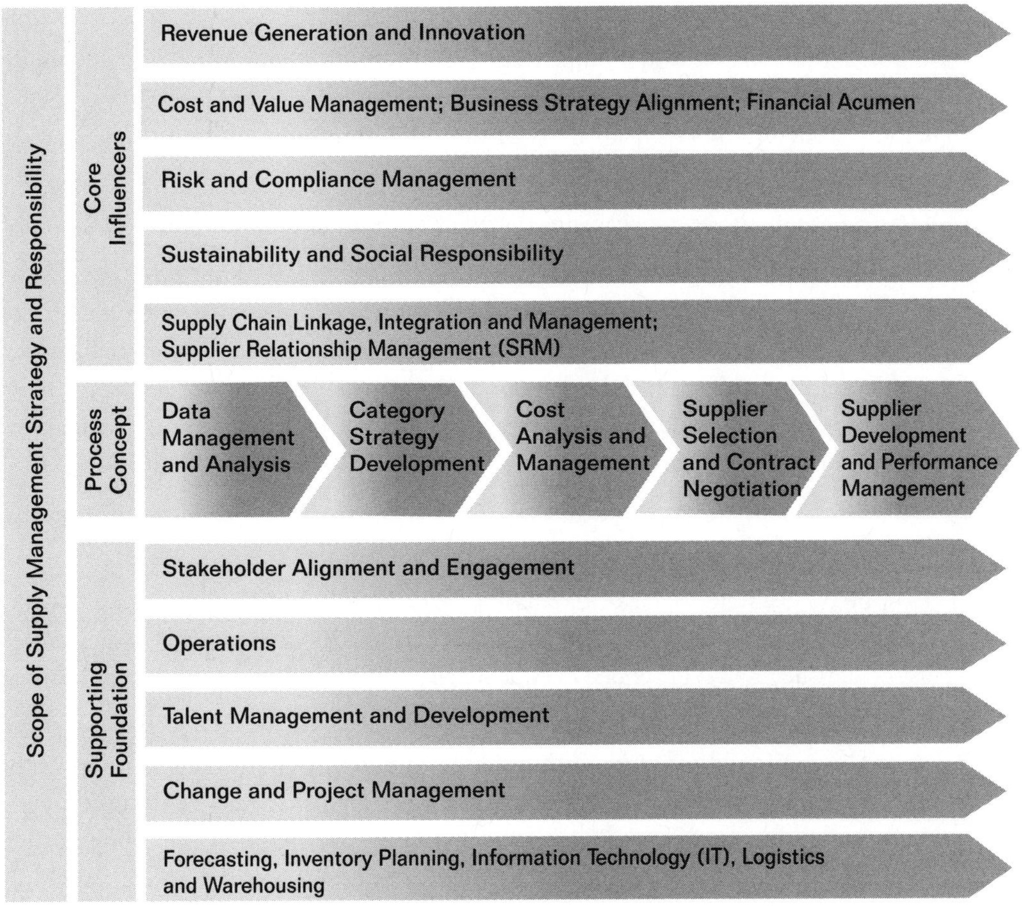

Scope of Supply Management Strategy and Responsibility

Core Influencers:
- Revenue Generation and Innovation
- Cost and Value Management; Business Strategy Alignment; Financial Acumen
- Risk and Compliance Management
- Sustainability and Social Responsibility
- Supply Chain Linkage, Integration and Management; Supplier Relationship Management (SRM)

Process Concept:
Data Management and Analysis → Category Strategy Development → Cost Analysis and Management → Supplier Selection and Contract Negotiation → Supplier Development and Performance Management

Supporting Foundation:
- Stakeholder Alignment and Engagement
- Operations
- Talent Management and Development
- Change and Project Management
- Forecasting, Inventory Planning, Information Technology (IT), Logistics and Warehousing

Near the top of the figure, immediately inside the "Supply Management Strategy and Philosophy" box, is "Core Influencers," which covers five categories of major issues that supply management professionals face today:

- Revenue Generation and Innovation
- Cost and Value Management; Business Strategy Alignment; Financial Acumen
- Risk and Compliance Management
- Sustainability and Social Responsibility
- Supply Chain Linkage, Integration and Management; Supplier Relationship Management (SRM).

Supply management professionals must consider all five of these major issues in their strategic decision-making. While supplier relationship management and cost management have long been recognized as important by most progressive organizations, these have been expanded upon, and additional influencers added — which have taken on new importance in recent years. Because of their overarching nature, these influencers are touched on in each of the three books in a variety of ways. More specifically, supply management professionals must ask the following questions:

1. How can we in supply management contribute to the organization's revenue generation and innovation strategies, directly supporting the organization's financial success?

2. How can we contribute to the organization's cost savings goals while retaining or increasing the value that purchased goods and services deliver to the organization and its customers? This must be done in such a way that it demonstrates supply management's understanding of the financial implications of its actions and its alignment with business unit strategy.

3. What risks might the organization face, and how can we plan, prepare for and manage these risks?

4. How do the decisions we make and the actions we take fit with the organization's social responsibility and sustainability objectives? This includes environmental issues as well as social issues, and is grounded in ethical behaviors that are part of an organization's culture.

5. How closely should we work with others in the supply chain? How should we be linked in terms of physical, financial and information flows? Related to this, how do we manage our supplier relationships and segment our suppliers according to their importance, potential contribution to innovation and success, and the potential supply chain risk they present?

Within supply management, some basic process steps must occur, as illustrated in the middle of the figure and labeled "Process Concept." Virtually all organizations have a model for the execution of the supply management process that includes all these activities, although they may be segmented into a different number of steps depending on the needs of the organization. The process begins with a thorough analysis of internal and external data to better understand the threats and opportunities in the internal and external environment. Next, specific strategies are developed for the particular purchase category — including services — and tactics for implementing those strategies are identified. Closely related to this, the organization engages in a cost analysis, looking for ways to better manage and reduce costs, and increase value. It then narrows down the choice of suppliers through data analysis (and bidding if appropriate), negotiates if appropriate and develops the contract. Finally, ongoing supplier measurement and management occurs, and may include supplier development efforts to improve supplier performance.

Finally, there is a "Supporting Foundation," a structure that the business and supply management organization should have in place to facilitate success. As shown at the bottom of the figure, a supply management professional must engage in the following activities:

1. Identify key stakeholders, then align with and engage stakeholders so supply management understands and supports their success — and also works with them as partners. Stakeholders can include internal customers, research and development, finance, marketing, and other areas that affect and are affected by supply management activities.
2. Work closely with operations. Operations is core to supply management performance, as supply management supplies operations with materials to meet its objectives.
3. Have an exceptional talent management and development program in place to attract the best people in the organization and offer the opportunity for both growth and advancement, creating an excellent system for managing and developing the organization's most valuable resource — its people.
4. Be skilled in change management and project management, as both are essential elements in the success of supply management initiatives.
5. Work closely with the people or groups in charge of forecasting, inventory planning, information technology (IT), logistics and warehousing, and seek alignment of objectives. These areas form the foundation for supply management decision-making and successful execution. IT provides the systems to link information quickly and accurately so supply management can successfully execute the strategic sourcing process.

These elements, integrating the internal business needs with external forces, become the foundation on which supply management builds success.

Volume 1, *Foundation of Supply Management,* deals with several of the more traditional areas of concern for supply management, yet looks at these issues from a leading-edge perspective. This volume covers the various sources of data and its analysis, budgeting, cost management — including cost/price analysis and total cost of ownership analysis, and leasing arrangements. This book also provides an in-depth view of sourcing, negotiating and contracting with suppliers, and the management of those contracts. Taken as a whole, these chapters provide an excellent perspective on the process steps associated with strategic sourcing. The final third of the book focuses on three of the overarching concerns of supply management: supplier relationship management; social and legal responsibility emphasizing supply management's role in sustainability; and international issues, including global sourcing, logistics and exchange rates, and countertrade issues. Volume 1 is a critical read for those who might be relatively new to supply management, those who have not had a formal education in supply management, and anyone who wants to stay abreast of the latest practices in supply management.

Volume 2, *Effective Supply Management Performance,* focuses on many of the operational issues that are part of a successful supply management performance. The latest surveys show that supply management professionals are responsible for a majority of the components of supply management; many of these are detailed in the definition of supply management provided previously. These are new areas of interaction for many supply management professionals. Volume 2 provides coverage of many operational issues such as project management, new product and service development, forecasting, warehousing, materials handling, logistics and international transportation, asset and inventory management, and quality. These all provide supporting structures for supply management. The book closes with an in-depth discussion of supplier performance management and metrics, information systems, and how technology can support the supply management professional in the integration of knowledge within and across organizations. This book is a must-read for anyone newly assigned to operations-oriented issues or who supervises or manages transportation, logistics or inventory management personnel as part of his or her supply management responsibilities.

Volume 3, *Leadership in Supply Management*, focuses on many of the human resources issues that supply management professionals face. The first half of the book explores management issues within the supply organization, such as managing and leading, developing shared values, setting direction, creating alignment and creating commitment for the supply organization's shared vision. The chapters cover various leadership styles, and details on developing strategies, aligning with internal and external stakeholders, team building and managing conflict. These are critical supporting structures for supply management. The second half of the book focuses on risk management and mitigation, and developing business plans exploring supply's role in mergers and acquisitions. These are linked to the strategic sourcing process, including outsourcing, developing and staffing the supply management organization, providing rewards and professional development for supply management, and executing the strategic sourcing process. This section includes a look at issues related to the overarching concerns of supply management, the process steps of supply management and the supporting structures. Taken as a whole, this volume covers talent management and human resources as well as strategic issues of management that all supply management functions face. The implementation of supply management processes as they relate to legal issues, both domestically and internationally, are reviewed. This book should be read by anyone who manages the supply management function or who is involved in the supply management strategy setting and planning process.

It has been a challenge for all those involved to capture the vast amount of material represented in these three volumes. The extensive practical and theoretical knowledge and expertise of the original authors, along with those who participated in this revision for 2014, will provide the reader with both a broad and deep perspective of the topics covered here. ISM hopes you find these books both interesting and valuable as you study for the updated CPSM® examination or simply work on enhancing your own knowledge of supply management.

Institute for Supply Management®

Preface

The role and importance of supply management probably has changed more in the past 20 years than in its entire history. This is due in great part to the desire of most organizations to become and remain competitive on a global scale. To attain that global competitiveness, the best organizations work to create a best-in-class supply management process that develops mutually beneficial relationships with suppliers, effectively manages inventories and logistics, and sets up a solid information and communication system that provides transparency among supply chain members. Quality management programs are commonly in place to continuously improve procurement practices and supplier quality, and best-in-class measurement systems are tied to an organization's strategy.

Globalization also has resulted in organizations placing an emphasis on outsourcing for the best quality, lowest cost materials and services that can be efficiently delivered — which can be a very tall order! Organizations today are also working to lower the total cost of ownership. In other words, all the costs associated with making the sourcing decision, the purchase itself and post-transaction expenses are being considered in supply management decisions. Lastly, many see the supply function as a means to remain competitive because its performance affects overall corporate performance. Together, these factors make the role of suppliers and the sourcing process itself very important to organizations and, as a result, senior executives view supply management as a strategic partner on the executive team. Supply management initiatives are being factored into the organizational strategy; thus, organizations need a more effective supply management group.

Supply management professionals are developing multiple initiatives to deal with the different types of challenges that take place. One trend was to reduce or optimize the supply base to manage the remaining suppliers more easily and create closer relationships. A related phenomenon has been an increase in single or dual sourcing with suppliers. Organizations also are bringing supply management professionals and suppliers into the new product or service design and development process as team members. Advances in information technology have enabled supply management professionals to integrate their knowledge internally and, with suppliers, streamline the supply management process and make transactional processes seamless and transparent. Thus, today's supply management professionals are able to perform their jobs more effectively, efficiently and at a higher level.

The primary purpose of this book is to provide a framework for achieving strong supply management performance through the supporting structures of the strategic supply management concept (see Figure P-1). Specifically, this book should help organizations become more operationally competitive. Figure P-1 identifies those chapters that cover the key tasks a supply management professional should fully understand to successfully pass the Certified Professional in Supply Management® (CPSM®) examinations.

Figure P1: Strategic Supply Management Concept

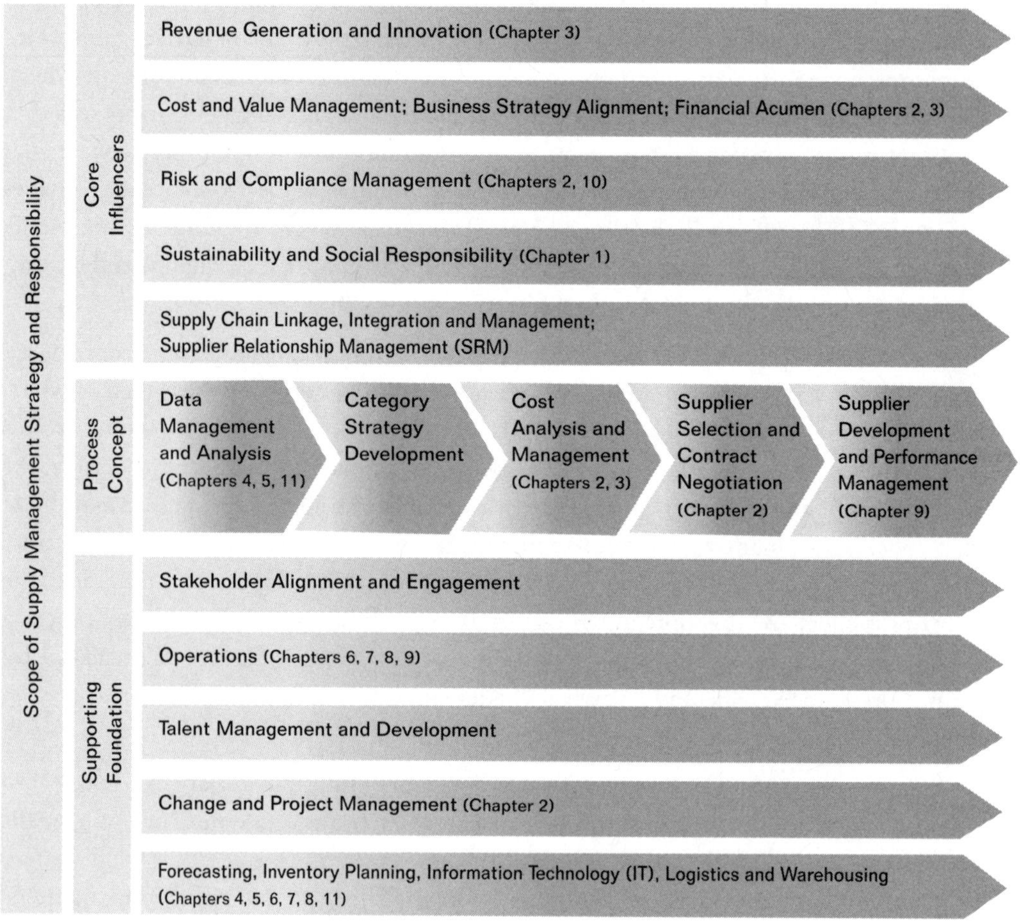

Scope of Supply Management Strategy and Responsibility

Core Influencers

- Revenue Generation and Innovation (Chapter 3)
- Cost and Value Management; Business Strategy Alignment; Financial Acumen (Chapters 2, 3)
- Risk and Compliance Management (Chapters 2, 10)
- Sustainability and Social Responsibility (Chapter 1)
- Supply Chain Linkage, Integration and Management; Supplier Relationship Management (SRM)

Process Concept

- Data Management and Analysis (Chapters 4, 5, 11)
- Category Strategy Development
- Cost Analysis and Management (Chapters 2, 3)
- Supplier Selection and Contract Negotiation (Chapter 2)
- Supplier Development and Performance Management (Chapter 9)

Supporting Foundation

- Stakeholder Alignment and Engagement
- Operations (Chapters 6, 7, 8, 9)
- Talent Management and Development
- Change and Project Management (Chapter 2)
- Forecasting, Inventory Planning, Information Technology (IT), Logistics and Warehousing (Chapters 4, 5, 6, 7, 8, 11)

About the Author

Linda Stanley, Ph.D. is a faculty associate of Supply Chain Management at Arizona State University and an adjunct professor of operations at Thunderbird, The American Graduate School of International Management. Since 1994 she has taught a wide range of courses including operations management, logistics, purchasing and supply chain management, negotiation and supplier management, and project management to MBA and Executive MBA students. Prior to her arrival at Thunderbird, she taught at Arizona State University — West Campus and Our Lady of the Lake University. Prior to entering academia, Dr. Stanley was a manager and auditor in the mortgage banking industry.

Dr. Stanley's research has focused on internal service quality, purchasing performance, and third-party logistics performance. She has published articles in several journals, including *Journal of Operations Management, Journal of Supply Chain Management,* and *Journal of Business Logistics*. She also has presented numerous papers at academic conferences, including Decision Sciences Institute, Production and Operations Management Society, and Academy of Management. She has coauthored several books including *Process Management: Creating Value along the Supply Chain, Transportation and Logistics Management,* and *Effective Supply Management Performance*. Her latest book, *Designing, Developing and Delivering Quality RFPs in the Public Sector*, is in development.

Dr. Stanley holds BS and Ph.D. degrees from Arizona State University and a BA from California State University, Sacramento.

Original Series Authors

Linda Stanley, Ph.D.

Darin Matthews currently serves as director of contracting and procurement for Portland State University. He is a past president of the Oregon Public Purchasing Association and a former board member of NAPM — Willamette Valley. Darin speaks throughout the world on a variety of procurement topics. His books include *Warehousing and Inventory Control, Logistics and Transportation,* and *Effective Supply Management Performance*. He has lectured at numerous universities throughout North America and serves on the faculty of Portland State University, School of Business Administration.

Darin is a Certified Public Procurement Officer (CPPO) and a Certified Purchasing Manager (C.P.M.). He holds a Bachelor's degree in Business/Political Science and a Master's degree in Acquisition Management.

Contents

Chapter 1: Supply Management Defined
Definitions 2
Historical Background 3
The Importance of Supply Management 6
    Return on Investment 6
    Profit Impact and Return on Assets 7
    A Source of Information 8
    Meeting Strategic Objectives 8
    Creating Goodwill 8
Making Supply Management Decisions 10
    Decision Tree Analysis 10
    Two-by-Two Portfolio Matrix 12
A Process View 13
Process Improvement Methods 16
    Six Sigma 16
    Lean Operations 17
Process Improvement Metrics 19
Summary 21
    Key Points 21

Chapter 2: Project Management
Defining Projects 24
Project Life Cycle 25
The Project Organization 28
    Functional Structure 29
    Projectized Structure 29
    Matrix Organization 30
Project Initiation 31
    Define the Problem 31
    Kepner-Tregoe Rational Process Analysis 34
    Cause-and-Effect Analysis 36
    Pareto Analysis 37
    Option Assessment or Alternative Analysis 37
    Stakeholder Analysis 42
    Project Approval 42
    Project Charter 43
Project Planning 45
    The Project Schedule 46
    Project Budget 48

Risk Management	50
Resource Requirements Planning	51
Supply Management's Role in Project Planning	52
Statement of Work Documentation	53
Statement of Work (SOW)	54
Project Execution	54
Requesting Sellers' Responses	55
Supplier Selection	57
Team Management	57
Change Management	58
Project Monitoring and Control	59
Contract Administration	59
Change Control	60
Project Performance Evaluation	60
Project Performance Reporting	63
Milestone Reviews	63
Project Closure	64
Contract Closure Process	64
Performance Evaluation	64
Summary	65
Key Points	65

Chapter 3: Product and Service Development

New Product and Service Development Process	68
Step 1. Generate and Screen New Product and Service Ideas	69
Step 2. Obtain Concept Approval	70
Step 3. Develop Product/Service Concept	72
Step 4. Validate and Test Products and Services	73
Step 5. Commercialize Product	73
Inputs to the Product and Service Development Process	74
Market Analysis	75
Production and Staff Capabilities	77
Logistics and Distribution Capabilities	79
Supplier Capability and Capacity Analysis	81
Supply Management's Role in Product and Service Design	83
Research and Development	85
Target Costing	86
Product Sustainability Evaluation	89
Summary	90
Key Points	90

Chapter 4: Foundations of Forecasting Practices

General Issues in Economics 94
    A Market Economy 95
    Closed Economies and Mixed Economies 95
The Global Economy 95
    Local Buying Preferences 96
    Risk Factors in the Geopolitical Climate 97
    Cultural Differences 98
    Exchange Rates and Currency Risk 99
    Import/Export Issues 100
Business Cycles 101
Economic Indicators 101
    Leading, Lagging and Coincident Indicators 102
    Implicit Price Deflator 106
    Custom Indexes 107
    Balance of Merchandise Trade 107
    Balance of Payments 108
Sources of Data Used in Forecasting 108
    ISM *Report On Business*® — Manufacturing and Non-Manufacturing 108
    U. S. Government Publications 112
    International Publications 113
    Private Publications 114
    Commercial Forecasts 114
    Regional Surveys 115
    Internal Historical Data 115
    Industry Sources 115
    Online Indexes and Search Engines 115
Using the Data 116
Summary 117
    Key Points 117

Chapter 5: Forecasting Models and Methods

Why Forecast? 120
    To Estimate Demand 120
    To Determine If Supply Can Meet Demand 121
    To Predict Technology Trends 121
    To Predict Prices 122
    To Predict Dependent Demand 122
    To Estimate the Supply Management Budget 125
Factors That Affect Demand Forecasts 125
    Lead Time 126
    Labor Markets 126

Material Shortages	127
Shifts in Technology	127
Weather Conditions	127
Demand Forecasting Process	128
Length of Forecast	129
Top-Down and Bottom-Up Forecasting	130
Qualitative Forecasts	132
Sales Force Composite	133
Market Research	133
Jury of Executive Opinion	134
The Delphi Method	134
Time Series Forecasting	135
Naive Approach	136
Moving Averages	136
Exponential Smoothing	138
Forecasting Seasonality	142
Forecasting a Trend	144
Simultaneously Considering Trends and Seasonal Patterns	149
Box-Jenkins Method	150
The Single-Period Model	151
Causal Modeling	154
Least Squares Regression Models	154
Forecast Accuracy	156
Tracking Signal	158
Managing Forecast Data With Suppliers	160
Overcoming Difficulties	162
Summary	162
Key Points	163

Chapter 6: Warehouse Management and Materials Handling

Warehousing Basics	166
Types of Warehouses	166
Distribution Center Versus Warehouse	167
Warehouse Location	168
Financial Considerations	168
Environmental Considerations	170
Governmental Considerations	170
Political Considerations	171
Warehouse and Materials Handling Design Factors	171
Facility Design	171
Space Requirements	173
Fluctuations in Warehouse Space Required	174

Materials Handling Equipment Requirements	174
Implementation	181
Warehouse Trends	182
Summary	184
Key Points	184

Chapter 7: Logistics Management and International Transportation

History of Logistics	189
Transportation Modes and Roles	189
Modes of Transportation	189
Trade-Offs Among Modes	191
Roles of Third-Party Providers	192
International Transportation Issues	193
Global Logistics	193
Trends in Global Logistics	194
Global Third Parties	195
Import and Export Documentation	196
International Commercial Terms (Incoterms®)	196
Security Considerations	200
Transportation Policies and Procedures	201
Transportation Restrictions	201
Freight Classifications and Rates	202
Freight Terms	202
Resolving Delivery Problems	203
Delivery Tracking and Tracing Systems	203
Visible Versus Latent Damage	203
Freight Claims	204
Resolution Process	204
Freight Bill Auditing	205
Carrier Performance Auditing	206
Logistics Performance Measures and Strategies	206
Logistics Metrics	206
Caterpillar Inc.	207
Logistics As a Profit Center	207
Productivity Reports	208
Using Scorecards	209
Summary	209
Key Points	210
Appendix: Transportation Terminology	211

Chapter 8: Asset and Inventory Management

Assets Defined 214
Asset Management 216
    Effective Asset Management Programs 217
    Asset Recovery 218
Importance of Inventory Management 219
Classifying Inventory 220
    ABC Classification 220
    Inventory Accuracy and Integrity 222
    Tracking Issues and Returns 222
    Verifying Inventory Levels 223
    Reconciliation 224
    Measuring Accuracy 225
Inventory Policies and Procedures 225
    Inventory Valuation 226
Replenishment and Priority Tools 227
    Inventory Holding Costs 227
    Inventory Ordering Costs 228
    Determining the Order Size 228
    Variable Order Systems 230
    Safety Stock 230
    Inventory Control Systems 231
Trends in Inventory Replenishment 232
    Inventory Consolidation 232
    Just-in-Time Inventory Management 233
    Inventory Scheduling 233
    Supplier-Managed Inventory 234
Inventory Disposition 235
    Investment Recovery Principles 236
    Surplus Material Categories 237
    Disposal Marketplace 238
    Disposition Methods 239
    Equipment Lending 241
    Value Stream Mapping 241
Summary 242
    Key Points 242

Chapter 9: Quality in Supply Management

Defining Quality and Its Role in Supply Management 244
    Supply Management's Role in Quality Assurance 244
    Quality Models 246
    Six Sigma 246
    Standardization Programs 248

    International Organization for Standardization (ISO) 250
    Other Standards Organizations 252
Quality Tools 253
    Plan-Do-Check-Act Cycle 253
    Histograms 254
    Pareto Analysis 254
    Fishbone Diagram 256
    Run Charts 256
    Statistical Process Control 258
    Capability Indexes 258
Improving Supply Management Performance 260
    Capability Maturity Model Integrated 262
    Contract Management Maturity Model® 263
Measuring and Evaluating Supplier Performance 264
    Improving Supplier Performance 265
    Focus Groups 265
    Gauge Internal Requirements 266
    Developing Supplier Measures 269
    Supplier Audits 271
    Effect of Legal Requirements 272
    Supplier Selection Factors 272
    Service Level Agreements 274
    Minimizing Risk of Counterfeit Components 278
Summary 279
    Key Points 279

Chapter 10: Performance Evaluation

Overview 282
    What to Measure 283
    Interrelation of Measurements 285
    Measurement Creation 285
    Results Evaluation 286
    Key Performance Indicators 286
    Performance Management Systems 288
    Corrective Action Processes 290
Supply Management Audits 290
    Compliance with Current Policies 294
Evaluation of Employees 296
    Determining Appraisal Factors 298
    Conducting Interviews 298
    Staff Development 299
Summary 301
    Key Points 301

Chapter 11: Knowledge Integration

Definitions 304
Information Technology Systems 306
      Other Considerations 309
      Materials Resource Plan 310
      Enterprise Resource Planning 310
      From ERP to ERP Cloud 314
      ERP and Implementation Considerations 314
Technology Trends in Supply Management 315
Summary 316
      Key Points 317

Endnotes 319

References 345

Index 353

CHAPTER

1

Supply Management Defined

This chapter provides the foundation for the remainder of the book, beginning with some supply management definitions and a discussion of the historical foundation of supply management. Next, the importance of supply management is discussed. Leading edge process improvement methods that are being used today and supply management's role are then described. Lastly, the measurement of process performance, which is key to continuous improvement and attaining organizational objectives, is discussed.

Chapter Objectives
- Define the field of supply management.
- Provide a historical background of supply management.
- Describe the benefits of a high-performing supply management organization.
- Explain the value of risk analysis.
- Describe the importance of a process view.

Definitions

Although the field of supply management has evolved significantly, no universally accepted or used descriptor exists. Rather, organizations vary in their use of titles to describe the supply management field, including purchasing, procurement, materials management and materiel. However, some distinctions are apparent and, in reality, these other terms are really subcomponents of supply management. The following definitions from the ISM *Glossary of Key Supply Management Terms* (2014) should help the reader delineate among the terms.

Purchasing is "a major function of an organization that is responsible for acquisition of required materials, services and equipment," while *procurement* is broader — an "organizational function that includes specifications development, value analysis, supplier market research, negotiation, buying activities, contract administration, inventory control, traffic, receiving and stores." *Materials management* is broader still because it extends beyond the actual purchase and is defined as "a managerial and organizational approach used to integrate the supply management functions in an organization. It involves the planning, acquisition, flow and distribution of production materials from the raw material state to the finished product state. Activities include procurement, inventory management, receiving, stores and warehousing, in-plant materials handling, production planning and control, traffic, and surplus and salvage. In spite of a slight difference in meaning, this term is often used interchangeable with 'supply management.'" *Materiel* is a military and government term that generally includes the same activities as materials management. More on materials management can be found in Chapter 6.

Historically, the use of the word *supply* in North America referred to the storing or warehousing of materials and supplies for internal usage. Others including government agencies, the United Kingdom and Europe, however, have interpreted the use of the word *supply* in a broader context to encompass purchasing, storing and receiving materials and supplies. In 2002, the National Association of Purchasing Management changed its name to Institute for Supply Management® (ISM®) to incorporate that broader meaning, and has defined *supply management* as "the identification, acquisition, access, positioning and management of resources and related capabilities the organization needs or potentially needs in the attainment of its strategic objectives." The components of supply management are listed below:

- Disposition/investment recovery;
- Distribution;
- Inventory control;
- Logistics;
- Materials management;
- Operations;
- Packaging;
- Procurement/purchasing;

- Product/service development;
- Quality;
- Receiving;
- Strategic sourcing;
- Transportation/traffic/shipping; and
- Warehousing/stores.

This text covers these multiple components of supply management. For example, the subject of product/service development is discussed in Chapter 3; materials management is covered in Chapter 6; transportation/traffic/shipping, receiving, warehousing, distribution, inventory control and asset recovery in Chapters 7 and 8; and quality in Chapter 9. To identify sources of supply, supply management professionals also must be involved in some forms of forecasting. Thus, the importance and role of forecasting to supply professionals is found in Chapters 4 and 5. In addition, supply management professionals act in a boundary-spanning position, meeting the needs of internal users and end customers through their interactions with external suppliers. Thus, knowledge integration through information technology is important; further discussion can be found in Chapter 11.

Lastly, supply chain management is defined as "the design and management of seamless, value-added processes across organizational boundaries to meet the real needs of the end customer. The development and integration of people and technological resources are critical to successful supply chain integration" (ISM *Glossary* 2014). Supply chain management involves the multiple stakeholders, including supply management, that are involved in planning and executing the delivery of an organization's products and services to the end customer.

Historical Background

The interest in supply management really developed in the latter part of the twentieth century, although the U.S. railroads realized the importance of the function as early as the mid-1800s. A railroad executive actually authored the first handbook on purchasing — *The Handling of Railway Supplies: Their Purchase and Distribution* — in 1887. By 1915, several other books and articles on purchasing were written. However, purchasing was still viewed primarily as a tactical activity. During World War I and World War II, the status of purchasing actually increased because effectively buying the materials and services needed to run the factories was essential to organizational success. Following World War II, and into the 1960s, the processes to make purchases continued to be refined, and more people were hired and trained. Thus, the decision-making process improved. More organizations improved the status of purchasing, and a chief purchasing officer could hold the title of vice president of purchasing or purchasing director, among others.

In the early 1970s, organizations were facing a global shortage of most basic raw materials required for operations, with accompanying price and interest rate increases beyond what had been experienced after World War II. OPEC's oil embargo in 1973 resulted in additional shortages and price increases. At the same time, countries were working to ease trade restrictions, which opened up world trade but also increased competition. Organizations began outsourcing materials and parts from countries with lower cost structures to gain a competitive advantage. Thus, throughout the 1970s and 1980s, the focus again was on purchasing, which could spell the difference between successful organization performance or dismal failure.

Beginning in the 1980s, the purchase of services was increasingly taken over by supply management. In the past, buying services was often left to other functions to handle, but changed in part because of the impact of downsizing and the willingness of other functions to give up noncore activities. Purchasing was also found to be best positioned within an organization to take over the responsibility based on its expertise in cost reduction.

Early in the 1990s, purchasing also became more integrated into corporate strategy as organizations faced greater domestic and global competition. Senior executives realized that cost control, improved quality and supplier services could be attained through a stronger purchasing group. Some organizations have since changed the functional name to purchasing and supply management, or simply supply management, to reflect a more process-oriented, strategic focus.

The American Red Cross, led by vice president and chief procurement officer, Jill Bossi, revamped its supply management organization beginning in 2009. The transactional procurement team, contract administration and the technical team were unified into one supply management group. This "center-led hybrid" group supports two main divisions of the organization. The change has helped create synergies between supply management and the business units, where they both see value in the relationship. A just-in-time approach is used to support The Red Cross's Disaster Services division so the organization can quickly identify, source and contract with suppliers to provide shelter and food when a disaster occurs. Local chapters, the first responders to a disaster, take advantage of national contracts to provide ready-to-eat meals, blankets and other services.[1]

In the twenty-first century, supply management is increasingly becoming more integrated with its network of suppliers through the advances in information technology. Organizations are using commodity teams, category management and cross-functional teams to make purchases, and supply management professionals are incorporating e-commerce options and networking solutions into their daily operations. Outsourcing is commonplace, and supply management professionals have moved away from simply a reactive approach to buying to an increasingly integrative strategy as they gain experience in the complexities of sourcing from international suppliers. In the twenty-first century senior executives have come to expect the role of supply management to lead innovation and transformation initiatives; positively impact top line revenue growth; effectively manage risk; and engage industry, business and suppliers in new unique ways to add value to the organization. A great deal of change is occurring in the profession, more in the past ten years than in any other period in history. Traditional entry-level positions are disappearing as companies search for cheaper labor in other markets (for example, labor arbitrage) due to outsourcing and offshoring. Software applications also handle many of the repetitive processes once done by people. Supply management organizations are threatened by specialty companies that now provide strategic sourcing as a core competency. Into the future, organizations will need supply management professionals who are strategic thinkers and contributors with excellent communication skills. Leaders will also need to be agile and adaptable.[2] Thus, supply management has been integrated to a greater extent into an organization's strategic planning process than ever before.

In a 2011 CAPS Research study, the following megatrends are expected to impact supply or value chain strategies in the next decade:
- Increasing availability and price pressures on basic materials and commodities;
- Increasing risk in globally extended supply/value chains;
- Intensifying global competition;
- Changing population/workforce demographics;
- Increasing demand for "green" products and services;
- Shifting economics of information and knowledge;
- Changing geopolitical landscape;
- Changing technology landscape;
- Increasing customer value expectations;
- Increasing political/social unrest; and
- Growing stakeholder demands on business.[3]

As a result of the megatrends, there are some critical supply challenges and strategies that organizations will be implementing, developing and executing over the next five years:
- Value-focused purchasing and supply — includes complexity, linkages to business strategy and end customer priorities, supply market changes and reliance on supply markets for value creation.
- Innovation — includes decreased product life cycles, innovation from multiple sources, new technologies, demand for complex products, reverse innovation, research and development budget restrictions, need for supplier collaboration and strong relationships with strategic suppliers.
- "Green" supply — includes from an operational perspective reducing costs and creating "green" benefits such as reduced energy and water usage, reduction in greenhouse gases and other emissions, and reduction in landfill. From a product perspective, must be good for the consumer and the world, must be neutral or good for the organization's bottom line, total life cycle assessment should be considered and varied consumer demand must exist.
- Extended global supply networks — includes market segmentation, complex logistics, insourcing/outsourcing balance, and global versus local versus regional supply strategy.

- Supply chain analytics — includes differences between descriptive versus predictive analytics, lack of understanding on how best to use analytics, lack of time to implement and lack of available skill, inability to get data, and lack of executive sponsorship.
- Metrics and measurement systems — includes disagreement over metric definitions and interpretation, fragmented databases, timeliness of data, consistent calculation of metrics; and need to measure internal and external total costs, measure supply chain total costs, and provide executives with valid and trackable measures of supply chains contributions.
- Talent management — includes "baby boomers" reaching retirement age, different job and career aspirations for "millennials," finding talent in developing economies, and providing training and development for all economies.
- Transformation and business strategy alignment — includes limited linkages to business and customer strategies, company and supply culture limiting change, measurement systems, price as the only focus, and inadequate resources in both capabilities and capacity.[4]

In terms of technological advances, the use of software as a service (SaaS) solutions to support supply management's operations has become more prevalent. However, transactional systems are also important and in use. For example, in the past the retail industry relied on stand-alone inventory management systems. Today these systems have been integrated into an enterprise resource system (ERP), allowing an organization to automatically calculate inventory reorder points and preferred stocking levels, and create purchase orders.

The billing process is software-supported, and orders are transmitted via the Internet — which interfaces with an enterprise resource system. More on knowledge integration can be found in Chapter 11.

The Importance of Supply Management

Several quantifiable benefits are attributed to high-performing supply management organizations, including lower operating costs, improved return on investment (ROI) and return on assets (ROA), and a direct positive impact to the bottom line. However, there are also other less tangible benefits. Some of these tangible and intangible benefits are discussed further in the following sections.

Return on Investment

A *return on investment* is defined as "the ratio of annual operating income to the total capital invested in the business" (ISM *Glossary* 2014), and has been applied specifically to supply management. A 2010 in-depth study of procurement practices conducted by CIPSA and The Hackett Group found that best-in-class supply management operations were able to produce a return on investment of 176 percent higher within their supply organizations than their peer group. Best-in-class organizations also were spending significantly less on total supply costs than their peers and allocating more staff to high-value activities.[5]

Profit Impact and Return on Assets

Return on assets is defined by the ISM *Glossary* (2014) as "a profitability ratio used to measure how hard the assets of an organization are working. ROA is calculated by dividing the net income by total assets." Reducing purchasing costs by 5 percent, for example, improves profitability by 2.5 percent and increases ROA by 5.225 percent. The following provides an example, illustrating the benefit of lowering purchasing costs.

The calculation of return on assets requires three steps:

1. Calculate investment turnover by dividing sales by total assets. In this example, investment turnover improves if inventory can be reduced by 5 percent.

	2013 (in US$)	Investment Turns	Less 5%	2014 (in US$)	Investment Turns
Sales	$1,300,000			$1,300,000	
Inventory	$ 200,000		$10,000	$ 190,000	
Total Assets	$ 650,000	2.0*	$10,000	$ 640,000	2.03

*$1,300,000/$650,000 = 2.0

2. Calculate the profit margin by dividing profit by sales. Because purchasing costs were reduced by 5 percent, profit margin in 2014 improved by 2.5 percent.

	2013 (in US$)	Profit Margin	2014 (in US$)	Profit Margin
Sales	$1,300,000		$1,300,000	
Total Costs	$1,235,000*		$1,202,500***	
Profit	$ 65,000**	5%	$ 97,500	7.5%

*Total costs include purchasing costs which account for 50 percent of sales, or US$650,000.
**US$65,000/US$1,300,000 = .05 × 100 = 5%
***Total costs = US$1,235,000 − (US$650,000 × 5%) = US$1,202,500

3. The return on assets then is calculated using the investment turnover and profit margin calculations. In 2014, the ROA improved by more than 5 percent.

	2013	2014
Investment Turnover	2.0	2.03
Profit Margin	5%	7.5%
ROA	2.0 × 5% = 10%	2.03 × 7.5% = 15.225%

A Source of Information

Supply management provides valuable information to others within an organization because of its heavy contact with market information sources such as suppliers, external research reports and trade shows. The availability of goods and services, new sources of supply, replacement parts and emerging technologies are important to those in production and operations, marketing and new product design, among others.

Meeting Strategic Objectives

The supply management department's performance is a key element to the success of an organization in terms of its contribution to the strategic objectives. A significant percentage of sales revenue is spent with suppliers — generally ranging anywhere from 30 percent to 70 percent. Any improvement in supply management's effectiveness in terms of reducing the cost of materials, ensuring suppliers meet delivery and quality specifications for incoming products and services, or improving the internal operating efficiency of the supply management function can translate to improved organizational performance.

Creating Goodwill

Any actions taken by supply management personnel with suppliers reflect on the public image of an organization. Thus, conducting business in a professional and socially responsible manner with suppliers should generate a positive reputation and an ability to attract new and better suppliers. ISM has published the *Principles of Sustainability and Social Responsibility* that covers 10 areas including ethics and business conduct (see Figure 1-1 for a synopsis).[6] Supply management organizations, for instance, can incorporate specific and measurable practices across the supply chain by (1) supporting sustainability and social responsibility principles and initiatives; (2) committing resources to support sustainability and social responsibility principles, practices and education; (3) building and integrating programs throughout the organization and cascading them throughout the supply chain; (4) engaging and involving executive management to ensure sustainability and social responsibility initiatives are integral to the culture and decision-making of the organization; (5) ensuring the sharing of strategies, policies, procedures, best practices and other relevant material to assist organizations working to improve sustainability and social responsibility behavior internally and with suppliers; (6) encouraging building and integrating a program throughout the organization and the supply chain; and (7) making enlightened business decisions that often move beyond the "letter of the law."

Figure 1-1: ISM *Principles of Sustainability and Social Responsibility*

Anti-Corruption
Corruption in all its forms, including extortion and bribery, will not be tolerated.

Diversity and Inclusiveness — Workforce and Supply Base
Workforce. Workforce diversity and inclusiveness is the attraction and retention of a workforce that reasonably represents the customer and communities in which the organization operates.
Supply Base. Attraction and retention of a diverse supply base is the responsibility of each supply professional.

Environment
Supply management promotes protection, preservation and vitality of the natural environment.

Ethics and Business Conduct
Every supply management professional is responsible for behaving ethically and actively promoting ethical conduct throughout the supply chain.

Financial Integrity and Transparency
Financially responsible supply management is characterized by integrity and transparency in all supply-related dealings and decisions.

Global Citizenship
Global citizenship is the ethical and moral obligation to act for the benefit of society locally, globally and virtually.

Health and Safety
Health and safety is the condition of being protected or free from the occurrence of risk of injury, danger, failure, error, accident, harm and loss of life.

Human Rights
Human beings have universal and natural rights and status regardless of legal jurisdiction and local factors.

Labor Rights
Supply management is committed to protecting and respecting labor rights globally.

Sustainability
Sustainability is the ability to meet current needs without hindering the ability to meet the needs of future generations in terms of economic, environmental and social challenges.

Source: Institute for Supply Management®, ISM *Principles of Sustainability and Social Responsibility with a Guide to Adoption and Implementation,* 2012, Tempe, AZ.

Making Supply Management Decisions

As evidenced by the previous discussion, supply management is multifaceted and faces many complex decisions in its daily operations. One of the most common questions that must be addressed is whether an item or service should be made in-house or outsourced — the classic *make-or-buy* or *insource/outsource* decision. If the item or service will be outsourced, suppliers must be evaluated and selected. Furthermore, another decision is whether to source from one, two or multiple suppliers (if there is a choice). The methods to use to negotiate prices, deciding whether contracts will be short-term or long-term, and other issues related to the purchase of those goods and services will require additional decision-making as well. For example, supply management professionals might use reverse auctions to purchase commodity parts but carry on lengthy negotiations to buy more strategic services such as healthcare coverage for employees. They also must select transportation modes and carriers, determine when deliveries of materials should be taken and where inventory will be stored (with the supplier, or in public or company-owned warehouses). The process of making these decisions is known as *risk analysis*, which is "the process of identifying elements or factors, and their probability of occurrence that could lead to injury, damage, loss or failure," according to the ISM *Glossary* (2014). Two forms of risk analysis include *decision tree analysis* and the *two-by-two portfolio matrix*. Both are discussed in more detail in the next section.

Decision Tree Analysis

The *decision tree* is one means to help supply professionals make interdependent decisions under uncertain conditions. A *decision tree* is "a decision-making tool that maps alternative courses of action and their consequences. Its components include decision forks, outcome forks, outcome probabilities, outcome rewards and expected values" (ISM *Glossary* 2014). Decision trees are useful because they give some structure to decision-making and provide a more objective way of analyzing the alternatives. Software packages are available to build decision trees, which makes the process relatively easy.

The diagram is read from left to right; to make the evaluation, however, the diagram values are calculated beginning on the right side. The alternative with the highest value is selected. For example, a decision tree as shown in Figure 1-2 might be used to make the choice between two different suppliers.

Figure 1-2: Decision Tree Analysis (in US$)

The new product design team at the Jones Company has developed a new product requiring a new part not used in other existing products. The supply professional does some research and has narrowed the selection of a supplier for a new part down to the top two. She uses decision tree analysis to help her choose between the two suppliers based on expected cost, beginning with an estimation of the possible demand for the part and the expected price/unit (based on demand).

ALTERNATIVE	DEMAND	PRICE/UNIT	TOTAL COST
Supplier 1			
Strong demand	150,000	$50	$7,500,000
Medium demand	100,000	$60	$6,000,000
Modest demand	50,000	$75	$3,750,000
Supplier 2			
Strong demand	150,000	$45	$6,750,000
Medium demand	100,000	$55	$5,500,000
Modest demand	50,000	$80	$4,000,000

The owner then creates a decision tree. The value shown under each decision is the dollar amount the Jones Company should expect to spend, using probability analysis.

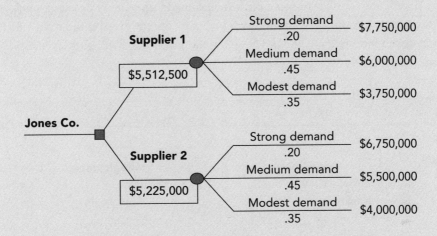

The calculations are shown in the following table:

ALTERNATIVE	CALCULATION	RESULT
Supplier 1	$7,500,000 x 0.20 + $6,000,000 x 0.45 + $3,750,000 x 0.35	$5,512,500
Supplier 2	$6,750,000 x 0.20 + $5,500,000 x 0.45 + $4,000,000 x 0.35	$5,225,000

Although Supplier 2's price/unit for 50,000 is higher than Supplier 1's, the expected cost still is lower, making Supplier 2 the preferred supplier. Other factors, of course, would be considered, including quality and delivery.

Two-by-Two Portfolio Matrix

While supply management has become more strategic, all purchases cannot simply be lumped into one category; thus, strategies must be tailored to the type of buy. Peter Kraljic, Director Emeritus at McKinsey, developed a two-by-two portfolio matrix to help supply management personnel develop an appropriate sourcing strategy for items purchased, based on profit impact (low to high) and supply risk (low to high).[7] As shown in Figure 1-3, items under review are classified in one of four risk categories: (1) *noncritical items*, (2) *leveraged items*, (3) *bottleneck items*, or (4) *strategic items*. Noncritical items are considered low-value, commodity-like because they can be easily standardized, are highly substitutable and are purchased using simple contracts or procurement cards (which are multipurpose bank cards with predetermined organization-set policies and procedures that eliminate the traditional requisition/purchase order process). The University of California has used p-cards since the late 1990s with success. The university estimates it saves between US$50 and $75 per transaction, which can add up quickly based on more than 768,000 transactions. In 2009 alone, the university system saved more than US$39.4 million, received incentive income of US$6.3 million from the bank and saved money in administrative costs.[8]

Figure 1-3: Kraljic's Two-by-Two Matrix

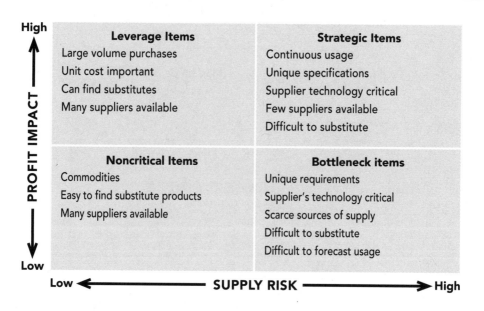

Source: Adapted from Peter Kraljic, "Purchasing Must Become Supply Management," *Harvard Business Review* 61(5), 109–117.

Some examples of leveraged commodities are injection moldings, metals, stampings, resins, insurance benefits, travel, telephones, car fleets and temporary employment organizations. Relationships with suppliers of leveraged goods and services will, in most cases, be arm's length, unless the supply management professional has created a short-term preferred relationship. Because of the large amount of expenditure in this area, a supply management professional could realize substantial savings through continually lowering costs. Supply management professionals may make a site visit to such a supplier, focusing on cost and continuous improvement. The payback potential for a site visit is high as these items are normally purchased in high volumes. Substitution is possible, however, because the marketplace is competitive with multiple sources of supply.

Bottleneck items, on the other hand, are unique high-risk products with customized specifications and technologies. Items in this category generally are purchased in larger quantities, and inventory levels are monitored more closely to avoid interruptions to supply. The relationship with the supplier is important to the buying organization, but supply management professionals will search for alternative suppliers to avoid the risk of supply interruptions.

Lastly, strategic items are extremely important to production or service delivery because of their unique characteristics. Only a few suppliers — perhaps only one — have the technical capability and capacity to meet the buying organization's needs; therefore, it is difficult to switch suppliers. Expenditures for strategic items also generally are high. Thus, these items normally are managed through closer, win-win, partnership-type relationships.

Another important decision is how to improve supply management processes by taking a process view. The following section discusses this topic in more detail.

A Process View

First, organizations must think in terms of processes instead of functions. An organization has literally hundreds of processes operating simultaneously. The goal is to add value for customers through these processes. Some examples of processes include order fulfillment, supplier selection and contract management. Managers need to define, understand and improve those processes that are most essential to their strategies and customer value proposition, support the mission and contribute to improving the bottom line. Process mapping is a good place to start in terms of defining and understanding an organization's processes.

Organizations will map processes as part of continuous improvement efforts. Process mapping, which involves creating a visual depiction "of a process (such as manufacturing a component or ordering a part), that breaks the process into key activities, transfers, decisions and approvals. Process maps enable analysis of the inputs, outputs and interrelationships of each process to understand how processes interact in a system, locate process flaws that are creating systemic problems, evaluate which activities add value for the customer, mobilize teams to streamline and improve processes, and identify processes that need to be reengineered" (ISM *Glossary* 2014).

Generally, a team of people familiar with the process will be assigned to map it; they may come from many parts of the organization. Cross-functional teams usually begin by taking a high-level view of the major core processes and then breaking those core processes into the subprocesses and sub-subprocesses. High-level process mapping is frequently used first to identify an organization's core and supporting processes. Organizations typically have five to eight core processes with five to seven supporting processes for each core process, although this is not always true. For example, Bronson Methodist Hospital, a 2005 recipient of the Malcolm Baldrige National Quality Award, identified only one key core process, Healthcare Service Delivery, with six supporting processes: (1) materials management, (2) environmental and safety management, (3) financial management, (4) human resources management, (5) information management, and (6) guest services management. A partial process map is illustrated in Figure 1-4.[9]

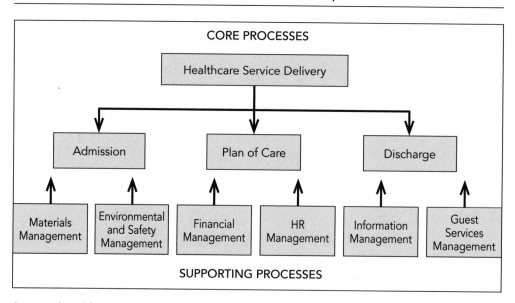

Figure 1-4: Core Processes for Bronson Methodist Hospital

Source: Adapted from Bronson Methodist Hospital Malcolm Baldrige National Quality Award Summary, 2005, available from www.quality.nist.gov/PDF_files/Bronson_Methodist_Hospital_Application_Summary.pdf.

More detailed maps then are used to identify the inputs, each step of the process as it currently exists and the outputs associated with each step. For example, Figure 1-5 is a process map for a generic order fulfillment process. Note that the process crosses over functional boundaries, including customer service, logistics, transportation and supply management. The map then can be used to identify and minimize nonvalue-adding activities, streamline the process or convert the process from a manual to an automated one.

Figure 1-5: Order Fulfillment Process

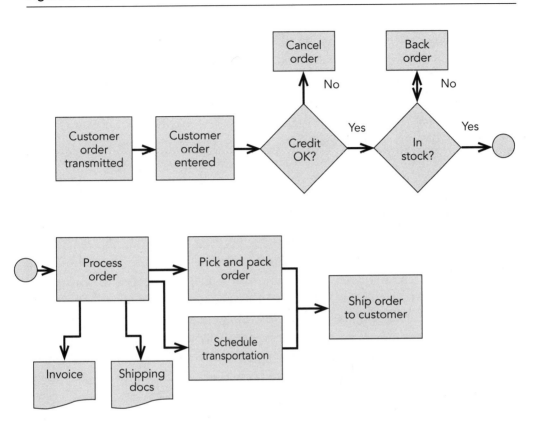

A common method used to identify process steps is to use Post-it® Notes to create the process map on a wall. As more of the process is revealed, the team can easily move or rearrange the Post-it® Notes. Software, such as iGrafx® FlowCharter 2013, SmartDraw 2014 or Microsoft® Visio, as well as web-based programs, are available to create process maps. Citibank, for example, sets up process mapping teams comprised of 30 to 50 people from every unit that makes a contribution to the process. The teams are empowered to make any process changes that will reduce cycle time and make customers happier.[10]

The difficulty for many organizations lies in identifying those core processes and then working to excel at the ones that will support the organization's strategy and customer value proposition. A good approach to identifying an organization's core and supporting processes is to document all information and material flows that occur throughout the organization and with suppliers and customers. Part of the mapping process will initially involve collecting supporting data, including organization documents such as process descriptions, strategy documents, past presentations or training documents. These documents then can be used to create the process maps.

These internal work processes, however, do not take place in isolation. Organizations must possess a good understanding of how their internal processes interact with each other and with the processes of other external organizations, including customers, suppliers, distributors and competitors. These interactions usually are clarified as mapping is performed. Then, with a firm understanding, organizations can begin to integrate their processes internally and with customers and suppliers.

Moreover, an organization must analyze these processes and identify those key value-added activities. These include strategic activities that are critical to achieving existing organizational strategies and that significantly impact customer satisfaction and product quality. Also, those business activities that usually support high value-added strategic activities and are critical to attaining general business operations are important. Lastly, organizations need to focus on those process improvements that extend from the suppliers' suppliers to the customers' customers, or the supply chain. This is only possible when a disciplined, structured approach is in place that applies quality management principles.

Once identified, each process should be named, along with a definition of its unique purpose and any links to other processes. Measures of effectiveness can be created for each process, and the maps can be used as a basis for training and discussion. *Process flow costing*, which tracks those process costs across functions for each process using activity-based costing, also can be used. Costs are typically separated into value-added and nonvalue-added categories.[11] Organizations then look for ways to minimize or eliminate those nonvalue-added costs by performing an appraisal of each process. Organizations also have adopted several broad-based initiatives to improve processes; these are discussed in the next section.

Process Improvement Methods

Organizations have adopted a number of assessment and improvement initiatives within the past 15 years; the two most commonly found in the popular press include Six Sigma and lean operations. The *Six Sigma methodology*, a quality improvement initiative originally developed by Motorola, has experienced widespread adoption by manufacturers worldwide while having a more limited, but growing, implementation by service industries.[12] *Lean operation* is an operations philosophy that stresses creating customer value through the elimination of waste. If a supplier is running out of capacity, if its total lead time is too long, or if the quality of its products and services does not consistently meet buyer specifications, Six Sigma and lean operations can help uncover the solutions to these problems. This review and identification process requires the involvement of supply management.

Six Sigma

Six Sigma is a data-driven framework designed by Motorola to make breakthrough, rather than incremental, quality improvements in an organization's value-adding processes while simultaneously saving money or increasing revenues (see a fuller discussion on Six

Sigma in Chapter 9). This represents the goal of having a defect occur in a process only 0.00034 percent of the time, or 3.4 times out of every one million measurement opportunities. Six Sigma is also meant to embody a philosophy or culture in which everyone from the CEO to the frontline service employee is involved in improving quality using a project management approach. Best-in-class organizations have implemented Six Sigma programs to come as close to Six Sigma as possible in their processes, including Honeywell International, Inc., Bank of America, the Vanguard Group, General Electric Co., the Dow Chemical Co. and others.

Lean Operations

A *lean operation* is a phrase coined in the United States but is based on the Toyota Production System (TPS) and a philosophy of continuous improvement. The TPS follows a philosophy of continuous learning and keeping things simple. An organization should make the best use of its time, people and physical assets to optimize productivity. Organizations also work to connect each value-added step in a process, in the best sequence and most effective way possible without interruption, at a point in time when another entity places an order somewhere downstream. That entity might be the customer or another point in the production system. Thus, lean principles can be applied to both services and manufacturing, with the ultimate goal to make lean thinking pervasive throughout the supply chain. Capital One Financial Corporation (COF) started the process of implementing lean processes within its global procurement services (GPS) function in 2009. According to the vice president of national lending and key sponsor of Capital One's lean initiative, "Visual tracking has become a near religion, with several wall segments illustrating the workflow of six different functional areas: fast-track contracting, medium/high complexity contracting, key sourcing initiatives, purchasing, goal-tracking and process improvement." As a result, cycle times have been significantly reduced without hiring additional staff, demand increased by 75 percent, and both internal customer and associate satisfaction has improved.[13]

The Lean Enterprise Institute identifies a five-step process to eliminate waste, as illustrated in Figure 1-6. To develop lean operations, organizations first must understand what value means to the end user or customer. Then it is important to uncover the various forms of waste that can occur, such as those shown in Figure 1-7. Value stream mapping is an effective tool to uncover waste, and is covered in more detail in Chapter 8. Organizations then work to eliminate waste and tightly sequence the remaining value-adding steps. Implementing a pull system such as just-in-time production or service delivery is important to manage the flow of incoming work. The 5S system — Seiri (Sort), Seiton (Set in Order), Seiso (Shine), Seiketsu (Standardize), and Shitsuke (Sustain) — also helps to improve productivity. Ideally, organizations repeat this process until all waste is eliminated.[14]

Figure 1-6: The Lean Process

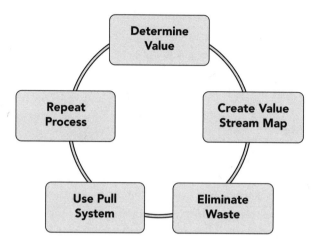

Source: Adapted from: Lean Enterprise Institute, accessed December 13, 2013, http://www.lean.org/WhatsLean/Principles.cfm.

Figure 1-7: Areas of Organizational Waste

EXAMPLES OF WASTE	
Long internal lead times	Excessive inventory
Bottlenecks at critical processes	Long setup times
Long wait times	Unnecessary steps
Redundant processes	Reporting errors
Systems failures	

Sources: Adapted from L. Arneth, "Transforming Traditional Lean Principles," *Inside Supply Management*® (August 2011); T. Coats, "Celebrate the Waste!," *Inside Supply Management*® (December 2009); and R.M. Monczka, R.B. Handfield, L.C. Giunipero and J.L. Patterson, *Purchasing and Supply Chain Management*, Brooks/Cole, a part of Cengage Learning, Inc., 2012.

Some organizations have taken lean operations a step further and combined it with Six Sigma, also known as *lean six sigma*, to eliminate waste and achieve major cost, inventory and lead time reductions in less than one year (ISM *Glossary* 2014). The rationale is that a lean operation is incapable of bringing a process under statistical control while Six Sigma is unable to greatly improve process speed or significantly reduce capital expenditures.

Some areas where supply management organizations can apply lean six sigma include the procure-to-pay (P2P) source-to-pay (S2P) process, sourcing events, contract negotiations and change orders.[15]

Lean supply management is "an overall methodology that seeks to minimize the resources required for supply chain activities by eliminating waste (nonvalue-added activities) that inflate costs, lead times and inventory requirements, and by emphasizing the use of quality improvement programs and flexible workforces and facilities" (ISM *Glossary* 2014). Lean supply management involves optimizing the size of the supply base and then working collaboratively with key suppliers on product or service development. A systems approach is then developed by focusing on the total cost of ownership and total supply lead time responsiveness, beginning with the raw material supplier and an attitude of continuous improvement, all with a customer focus. (More on product and service development can be found in Chapter 3.) This is achieved by using *value stream mapping*, a "lean manufacturing technique in which the transformation of materials is traced from beginning to end to determine if there is waste in the process either in the form of a step where no value is added or a point of 'wait time' when material is being stored to await further value-adding transformation. This concept also may be applied to services" (ISM *Glossary* 2014). It provides a blueprint for implementing any improvements, helping those involved visualize all the flows in a process.

Some organizations are also taking a *lean supply chain* approach by applying lean principles cooperatively throughout the supply chain. Together, supply chain members identify product/service value and target costs for each product or product family. They then work to find and eliminate waste within the supply chain to meet joint target cost and return-on-investment goals. As they meet their target costs, they continue to search for new forms of waste and then set new target costs. Supply chain members also strive to align their key processes and inventory policies with a goal to deliver an uninterrupted flow of goods and services. Lastly, because transparency of all activities in the supply chain is very important, information support is key.

As an organization strives to improve its processes, it needs an effective system to measure and assess its current state, create goals and move toward a world-class organization. The following section provides a description of this process.

Process Improvement Metrics

Supply management uses measures and measurement systems to help develop strategies, evaluate process performance and reward personnel. Measures have been extensively revised as supply management has become more visible and strategically important to organizations. Thus, it is imperative that valid and reliable measurement results, tied to strategic goals, are communicated regularly to senior management. Figure 1-8 provides some examples. It is also important that these measures and goals are jointly determined by the chief supply management officer and senior management.

The measurement process begins once a corporate strategy has been set. Supply management then works closely with the strategic business units (SBUs) and other functional areas — such as operations, new product development and accounting — to develop measures and goals that will determine organizational priorities, motivate personnel and effectively track each process. Good measures help focus personnel on the most important process activities and outcomes. More on performance evaluation can be found in Chapter 10.

Figure 1-8: Lean-Driven Supply Chain Metrics

- Working capital as a percent of sales as compared to that of our peers
- Actual supplier lead time
- First-pass yield (also known as the "perfect order")
- Error rates including overages, shortages, delivering wrong product, invoices
- Process error rates and process lead times
- Number of touches — how many times one of the products hits the facilities
- Supply expense as a percentage of operating revenue
- Supply expense per patient discharged (hospital)
- Supply chain management impact savings — what something should have cost compared to using SCM methodologies in what we actually pay
- Repair turnaround time
- Changeover time (setup time)
- Supply chain cost per output unit — encompasses transportation costs, fulfillment cost, inventory planning cost
- On-time delivery
- Percentage of suppliers on pull systems
- Percentage of invoices that go through accounts payable without any human intervention (touchless)
- Percentage of touchless purchase orders
- Purchasing department spend as percent of sales, general and administrative (SG&A) expenses
- Percentage supplier spend from approved supplier list
- Percent of supply base that is optimized

Source: G.A. Zdisian, "Lean Implementation," *Inside Supply Management*® (19:11), November 2008, 36.

Summary

This is an exciting yet challenging time for those in the supply management field. For example, approximately 70 percent of consumer goods have a life cycle of less than 18 months, and 20 percent will be marketable for three to four years. As a result, supply management professionals will be seeking innovation at an even faster pace. The market potential of the five billion people worldwide earning less than US$2,000 annually is also being seriously tapped. As a result, total cost of ownership models will become even more critical to procurement decisions. Another key trend is the need for knowledge workers in central locations to optimize supply chains globally. For example, a Fortune 500 corporation might create a supply management "center of excellence" located in Brazil, a supply chain analytics center in Singapore and supply chain planning in the United States.[16] All this and more means supply management professionals today must be more prepared than ever to meet an organization's demands for higher levels of performance.

Supply management has increased its presence at the executive table in the areas of planning, forecasting and new product/service development. In addition, better integration and performance in the supporting operational areas of inventory management, materials management, warehousing, logistics and transportation through knowledge integration is expected of the supply management organization. Initiatives to increase that involvement, create value and improve operations will require a project orientation; thus, supply management professionals are contributing members to project teams. To make measurable improvements, however, effective performance measurement systems — covering both supply management and supplier performance — will be required. This book covers these topical areas as a basis to increase the supply management professional's knowledge and as a foundation for organizational improvement.

Key Points

1. A number of terms are used interchangeably to describe the subcomponents within supply management, including *purchasing, procurement, materials management* and *materiel*, but each has a slightly different meaning. The terms *supply management* and *supply chain management* sometimes are used interchangeably.
2. *Supply management* is "the identification, acquisition, access, positioning and management of resources and related capabilities the organization needs or potentially needs in the attainment of its strategic objectives" (ISM *Glossary* 2014).
3. *Supply chain management* is "the design and management of seamless, value-added processes across organizational boundaries to meet the real needs of the end customer. The development and integration of people and technological resources are critical to successful supply chain management" (ISM *Glossary* 2014).
4. The interest in supply management really developed in the latter part of the twentieth century, although the U.S. railroads realized the importance of the function as early as the mid-1800s.

5. Beginning in the 1980s, purchasing began to assume greater responsibility for the purchase of services, in part because of the impact of downsizing and the willingness of other functions to give up noncore activities, while in the 1990s purchasing became more integrated into corporate strategy as organizations faced greater domestic and global competition.
6. Several quantifiable benefits are attributed to high-performing supply management organizations, including lower operating costs, improved return on investment (ROI) and return on assets (ROA), and a direct positive impact on the bottom line.
7. Some of the intangible benefits associated with supply management recognize that the supply management group (1) serves as a good source of information, (2) assists in meeting an organization's strategic objectives, and (3) helps create goodwill.
8. One of the most common questions that organizations must address is whether an item or service should be made or created in-house or outsourced — the classic make-or-buy decision.
9. Two common forms of risk analysis include decision tree analysis and the two-by-two portfolio matrix.
10. Organizations have adopted a number of assessment and improvement initiatives within the past 15 years. The two most commonly adopted include Six Sigma and lean operations. Some organizations also are taking a *lean supply chain* approach by applying lean principles cooperatively throughout the supply chain.
11. It is imperative that valid and reliable measurement results, tied to strategic goals, are communicated regularly to senior management. It is also important that measures and goals are jointly determined by the chief supply management officer and senior management.

CHAPTER

2

Project Management

Today, more than ever, supply management professionals are active participants in a variety of projects. They may be involved in enterprisewide projects; projects with other functions including engineering, operations, marketing and sales; or their own internal projects. Most often they are concerned with the acquisition, purchase and value to the organization of those goods and services that will be needed to deploy any organization-related project plans. Some supply management professionals work in a project environment on a full-time basis while others are brought into a project as needed. Examples of projects where supply management lends expertise and will most likely be involved include those listed below:

- Creating a supplier certification program;
- Assessing an international supplier program;
- Selecting and recommending materials or developing a statement of work for a new product or service;
- Contract preparation and negotiation; and
- Developing a key supplier.

Thus, it is important to understand the discipline of project management and its application to the strategic supply management process framework, particularly the overarching concerns of risk management and supplier relationship management, as well as the fourth process step, negotiate and contract (see Figure S-1, Strategic Supply Management Concept). This chapter will begin by looking at the role of supply management professionals in a project environment, introduce some definitions and take a look at the life cycle of a project. The next section will examine the types of organizational structures that exist to support projects. The remainder of this chapter will discuss the project processes and supply management's role within each process.

Chapter Objectives
- Define the field of project management.
- Describe the role of supply management during a project's life cycle.
- Discuss the tools available to assess projects.

Defining Projects

The Project Management Institute (PMI), a nonprofit organization devoted to the education and certification of project management professionals, has defined a *project* as "... a temporary group activity designed to produce a unique product, service or result."[1] The ISM *Glossary* (2014) defines a *project* as "a special piece of work outside the normal flow of daily activities that has a specific objective and a time and budget limit." Note the key characteristics of a project common to both definitions. First, each project has a beginning and an end, although the length of time may vary from a few days to several weeks, months or even years. Second, each project is distinctive in some respects from other projects. For many supply management professionals, project management is a way of life, as most of their time is spent developing new suppliers, negotiating contracts or supporting new products or services. Each contract, for example, has its own unique terms and conditions including quantities purchased, pricing, delivery dates and performance requirements, among others.

Projects are typically created to meet at least one of five objectives: (1) create a change in an organization, (2) exploit new opportunities, (3) implement the strategic plan, (4) fulfill a contractual agreement, or (5) solve some problem. Thus, for projects to be successful, projects take more planning as a rule of thumb than the typical day-to-day routines found in most organizations.

Because organizations run so many projects, project management has evolved into a specialized field. *Project management* has been defined in the ISM *Glossary* (2014) as "the process of coordinating the organization, planning, scheduling, controlling, monitoring and evaluating of activities so that the objectives of a project are met." Project managers set specific targets and allocate resources such as time, money, people, energy and space over the course of a project.

Project Life Cycle

As shown in Figure 2-1, each project typically will go through a sequence of activities throughout its life to accomplish specific goals and objectives; this is known collectively as the *project life cycle*. A project's life cycle activities are usually divided into several phases or stages for better control, beginning with an initial planning phase, progressing through at least one intermediary phase where the plans are executed, and ending in a final phase that terminates the project. When a phase contains many complex activities, it may be broken down into smaller subphases for better monitoring and control. During each phase the project management team will be faced with prioritizing tasks, minimizing sources of conflict such as schedules or cost, and identifying those critical factors that will make the project successful. The end of each phase is usually defined by the completion and acceptance of one or more *deliverables* (a measurable, verifiable work product). If a deliverable is not acceptable, additional work still may be needed, delaying the move on to the next phase. For example, during the initial phase, *stakeholders* (parties with a vested interest in the project) should review the description of the project's scope (a deliverable) to be sure it meets the acceptance criteria.

Figure 2-1: Project Life Cycle

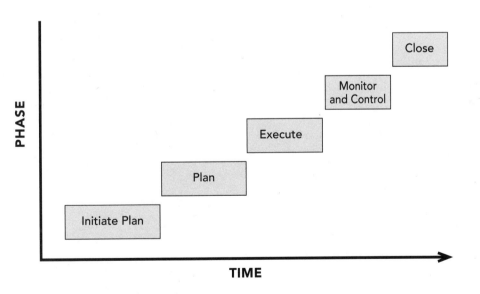

Not all projects will complete their life cycles. Some projects will fail before they are completed, perhaps because of budget overruns, a change in organizational direction or personnel issues. Other projects may skip the project's initial planning stage and move immediately into project execution with no prototyping or testing and little monitoring or control. Still other projects may go through project planning, execution and testing several times before termination.

Projects also can be thought of as sets of interlinking processes. PMI breaks down projects into five process groups, each with a set of interrelated project activities. These activities are typically performed during each phase of a project (although that is not always the case). A project should be tailored to meet its necessary objectives. For example, the initiating process may take place only at the onset of a project. The five process groups are further described in Figure 2-2.

Figure 2-2: Project Management Process Groups

PROCESS GROUP	DESCRIPTION	ACTIVITIES	DELIVERABLES/ OUTPUTS
Initiating	Processes for formalizing authorization to begin new project or project phase	Evaluate alternatives Clarify objectives Develop project scope Develop project charter Identify available resources	Project charter Preliminary project scope statement
Planning	Planning and managing a successful project	Gather information Finalize scope Develop cost budget Develop schedule Identify risks Establish quality requirements Plan purchases	Project management plan Scope management plan Staffing plan Budget Quality control plan Supply management plan Contract statement of work
Executing	Processes to complete the work and meet project requirements	Coordinate people and resources Perform project activities Obtain information, bids, quotes, proposals from suppliers Select suppliers Implement any approved changes	Updated plans Implemented changes Team performance assessments Project-specific deliverables Supplier proposals Contract Contract management plan
Monitoring and Control	Processes to examine project execution, identify problems and take corrective action	Observe/monitor Review supplier performance Measure against project plans and performance baselines Implement corrective actions Establish preventive measures	Performance reports Updated supply management plan Updated contract management plan
Closing	Formal termination of a project or project phase; handing off a project; canceling a project	Finalize all process group activities Close out contracts Resolve contract issues	Closed contract Final product, service, result

Source: Adapted from Project Management Institute, *A Guide to the Project Management Body of Knowledge (PMBOK® Guide)*, Project Management Institute, Inc. 5th edition, 2013. Copyright and all rights reserved. Material from this publication has been reproduced with the permission of PMI.

PMI's PMBOK® Guide also describes nine knowledge areas of project management as shown in Figure 2-3. The knowledge area of project procurement management includes a discussion of the following:

- Plan purchases and acquisitions;
- Plan contracting;
- Request seller responses;
- Select sellers;
- Contract administration; and
- Contract closure.

Figure 2-3: PMI Knowledge Areas

KNOWLEDGE AREA	DESCRIPTION	EXAMPLES
Integration Management	Processes and activities that integrate project management elements	Develop project charter Develop preliminary project scope statement Monitor/control project work
Scope Management	Processes used to make sure project work matches project scope	Planning and defining scope Verifying scope Controlling scope
Time Management	Processes that ensure project is completed in a timely manner	Defining project activities Sequencing activities; estimating resource requirements Estimating activity duration
Cost Management	Processes that ensure project is completed within the planned budget	Planning and estimating costs Budgeting Controlling costs
Quality Management	Processes that ensure project will meet quality objectives	Quality planning Quality assurance Quality control
Human Resources Management	Processes to organize and manage the project team	HR planning Select and develop project team Manage the project team
Communications Management	Processes for the collection, dissemination and disposal of project information	Communication planning Distributing information Reporting performance Manage communication to stakeholders

KNOWLEDGE AREA	DESCRIPTION	EXAMPLES
Risk Management	Processes to oversee risk management	Risk management planning Identifying risks Qualitative and quantitative risk analysis Risk responsive planning Risk monitoring and control
Procurement Management	Processes to acquire materials and services to support the project and manage contracts	Purchase and acquisition planning Contract planning Requesting supplier responses Selecting suppliers Administering contracts; closing out contracts

Source: Adapted from Project Management Institute, *A Guide to the Project Management Body of Knowledge (PMBOK® Guide)*, Project Management Institute, Inc., 5th edition, 2013. Copyright and all rights reserved. Material from this publication has been reproduced with the permission of PMI.

A supply management professional may be involved at one time or another in one or more of the other knowledge areas shown in Figure 2-3. He or she may need to work on critical issues in cost management, quality management or risk management, for example. This discussion will focus on the procurement management knowledge area for purposes of illustration. Further discussion of the six knowledge areas for procurement management can be found in the sections on project planning, execution and closeout.

The Project Organization

Projects are most often configured within the constraints of the overall organizational structure. Figure 2-4 identifies three generic approaches to organizing projects.

Figure 2-4: Project Organizational Structures

	FUNCTIONAL	MATRIX	PROJECTIZED
Project Manager's Authority	Little or none	Limited to high	High to almost total
Percent of Performing Organization's Personnel Assigned Full-time to Project Work	Virtually none	0–95%	85–100%
Project Manager's Role	Part-time	Part-time to Full-time	Full-time

Figure 2-4: Project Organizational Structures *continued*

	FUNCTIONAL	MATRIX	PROJECTIZED
Common Titles for Project Manager's Role	Project Coordinator/ Project Leader	Project Coordinator Project Manager Project Officer Program Manager	Project Manager Program Manager
Project Management Administrative Staff	Part-time	Part-time to Full-time	Full-time
Level of Commitment	Inside group: high Outside group: low	Varies	Highest
Communication	More difficult	More difficult	Least difficult More structured
Priority	Inside group: high Outside group: low	Varies	Highest
Potential Conflicts	Low	High	Low

Source: Adapted from Project Management Institute, *A Guide to the Project Management Body of Knowledge (PMBOK® Guide)*, Project Management Institute, Inc., 5th edition, 2013. Copyright and all rights reserved. Material from this publication has been reproduced with the permission of PMI.

Functional Structure

Organizations less familiar with the discipline of project management usually begin by creating task forces or committees within each function to tackle problems, known as a functional structure. The majority of organizations operate with functional areas such as marketing, accounting, operations, supply management and so on. The advantage of a functional structure is that the employees generally are more dedicated to the project because they see that the potential results will directly affect them. A disadvantage with these types of structures is that the organization's goals often are subordinated to the needs of the functional area. A second disadvantage is that those outside the functional area, such as supply management personnel, also may be requested by the functional department at times when their skills are needed; however, they may not always be available when needed, thus possibly impeding the success of the project.

Projectized Structure

Organizations also may adopt a *projectized structure* to implement projects. In this type of structure, full-time project managers recruit people from the various functional areas who are then relieved of their regular duties and assigned to the project. Large accounting firms and construction organizations are just two examples of organizations that operate in this type of environment. These project managers often report directly to a senior executive and, as a result, the approved projects are more cohesive in nature, are aimed at common organizational goals and have a higher success factor. In this type of environment, supply management personnel and others are assigned directly to the project manager.

While the projectized form of project management has its advantages, there are some disadvantages. First, there probably will be some overlap in human resource needs, as individuals will be assigned to each project on a full-time basis and pulled away from day-to-day activities. Secondly, there may be duplication of equipment and facilities among the many projects. Both duplication of people and equipment will result in higher costs during a time when organizations are trying to trim costs. Lastly, there is always the issue of what to do with personnel once the project is completed. If another project is not available, an employee may be temporarily without work or, at worst case, permanently without a job.

Matrix Organization

To overcome some of the disadvantages of functional and projectized structures, a third option is the *matrix organization*. Personnel are not assigned to a project full-time but rather are shared with the functional department. A project manager is assigned to a project — either full-time or part-time, depending on the size of the project — and then must negotiate for the services of individual team members with each appropriate functional manager. For example, the project manager might talk to the supply management director about using a specific commodities specialist on his or her project. The two managers must work out the details of the arrangement, such as project time requirements.

There are some significant advantages to the matrix organization. First, the project manager's control of any resources allocated to the project increases his or her accountability for completing the project. The project manager also has some flexibility in how the project funds are used. Moreover, because the functional manager has been included in the process, he or she tends to be more supportive of the project. Lastly, if a person has been assigned to the project full-time, the functional manager should be holding the person's job for him when he or she completes the required project activities. However, when personnel are assigned to a project on a part-time basis, there is a greater chance for conflict if the functional manager feels the project is using too much of the assigned person's time. The matrix organization also requires more personnel, thus increasing the costs.

In an effort to improve project performance, a large engineering organization moved from a functional organization to a matrix structure. As a result, a program manager was given responsibility for all projects that fell under one of four areas: wastewater, street, storm water and municipal facilities. Project managers were assigned to individual projects with responsibility for a project's scope, budget and schedule. Each functional manager negotiated the scope, budget and schedule for the technical tasks that were needed to complete his or her portion of the project. Functional managers also supervised the staff assigned to a project and participated in project information meetings. As a result, project costs did not change significantly, and projects were completed within the budget cycle more consistently.

Because projects come in all shapes and sizes, most organizations will adapt by incorporating more than one of the structures described previously. This adaptation is known as an organic structure, which responds to the needs of the organization by using a combination of functional, matrix and projectized structures. For example, some supply management professionals may be assigned some projects on an ad hoc basis, while others are involved in contract negotiation full-time.

The organizational and project structures set the stage for how tasks will be performed, what will be required to complete the tasks, and how the organization will meet the project's objectives. It is also directly related to the planning and execution of a project. The following sections describe the stages of a project from a process point of view, beginning with the initiation of a project.

Project Initiation

Projects, as stated at the beginning of this chapter, often are created because a problem has arisen or a new process or procedure needs to be developed — there is a specific organizational need or internal requirements or some law has changed. For example, a supply management team may be experiencing performance problems with one of its suppliers. In other instances, an organization might face a change in an environmental law, which requires it to alter the disposal process for certain chemicals. In these instances, a team generally is assigned to identify and then solve problems.

Define the Problem

Usually someone — an individual, a department, senior management or the CEO — realizes that a complex issue is affecting the organization. In these situations, it is a good idea to clarify that complex issue in writing. For example, a U.S. hospital created the following problem statement: "Ten percent of the InVision (healthcare information software) system updates last month had to be backed up, resulting in an 18 percent increase in service issues."[2] The statement is concise and gets to the root of the problem.

While it may sound simple, projects often fail because a complex issue has incorrectly been identified. A project team may be assigned to solving a problem that does not really exist or is insignificant compared to other, more important problems. In other instances, a manager clearly "sees the problem" but is unable to make it clear to the rest of the team. Because the manager is the manager, the team often follows along without argument even though they might disagree, something known as the *Abilene Paradox*.[3] As a result, the scope of the project does not address the manager's real concerns and fails.

To make the best use of a team's time and address problems that will improve an organization's competitiveness, a manager should work together with the team to uncover and define an actual problem and its underlying or root causes using some form of data collection and analysis. This also may be the time to bring in outside "experts" in the form of consultants or contractors, who can provide an outsider's perspective. The process often starts with a *SWOT analysis* as described in the following section. (*Leadership in Supply Management*, Volume 3 of the ISM *Professional Series*, also includes a discussion of SWOT analysis.)

SWOT Analysis. SWOT analysis is a macrolevel evaluation of an organization's internal and external forces — its strengths, weaknesses, opportunities and threats — to help senior management evaluate the organization's current environment that triggered the need for this particular project. A relatively simple form of risk assessment, a SWOT analysis provides direction and serves as a basis to create a *project business case*, which is a written justification for the project's deployment. The analysis also can be used to help the project team accomplish its objectives or overcome some obstacle.

Both internal and external characteristics of an organization's business environment are in flux. For example, internally an organization's vision, strategy or objectives change over time. An organization experiences problems with its current processes or technologies. Externally, new technologies become available, creating an opportunity to improve competitiveness. Other external changes also may be occurring in the legislative or environmental arena. Still other external pressures may come from the competition, shifts in consumer preferences or changing economic cycles.

Strengths and weaknesses are the internal things an organization currently can and cannot do, respectively. A strength is something the organization does well, from both the customer's as well as the organization's viewpoint. A weakness can be something the organization is doing poorly or something that can be improved. In evaluating those strengths and weaknesses, it is important to be realistic — in other words, not be overly critical but be modest in the assessment.

On the other hand, opportunities and threats are the potentially favorable and unfavorable conditions in the external environment. Thus, every organization should make an evaluation. Figure 2-5 illustrates a SWOT analysis created by Tesco PLC, a grocery food chain based in the United Kingdom.[4] Tesco identified opportunities that were a good fit to its strengths but also would help overcome internal organizational weaknesses. Organizations should use their strengths to reduce vulnerability to any external threats. At the same time, they should create a defensive plan to prevent weaknesses from making them highly susceptible to external threats. Once the SWOT analysis has been completed, the team should have a better understanding of the environment that created the problem(s) and be able to identify projects that will minimize or eliminate these problems which, as a result, will improve their competitiveness.

CHAPTER 2: Project Management

Figure 2-5: SWOT Analysis Matrix at Tesco PLC

STRENGTHS	WEAKNESSES
Powerful retail brand Substantial financial power Well established customer base Loyal, trusting customers Reputation, value for money Great store locations Superb warehousing and logistics capabilities Club card scheme enhances customer loyalty Quickly expanding Different store types match customer demand Economies of scale	Inefficiencies in bureaucracy because of size Large amount of debt Highly dependent on UK market Lack of integration between online and offline resources Too much product diversity Large capital expenditures on new stores and infrastructure, resulting in less cash to innovate New areas (personal finance) lack experience and expertise
OPPORTUNITIES	**THREATS**
Improve customer relations Increase sales through better integration of Internet resources Integrate offline and online data to better serve customers Form strategic alliances with other organizations to improve experience and expertise Add new locations (Eastern Europe, southeastern United Kingdom)	A tax increase on alcoholic beverages Possible takeovers Tax on food and books Expansion of low-cost supermarkets A weakening economy An increase in unemployment Bigger supermarkets (Walmart stores) taking them on Customer worry over the end of local shops; Tesco becomes brunt of blame Monopolies and Mergers Commission finds Tesco is too powerful and splits up the organization

Source: Adapted from Paul Evans, An Analysis of Tesco PLC: Structure, *Hierarchy and Organisation*, December 2006, available from www.321books.co.uk/catalog/tesco/swot-analysis.htm.

At this point, the team may decide that one particular problem stands out but is multifaceted and just too large to tackle in one project, or that multiple unrelated problems exist. The team then should resort to brainstorming with a group of stakeholders, which may include the process users, managers, customers and suppliers, to further understand the problem. Based on its analysis, the team should determine which problems should be tackled or what areas of a much larger problem should be addressed. During the brainstorming session, any ideas should be written down without prejudice. Three important issues should be addressed for each problem under consideration for a project:

1. How frequently does the problem or complex issue occur?
2. How important is the problem or complex issue?
3. How likely is it that we can resolve the problem or complex issue (feasibility)?

The frequency of the problem can be estimated by collecting some data, while the importance and feasibility can be evaluated using a Likert-type scale. The results then can be rank-ordered using a prioritization matrix. Figure 2-6 provides an example.

Figure 2-6: Prioritization Matrix

Problem Description	(1) Frequency of Occurrence	(2) Importance	(3) Feasibility of Resolution	(4) Total Score
Delivery Problems with Supplier X	3	3	2	18

Ranking:

1 = Low   2 = Medium   3 = High

To obtain score, calculate the product of columns 1, 2 and 3. For example, in the instance of delivery problems, the total score is calculated as 3 × 3 × 2 = 18.

Kepner-Tregoe Rational Process Analysis

Kepner-Tregoe Rational Process Analysis, developed by Charles Kepner and Benjamin Tregoe in *The New Rational Manager* (1981), is a set of systematic procedures "to apply critical thinking to information, data and experience for the purpose of solving problems, making decisions, anticipating future problems and appraising situations" (ISM *Glossary* 2014). Kepner and Tregoe identify four patterns of thinking that managers use every day and can be applied to specific problems that might require a project approach:

1. The project team needs to assess what is going on. In other words, what is the current environment? Answering this question helps managers regain order when there has been uncertainty or confusion, establish priorities and determine the project parameters that will have good results.
2. The team needs to be able to determine the causes of the problem. Why did this happen?
3. The team will determine what course of action should be taken to help them meet their project goals.
4. The team should determine what lies ahead. What kinds of decisions will the team have to make in the future?

The first question requires a *situation appraisal* — looking at the actual situation at hand and identifying any problems that need to be solved. The second question requires a problem analysis. As shown in Figure 2-7, by focusing on a specific issue, the team begins by identifying a problem and then describing it — otherwise known as a *deviation statement*. This stage is important because the problem description will be the basis for the scope of the project. With the deviation statement in hand, the team then can describe the identity, location, timing and magnitude of the problem. It is important to develop a good understanding of both what the problem *is* and *is not*, by asking how often it is happening, where the problem is occurring, when it is happening, what the extent or degree of the problem and its occurrence is, and who is involved in the situation/problem. This process helps the team narrow down the possible causes of the problem, and the team then can develop a project to address the third question. Kepner and Tregoe refer to this as decision analysis. The last question helps organizations anticipate the future and requires a *potential problem (opportunity) analysis*.[5]

Figure 2-7: Kepner-Tregoe Problem Analysis

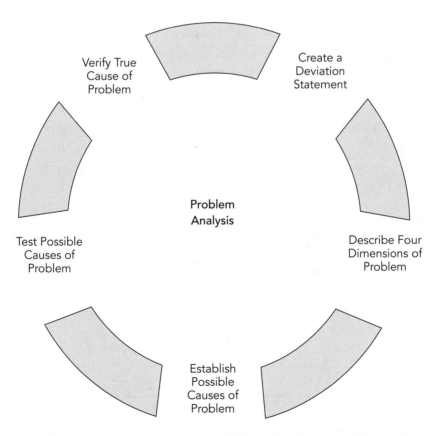

Source: Adapted from Charles H. Kepner and Benjamin B. Tregoe, *The New Rational Manager* (Princeton, NJ: Princeton Research Press, 1981).

Richmond, Virginia-based Interbake Foods LLC, maker of baked goods such as Girl Scout cookies, ice-cream cones and crackers, had acquired two other organizations, resulting in an attempt to mesh three different ways of doing business, three different cultures, disparate sales forces, an inefficient distribution system and less-than-ideal manufacturing locations. The new organization used project management along with Kepner-Tregoe's Rational Process Analysis to successfully complete the integration process. Teams were assembled from the three different cultures, including members from different functions and management levels to address all the issues. As a result, costs in distribution and manufacturing dropped significantly, and revenues increased by 30 percent within two years of the acquisitions.[6]

Two other Six Sigma process analysis tools that can help a project team uncover and pinpoint the reasons a problem is occurring are cause-and-effect analysis and Pareto analysis.

Cause-and-Effect Analysis

A cause-and-effect diagram, also known as a fishbone diagram, is a chart "that captures all the possible causes of a problem in a format designed to show their relationships to the problem (the effect) and to each other. The diagram resembles the skeleton of a fish" (ISM *Glossary* 2014). For example, a commodity manager might receive continuing quality problem reports from manufacturing with regard to a particular part he or she purchases from a supplier. The cause-and-effect diagram can be an effective tool for some initial brainstorming. Its use, however, also can result in an oversimplification of the problem or too much detail for a realistic analysis. Figure 2-8 provides an example of a cause-and-effect diagram. To create the diagram, a team identifies key problem categories. Causes usually are categorized by machine, manpower, management and materials, but other categories may be identified. For each category, the team then would brainstorm a list of possible causes of this problem category. The team could be even more specific and list the causes of a cause.

Figure 2-8: Cause-and-Effect Diagram

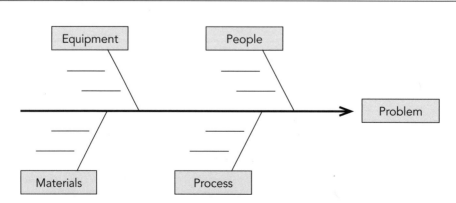

Pareto Analysis

Pareto analysis is a "process of determining the small minority of a population that accounts for the majority of a given effect. For example, in inventory management, 20 percent of the inventoried items account for 80 percent of the total dollars" (ISM *Glossary* 2014). A Pareto analysis typically is performed once a cause-and-effect diagram has been created. Data are collected to determine the frequency of each possible cause of the problem. The collected data then can be plotted to create a Pareto chart. A Pareto chart is a combination bar chart and cumulative percentage chart, "showing the frequency with which events occur, arranged in order of descending frequency. It is used to rank-order the issues so that resources can be applied first to those with the largest potential return" (ISM *Glossary* 2014). The Pareto chart should help the team determine the biggest issues facing it and where it should place its greatest efforts. An example of a Pareto chart is provided in Figure 2-9.

Figure 2-9: Pareto Chart Example

Adams Automotive Parts sells automotive supplies to retailers. In the past three months, the owner has noticed the number of customer complaints has increased. He assigns a team to investigate the problem. The team collects the customer complaint data and creates a Pareto diagram. The bars indicate the number of complaints attributed to each problem and the line indicates the cumulative percentage of complaints. The team concludes that 62 percent of the complaints can be attributed to damaged or late deliveries.

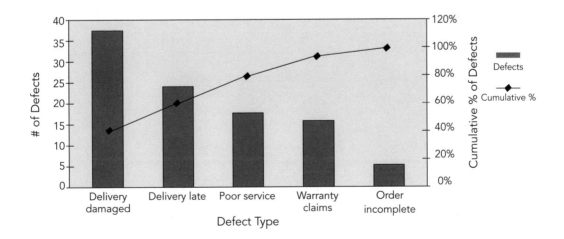

Option Assessment or Alternative Analysis

Once the problem or opportunity under consideration for the project has been identified, the possible solutions — in the form of project proposals, with their related benefits, costs, risks and feasibility — should be listed. The benefits and costs may be financial and qualitative, with some examples provided in Figure 2-10 and Figure 2-11.

Figure 2-10: Examples of Project Benefits to the Business

BENEFIT	DESCRIPTION

Financial	$ of new revenue generated
	$ cost savings
	% increase in profit margin

Market	% gain in market share Estimated increase in competitiveness % increase in customer awareness
Customer	% increase in customer satisfaction % increase in customer retention Increase in customer loyalty
Supply Management	% increase in efficiency % improvement in supplier quality % improvement in supplier delivery

Source: Adapted from Jason Westland, *Project Management Life Cycle* (London: Kogan Page, Ltd., 2006), 19.

Figure 2-11: Examples of Project Costs

COST	DESCRIPTION
Project Participants	Project staff salaries Training costs for employees Purchasing costs of contractors or consultants
Internal Organization	Downtime during testing Losses in productivity during transition Resistance to change New manuals
Physical Assets	Equipment and materials Software, phones, printers Office space dedicated to project
External Suppliers	Training costs Temporary losses in productivity or service delivery Resistance to change Search costs for new supplier(s)

Source: Adapted from Jason Westland, *Project Management Life Cycle* (London: Kogan Page, Ltd., 2006), 19.

Risks generally are associated with the project itself, such as the risk that the project will not be completed on time or that the funding needed to complete the project is not available. The team should assess the probability that the risk will occur, the potential effect of the risk and any countermeasures the team would need to take in the event a risk occurs. An example of a survey form used in risk analysis is provided in Figure 2-12. Additional risk assessment should be performed during the planning stage, and is covered later in this chapter.

Figure 2-12: Project Risk Analysis Survey

Project Name: Supplier Development

1. Description of risk: Funds will not be available in the budget for the project.

   Rate the following based on a scale of: High = 2; Medium = 1; Low = 0

2. a) Risk probability score: _____

   b) Impact of risk score: _____

           Total: _____

3. a) Difficulty in avoiding risk: _____

   b) Probability of avoiding risk: _____

           Total: _____

4. a) Difficulty in mitigating risk: _____

   b) Probability of mitigating risk: _____

           Total: _____

5. If steps are taken to avoid the risk, what will be the impact on project costs?

   _____ Remain the same   _____ Increase 1% to 5%   _____ Increase 6% to 10%

   _____ Increase more than 10%

6. If steps are taken to mitigate the risk, what will be the impact on project schedule?

   _____ Remain the same   _____ Increase 1% to 5%   _____ Increase 6% to 10%

   _____ Increase by more than 10%

7. Recommendation:

   _____ Take no action   _____ Avoid the risk   _____ Mitigate the risk

   _____ Do further analysis

Based on each solution's benefits, costs and risks, a *feasibility study* will help limit the number of solutions under consideration by determining the chance that each solution actually will solve the problem at hand or take advantage of an opportunity. Several aspects of each solution should be considered, and some method should be used to assess the feasibility of each aspect. Figure 2-13 provides an example of a feasibility study for one alternative solution.

Figure 2-13: Feasibility Study for Solution "A"

CATEGORY	RATING	METHODOLOGY USED
Additional people needed to complete project.	7	Survey available employees take to identify skill sets.
New processes will have to be adopted.	4	Processes at other organizations were benchmarked.
New capital equipment will have to be purchased.	8	Current capital equipment was inspected.
New technology will be needed to complete the project.	8	A team created a technology prototype.

Feasibility Rating:
1 = extremely low feasibility
10 = extremely high feasibility

Managers also may incorporate *net present value* (NPV) and *internal rate of return* (IRR) analyses into their feasibility study, which generally are used for capital improvement projects. Net present value is the difference between the present value of all cash inflows and the present value of all cash outflows during the life cycle of the improvement. Cash outflows generally include the cost of the project itself and other expenditures that result from implementation of the project. Cash inflows occur after the project has been completed and could be either additional revenues or cost savings. If the NPV is positive, this indicates that a project should be approved because cash flows will be positive. The formula for net present value is:

$$NPV = \sum_{t=1}^{T} \frac{C_t}{(1+r)^t}$$

where

C_t = net cash flow for year t

r = expected rate of return

t = year

T = number of years under analysis

For example, imagine a supply management team is reviewing a project proposal to investigate substituting a less expensive component part in an existing product. Marketing has informed the team that the product will be on the market for another four years. The project is expected to take one year. The proposal contains a net present value analysis based on an expected 8 percent return each year (as shown in Figure 2-14). Because the sum of the net present values is a negative number, the project would likely be rejected.

Figure 2-14: Net Present Value (in US$)

YEAR	COST SAVINGS	EXPENSES	NET CASH FLOW	NET PRESENT VALUE
0	$ 0	$150,000	−$150,000	−$150,000
1	$50,000	$ 5,000	$ 45,000	$ 41,666
2	$50,000	$ 5,000	$ 45,000	$ 38,580
3	$50,000	$ 5,000	$ 45,000	$ 35,722
4	$50,000	$ 5,000	$ 45,000	$ 33,076
			Sum of NPVs =	−$956

The internal rate of return (IRR) is the rate of return that would make the present value of future cash flows plus the final market value of an investment or business opportunity equal to the current market price of the investment or opportunity. In other words, the IRR answers the question: At what rate of return will the project break even? Basically, the IRR is the return that an organization would receive in the event it invested in itself rather than elsewhere. The IRR is calculated similarly to NPV, but the NPV needs to be set to zero; one can then solve for the IRR. Using the values provided in Figure 2-14, solve for the IRR as follows:

$0 = -\$150{,}000 + \$45{,}000/[(1 + r)/100]^1 + \$45{,}000/[(1+r)/100]^2 + \$45{,}000/[(1+r)/100]^3 + \$45{,}000[(1+r)/100]^4$

IRR = 7.71%

Because of the complexity of solving for the IRR by hand, electronic spreadsheets with built-in formulas, such as Microsoft Excel, can simplify the process. Experts do not recommend that the IRR be used to compare different projects unless the discount rate is the same, cash flows are predictable, the projects share an equal amount of risk and the project length is relatively similar. They argue that discount rates vary over time and the IRR assumes only one discount rate. Thus, it would be difficult to judge a one-year project against a five-year project. On the other hand, the NPV can be used to compare various projects, and a different interest rate can be used each year or for only certain years.

Stakeholder Analysis

A stakeholder analysis also assists a project team in assessing the project environment by identifying each stakeholder and his or her role as well as that person's level of interest and influence in the project. Moreover, this analysis should help the team determine the level of risk and variability that could occur in the project, ultimately affecting the chance of project success.

A project typically will have *primary stakeholders* (those ultimately affected by the project's deliverables) and *secondary stakeholders* (intermediaries who aid in the project delivery process). For example, if a supply management team is conducting a project to create a supplier development program, the primary stakeholders would be the supply management department, the affected suppliers and possibly the internal stakeholders. Some secondary stakeholders would include the project manager and the project team.

A stakeholder analysis can help the team identify any potential conflicts among the stakeholders, which could negatively affect the project's success. These types of conflicts must be resolved early in the project. Conversely, if there are already some strong positive relationships that exist between stakeholders, the team can build on those relationships to strengthen project sponsorship and cooperation. Lastly, the analysis can be used to help a team assess the appropriate level of participation of the various stakeholders during successive stages of the project life cycle. Some questions to consider during the analysis include those listed below:

- What are each stakeholder's expectations with regard to the project?
- What are the likely benefits each stakeholder will accrue from the project?
- What resources will the stakeholder want to commit (or avoid committing) to the project?
- What other interests does the stakeholder have that could conflict with the project?
- How does the stakeholder feel about other stakeholders involved in the project?

Project Approval

Once the problem has been defined and studied, project proposals are submitted for approval. If a project is relatively small and will be assigned to a single person, approval is fairly simple. Contract renegotiations also may be an automatic process and may not require preapproval. However, larger projects typically require a more formal presentation — either to a project sponsor, senior management or the client. For midsize projects that require some funding, organizations may have a project management group in place that does nothing but review project proposals and decide which projects will move forward.

For larger, more complex projects such as road construction or building a new facility, senior management often will develop a *project business case*), which is presented to the client and incorporates the process described so far into one document. The project business case essentially justifies the deployment of a project. According to Jason Westland, author of *Project Management Life Cycle*, a business case should include the following:

- A description of the problem under consideration;
- The options available to solve the problem;
- The benefits, costs, risks and feasibility for each available option; and
- The recommended solution.[7]

Project Charter

Once a project is approved, a *project charter* often is developed. A project charter defines the project, but also establishes the authority of the project sponsor to the project manager and is used to announce the project to relevant stakeholders. Generally reserved for larger projects, it is a good referral document and begins the "paper trail." Team members also can use the project charter as a guide if in doubt as to the project scope.

Usually, the charter is created by the project manager and project sponsor, although others may be involved. While there is no set format, a general template may be followed (see Figure 2-15). The project charter may be in the form of a memo, an email or a more formal document, any of which should be kept with the project documentation. However, some important areas should be addressed. For example, the project's scope and any constraints, the project's important *milestones* (important deliverables or events that signify noteworthy progress on the project), the assigned project manager and team members, and a risk analysis should be included. The charter also should be signed and dated by the project sponsor or other responsible party as a formal indication of project approval.

Figure 2-15: Project Charter Template

Project Title			
Project Manager:		Project Team Members:	
Problem Statement:		Goal Statement:	
Problem Scope Statement: Constraints:		Stakeholders:	
Project Risks: 1) 2) 3)		Risk Strategy:	
Project Milestones: 1) 2) 3) 4)	Deliverables:	Target Completion Date:	Actual Completion Date:
Sponsor Signature:		Date:	

Project Planning

Planning provides the roadmap for a project once it has been approved. Projects should have a formal project plan that provides each project team member with the project details. Certain essential planning steps will increase the chances that a project will be successful.

Project planning generally begins with the project team writing a description of the project along with a clear statement of the project objectives. The team then creates a *work breakdown structure* (WBS) with a corresponding project *organization and functional responsibility chart*. The WBS provides an illustration of the project's scope, and all tasks become the basis for monitoring the project's progress. The organization and functional responsibility chart identifies the project team and shows the responsibilities assigned to the team members for the various tasks. A project schedule also will be prepared and resource requirements will be planned (also known as *resource loading*). Resource loading involves scheduling the necessary resources (people and equipment, for example) for given project activities at given times.

The results of these planning efforts then should be compiled into a document known as the *project plan*. A project plan should be *written*, even if only one person is involved, so the project member(s) can track the progress of the project. In other words, at any point during the project the plan provides the stakeholders information on what tasks need to be completed at what time, when they should be completed and by what person or team, and what other resources have been assigned to the task at hand. The project plan goes through a review and approval process, which will be individual to each organization. Small functional projects may simply need the approval of the functional manager. For larger projects, the project manager and/or project sponsor may be responsible for approving the project. In the public sector, project plans often go through a formal review process. Once the review and approval of the project is complete, however, the project now is ready to be executed.

In one organization, executives initiated discussions to improve intercompany collaboration and visibility across their supply chain and to cut supply chain costs by reducing inventory levels. They concluded that collaborative planning, forecasting and replenishment (CPFR) could be a viable solution; a joint organization team developed a business case to gain management support and obtain the resources needed to complete the project. (See Chapter 5 for an additional discussion of CPFR.) Once approval was received, the project team developed a list of activities that would need to be performed before CPFR could be implemented. This list became the basis for the project plan; the team assigned task responsibilities to cross-company teams and time lines for each activity with target completion dates. The project plan was the blueprint for the teams and was central to the timely completion and success of the project.

The nine essential elements of a project plan are listed below:
1. *Overview*. Short project description; deliverables; major milestones.
2. *Objectives*. Details of project deliverables.
3. *Technical and managerial approaches*. Special practices beyond normal procedures.
4. *Contractual agreements*. Detailed description of agreements with client and suppliers.
5. *Project schedule*. Time line of all project-related activities and major deliverables; milestones.
6. *Project budget or resource requirements*. Capital and operating expenses or a list of the project members and skill requirements.
7. *Risk management*. Solutions to eliminate or mitigate potential problems.
8. *Risk assessment*. Steps to mitigate potential project problems.
9. *Evaluation methods*. Evaluation standards and procedures; monitoring requirements.[8]

The following sections provide a more detailed discussion on the project schedule, project budget, resource requirements and risk analysis.

The Project Schedule

A project consists of many interdependent tasks involving multiple functions including supply management. Thus, supply management professionals should be involved in the development of the project schedule as it relates to those supply management activities required in the project. The project manager and team members should identify all required tasks to complete the project, estimate the duration of each task, and compile them into a schedule that is logical and meets delivery requirements. Once the schedule is complete, the project manager, with supply management and other team members, should use the schedule to monitor and control the project tasks to assure they stay on schedule and complete the project on time.

Project teams generally start with a *work breakdown structure* (WBS) as a basis for the project schedule, which is a collection of all project activities grouped in some logical fashion under major categories. Figure 2-16 provides an example of a WBS.

Figure 2-16: Work Breakdown Structure (WBS)

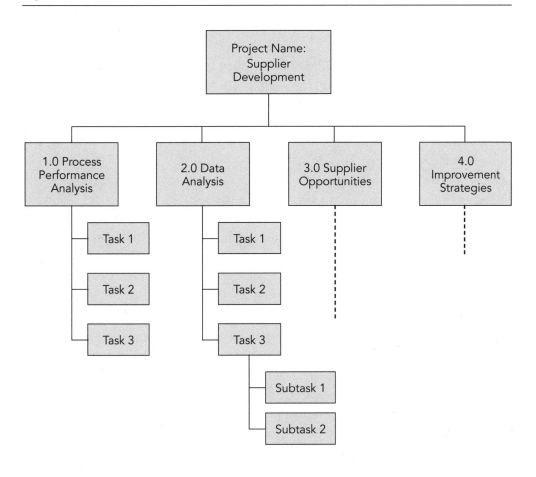

The WBS then becomes one input to the schedule. Other inputs are the expected task times and any time or resource constraints to the schedule. For example, the supply management professional assigned to the project may be available only for a certain number of hours each day, which would extend the expected time to complete the assigned tasks. Ideally, task time estimates should be determined based on historical data and estimates from the people who will actually be performing the tasks. In reality, these estimates often are based on the project due date (and often the reason for many late projects).

Based on this information the schedule is created, and shows each project activity along with start and end times. Many organizations use *Gantt charts* because they are relatively easy to create and read. The Gantt chart is a "horizontal bar chart used in project management that is commonly used to plot planned and actual progress of project activities" (ISM *Glossary* 2014). These forms may include any standard contract templates, descriptions of the items or services that will be purchased, all nondisclosure agreements, and evaluation criteria for the proposals.

The disadvantages of these charts lies in the difficulty of interpreting them when there are several activities that begin and end at the same time, and visually determining the *critical path*. The critical path is the set of those tasks that cannot be delayed without delaying the entire project.

The *Critical Path Method* (CPM) and *Program Evaluation and Review Technique* (PERT) are two similar forms of network diagrams that graphically portray the sequential relationships and interdependencies between the project tasks. The CPM is "a mathematical-based algorithm for scheduling a set of project activities that shows the longest path of planned activities to the end of the project, and the earliest and latest that each activity can start and finish without making the project longer. A CPM model includes a list of activities or work breakdown structure, the time that each activity takes to complete and the dependencies between the activities" (ISM *Glossary* 2014). The PERT is "a network planning technique used for controlling the activities in a project. Each activity is assigned a pessimistic, probable and optimistic estimate of duration. The critical path and project duration are determined and progress monitored using this data" (ISM *Glossary* 2014). The diagrams look much the same, with precedent and subsequent tasks clearly identified in the network and the time duration and function of each task included. The networks also are used to identify the critical path.

However, the method used to calculate the estimated start and end times for each task differs between the CPM and the PERT. The CPM uses concrete time estimates while the PERT uses probabilistic time estimates. The advantage of the CPM is time savings in the calculations, while the PERT should offer more realistic time estimates. The PERT also allows for what-if analyses by changing the probabilities. Today, Gantt charts and CPM and PERT diagrams usually are created using Excel spreadsheets or other software programs for simpler projects, and project scheduling software such as Microsoft Project™ or Primavera™ for complex projects. The benefits of using a project management software tool include the following:

- Increased ability to effectively manage and understand project schedules;
- Improved ability to become productive quickly;
- Increased capability to build effective charts, graphs and diagrams;
- Better communication within the project team;
- Improved understanding of change impacts;
- Increased control over finances and the resources allocated to the project; and
- More effective tracking according to the project team's needs.[9]

Project Budget

The *budget*, a plan to allocate resources to the project, must be developed to gain approval for the project plan. Once developed, the budget is used by senior management to monitor and control the project. To make the budget meaningful and relevant, data on expenditures need to be collected and then reported in a timely fashion. Otherwise, current or impending financial difficulties with the project will be missed, possibly shutting down the project when these problems eventually are uncovered. Thus, the budgeting system must be carefully designed so the numbers are accurately reported at specific times needed for decision-making.

While traditional budgets are organized by activity such as phone, electricity and salaries, project budgets are more relevant and easier to understand by the project team and senior management if they are organized by project task and the expected timing of the expense associated with that task. Project expenses then can be separated from those of regular operations. Figure 2-17 provides an example of a project budget. Supply management's role in the budgeting process is to provide information on contracted prices for materials and services, and estimates for related human resources expenses to solicit, negotiate and manage any contracts.

Figure 2-17: Project Budgets

Task	Cost Estimate	MONTHLY BUDGET (IN US$)					
		1	2	3	4	5	6
1	$ 8,000	$4,500	$3,500				
2	$10,500		$5,500	$5,000			
3	$12,000		$6,700	$3,000	$2,300		
4	$ 7,000		$1,000	$3,300	$2,700		
5	$14,000			$5,400	$5,400	$3,200	
6	$ 1,500				$1,500		
7	$ 8,000			$4,000		$4,000	
8	$ 3,500				$3,500		
9	$ 9,000				$6,200	$2,800	
10	$ 7,500					$5,000	$2,500
Totals	$81,000	$4,500	$16,700	$20,700	$21,600	$15,000	$2,500

There are many examples of projects that run over budget. No matter how much time and effort is spent on the process, the budget is still a forecast and, as a result, subject to error. Thus, it is important to look at some of the project issues and address ways to overcome them during the planning process. One of the most common reasons for budget overruns is that unexpected expenses are incurred during the project in the form of machinery, equipment or personnel. To avoid underbudgeting, either an additional percentage is sometimes added to the budgeted amounts or the project manager identifies the items that have the most significant impact on the budget and then estimates a price change rate for each one.

There are also other reasons budgets are inaccurate. Waste, in the form of rework and defects, often is overlooked and should be factored into the budget. Also, as the project progresses, additional workers may be hired to meet deadlines; these workers then must be trained. As is often the case, existing workers are expected to train the new workers, which takes time out of their schedule and lengthens the project time. Lastly, estimators may be overly optimistic at the beginning of the project or there may be pressure from upper management to keep costs down, resulting in eventual budget overruns. Past experience, common sense and procedures can help overcome these problems.

Risk Management

Risk management in general is the process of "directing or conducting the activities necessary to reduce, eliminate or mitigate the impact of factors that could lead to injury, damage, loss or failure" (ISM *Glossary* 2014). When applied to project management, risk management is the identification, analysis and planned response to potential project risks. (An additional discussion of risk is covered in *Leadership in Supply Management*, Volume 3 of the ISM *Professional Series*.) As mentioned previously in this chapter, some initial risk analysis should be undertaken to assess the possible chance that a project will not be successful. A more detailed risk analysis then should be performed and documented during the project planning stage. Possible risks may be associated with the project team itself, the customer, senior management, the budget, quality issues or acts of nature, to name a few. There also may be risks that are interrelated, and those connections need to be addressed. For example, the risk of a shortfall in the budget may be related to project quality. Supply management's assessment of risk is an important part of the analysis, because there is the chance for supply interruptions or delays, or the threat of rising prices for goods or services (among other risks), particularly for longer projects.

To identify the possible project risks, meeting with the stakeholders — either through a brainstorming session or individual interviews — is important. The project manager may incorporate *scenario analysis* into the interviews and meetings, where possible sequences of events are generated. An analysis of the schedule by reviewing the network diagram or Gantt chart also may turn up possible risks. Lastly, reviews of similar past projects may help the team identify potential risks for the current project. With collected data in hand, the project team can develop a risk profile that contains a list of the possible risks and the possible magnitude of the risks. Figure 2-18 provides an example of a risk assessment document that may be used to track associated project risks. The most important risks should be kept at the top of the document, and at least one person should be assigned the responsibility for monitoring and managing that risk. This record should be updated regularly. A *risk matrix* (see Figure 2-19) also may be helpful in visually assessing the various project risks in terms of the probability of each risk occurring and the consequences of that risk.

CHAPTER 2: Project Management

Figure 2-18: Risk Analysis

Risk #	Description of Risk	Related Risk(s)	Probability of Risk Occurring	Consequences of Risk	Rank	Actions to Manage/ Mitigate Risk

Figure 2-19: Risk Matrix

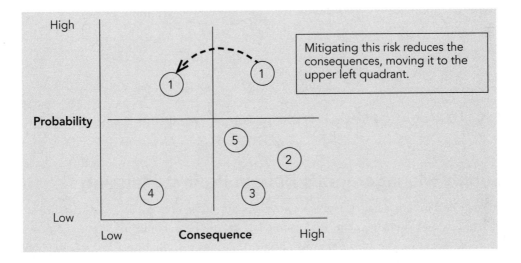

Resource Requirements Plan

The project manager will need to select the project management team(s), and each project team member will have certain roles and responsibilities throughout the life of the project based on his or her expertise. A *responsibility matrix* is a referral tool that will help the project manager, particularly in complex projects. Shown in Figure 2-20, it identifies the responsibilities for each person or group for the major project activities. It also should show the interactions that will take place across the various departments and organizations involved in the project. Sometimes coding of responsibilities for each task is helpful for the project team. Coding activities might include (1) direct responsibility, (2) needs notification, (3) issues approval, or (4) support. The project manager must determine or forecast any necessary resources to complete the project; these resources become the basis for the budget discussed previously.

Figure 2-20: Responsibility Assignment Matrix

Project Phase	Task	Project Manager	PROJECT TEAM Supply Mgt. — Contracts Team	Technical Team	Operations Improvement Team
Analyze Need	A1	○	●	●	●
	A2	●	○	○	◆
	A3	◆	●	●	●
Solicit Quotes	B2	○	◆	●	
	B2	■	○	●	
Write RFP	C1		■	◆	○
	C2	◆	◆	■	○
• • • •					

Coding: ○ Approval   ● Responsible   ◆ Notification   ■ Support

Supply Management's Role in Project Planning

During the planning stage, the project manager should involve the relevant stakeholders, including supply management, to decide what should be outsourced. While the project team may develop the specifications and/or drawings for all contracted work, supply management should be included in these meetings to offer its expertise. For example, supply management professionals provide needed input on the contractual aspects of the project plan such as contract type preferred (examples include cost, time-and-materials or fixed-price), terms and conditions, and their expertise on product or service specifications.

Generally, purchase and acquisition planning starts because the project team has performed an insourcing/outsourcing analysis and determined that at least some portions of the project will be outsourced to a third party. Outsourcing usually occurs when an organization does not have the internal expertise, time or all the resources required to complete the project on its own. In this event, the team can use the resource requirement estimates performed during this stage to solicit and review incoming proposals from potential suppliers.

The insourcing/outsourcing analysis is performed by estimating the resources, skills, equipment and services that will be required, as well as any time constraints placed on the project. At this stage, supply management personnel may draw up a *procurement management plan*. This plan details how supply management will oversee the procurement process. According to the *PMBOK®*,[10] the plan may include the following:

- The types of contracts that will be used;
- The person(s) assigned to any required estimates;
- The responsibilities of the project team related to procurement;
- Documentation that will be used;
- Coordination between supply management, scheduling and performance reporting;
- Management of lead times;
- Management of risk;
- Format for statements of work;
- Process to identify qualified suppliers; and
- Performance metrics that will be used to manage the contracts and evaluate suppliers.

Supply management professionals prepare any documentation needed to define the statement of work, request responses from suppliers and select the suppliers that will be contracted for the project, develop the project schedule for supply management-related activities, and create the budget. Some examples of these documents are discussed in the next section.

Statement of Work Documentation

The assigned supply management professional or team typically develops a description of the work that will be required of each supplier/contractor, otherwise known as the *statement of work*. This supply management person or team also will have to determine the terms of the contract and how the supplier/contractor will be evaluated. All requirements will be developed into a document that could be a *request for proposal* (RFP), a *request for quotation* (RFQ) or an *invitation for bid* (IFB). According to the ISM *Glossary* (2014), an RFQ is "a solicitation document used to obtain price quotes for a specified product or service. These are often a follow-up to an earlier Request for Information (RFI). The law may or may not treat a quotation as a binding offer." RFQs often are used in the event supply management is buying commodities or services that can be priced on an hourly basis. If the project team already knows the scope of work required, such as in the case of a road construction project, an IFB is appropriate. An IFB is "the request made to potential suppliers for a bid on goods or services to be purchased" or, for government procurement, "the solicitation document used in sealed bidding and in the second step of two-step bidding" (ISM *Glossary* 2014). The RFP, defined by ISM as "a solicitation document used to obtain offers of price and proposed method of execution of a project," often is used when the complete statement of work has not yet been determined and the project team needs the supplier's technical expertise in this area (although this is not always the case). RFPs often are used for information technology or research projects.

CoreLogic, a U.S.-based provider of consumer, financial and property information, analytics and services to businesses and government entities, faced a need to transform its procurement function to a best-in-class organization. Deloitte's consulting group was engaged to negotiate an outsourcing contract with a service provider that could establish best practices and establish formal governance. Once the parameters were defined, Deloite created and advertised an RFI to evaluate the capabilities of the available service providers, and to determine solutions and best practices in the marketplace. After all responses were received, Deloitte then developed an RFP and sent it to a short list of service providers.[11]

The *statement of work* (SOW) becomes an attachment to a request for proposal and is described in more detail in the following section.

Statement of Work (SOW)

The SOW is "a statement outlining the specific services a contractor is expected to perform, generally indicating the type, level and quality of service, as well as the time schedule required," according to the ISM *Glossary* (2014). There are actually four types of SOWs. The first type, a *design SOW*, provides precise design specifications and how the work will be performed. The second type, *level-of-effort SOW*, defines the number of personnel in each labor category (project managers, design engineers and account managers, for instance) and hours required to perform the work, and is used for service contracts. A third type is the *performance SOW* that states what will be needed — the technical standards — but does not include a description of how the work, will be accomplished. The fourth type is the *functional SOW*, which does not include performance or technical standards but simply states the purpose of the purchased product. With a functional SOW, the responsibility falls on the supplier to develop the performance standards that will meet the project needs. To prepare the SOW, the supply management professional typically works with the project manager to determine his or her perception of the marketplace and glean any past experiences with acquisitions of this nature. It is important to remember that the SOW is subject to contract law. Thus, it needs to be understandable to the reader and not ambiguous.

The SOW will help potential suppliers to cost or price their proposal as accurately as possible. It also can be used as a benchmark to help supply management evaluate the contractor's performance during its administration. A well written SOW will minimize the need for change orders and reduce the number of contract claims and disputes that may arise. Once the RFPs have been reviewed and a bidder has been selected, the SOW is incorporated into the contract along with other parts of the bidder's proposal, and any changes or conditions.

Project Execution

Once the project plan has been approved, the team moves into the next phase — the actual deployment of the project. If the project was initiated for organizational process improvements or supplier process improvements, for example, a specific time line (developed during the project planning phase) is followed for the process improvement implementation.

When the project results require the procuring of a good or service from a new or existing supplier, supply management professionals, with plans in hand, begin the actual solicitation of suppliers and negotiation of contracts to support the project. This is one of the Process Concept steps in the Strategic Supply Management Concept framework found in the "Series Overview" of this book.

Requesting Sellers' Responses

The supply management team member, with any specifications provided by the project manager, develops a list of suppliers that should be qualified to meet the project's sourcing needs. The department should have on hand a list of suppliers it has dealt with previously, along with each supplier's performance ratings. If the project need is new, the supply management professional may have to find and qualify new suppliers. The supply management professional can use a number of sources to locate new suppliers, including trade journals, supplier catalogs, trade shows, trade registers and Internet searches. He or she also might talk to supply management professionals at other organizations or to salespeople within his or her own organization to obtain leads. Another option is to advertise in the newspaper, online or on the organization's website. Once a pool of possible suppliers is assembled, the supply management professional(s) and project manager analyze each supplier to assess whether its actual technical and manufacturing capabilities, and financial stability, will meet the project need. There is generally a direct correlation between the complexity and the expected cost to meet a project's need, and the time spent on this assessment.

Supply management personnel will develop a *qualified sellers list*, which contains those suppliers that will be asked to submit a proposal or quote. The requests for proposals or quotes will be sent to those on the qualified sellers list, and those interested suppliers will prepare and submit their written proposals. The project team also may request an oral presentation if a potential supplier is new to the organization. Once the analysis is complete, supply management should have a list of desirable suppliers from which to select.

Before the proposals have been prepared and sent to potential bidders, there also should be a time period for suppliers to ask questions regarding the customer's requirements. The project team or the supply management team in charge of the contract may set up a meeting for the potential bidders, also known as a *bidder's conference* or *pre-proposal conference*, to entertain questions. Alternatively, potential bidders may simply present questions in writing. The questions raised during this time period can be used to clarify the supply management documents in an addendum. For example, suppliers may need clarification on the statement of work requirements, the deliverables or special terms and conditions. Suppliers will be especially interested in how they will be evaluated in the selection process and, in particular, how prices will be scored.

Once these activities are concluded, supply management now is ready for the next stage of the process — proposal solicitation.

Proposal Solicitation. There are actually three steps to proposal solicitation: (1) origination, (2) qualification, and (3) negotiation.

ORIGINATION. At this point, supply management has determined the type of contract that will be used during the planning stage such as cost, time-and-materials, or fixed-price. In the case of standardized items or commodities, a purchase order will most likely be a fixed price with no negotiation involved. In other situations with relatively low-value items, the project manager may provide a set of needs to the supply management team member. It is then up to that person to determine the materials, supplies or services that will meet the project needs and request quotes from different suppliers on a given contract. The supply management professional will review the credentials of available suppliers, select the ones that seem most capable of fulfilling the project manager's needs and send the request for quotes.

QUALIFICATION. Once the quotes are received, they are reviewed and one is selected. In certain instances, there may be large monetary gaps between the quotes, requiring the supply management professional to do some negotiating to resolve issues and settle on a price.

When the materials or services are relatively complex, the supply management professional will make a request for proposal as described previously. RFPs may have already been prepared during the planning stages to help with the budgeting process.

NEGOTIATION. If the project need is relatively simple, one person may be assigned to negotiate the terms of the contract with the supplier. However, for more complex, high-dollar value needs, a team often is assigned to the negotiation. A contract specialist generally is assigned to lead the negotiation, but the team also should include the project manager who most closely understands the project requirements. Additional team members may represent various departments, including engineering, marketing, legal and cost accounting, depending on the specific project. Face-to-face negotiation is a complex process requiring a great deal of upfront preparation and training, beyond the scope of this chapter (additional information can be found in *Foundation of Supply Management*, Volume 1 of the ISM *Professional Series*). The objective of the negotiation, from the project manager's standpoint, is to secure a fair, reasonable price while at the same time feeling confident that the supplier will meet the contract requirements within the time and performance constraints. The supply management department wants to be sure that the contract allows it control over the execution of the contract terms while still maintaining good relations with the supplier. Cooperation is important during those times when contentious issues arise during the project. Supply management also is looking at the possibility of future dealings with the supplier beyond the current project.

Supplier Selection

Once the bids are in, one supplier is selected based on interviews, presentations, negotiation or some combination of the three. For larger contracts, a team generally is involved in the selection process and may include the project manager, a supply or contracts manager and technical specialists. In the event a bidding process is used, the lowest bidder usually is selected if it is capable of meeting the terms of the contract.

An important process step is developing the written contract. It is important that contract clauses expressly limit the liability exposure to the procurement organization. Once the contract is prepared, it will be sent to the supplier for signature. If the contract is signed, supply management then will administer the contract. Should the supplier refuse to sign the contract for some reason, the negotiation process begins again. A supplier may also *conditionally* accept the contract. At this point, the team has the option of accepting these conditions, refusing them or entering into additional negotiations. Any details specific to the contract(s) are included in the project plan and the contract is administered, a subject covered later under "Project Monitoring and Control" in this chapter. (A discussion of contract administration can also be found in *Foundation of Supply Management*, Volume 1 of the ISM *Professional Series*.)

Team Management

As the previous sections suggest, a great deal of teamwork is required to successfully qualify suppliers and negotiate contracts for a project. However, large projects with cross-functional teams are normally comprised of a mix of people with different backgrounds, skills and attitudes, which must be managed effectively if the project is to be a success. The team members' working relationships will affect individual and project productivity, and impact the project customer and other stakeholders. Thus, the project manager should initially perform appropriate team-building exercises. Often a project kickoff meeting is used to generate excitement for the project and create a team environment. During the project, the project manager needs to quickly identify potential and actual conflicts and rectify them before they deteriorate too far, jeopardizing the project. During project execution, the project manager must not only be task-oriented — working on completing the project on time within cost and quality constraints, but also people-oriented — keeping the team members satisfied and motivated to stay on task.

There is also the matter of working with the suppliers that provide supporting materials and services. Outside suppliers are, in one sense, part of the project team. They are part of the project management process and the decision-making process. They become internal stakeholders because they have a vested interest in the project outcome, and are providing valuable inputs to the project. As such, it is important that the avenues of communication remain open, and suppliers are treated honestly and with respect to increased mutual trust. As a result, suppliers should recognize the reciprocal benefits of being involved in the project.

On the other hand, suppliers are independent contractors, there to fulfill their contractual obligations. Their commitment to the project may not be to the same degree as other internal stakeholders and they may, rightly so, be concerned about their own organizations' welfare and needs. In most cases, however, suppliers will recognize the benefits of a good working relationship because satisfying the project manager's needs increases the chances for additional business. Thus, the project manager must manage and motivate the suppliers similar to the way he or she interacts with the other team members, recognizing the differences mentioned.

Change Management

Changes are inevitable with projects, mostly because the occurrence of some events will not always be anticipated. Change requests are more likely to occur as the complexity of a project increases or the project extends over a number of years, as in many construction and technology improvement projects. If the project becomes larger as a result of change or there are changes occurring outside the control of the project team, the phenomenon known as *scope creep* has occurred. Completely eliminating scope creep is impossible, but a good planning and control process is important to avoid excessive scope creep. Change requests are also the biggest reason for increases in project budget overruns. It is important, then, to establish who will have the authority to initiate change requests, what will be the procedures for processing and funding any changes, and who will have the final authority to approve changes. It will be up to the project manager to control the change process.

Project changes also can affect the contracting process. Thus, the terms of the contract are very important because they can be written in such a way that is too restrictive. To increase project flexibility, contracts for complex multiple-year projects often are written on a cost-plus basis rather than with a fixed price. For example, a *cost-plus-percentage-of-cost* contract means that the supplier will be reimbursed for allowable costs based on contract performance plus an agreed-on additional percentage of the estimated cost, or profit. A *cost-plus-fixed-fee* contract is similar to the cost-plus-percentage-of-cost contract but the supplier receives a fixed fee, which remains the same unless the scope of work changes. In both instances, the buyer assumes a great deal of risk because the supplier has no incentive to contain its costs and the buyer will need to pay special attention to charges for materials and labor during the contracted period. A more favorable contract is the *cost-plus-incentive fee*. In this instance, the supplier receives a bonus if a cost savings is realized to the buyer based on a prenegotiated formula. Perhaps even more favorable to the buyer but more complex is the *fixed-price-with-incentive fee* contract. In this instance, a target cost, target profit, target price, ceiling price and share ratio are negotiated. The procurement organization agrees to pay no more than a specified ceiling price. However, if the supplier's costs are less than the target cost, any savings will be shared based on the negotiated formula. The following example illustrates how this works:

Organization X and Supplier A have negotiated a fixed-price-plus-incentive fee contract. The two parties agree to the following:

Ceiling price:	US$220,000
Target price:	US$210,000
Target cost:	US$200,000
Target profit:	US$ 10,000
Share ratio:	65/35

In this instance, if Supplier A's costs exceed the ceiling price of $220,000, it will make no profit. If Supplier A's target costs are $190,000, it will make the $10,000 profit, plus it will split the cost savings of $10,000 ($200,000 – $190,000) with the buyer at a share ratio of 65 percent to 35 percent. Thus, it will make an additional US$3,500 ($10,000 × 35%).

The terms for making changes to the contract also should be clearly specified within the agreement, including those parties allowed to initiate and authorize changes.

Project Monitoring and Control

Once the project tasks are under way and any contracted work has begun, the project must be administered. This phase includes monitoring the project by collecting, reporting and documenting any project information that is important to the project manager and other stakeholders. The project manager then uses that information to control the project by making sure actual performance meets the plan. In other words, the project manager should make sure that the project meets cost, time and performance constraints. If the project is not meeting these constraints, it is up to the project manager to take whatever action is necessary to bring the project back on track. Part of the monitoring and control process is overseeing any contracts. The project manager, in conjunction with supply management, is typically responsible for monitoring the contract(s).

Contract Administration

The project manager typically will supervise any work that is performed under the terms of the contract and by others on the project team who often interact with the suppliers as part of their project tasks. Contract administration responsibilities will include approving invoices from suppliers as the work is completed, preparation and processing of change orders, and any interpretation of contract terms that might be required, among other tasks.

To administer the contract, the supply management professional and project manager should create and then follow a set of control procedures to assure compliance with current contracting and compensation policies. All work should be properly authorized, and certainly no work should begin without a signed contract. The supply management professional should set up a contract file that contains the contract, budget, any constraints, work authorizations and scope change authorizations.

The supply management professional and the project manager also should perform periodic inspections to ensure the terms of the contract have been met. The required quality specifications should have been written into the contract, and provide a basis for the inspections. There also should be remediation and warranty clauses within the contract, in the event the supplier's work does not meet set quality standards. In projects, time is of the essence, so setting time constraints for warranty work is important.

Additionally, a system should be set in place to deal with change orders because, as mentioned previously, they can make a difference in the total cost of the project. A complete review of each proposed change should be conducted either by the project manager or in a team meeting. Any concerns should be addressed, as well as the impact of the change on the project schedule, performance and cost. An information system that tracks cost variances — the difference between budgeted cost and actual cost based on the proposed change — can be useful. Each change should be documented and authorized along with any associated price changes, and then be incorporated into the project plan. The following section provides a further discussion of creating a *change control system*.

Change Control

Changes, as mentioned, generally come about because a stakeholder, usually the client or user, wants to improve the outcome of the project. As the project progresses, the stakeholder may become aware of a new material or technology he or she would like to use, for example. The team also may face changes in organization protocols or external requirements that affect the project's scope. As a result, changes may be requested that affect the project's plan, its processes, the budget or schedule, or one or more deliverables.

Thus, the project plan should include a change control system that will handle the processing and consideration of all change requests. The change control process begins with a written change order, which provides a description of the changes along with proposed changes to the plan, process, budget, schedule or deliverables. To maintain control of the change process, all change approvals should be in writing and signed off by those affected by the change, such as the client and a senior manager. Although the project manager's approval is not required, he or she should be included in the discussion on any proposed change before it is formally sent for approval. If the change is approved, any portions of the project plan affected by the change need to be revised.

Project Performance Evaluation

The project manager and other stakeholders have a vested interest in how the project is progressing; that is, they want to know the status of the project in terms of meeting delivery, performance and cost objectives. One means to evaluate a project is by using an *earned value management system* (EVMS) which, "with related subsystems is implemented to establish a relationship between cost, schedule and technical aspects of a project, measure progress, accumulate actual costs, analyze actual costs, analyze deviations from plans, forecast completion of events, and incorporate changes in a timely manner" (ISM *Glossary* 2014).

Earned value is a measure used to ascertain project progress in terms of these three constraints (delivery, performance and cost objectives). Earned value is computed by multiplying the budgeted cost of each task by the estimated percentage completed of that task. The values for each task then are summed together. Earned value is calculated periodically through the life of the project. A graph can be created to provide a visual representation of the project's actual progress, known as the *actual cost of work performed* (ACWP) against the cost-schedule plan (*budgeted cost of work scheduled* or BCWS) and the *budgeted cost of work performed* (BCWP) as shown in Figure 2-21. The cost variance is the difference between the BCWP and ACWP, while the schedule variance is the difference between the BCWS and BCWP.

Figure 2-21: Earned Value Graph

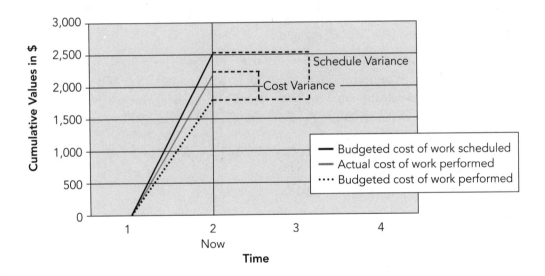

Note: The graph indicates that project is over budget (actual cost of work performed is greater than budgeted cost of work performed) and behind schedule (budgeted cost of work performed is less than budgeted cost of work scheduled).

There are two difficulties in calculating earned value, first in estimating the percentage completion of a task (it is, at best, an educated guess) and the cost (money is often spent in "clumps" and is not a good indicator of project progress). Thus, project managers may calculate efficiency indicators or variances that reflect cost and schedule performance. A cost performance index (CPI) — which is BCWP/ACWP — also can be calculated to determine cost overruns or underruns, while a *schedule performance index* (SPI) — calculated as BCWP/BCWS — helps organizations estimate the project's scheduling efficiency. Any value less than 1.0 is considered unfavorable.

For example, suppose that the expected cost to perform a cost analysis, one of the project tasks, is US$2,500 (BCWS) and the supply management professional assigned to the task was scheduled to finish the analysis today. In actuality, $2,250 (ACWP) has been spent and the task is about three-quarters completed (BCWP = $2,500 × 3/4). The project manager performs the following calculations:

Cost variance = BCWP − ACWP = ($2,500 × 3/4) − $2,250 = $1,875 − $2,250 = −$375

Schedule variance = BCWP − BCWS = ($2,500 × 3/4) − $2,500 = $1,875 − $2,500 = −$625

CPI = ($2,500 × 3/4)/$2,250 = 0.83

SPI = ($2,500 × 3/4)/$2,500 = 0.75

From the calculations we can conclude that more was spent on the cost analysis than what was originally planned, and the supply management professional is not making as much progress on the task as was expected.

These calculations also can be used to estimate the *estimated (remaining cost) to completion* (ETC) and the *projected (total cost) estimated at completion* (EAC) in the event nothing is done to rectify the situation. If we assume that the *budget at completion of the project task* (BAC) is US$2,500 and the BCWP is US$1,875 (US$2,500 × 3/4):

ETC = (BAC − BCWP)/CPI = ($2,500 − $1,875)/0.83 = $753

The total cost to finish this task will be:

EAC = ETC + ACWP = $753 + $2,250 = $3,003

Thus, the additional cost to finish this task is projected to be US$753. When this cost is added to the money spent to date of US$2,250, the total cost to complete the task is now US$3,003 rather than the original cost estimate of US$2,500.

Other performance measurement tools include *trend projections* and the *critical ratio*. A trend projection is a visual progress report in graphical format where actual values are plotted against the budget or schedule. The critical ratio is the product of the schedule performance index and cost performance index for a particular task, process or the entire project, and is calculated as follows:

Critical ratio = SPI × CPI

James Lewis, author of *Project Planning, Scheduling and Control*, suggests an interpretation of the results:

0.9 − 1.2: Task, process or project is okay.

0.8 − 0.9 or 1.2 − 1.3: Review progress and make corrections.

Less than 0.8: Red-flag the task, process or project.

Less than 0.6: Inform management of serious project problems.[12]

However, it is important to look at both the numerator and the denominator. For instance, a project task may be behind schedule but running below cost, suggesting that the project could be okay if that task is not on the critical path.

Using the previous example, the critical ratio can be calculated:

Critical ratio = $0.83 \times 0.75 = 0.63$

Because the critical ratio is close to 0.6, this indicates that the project task is in trouble and needs attention. If this were the critical ratio for the entire project, it is highly likely that the project manager would report the problem to management. However, because this is a single task, the project management team should be able to resolve the issues.

Project Performance Reporting

Part of the challenge of working on a project can be all the reporting that must be completed. However, for complex projects, project managers need to maintain a good reporting system to ensure that project requirements are being met within the project's constraints. These constraints include the project scope, quality, schedule, budget, resources and risks. An important factor to consider is what performance data should be collected and what process should be used to collect that data. For example, should special forms be created to collect the data? At what points in the project should the data be collected?

Once the data has been collected, it must be analyzed and then organized into a reporting format. The most common formats are project status reports, variance reports, time/cost reports and updates. The level of detail and reporting frequency should be appropriate for the target audience. For example, data often is aggregated and reported in a summary form for senior management, but is provided in more detail for the project team. All stakeholders should be included in the reporting system, but not necessarily to the same degree. The client and supply management professional may be more interested in cost and scheduling performance, while the supply management professional and engineering also may want to know if suppliers are meeting technical specifications.

Supply management professionals should keep track of their suppliers' costs, delivery and cost performance throughout the life of the contract. A file for each supplier and subsupplier helps the project manager monitor the contracts and provides the necessary information for a final evaluation.

Milestone Reviews

The project schedule, as noted earlier, should identify the major milestones or points in the project where an important deliverable should be completed or a decision should be made whether or not to continue the project. An important part of project monitoring and control is to track the project's milestones, evaluate project progress, make any needed inspections and maintain a file of the milestone reviews. A specific person should be assigned this task, and milestone reviews should be kept with the other project documentation.

Project Closure

The last step in the project life cycle is closing out the project. At this point, all personnel involved in the project will be transferred back to their functional areas or reassigned to a new project. The completed project also is transferred to the client or user department. An important step at this stage is closing out the contract.

Contract Closure Process

The contract will be closed out at this stage of the project. Supply management, the client or user and other experts generally make the final inspections to ensure the work has been completed to their satisfaction and met the terms of the contract. Any deficiencies are noted and corrected by the supplier. Any corrections to the work should be performed before final payment is made.

The supplier typically submits a request for final payment along with a release of liens and certification that all bills have been paid. Any work guarantees for materials and workmanship also should be supplied at this time. Other documentation may be required per the project plan or contract and also must be submitted before payment is made. Assuming the supplier has met the contract requirements and submitted the correct documentation, and the final product or service has been accepted, final payment then is processed and delivered. At this point, supply management also should dispose of any inventory, property or other resources not used in the contract. Once the contract is closed, supply management should evaluate the performance of each contractor/supplier.

Performance Evaluation

Supply management professionals also should evaluate their suppliers' performance to determine the extent to which they met the terms of the contract. The supply management professional can use the performance file established for each supplier as a basis for a final evaluation. This evaluation then can be used to determine the likelihood that a particular supplier will be considered for future contracts; this information can also be used as a feedback tool to determine the lessons learned and anything that will improve current practices to manage future contracts.

These evaluations become a part of the *post-project audit*. Essentially, the post-project audit is a constructive review of all aspects of the project — management, methodologies used, procedures, budgets, expenses, recordkeeping and progress. In summary, it compares what actually happened to what was supposed to happen. To measure the project's success, the project team may refer back to the schedule, milestone reviews, resource usage reports, change order documentation and progress reports. If systems were not in place or documentation is incomplete or missing, these are clear indicators of things that need to be addressed in future projects. The audit also allows the project team to identify any best practices and lessons learned. The results of the audit should be formalized into a written document, placed in the project plan file, and distributed to the project team and appropriate stakeholders.

Unfortunately, the post-project audit is probably the most neglected element of the project life cycle simply because project members already have been reassigned to other projects or moved back to their functional area. A post-project audit, however, gives the project manager and the organization an excellent opportunity to improve the process, retain those best practices and further develop the project areas that were lacking.

Summary

Project management is an exciting field, and supply management professionals play an important role in the success of complex projects. This chapter provided a discussion of the key phases that most projects follow, along with supply management's contribution at each stage of the process. Probably the key factor that will determine a project's ultimate success or failure is the degree of planning. Supply management personnel provide the expertise in contract planning for any materials or services that will be outsourced.

However, monitoring and controlling a project through the execution stage is also important. Supply management should be an integral part of the project as it administers any contracts. Lastly, a postproject audit will help an organization identify best practices that can be applied to future projects. Supply management professionals can use this opportunity to constructively review the contracting process and suppliers involved in the project.

Key Points

1. Projects are typically created to (1) create a change in the organization, (2) implement the strategic plan, (3) fulfill a contractual agreement, or (4) solve some problem or critical issue facing the organization.
2. Projects go through phases, which consist of several interrelated activities.
3. Each project has a life cycle.
4. Organizations generally align supply management's organizational structure with their project structures.
5. A project business case should be created to justify the approval of a project.
6. Supply management is involved in projects at the planning stage through source solicitation, planning and selection.
7. Supply management continues the selection of suppliers and awards contracts during the project execution stage.
8. The monitoring and control of project contracts is the responsibility of supply management and the project manager during project monitoring and control phase.
9. The project closeout requires supply management to complete any inspections, ensure the terms of the contract have been met and make final payment to the supplier.
10. A post-project audit allows supply management to constructively review the project and make adjustments for future project contracts.

CHAPTER

3

Product and Service Development

Successful new products and services not only serve some purpose and meet specific quality, design and service performance requirements, but also should introduce some unexpected innovative feature that drives customers to buy them. Today, the consumer appears to have an insatiable need for new products and services, which is evidenced by the shelves at Walmart and other "big box" stores. Organizations need more than one product or service to remain financially successful and competitive. Thus, organizations require some type of framework to help them meet the demands for both innovation and product and service development speed.

According to Steven Wheelwright and Kim Clark, authors of *Leading Product Development*, "By the time a product reaches market, it will have passed through every function, to one degree or another, in the business."[1] The traditional way to manage the process was for each affected function to work independently and then pass its assigned portion on to the next function, or what's known as the "over-the-wall" approach. However, this process proved to be slow and cumbersome. Operating with cross-functional teams has proven to be more efficient and is being used to manage the product and service development process. A number of benefits have been attributed to the use of these teams as cited by P. Fraser Johnson, Ph.D. and colleagues, authors of *Purchasing and Supply Management*, including shorter development times, resulting in lower costs and an improvement in quality.[2]

Supply management professionals have become key members on product development teams across many industries. With worldwide production facilities, BorgWarner Morse TEC manufactures power transmission, driveline systems and engine timing technologies for the automotive and light vehicle industry using more than 80,000 metric tons of commodities each year. According to the company, "most are procured as raw materials or within manufactured components purchased from its supply base." In October 2010, the company created the BorgWarner Morse TEC Global Supply Management (GSM) team because senior management needed to determine the impact of commodities on the company's business and financial forecast. "The team began developing the infrastructure for a commodity engine database integrated electronically with its ERP software. After initial design validation, the software launched in October 2011 and has delivered significant value since then."[3]

This increasingly important role in product and service development today has come about for two main reasons: (1) organizations have increased their focus on new product and service development as a means to compete, and (2) organizations have moved further away from vertical integration in which several steps to produce and deliver a product or service are controlled by one organization. A significant percentage of product costs are outsourced to outside suppliers. As a result, the role of suppliers has increased and organizations are involving them early in the planning process. A 2013 study by the IBM Institute for Business Value of Chief Procurement Officers showed that 73 percent of top performing procurement organizations are effective at gathering insights from the supplier community, compared to only 16 percent of lower performing counterparts.[4] Because of these factors, supply management takes a central role in collaborating and managing those key suppliers.

Thus, the subject of product and service development is important to supply management and will be covered more fully in this chapter. The first part of the chapter will include a general discussion of the product and service development process. The next sections will describe many of the inputs that go into the process. Finally, the chapter concludes with a discussion of the role of supply professionals in the process.

Chapter Objectives
- Describe the product and service development process.
- Define the inputs to the product and service development process.
- Explain the role of supply management in the product and service development process.

New Product and Service Development Process

The product and service development process is a series of overlapping, interdependent steps or phases beginning with the generation of new or revamped product or service ideas as shown in Figure 3-1. Although it is sometimes difficult to distinguish between the steps, there are usually checkpoints between each phase where it is determined whether or not the project should move forward. Any outstanding issues are resolved at these checkpoints, if possible, before the project moves on to the next step. While some may argue about the actual number of steps, this text identifies and describes five in more detail in the following section.

Figure 3-1: New Product or Service Development Process

Generate and Screen Ideas	Preliminary Market, Financial and Technical Assessment	Develop Product/ Service Concept	Validate and Test Market	Launch, Commercialize
Market research	Business plan	Preliminary production plan	Marketing plan	Market response data
Forecast	Staffing requirements	Preliminary staffing plan	Formal production plan	Revised marketing plan
Product design	Logistics capabilities	Preliminary distribution plan	Formal staffing plan	Revised distribution plan
Service specifications	Supplier capabilities	Supply contracts	Formal distribution plan	Revised staffing plan
	Production capabilities			

INFORMATION INPUTS

Step 1. Generate and Screen New Product and Service Ideas

New product or service ideas fall into four general categories:[5]

1. *Breakthrough ideas.* Breakthrough ideas usually redefine a family of products or services. If successful, these products or services result in an organization making significant strides in passing its competition and improving profitability. This was the case when Ford created the Taurus in the 1980s, IBM invented the SmartPhone in the 1990s and Colgate developed and introduced Optic White teeth cleaning products in 2013.

2. *Incremental ideas.* Incremental ideas are process changes that improve the delivery or quality of an existing product and service while reducing costs. For example, digitization — the replacement of human effort with computers and networking — has resulted in a shift to online banking, increasing customer convenience at a significant cost savings for financial institutions.

3. *Derivative ideas.* These ideas result in add-on features that extend, improve or modify existing products, services or processes. For example, airlines provide ATM-style kiosks at their ticket counters that allow customers to check in without the help of a gate agent. In many countries, cell phones now also function as credit cards, train commuter passes, stream video and are video-chat capable. [6]

4. *Customized ideas.* Organizations also develop ideas that result in products and services that are uniquely created to meet the specific demands of one customer. These ideas may also result in customized add-on features to new or existing products. For example, Apple Care Professional Support, with headquarters in California, will help an organization assess its current legacy system and then tailor software applications to meet its technological needs, providing a turnkey service.[7]

To generate new ideas, marketing and design teams begin by evaluating the need for the product, service or process. Organizations may have their own research and development in-house, or they may contract for design services or new product ideas. For example, an entrepreneur may need some help creating the interior design for a new restaurant concept. IDEO, a global organization headquartered in California, helps organizations innovate by providing leading-edge ideas and designs for products, services and spaces with interactive designs that bring ideas to life. If an organization requires design services, supply management will be involved in the process, searching for potential suppliers, developing requests for proposals and negotiating the final agreement.[8]

An organization also will often use customer input for ideas. Many organizations offer a toll-free number or online customer service that consumers may use to register complaints or make suggestions to improve an existing product or service. Most organizations also collect data through customer surveys, focus groups and interviews. The development of "green" mutual funds such as the Alger Green Fund[9] or the Socially Responsible Investment Funds offered by the Netherlands' Triodos Bank,[10] for example, was driven by individuals who wanted to invest their funds in a socially responsible manner. In some instances, business customers may make a direct request for a specific product, using an RFP with specifications attached. They usually are looking to their suppliers for new product or process technologies that would support the team's development efforts. However, suppliers also may develop product or process ideas internally in anticipation of an expected customer need. For example, an automotive supplier developed a window frame module that replaced 15 separate parts used previously in car designs. Rather than wait to hear from the automakers, the supplier approached the customers' designers directly to convince them to use the new module in future cars.

The design team may use some other tools to help it screen new product ideas. Some of these tools will be discussed later in the chapter.

Step 2. Obtain Concept Approval

Once the product or service idea is more fully developed, the design team presents its proposal for approval to fully develop and commercialize the product or service (see Steps 3 through 5). The best performing organizations take a systems approach, creating a portfolio process to choose projects based on the organization's strategic objectives.[11] The advantage of product portfolio management is that it incorporates some discipline and rigor to the selection of projects and helps guide an organization in the allocation of resources. Using this approach, product ideas generally are broken down into the four categories (as discussed in Step 1). Screening and evaluation then are tailored to the specific product or service category. For example, financial measures such as payback or expected profitability might be applied to derivative and incremental ideas, while a more comprehensive set of qualitative and strategic criteria could be used to evaluate innovative and customized ideas.

To increase the chances for project acceptance, the design team should develop a *business case*, which outlines the justification for marketing the product or service based on a *needs analysis*, technical requirements, cost analysis, any environmental constraints, market size and potential, projected revenues and expected profit. A needs analysis identifies the target audience, the *customer benefit package* (the tangible and intangible product or service features desired by the customer), sales projections, and the product's or service's expected fit with the organizational mission, vision and strategy. The business case also should include the customers' reaction to the proposed product characteristics and to pricing.

An organizational team or the owner (if the organization is relatively small) will assess the feasibility of the product or service design. For innovative ideas, the more completely a design team develops the business case, the better chance the product or service concept has for getting approved. When senior management is involved, it may use a scorecard to evaluate the project (as shown in Figure 3-3). The criteria used in the scorecard should be easily found in the business case.

Figure 3-3: Sample Scorecard Criteria for Product and Service Selection

Criteria 1: Fit With Mission and Strategy	Criteria 2: : Competitive Advantage
Alignment with mission	Degree of unique customer/user benefits
Importance to strategy	Degree of value to customer (value proposition)
Fit with strategy	
Effect on business strategy	Degree of differentiation from other products/services in the market
Effect on mission	Customer feedback
Criteria 3: Market Evaluation	**Criteria 4: Core Competencies**
Current size of market	Potential for leveraging core competencies and strengths in:
Potential for market growth	
Degree of competition	• Technology
Profit margins (if similar products sold by competitors)	• Operations • Distribution • Sales Force • Marketing

Figure 3-3: Sample Scorecard Criteria for Product and Service Selection *continued*

Criteria 5: Technical Capabilities	Criteria 6: Financial Impact
Current capabilities	Return on investment (NPV, IRR, and so on)
Gaps	Soundness of financial estimates
Barriers	Potential financial impact
Past track record	Level of risk
Technical results, to date	Ability to mitigate risks
Scoring:	
0 – poor or low	
10 – excellent or very high	

Source: Adapted from R.G. Cooper and S.J. Edgett, "Ten Ways to Make Better Portfolio and Project Selection Decisions," Product Development Institute Inc.®, (June 2006), accessed December 13, 2013, http://www.stage-gate.net/downloads/working_papers/wp_24.pdf.

Step 3. Develop Product/Service Concept

If the proposal is approved, the product or service concept is fully designed and the specifications are firmed up. A prototype is built in the case of a manufactured product and the manufacturing process is designed and integrated into the current environment. Alternatively, with services, the delivery system is created, which includes both the tangible and intangible elements. Marketing also may do some preliminary testing to determine a price point for the new product or service.

Fast-casual restaurant chain Captain D's, for example, was experiencing a shrinking core market and not attracting younger people. In response, the organization introduced a new store prototype in 2006 that included a name change from Captain D's Seafood to Captain D's Seafood Kitchen, a new logo, a new store design and an updated menu. As a result, "Guest counts are up significantly" and "customer feedback has been positive."[12] REpower Systems AG of Hamburg, Germany, approved the idea of a larger wind turbine to produce electricity that could be positioned on offshore wind farms. A prototype was first tested in 2003 at the organization's onshore test site in Brunsbüttel, Schleswig-Holstein, for maintainability and ease of service. Subsequently, the product was successfully introduced into the market in 2006 with its first installation in Scotland.[13]

In the event a supplier is developing a major component or module, the product development team will need to see a prototype to evaluate its performance. With the aid of *computer-aided design* (CAD) and *computer-aided manufacturing* (CAM) software, prototyping has become an easier process. The supplier submits its plans and design specifications for its portion electronically to the design team, which then is "preassembled" and evaluated against the organization's own design. Tower Tools, a Leicester, England-based company specializing in molds for rubber products such as aerospace seals, used CAD/CAM to design the tooling for the cargo door for Boeing's 777 freighter. Tower was able to deliver the first seal six weeks earlier than the norm for a seal of that size, and the seal fit as promised.[14]

Step 4. Validate and Test Products and Services

Once the concept is fully developed into a product or service, it should be validated and tested in the marketplace. Testing assures that the product or service meets the defined user's needs. For instance, in 2005, Canadian-based Dairy Fresh Farms, Inc. partnered with Lucerne Dairy and Safeway Stores, Inc. to test a unique patented dairy process that combines skim milk with canola oil to create a new 2 percent milk-equivalent product. The product was tested in 205 Safeway stores in Canada by offering demonstrations, samples and educational materials to 300,000 consumers.[15] Validation provides proof that the product or service is being used as intended with the expected outcome. For example, sunscreen manufacturers must validate the sun protection claims made on their products through clinical and/or in vitro testing.

There are several ways to improve product validation and testing. First, an organization should create a standardized system for product and service validation and testing. In other words, each product or service should be validated and tested using the same survey questions, sampling plans and analytical methods. As an organization continues to test, over time some normative data will develop, which will help it to interpret any test scores. An important issue to address is how good the product or service is against the norm for other like products or services developed in the past. The product or service also should be validated and tested in a "real" environment because the results are usually more accurate than the results from lab tests. Tire organizations, for example, road test their tires on streets and freeways; cleansers or detergents are tested in the home; and new menu items usually are tested in restaurants.[16]

Step 5. Commercialize Product

If the response to the product or service is positive, production is ramped up and distributed in Step 5. Experience shows that organizations generally should start small and then change production and delivery as evidenced by demand patterns. New services may be initiated in selected markets; if they are successful, they may be expanded throughout the enterprise.

To increase the success rate of the development process, organizations should optimize the analysis process and evaluation of its current capabilities. The next section describes some of the inputs to the product or service development process.

Inputs to the Product and Service Development Process

As shown in Figure 3-4, the product and service development process relies on a number of inputs for success. The product or service design should be in line with the organization's mission, vision and strategy. (See *Leadership in Supply Management*, Volume 3 of the ISM *Professional Series*, for additional discussion on organizational strategy.) Any new product or service ideas should be developed in consideration of the current product line or services being offered; generally, a new product or service is most successful when it is an extension of, or complementary to, the existing product or service. Customer needs and desires should certainly be a major factor in developing new product and service ideas. However, product and service development will be constrained by either an organization's own internal capabilities or those that can be attained from outside suppliers. For example, an organization will have a given body of knowledge and technology that will serve as a boundary, which can be extended through an external supplier's expertise.

Figure 3-4: Inputs to New Product or Service Development Process

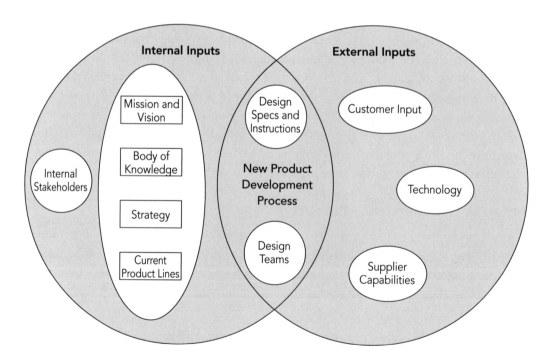

An organization should evaluate a number of areas to help it develop products and services that will be commercially successful. This includes an analysis of the marketplace, whether international or domestic, as well as the current capabilities of its functions such as operations, staff, supply management and logistics. These areas will be discussed in more detail in the following sections.

Market Analysis

First, an organization should perform a market analysis. Three popular methods employed to understand the marketplace more fully are the SWOT analysis, Porter's Five Forces analysis and benchmarking. The *SWOT analysis*, an analysis of an organization's strengths, weaknesses, opportunities and threats, is frequently used and was discussed more fully in Chapter 2. Porter's Five Forces analysis and benchmarking are other tools, which will be described further in the following section.

Porter's Five Forces Analysis. Michael Porter, a Harvard Business School professor and pre-eminent scholar in the field of management, developed the five forces model to help organizations develop a competitive strategy by examining their environment.[17] At the center of the model is the specific industry and level of competition or rivalry among the organizations. Other environmental forces that affect the level of intensity among the competition are the existing rivalry among competitors, the potential for new entrants into the marketplace, the threat of substitute products or services, the relative bargaining power of buyers, and the relative bargaining strength of suppliers. Porter's Five Forces analysis model suggests the importance of the role of supply management early on in Step 1 of the product or service development process.

Rivalry happens when one or more existing competitors realize an opportunity to improve their position, or when they are responding to the pressure from other competitors. Pressures may come in the form of new product and service introductions, mergers or acquisitions, or price cuts. Much of the rivalry and jockeying for position depends on the size of the industry (number of competitors), the pace of industry growth (slow to fast), and the extent of product differentiation (low to high), to name just a few factors. For example, in the running shoe industry in the mid-2000s, there were two major competitors — Adidas and Nike — and many smaller ones. Industry growth was relatively flat while product differentiation was generally based on branding strategies. German-owned Adidas acquired Reebok International, Ltd. in 2006 to gain market share, increasing pressure on U.S.-owned Nike and other rivals. Adidas also has been aggressive in developing new technologies to increase sales. In 2013, it introduced Springblade shoes — which are extremely light, have a sock-like feel and contain sixteen high tech polymer blades intended to improve a person's stride.[18]

New entrants in an industry look to gain a share of the market, but also to bring in added capacity. They may introduce products or services by undercutting current prices, thus reducing profitability for the industry. However, the extent of new competition depends on existing barriers to entry, which include restricted or closed distribution channels; economies of scale; existing customer loyalties; the need for large financial investment; the cost for the customer to switch to another product or service; other cost issues such as proprietary technologies, favorable access to materials, locations or government subsidies; and government policies. Another related issue is the response from existing competitors. For example, Harris Teeter, a regional grocery chain in the Southeast U.S., announced in 2013 that it was looking for a buyer. Kroger, a large U.S.-based grocery chain, purchased Harris Teeter to improve its competitive stance against Publix, another regional chain, and Walmart.[19]

Suppliers can exert power by threatening to reduce the quality of their products and services, or raise prices. When the supplier is powerful relative to the industry, such as the only supplier or one of a handful of suppliers, its threat is all that much greater. If the industry is not that important to the supplier's business, the supplier provides a product or service important to the buyer's survival, there is a lack of substitute products, switching costs for the buyer are high or the supplier has the potential to integrate forward into the buyer's business, the supplier becomes all that more powerful. For example, De Beers, a family of diamond exploration, mining and trading organizations with headquarters in Johannesburg, South Africa, had a great deal of influence in the diamond industry because it controlled the most productive diamond mines. However, the diamond industry has become much more segmented, which has significantly reduced De Beers' power.[20] Even a supplying country can exert power. In 2012, China reduced its total exports of rare earth metals, causing an abrupt and large spike in cost and a scramble by other countries to reopen old mines or plan new ones.[21] Supply management organizations also can exert influence over their suppliers for a number of reasons. According to Michael Porter, the buyer is more powerful when the volume of purchases is larger compared to the supplier's sales, the cost of purchases is significant, the product purchased is considered a commodity, switching costs are low, profit margins are low (increasing pressure to negotiate lower prices) and there is a threat of the buyer integrating backward toward the supplier.

Lastly, substitute products essentially limit the extent of price increases to the customer. The price of aluminum cans, for example, is constrained because there are several substitutes including glass, plastic and steel. The price of televisions continues to come down as competition increases between organizations that produce plasma, LCD and LED formats.

Benchmarking. According to the ISM *Glossary* (2014), a *benchmark* is "a standard or point of reference used in measuring or judging an organization's performance according to selected criteria." A benchmark also is considered the standard of excellence for a particular business process. Any benchmarking should always be conducted with the customers' expectations in mind, which can be gathered through surveys or interviews.

The results of the benchmarking process help organizations measure their own performance by examining other processes within their own organizations or against other outside organizations considered "the best" at what they do. In other words, benchmarking is "a process by which selected practices and results of one organization are compared to those of one or more other organizations to establish targets for improvement. Benchmarking can be performed by identifying world-class organizations and visiting them for information-gathering and comparison or by responding to surveys from third-party independent research organizations that collect, aggregate and disseminate benchmark data" (ISM *Glossary* 2014).

Production and Staff Capabilities

When new products or services are being added to an organization's product line, this will potentially impact production and/or staffing requirements if capacity is being fully utilized. Thus, it is important to go through a structured planning process to estimate human resources, production or new equipment needs based on the addition of new products or services. These plans essentially translate an organization's *business plan* into an *operational plan*, often referred to as production and staffing plans. A business plan includes the organization's projections for income, expenses and profit, which are supported by budgets, a projected cash flow statement and a pro forma balance sheet. The plan should provide information on any new product introductions, expected market share gains and capital investments.

A number of inputs go into the staffing and production plans, as shown in Figure 3-5. An important component to successful planning is feedback from the product development team, including new product/service introductions and any planned changes to product or service designs. Distribution and marketing also provide important information, including demand forecasts and firm orders. This type of feedback and more will be collected to start the planning process. In general, a team will review the demand requirements, period by period, over the planning horizon. The length of the period will depend on the organization, and could be a week, a month or a quarter.

Figure 3-5: Inputs to Production/Service Delivery and Staffing Plans

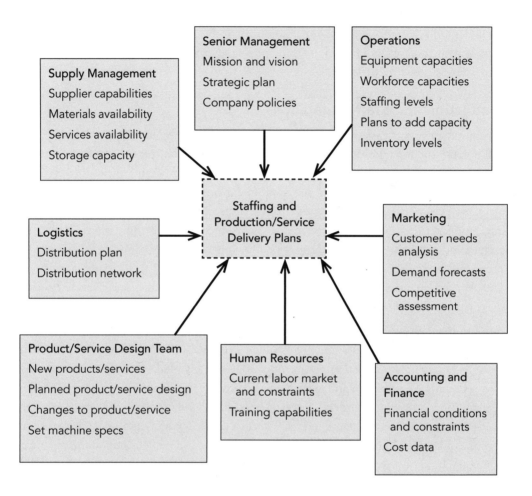

The team then will identify the constraints and costs of the plan, as well as possible alternatives that might improve the plan. Constraints include the current operational capacity and capabilities of any equipment and the workforce based on the existing line of products or services. Operations should have the data on the use of current capacity (80 percent, for instance) and desired *capacity cushion*. The capacity cushion is "the amount of reserve capacity that a firm maintains to handle sudden increases in demand or temporary losses of production capacity," and will vary from industry to industry.[22] U.S. manufacturers, in general, keep an average cushion of 18 percent; electric utilities prefer a cushion of 15 percent to 20 percent to avoid loss of service; hotels experience customer service problems if the capacity cushion drops below 20 percent.[23] In conjunction with capacity cushion estimates, an organization needs to know how much flexibility the operations team has in its ability to respond to change. For example, does operations have a trained temporary workforce available in the event demand for a new product or service is higher than initially anticipated? How quickly can new workers be trained or temporary workers be brought on board to fill the gap? If capacity is limited, an organization might decide to outsource the design and production of certain parts, components or even the entire product to avoid additional capital investments if the supplier can provide equal or higher levels of quality at a lower cost. A service provider may decide to expand its hours or hire additional workers to increase capacity, take reservations or make appointments to control demand — or simply let customers wait.

Based on organizational needs and constraints, the plan then is prepared, usually through a series of revisions, until it is found to be acceptable. Once the plan is approved, the plan may be changed or updated as circumstances change.

Logistics and Distribution Capabilities

The capabilities of both inbound logistics and distribution are also important when evaluating a new product's or service's potential for successful market introduction. If the product or service cannot reach the marketplace because of distribution problems, certainly customers cannot buy it. Book publishers have been forced to rethink book distribution because many towns and cities no longer have brick-and-mortar bookstores. Even the large chains are disappearing. Borders was liquidated in 2011 and HMV sold Waterstone. Large retailers like Walmart and Target filled the void to a certain extent, but demand only the best-selling book titles. To fill the gap, publishers have moved to electronic publishing.[24] Leapfrog Enterprises, Inc., a small U.S. toy manufacturer, ran into distribution problems as it introduced 15 new toy products for the 2004 Christmas season. As a result, fourth quarter sales dropped 23 percent from the previous year as Mattel drained off market share with competing products.[25]

The best organizations integrate logistical decisions with all other aspects of new product or service development. For example, IBM introduces new product platforms approximately every 12 to 18 months, with small upgrades in between. When a new product is planned for production in one of its global factories, IBM must determine if there will be enough transportation capacity for inbound shipment of parts, and then enough outbound transportation to ship product to its international markets.[26] Some important factors, however, must be considered. For example, what will be the distribution channel(s) for the new product? Banks offer new products, such as certificates of deposit and other investments, through brick-and-mortar facilities and online, or just online. The Coca-Cola Company distributes its line of soft drink and water products through several channels, including vending machines, grocery stores, gas stations and restaurants. Each channel has different transportation and storage requirements. Two other important issues are whether a new channel must be created and if the current system has the capability to add the new product. For example, a beverage organization used a third-party logistics provider (3PL) to distribute its line of refrigerated drinks. The organization launched a new shelf-stable drink; however, it did not own dry van carriers and projected demand for the new drink was highly uncertain, so it faced difficulties in developing contracts with new carriers. As a result, the organization went back to its 3PL and asked it to develop a carrier base for the new product based on some very rough demand estimates.

Logistics also needs to have a good understanding of the organization's manufacturing (or service) strategy for the product. This is why it is important to have cross-functional design teams. If an organization plans to use a just-in-time or lean strategy for manufacturing, for example, the approach to inbound logistics will vary from using a more traditional strategy. On the outbound side, if the organization plans a mass customization strategy, logistics requirements will differ from traditional manufacturing approaches. Because Hewlett-Packard (HP) sells computers and peripherals (including printers), it uses a mass customization strategy. Thus, power cords are packed right before shipment and instruction manuals can be found online.

U.S.-based printing solutions provider Lexmark International, Inc. developed cross-functional teams to improve the new product development process, with several goals in mind: (1) increase design flexibility to allow for more product differentiation at the point of distribution; (2) significantly reduce the number of times a product is touched during final assembly and distribution; (3) incorporate an early review of size and weight requirements to reduce shipping costs; and (4) improve pallet configuration at the factory so handling at the distribution center could be streamlined. As a result, the team came up with a two-pronged approach to supply chain management. The organization's high-end printers, with many features, are produced using a mass customization strategy, postponing final assembly until an order is received. Inexpensive inkjet printers, with fairly predictable demand, are mass-produced and shipped directly to retail outlets.[27]

Logistics also needs to be involved in product design when it comes to packaging. Packaging not only is a tool to help sell a product, but it also provides protection during shipment. Proper packaging can help reduce transportation costs as well. Packaging should be designed to fit on pallets and maximize the use of shipping space within a container, truck, train, ship or plane.

To minimize waste, organizations should perform packaging optimization, which can eliminate the use of unnecessary packaging by balancing the use of packaging materials against the protection each material will provide. The goal is to use the least amount of packaging that will provide an adequate level of protection within the shipping environment. Organizations should also seek solutions that reduce the need for landfills. The benefits of optimizing the packaging include a reduction in waste as well as cost savings in packaging materials and shipping costs. In one of its sustainability initiatives, Coca Cola, for example, developed the packaging for the Coca Cola PlantBottle™ "from renewable resources that are 100 percent recyclable."[28]

The packaging optimization process begins by understanding the product, such as its value; its physical characteristics such as length, height, width and weight; and its fragility. It is also important to have information on the packaging materials that are available and the properties of each packaging material, along with the recommended application. Third, an organization should be familiar with the acceptable level of damage to the package, the modes of transportation that will be used and whether the package will be reused, possibly as a container. With all this in mind, the final decision will depend on the packaging budget.

Several important questions to consider during this process include: Does the existing or proposed packaging material just meet or exceed requirements? Will less protection still adequately protect the product? Is any cushioning material required, such as Bubble Wrap? If so, will less cushioning still protect the product from damage during shipment?

The packaging material and the product will normally be tested to evaluate the potential for damage during shipment. Typically, the packaging material will be continually refined until just the right amount is found to protect the product at the lowest cost. If a package must meet certain national or international standards, some outside professional help may be required. The ASTM International and the International Safe Transit Association (ISTA) have developed testing standards to assess the various transport packaging materials available today. Testing labs also are available that have been certified by the ISTA. These labs perform drop and vibration testing through ISTA's Transit Tested program. The ISTA also offers certification programs for packaged products and packaging professionals.

Lastly, logistics will need to plan for the expected lead times and initial inventory levels required to meet product launch requirements and storage locations. These decisions naturally tie in with the location of target markets, transportation requirements, product launch strategy and product availability. In some instances, current warehouse facilities may be adequate if the organization plans a slow ramp-up in production. If, on the other hand, the organization plans to "flood" the market, logistics may have to contract for additional warehouse space. Zara, a Spanish apparel company, creates and produces new fashion designs in 10 to 15 days, so its supply chain must be fast and flexible. Its distribution center in La Coruna, Spain then ships the new products twice a week to more than 1,600 company-owned stores located worldwide. La Coruna is located close to an international airport so merchandise can be flown overnight to stores in the U.S., South America and Asia. Trucks are used to quickly transport goods to stores in Europe.[29]

Supplier Capability and Capacity Analysis

One of supply management's responsibilities is to be knowledgeable about current supplier capabilities and to develop new suppliers. To make this happen, the supply management professional must understand the makeup and incorporation of any materials or resources that will be used to manufacture the product or support the service delivery process. Thus, specialists will be involved in assessing the capabilities and capacity of suppliers during the evaluation and selection process. Some questions that generally arise include: Which suppliers should be involved in the product or service development process? Will the supplier be able to meet our requirements? Does the supplier's "technology roadmap" align with ours? To what level should the supplier be part of the project, given the complexity of the product or service?

This analysis begins with *supply forecasts* to determine whether an adequate supply of the materials, parts or resources will be available to the buying organization in sufficient quantities to meet production or service delivery requirements, at the right quality and in the required time frame. Any forecasting should be balanced by economic conditions and trends that might affect supply such as those listed below:

- Fluctuating lead times due to demand increases, supply constraints or a supplier's poor financial condition;
- Uncertain labor conditions, because of strikes or threats of strikes;
- Restraint on capital, affecting the supplier's ability to meet production or service provision commitments;
- Political events, such as new environmental laws, changes in political appointments or inflation;
- Natural disasters, new discoveries or depletion of a commodity; and
- Changing trade rules or regulations.[30]

This information then can be used to develop a supply management strategy, including the insource/outsource decision. Once a strategy is set, a supply management team creates plans and options that are unique to each commodity. The forecasts, market conditions and proposed strategy are presented to the design team and management.

If the supply management professional determines it would be better to outsource, he or she begins the process of identifying, evaluating and selecting specific suppliers. Some suppliers may already have a working relationship with the supply management organization. Thus, those suppliers' past histories and prior experiences with the organization, as well as their industry reputations, would be evaluated. The supply management professional also may have to seek and develop new or alternate sources of supply for materials and equipment.

If an identified supplier has not been prequalified, supply management does so at this time, essentially performing a risk assessment. Under consideration would be issues such as whether the supplier has the capability to meet the necessary requirements to integrate into the product or service development process. Questions to look at for each potential supplier include: Does it have the technical capabilities, such as the necessary tooling? Does the supplier meet quality requirements? Does it have adequately trained personnel? Does it have the capability to meet the product or service development schedule? Can the supplier meet the lead time requirements for production and delivery? Will it meet the cost constraints?[31] This type of analysis may require a visit to the supplier's facilities. The supply management professional also might confer with colleagues at other organizations who have had a relationship with the supplier to estimate the supplier's capabilities.

More frequently today, suppliers are involved in product or service development from the ground up, as mentioned at the beginning of this chapter and described in the Boeing example cited earlier. *Early supplier involvement* (ESI), according to the ISM *Glossary*

(2014), is "a practice that brings together one or more selected suppliers with a buyer's product or service design team early in the product development process. The objective is to use the supplier's expertise and experience in developing a product specification that is designed for effective and efficient product or service rollout." Suppliers may offer substitute products, processes or technologies of equal quality.

Supply Management's Role in Product and Service Design

As mentioned throughout this chapter, supply management professionals can make a number of significant contributions to new product or service development. They can help in the insource/outsource decision, estimate supply chain requirements and recommend the best suppliers for a given project. Additionally, supply management professionals can help the product or service development team select a design based on the available alternatives. This will help reduce the amount of resources used, inventory holding costs and transportation and production costs; improve quality; and reduce time to market. Lastly, supply management professionals can contribute in planning for the expected obsolescence of component parts or resources as necessary, or the discontinuance of a specific service provision. This is especially important for organizations that create products and services with long expected life cycles but short component or resource life cycles, such as in the electronics industry. Some alternatives that organizations may use to mitigate the risk of obsolescence and the supply management's role include the following:

1. The organization decides to self-fund a lifetime buy of the component or resource. The supply management professional develops an agreement with the supplier to ensure that a component or resource will be available until the product or service is redesigned or discontinued.
2. An organization negotiates a commitment from the customer to financially support the future availability of a component or resource. The supply management professional negotiates with the supplier for a lifetime supply of the component or resource.
3. The organization does no preplanning for obsolescence. In the event a component or resource no longer is available, the supply management professional attempts to source for an alternate component or resource solution that will be an equivalent in form, fit and function.
4. The organization decides to redesign the product or service. At this point, the supply management professional sources the new components or resources.
5. The organization chooses to sunset the product or service because the component parts or resources are obsolete.[32]

As evidenced in this chapter, the supply management professional's role really extends across the entire product and service development process. However, many organizations involve supply management in varying degrees based on the type of product or service, the amount of required outsourcing, and their attitude toward early involvement and cross-functional teaming. Figure 3-6 illustrates a number of ways supply management may be integrated into the process.[33] On some projects, supply management professionals are needed full-time and are fully integrated into the development project, teaming with engineers on the design of many specific parts that require a particular technology. In the event the number of parts required is fewer, a supply management professional still may work closely with engineering but on a part-time basis. Supply also may team with internal customers on the development of statements of work (SOWs) or service level agreements (SLAs). When supply management expertise is only occasionally needed, someone may be called into the project on an ad hoc basis. While these first three scenarios involve a greater degree of supply management dedication, there are other instances where the supply management professional plays the role of coordinator. A supply management coordinator is on the project development team, managing a supply specialist external to the team. Sometimes, a supply coordinator, along with his or her team, act as product or service development team members on a part-time or full-time basis.

Figure 3-6: Supply Management's Involvement in Product or Service Department

Project Complexity	Small	Large
High	Supply management coordinator of others outside project team	Supply management coordinator integrated into team (part-time or full time)
Low	Ad hoc supply management involvement	Integrated supply management involvement

Project Size

Source: Adapted from Nicolette Lakemond, Ferrie van Echtelt and Finn Wynstra, "A Configuration Typology for Involving Purchasing Specialists in Product Development," *The Journal of Supply Chain Management* (Fall 2001), 11–20.

Early involvement of supply management is important for the success of the new product or service. *Early purchasing involvement* (EPI) is "a practice that involves purchasing professionals in the new product or service development process from its inception" (ISM *Glossary* 2014). Some attributes of EPI include the following:
- Participating in new product or service cross-functional teams;
- Helping evaluate and select suppliers;
- Working with key suppliers on new product or service provision projects;
- Using target costing to improve competitiveness; and
- Using a quality management system to improve performance.[34]

At Cisco Systems, Inc., headquartered in the U.S. in San Jose, California, supply management works closely with engineers to establish the technology needs for its future networking products such as integrated circuits and microprocessors. It also helps decide which suppliers will be involved in the new product development process, and then carefully oversees the suppliers' technology roadmaps to make sure they are investing in technologies based on Cisco's future needs.[35] In a CAPS Research study, McGinnis and Vallopra found that if suppliers are involved in the new product development process, success will be more likely if supply management also "has a significant new product development role."[36]

Supply management also may create a *qualified products list* (QPL), which will help it speed up the supplier selection decision. A QPL is a listing of products, product families, supplies and equipment that are known to meet the needs of the organization. Prequalified products or product families have been evaluated to verify that they meet all applicable specification requirements. These products usually have been tested in advance of purchase because they take some time to test and evaluate.

Thus, supply management might participate in a number of different activities. These activities are discussed in more detail in the following sections.

Research and Development

Benchmarking. Benchmarking, described in greater detail in Chapter 2 and earlier in this chapter, is a common approach for setting performance standards, objectives, measurements and processes. One form of benchmarking is to disassemble a competitor's product to uncover any clues regarding its superiority. If any organization is building a similar product, this may help supply management in the buying process.

To uncover information about competitors' products or services, supply management also may refer to trade journals, the Internet or other industry-related publications to gain information on top-notch organizations. Suppliers are also a good direct source of information. They can provide the names of organizations they find to be "the best" in a particular functional area or business practice. Lastly, supply management might benchmark by searching published industry databases.

Request for Information. Supply management also may gather information about available products, processes or technology by sending out a *request for information* to at least one supplier. According to the ISM *Glossary* (2014), a request for information, or RFI, is "a solicitation document used to obtain general information about products, services or suppliers. It is an information request, not binding on either the supplier or the purchaser, and is often used prior to specific requisitions for items."

Supplier Research. The purpose of supplier research is to learn more about current as well as potential suppliers in terms of the way they operate and their market positions. This knowledge helps supply management to develop and select a base of suitable alternative sources of supply, as well as prepare for the negotiation process.

Sources of information may include literature provided by the supplier, government reports, ThomasNet®, past supply management files on suppliers, or database searches via the Internet. Supply management also may discuss the situation with customers or users, economic development forums, foreign embassies and other colleagues in the supply management field.

Target Costing

Target costing is "a structured approach to determine the life-cycle costs at which a proposed product with a specified functionality and quality must be produced to generate the desired level of profitability over its life cycle when sold at its anticipated selling price" (ISM *Glossary* 2014). Supply management professionals use this approach to identify and communicate the allowable price for a supplier's product or service, and create performance guidelines. Target costing has the promise to improve both the cost and functionality of a new product. A CAPS Research study reported that "target costing is a critical tool for linking all the functions in an organization to support a common goal for new product development. Target costing is a way to ensure that all functions involved in new product development understand the customers' needs as well as the cost goals, and are all aiming at the same target."[37]

As shown in Figure 3-7, when a product is developed, the new product development team has to keep pricing in mind and consider not only whether the customer will buy this product, but at what price. Thus, a sales price will have to be set. The profit margin is the difference between the sales price and the costs to produce the product. Typically, organizations will start with a sales price — what the market will bear — and the desired profit.

CHAPTER 3: Product and Service Development

Figure 3-7: Target Costing Process Map

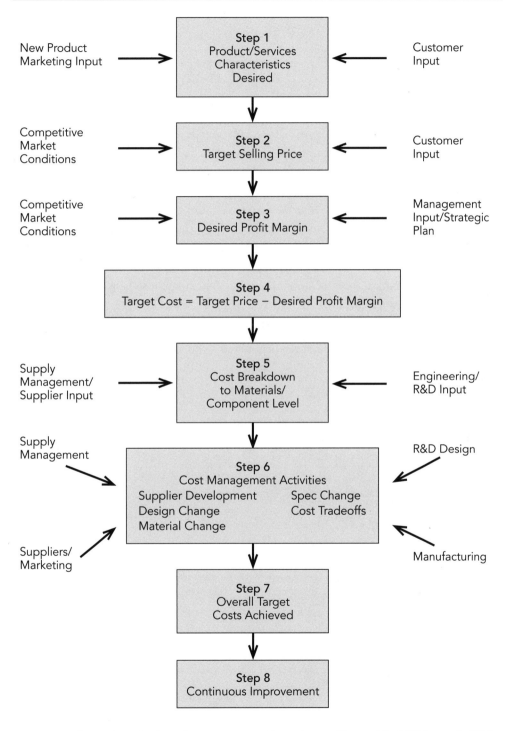

Source: Lisa Ellram, *The Role of Supply Management in Target Costing* (Tempe, AZ: CAPS Research, 1999) 16.

The target cost is calculated as follows:

Target cost = expected sales price − desired profit

The amount remaining is the total allowable cost to make that product or to perform that service, including materials. This cost then is allocated among all related purchases and internal costs, resulting in a target cost for each item.

Meeting the target cost, however, probably will require some cost management activities. Some changes may have to be made to the original design, specifications or materials. This will mean performing a cost trade-off analysis. Internally, negotiations may take place between design, engineering, marketing and others to compromise to reach the target cost. Supply management professionals also most likely will have to work with suppliers to be sure their prices come in at or below the target cost. Often, further analysis and negotiation is needed in an effort to remove costs from both the organization's and supplier's operations to reduce the price to an acceptable target level. The procurement organization may have to take a critical look at its own internal processes and make improvements. This process may require some additional supplier development to help the suppliers find ways to cut their own internal costs. The following example shows how a hypothetical manufacturer performed target cost analysis.

ABC, a Silicon Valley manufacturer, negotiated a contract to produce 15,000 units of one of its products for US$98/unit. ABC's normal profit margin is 25 percent. Thus, the target cost was calculated as follows:

Target cost = target price − expected profit margin
= 15,000($98) − .25(15,000 × $98)
= $1,470,000 − $367,500
= $1,102,500
The target cost/unit is:
$1,102,500/15,000 = $73.50

The product development team estimated the cost for materials and production at $80. Thus, there was a gap of:

$80 − $73.50 = $6.50/unit
or a total cost of:
$6.50 × 15,000 units = $97,500.

The team first analyzed material scrap and made recommendations to improve performance by 35 percent, which will reduce the unit cost by US$4. Some improvements in material handling also were made to reduce the distance materials traveled, and supply management negotiated with its suppliers in an effort to reduce their costs. These two efforts further reduced costs by US$1.50 a unit. The overall result was a cost savings of US$82,500. Management applauded the team's efforts and approved the contract, although the target costs were higher than expected. Later, management went to the marketing department to review the pricing structure for the product and some adjustments were made upward.

Product Sustainability Evaluation

While keeping costs down is certainly a priority, supply management professionals should keep in mind ISM's *Principles of Sustainability and Social Responsibility*. Specifically, best-in-class organizations in sustainability and social responsibility incorporate specific and measurable practices across their supply chain. They will:

1. Support sustainability and social responsibility principles and initiatives.
2. Commit resources to support sustainability and social responsibility principles, practices and education.
3. Build and integrate programs throughout the organization and cascade them throughout the supply chain.
4. Engage and involve executive management to ensure sustainability and social responsibility initiatives are integral to the culture and decision-making of the organization.
5. Ensure the sharing of strategies, policies, procedures, best practices and other relevant material to assist organizations working to improve sustainability and social responsibility behavior internally and with suppliers.
6. Encourage building and integrating a program throughout the organization and the supply chain.
7. Make enlightened business decisions that often move beyond the "letter of the law."[38]

In many instances, governments worldwide are putting common sustainability practices into law, such as the use of recycled materials; the disposal of waste materials; and compliance with local, regional and national regulations.

Supply management can influence the creation of sustainable products at a number of points in the product or service development process. However, involving supply management at the inception of all product development on the design team will make the biggest impact on the environment. For instance, in the product design stage, supply management may research and make recommendations regarding changing out product materials that contain less ozone-depleting substances or hazardous waste. It also may be possible to reduce the amount of materials used without reducing functionality. Life-cycle analysis also can be performed, which is the evaluation of all the inflows and outflows of materials on the bill of materials, as well as any byproducts of the production process. Supply management professionals can determine the potential to recycle or reuse the product once it reaches the end of its life cycle. Additionally, supply management professionals and senior management must work with suppliers to ensure they meet organization standards.

Suppliers should be implementing similar process improvement initiatives to reduce waste and emissions. They also need a formal environmental plan in place that supply management can review and evaluate, and make recommendations for improvement. Lastly, the organization should send the message that environmental responsibility is a priority and will be part of the suppliers' evaluations in determining future business dealings.[39]

Summary

Supply management professionals play an important role in the product and service development process. This chapter provides a discussion of the role of supply management in the development process. A general overview of product or service development was provided. The need for assessing the market and internal capabilities also was discussed at length. Lastly, supply management activities that can make a positive impact on the process were described.

Key Points

1. The product and service development process is a series of overlapping, interdependent steps or phases, beginning with the generation of new or revamped product or service ideas.
2. Organizations that perform best in product and service development take a systems approach, creating a systematic portfolio process to choose projects based on the organization's strategic objectives.
3. To increase the chances for project acceptance, the design team should develop a *business case*, which outlines the justification for marketing the product/service based on a *needs analysis*, technical requirements, cost analysis, any environmental constraints, market size and potential, projected revenues, and expected profit.
4. When new products or services are being introduced, an organization should go through a planning process to estimate human resources, production and other resource needs based on an organization's business plan. The team also should identify the constraints and costs of the plan, as well as possible alternatives that might work better.
5. An organization's logistical capabilities should be assessed. Factors that affect logistical capability include the availability of distribution channels, the effect of the manufacturing or service strategy on logistics, and packaging issues.
6. Supplier capabilities also should be determined. Some questions supply management professionals need to consider that affect supplier capabilities include (1) Which suppliers should be involved in the product or service development process?; (2) Will the supplier be able to meet our requirements?; (3) Does the supplier's "technology roadmap" align with ours?; (4) To what level should the supplier be part of the project, given the complexity of the product?

7. Supply forecasts are used to determine whether an adequate supply of the materials and supporting services will be sufficiently available to the buying organization to support production of the new product or delivery of the new service.
8. Suppliers today are involved in product or service development from the ground up, known as early supplier involvement (ESI), with the goal to use the supplier's expertise and experience in developing a product or service specification that is designed for effective and efficient rollout.
9. Supply professionals can contribute to the development process by establishing supply chain requirements, benchmarking, helping assess designs, and conducting supplier research and target costing.

CHAPTER 4

Foundations of Forecasting Practices

In today's world, organizations are operating in a dynamic environment with constantly changing conditions. Customers change their minds resulting in quickly needed adjustments to production, delivery and service provision schedules. Disruptions in supply also may occur because of any number of factors, including weather, political upheavals, terrorism or new restrictive government regulations, among others. Businesses go through acquisitions, mergers or changes in leadership. New opportunities for growth also may arise through new product lines, strategic alliances or expansion. Thus, organizations are faced with making decisions based on this continual change. Typically, decisions are based on a *forecast* — a prediction of the future or, as defined in the ISM *Glossary* (2014), "a prediction based on quantitative (numeric) or qualitative (non-numeric) data. Forecasters attempt to predict future activities, such as demand, with sufficient accuracy to be the basis of planning." The overall purpose of the forecast is to minimize uncertainty in the decision-making process. Inherent in this definition is the idea that forecasters are involved in first recognizing and then evaluating the various forms of risk, identified as one of the Core Influencers in the Strategic Supply Management Concept framework. (See the "Series Overview" at the beginning of this book.)

Forecasting is necessary to planning and operating any business, helping leaders take the proper course of action. Thus, it is important to make sure the forecasting process is effective. Poor forecasting can lead to customer service problems, understocking or overstocking of materials, underproduction or overproduction, too few or too many employees (among other issues) with negative financial implications. Large organizations usually have special forecasting units; however, whether large or small, organizations need some type of forecasting system that will support the decision-making process. Although forecasting will never be perfect, organizations should strive to come up with the best, unbiased view of the future.

Supply management professionals are actively involved in the forecasting process for two main reasons, beginning with the need to assure a sufficient supply of goods and services is available to run the organization. This means selecting and working with the most qualified suppliers so they are prepared to deliver the needed quantities of materials or services at the proper point in time. To better prepare the supplier, the best organizations share forecast data and jointly make adjustments as actual demand varies from that forecast. Second, supply management professionals must make sure that goods and services are available at an acceptable price and quality level. This is important because the price of intermediary inputs will have an impact on finished product and service prices, which may have an effect on demand.

Because of the importance of forecasting, two chapters are devoted to this subject. Chapter 4 begins with several basic economic issues and a discussion of business cycles. Next, a review of the evolution of the global marketplace is provided, followed by a discussion of the value of leading, lagging and coincident economic indicators, with some examples of each. Lastly, some sources of data used to develop forecasts are presented. Chapter 5 provides a discussion of the models and mechanics used to prepare demand forecasts.

Chapter Objectives
- Describe the economic factors that affect a forecast.
- Explain the impact of globalization on forecasting.
- Discuss the role of economic indicators in the forecasting process.
- Describe some commonly used publications and data sources used in the forecasting process.

General Issues in Economics

The world operates with a combination of economic markets, and it is difficult to find a standardization of terms. However, this section will briefly describe three common types of economies.

A Market Economy

A *pure market* or *free market economy* exists when the production and distribution of goods and services takes place through the mechanism of free markets guided by a free pricing system. In other words, businesses have the freedom to determine what materials and services they will purchase and what products and services they will produce and sell based on current prices, available supply, and demand. Likewise, consumers can freely buy what they want based on price, supply and demand. All labor, goods, services and capital are free from any government restriction or trade barriers so they can move freely across national borders.

In reality, no country operates with a pure market economy. Many countries have restrictions to prevent monopolies from forming, and some are privatizing state-run firms. For example, India has had state-run industries such as coal for many years, although it had plans to privatize them to improve the economy in 2013.[1] And, in 2013 Nigeria sold off its power companies to improve service.[2]

In general, economists believe that the government plays a legitimate role in a market economy, because it defines and enforces the basic rules of the market. However, there is some argument regarding the level of *protectionist tariffs* ("a discriminatory tax imposed on imported goods by customs authorities" according to the ISM *Glossary*, 2014), the amount of federal control over interest rates and the level of industry subsidies that should be imposed.

Closed Economies and Mixed Economies

Two other types of economies that exist in the world today are the *closed economy* and the *mixed economy*. A closed economy is one in which a country severely limits the amount of trade with the outside world, and relies on its own resources to support production and trade. While there are no completely closed economies in the world today, North Korea and Cuba exhibit many of the traits of a closed economy. Others operate with a mix of state-owned and private enterprises, otherwise known as a mixed economy. Most industrialized nations arguably operate within a mixed economy to varying degrees, including the United States, Sweden, France and Mexico.

The Global Economy

Even with these differing economic models, from a global perspective, trade is relatively open today. Organizations generally have the ability to market and sell products and services around the world with fewer forms of protectionism than ever before. From 2005 through 2011, world market trade increased 3.7 percent annually while world Gross Domestic Product (GDP) grew by 2.3 percent. The United States dominates, though, as a global trader in merchandise, with US$3,746 billion in imports and exports in 2011, and half of the world's exports come from North America and Europe.[3]

Organizations also are forming offshore partnerships and alliances. While the United States once dominated the global marketplace, its share today is between 26 percent and 27 percent. Because of lower trade barriers, international competitors have equal access to the least expensive forms of raw materials, labor and technology. As a result, they benefit from similar economies of scale. According to the World Bank, 20 years ago developing countries supplied 14 percent of the world's manufactured imports to industrialized nations, but today that number is up to 51 percent.[4] Thus, forecasting becomes more complex as organizations struggle to understand the nature of the economies of the country or countries in which they conduct business.

Globalization began after World War II in an effort to rebuild Japan and Western Europe. International agreements were created to encourage trade between all free nations. In 1947, the General Agreement on Tariffs and Trade (GATT) was formed, an informal organization that oversaw the multilateral trading system. The United States, Canada and Western European nations then signed the Organisation for Economic Co-Operation and Development (OECD) in 1960, which allowed for closer cooperation when economic problems arose (Japan, New Zealand and Australia later signed the agreement). In 1967, a round of multilateral trade negotiations hosted by GATT and known as The Kennedy Round, resulted in agreement among the world's major trading powers to significantly decrease tariffs on all manufactured goods.

The World Trade Organization (WTO; http://www.wto.org) replaced GATT in 1995 and has been a catalyst to improve trade relations. The WTO, comprised of approximately 159 member nations, is the only international organization that deals with the rules of trade between countries with the purpose of reducing trade barriers among countries. The WTO also provides a forum for trade negotiations, handles trade disputes, monitors national trade policies, and provides technical and trade assistance to developing nations. Its guiding principles are that the trading system should (1) function without discrimination between trading partners; (2) be more open to trade by lowering trade barriers such as customs duties (or tariffs) and discourage measures such as import bans or quotas that restrict quantities; (3) be predictable and transparent, without arbitrary trade barriers; (4) be more competitive, discouraging "unfair" practices such as export subsidies, product dumping and similar practices; (5) be more beneficial to less-developed countries; and (6) be protective of the environment. While the environment also includes public health, animal health and plant health, environmental protection measures should not be used as a means of disguising protectionist policies.[5] However, while trade barriers have decreased, tariffs and other forms of protectionism such as trading quotas still exist.

Local Buying Preferences

The issue of local buying preferences has changed over the past decade with the advent of advanced communication technologies and a changing political climate. In general, organizations take a two-pronged approach: standardize where possible while considering local needs. In 2013 Fiat and Chrysler Group, for instance, partnered with Chinese-owned

Guangzhou Group Company Ltd. to build one model of the Jeep for the Chinese market.[6] Walmart International, with stores in 26 countries, uses a variety of formats to ensure they are "relevant to our customers" and "to understand their unique preferences."[7] And white goods manufacturer Whirlpool Corp.'s Design Center "tests the relevance of its design vision and concepts to reflect local influences and market diversity."[8]

Other global organizations are looking at regional preferences within a specific country and then developing products to meet those needs and desires. Multinational organizations, for example, are looking for ways to market their products to Latin America, a diverse continent with poor rural farmers as well as urban multimillionaires. The affluent accept global marketing and standardized global products, but those in the smaller cities do not. The challenge is to adapt to the local preferences of the small cities as market expansion plans continue. Johnson & Johnson, for example, tailors its products to various regions it serves including Latin America. According to Santiago Cardenas, head of Strategic Marketing Services, "The single most important opportunity is to capture the hearts and brand preference of the emerging consumers." In particular, the Latin American consumers are brand loyal and want products that are sustainable.[9]

As organizations develop more complex product lines based on local buying preferences, forecasting becomes more difficult and often less accurate. Some organizations have tried to mitigate this problem by standardizing as much as possible, and adapting their manufacturing and distribution systems to market a global product to many country markets. Appliance manufacturers, for example, ship product without the power cord, and customers make an additional purchase based on local electrical current requirements. Software providers like Kaspersky have made software available in downloadable format.

Risk Factors in the Geopolitical Climate

As organizations continue to expand into global markets, geopolitical risks have increasingly made an impact on them. These risks stem from a region's history, geography, religion, government structure and socioeconomic factors. Some common risks include terrorism, war and political corruption.

Geopolitical factors — either locally or abroad — can affect demand. New administrations, shifts in the political climate and government takeovers are just a few of the changes that may alter an organization's original demand projections. For example, a branded pharmaceutical company may have difficulty entering the Brazilian market. The current Brazilian government, for example, favors generic pharmaceutical products over name brands, even if they are not patented. As a result, it can take twelve to fourteen months — several months longer — to register a branded product. What can be patented is also greatly restricted.[10] Organizations often use published reports to keep informed of changes in political conditions, subscribing to reports by groups such as the Congressional Research Service, a unit of the U.S. Library of Congress that publishes country-specific economic and political reports prepared by specialists. They also often take the predictions of university economics and finance professors and other experts into consideration when estimating future demand.

There is also the potential risk of interruptions in supply because of political problems, such as a change in the government leadership or shifts in political sentiment. While the risk generally is higher in lesser developed countries, disruptions can occur anywhere. Immediately following the terrorist attacks of September 11, 2001, U.S. border security was increased dramatically, creating significant delays at all customs checkpoints. Ford Motor Co. was forced to shut down its plants for several days because of a delayed delivery of engines and drivetrains from Canadian suppliers.[11] Thus, organizations must monitor the political conditions and create contingency plans in the event a disruption in supply occurs.

Cultural Differences

Organizations also need to consider the cultural differences when expanding globally. Much has been written about what constitutes intercultural competence, but disagreement exists. However, it is possible to go to almost any online bookstore to find a book that has exhaustive lists on the behavior appropriate for any given country. Because so many different situations exist among and between cultures, a list cannot possibly cover every situation. To adapt to the differences, it is first necessary to understand and value some general differences. In particular, it is important to understand differences in industrial histories, relationships to technology, and natural resources, religions and geography.[12]

Cultures also can be defined as high context and low context. According to Heather Keller, "When communicating, people from high-context cultures, such as China, Japan, South American countries and Arab countries, take into account the entire context of the communication event rather than focusing solely on the spoken word. The nonverbal aspects of communication, the relationship with the listener, the situation, the background and the environment are also taken into consideration. People from low-context cultures, such as the United States, Scandinavia, Australia and German-speaking countries, on the other hand, primarily focus on the words being uttered. That is, they use direct, verbal statements to convey meaning."[13] Understanding these differences, then, can enhance the forecasting process.

China's white goods manufacturer, Haier Co., Ltd., recognized cultural differences as its biggest challenge. The organization expanded into the United States, building niche markets with niche products. Haier also hired local talent to run local operations. However, as Chairman and CEO Zhang Ruimin said in a 2005 interview, "When we aimed to be one of the top 10 retailers in the United States, our American managers thought it would be impossible to get there in such a short time." He goes on to say that while localization is good, any gaps in communication or culture need to be addressed quickly to avoid problems later. Haier continues operations in the United States with headquarters in New York City and a US$40 million facility in Camden, South Carolina.[14]

CHAPTER 4: Foundations of Forecasting Practices

Exchange Rates and Currency Risk

International currency exchange rate fluctuations also play a role in global trade and forecasting. Manufacturers, for example, closely watch the exchange rates for the Chinese currency, the yuan. A strengthening of the yuan can make "Chinese goods 'relatively more expensive' to foreigners, which allows 'other countries to compete better with China's low-cost producers.'"[15] (The mainland China yuan currently fluctuates with the U.S. dollar, while the Hong Kong yuan floats freely.)[16]

Another important risk issue in global sourcing is whether the supply management organization should use its own currency or that of the country from which it is making the purchase. Thus, forecasting exchange rates is not uncommon. When payment will be made within a relatively short period of time, the choice is not that important. However, if the relationship with the supplier is long-standing or payments will not be due for an extended period of time, exchange rates can fluctuate considerably, adversely affecting the price that was originally negotiated. The most commonly traded currencies float freely today, and rates quickly can be affected by economic, political or psychological factors. Some countries also may choose to impose restrictions or controls on currency exchanges. (See the ISM *Professional Series* book, *Foundation of Supply Management*, for a more detailed discussion on exchange rates.)

In 2006 German automakers BMW, Volkswagen and Mercedes were hurt financially in the U.S. luxury car market by a strong euro against the U.S. dollar. Most production costs are based on the euro, making it difficult to compete on price against Japanese brands Lexus (owned by Toyota Motor Co.) and Infiniti (owned by Nissan). The Japanese yen was weak against the U.S. dollar, primarily because of slow growth and lower interest rates in Japan. The German automakers mitigated the problem by ramping up car production in the United States.[17]

The most conservative organizations pay with their own currency so they always know exactly what they will be paying. Larger, more aggressive organizations will pay in the suppliers' local currency, with caps on the amount of exchange rate fluctuation allowed; alternatively, they will trade using a *hedging* strategy to help reduce business risk. Hedging involves taking out an investment that will specifically reduce or cancel out the risk in another investment.[18] Global fast food retailer McDonald's Corp. has a financial markets group, which is responsible for hedging against the risks of international exchange rate fluctuations.[19]

Two types of hedging strategies are the purchase of *forward exchange contracts* and *currency options*. A forward exchange contract is a contract to exchange one form of currency for another at a specified exchange rate on some future date. Currency options give an organization the right to buy a given amount of currency at a specified exchange rate on or before a specified date, but do not require the organization to buy at the end of the period. Currency options offer some flexibility; however, they are more expensive than setting up a forward exchange contract.

Import/Export Issues

Organizations must consider a number of additional forecasting issues when they choose to buy and sell from others internationally. Sales will be affected first by how easy it will be to sell to international customers. Production costs also will be influenced by how costly and time-consuming it will be to purchase the supply of goods and services necessary to support the demand forecast. However, two other factors must be considered during the forecasting process as well, which increase the complexity of sourcing from international suppliers.

First, a number of costs exist that are not normally incurred in domestic sourcing, such as foreign taxes, payment costs (letters of credit fees, exchange rate differentials and translation costs), commissions to customs brokers, inspection costs, customs documentation fees and import tariffs. (Tax issues can be extremely complex, so a taxation expert generally should be involved in understanding materials flows between countries and developing the most favorable terms and conditions.) Transportation costs and the additional costs to buy and hold additional inventory to avoid stockouts also will be higher. Additionally, the higher cost of expedited delivery may be necessary at times to maintain production schedules or support service delivery. The risk of obsolescence, spoilage or theft also is naturally greater, because more forms of transportation are used and delivery times usually are longer.

Protectionism, by country, by industry and by product, results in the use of tariffs and surcharges in certain circumstances to protect local industries. In a 2013 report, "EU Report on Potentially Trade-Restrictive Measures," 150 new trade restrictions were introduced in one year — from May 2012 to May 2013 — and only 18 existing measures were taken off the books. Import duty hikes are increasing to a high degree, with Argentina, Brazil, Russia and Ukraine imposing the stiffest increases. Also, some countries such as Brazil and Indonesia protect "domestic industries from foreign competition to the disadvantage of their consumers and other industry sectors."[20]

Supply management professionals must understand and be able to apply the tariff schedules and calculate the tariff duties. There are also the additional costs to maintain the appropriate documentation related to customs requirements, international logistics paperwork and payment transactions. If these additional costs raise the price of a product too much, demand will be lower.

Legal issues also must be considered. In 1988, the United Nations passed the Convention on Contracts for the International Sale of Goods (CISG), which applies to the sale of goods between organizations in participating countries. The CISG differs in some respects to domestic codes such as the U.S. Uniform Commercial Code, so supply management professionals must be aware of international laws pertaining to the specified contract (not all countries have adopted the CISG). Complexities in the law may affect the ability to deliver goods and services.

The previous sections of this chapter state that a sound forecasting methodology is needed to help deal with the uncertainty in today's global economy. Effective forecasting begins with a firm understanding of the nature of business cycles. Knowing what economic indicators are important to further that understanding also is important. Lastly, organizations need some sources of information that will improve an organization's chances for creating more accurate forecasts. The remainder of this chapter delves into these topics, beginning with a discussion of business cycles.

Business Cycles

As mentioned previously in this chapter, every economy, regardless of country — whether free market, closed or mixed — experiences ups and downs. For periods of time, the economy will grow at a robust rate, with household income increasing, consumer spending on the rise, and organizations expanding and hiring. There also are periods when the economy will be relatively flat, with little growth in wages, spending or business expansion. A third scenario is *recession*, when the economy is shrinking. Most economists and journalists define a recession as "two back-to-back quarters of negative gross domestic product (GDP) growth."[21] The GDP, according to the U.S. Bureau of Economic Analysis (BEA), "measures the market value of final goods and services produced by labor and property in the United States, including goods that are added to or subtracted from inventories."[22] Alternatively, economists may use the gross national product (GNP) as a measure of economic health. The GNP is a "measure of a nation's total output, which is the total value of all finished goods and services produced anywhere in the world by its agencies and firms during a certain time period (typically one calendar year)" (ISM *Glossary* 2014).

Evidence of the business cycle is apparent from changes in the GDP, unemployment rates, price changes and profits. The swings in the economy are known as the business cycle. The *business cycle* has five phases:
1. The highest point of output before a downturn;
2. Recession, or shrinking of the economy;
3. Recession trough, or lowest point in economic activity;
4. Recovery, or resuming growth path; and
5. Expansion, beyond previous high point.

The difficulty lies in predicting a business cycle. Organizations generally use a mix of economic indicators as a basis to forecast long-term growth prospects. More on the economic indicators commonly used today can be found in the next section.

Economic Indicators

Understanding economic indicators helps supply management professionals identify those market forces that will affect the supply and demand for a particular commodity, product or service. "Economic data can be used to study past economic trends, analyze and understand current movements in markets, and predict future market trends," according to an

ISM publication.[23] DailyFX, an online company for market news and analysis, provides a daily economic calendar, known as Daily Forex, of economic indicators.[24] Some of these economic indicators are discussed in the following sections.

Leading, Lagging and Coincident Indicators

Because no one indicator can give a true picture of the economy, many are published and then analyzed by businesses and governments. For example, The Bureau of Labor Statistics publishes the Consumer Price Index for services, and The Conference Board releases the Index of Lagging Indicators.

A *leading indicator* is "a measure of economic activity that changes before the business cycle does and thus indicates its future direction" (ISM *Glossary* 2014). Some examples include the change in the number of building permits issued in a given period, the money supply (the amount of cash and bank deposits held by organizations and households), inventory level changes, changes in stock prices and the number of unemployment insurance claims. For instance, the town of Gilbert, Arizona issued twice as many residential building permits in 2012 as it did in 2011, indicating an upswing in the city's economy.[25] Mortgage organizations, construction organizations and subcontractors, and appliance manufacturers are just some of the businesses that would use this indicator in their forecasting process. Federal governments also use these indicators to determine whether to raise interest rates.

A *lagging indicator*, on the other hand, confirms that a change has occurred in the economy and tends to follow changes in the economy. In other words, if the economy is improving, the lagging indicators will confirm that phenomenon after the state of the general economy has changed. Some key lagging indicators include labor costs, business spending, prime interest rates, inventory book value, unemployment rates and outstanding bank loans. For example, if business spending is on the increase, this generally confirms that the economy is doing well. Lastly, a *coincident indicator* is "a measure of economic activity that changes concurrently with changes in the business cycle" (ISM *Glossary* 2014). Some examples include personal income, nonagricultural employment and industrial production.

Two commonly used U.S. families of indexes are the Producer Price Index (PPI) and the Consumer Price Index (CPI), which are discussed in the following sections.

Producer Price Index (PPI). The Producer Price Index (PPI) is actually a family of indexes published by many national agencies including the U.S. Bureau of Labor Statistics (BLS),[26] the UK Office for National Statistics (ONS)[27] and Statistics Finland.[28] The PPI, according to the BLS, "measures the average change over time in the prices received by domestic producers of goods and services."[29] The PPI is based on the selling price rather than on the actual cost to produce an item. For manufacturing, these indexes cover the different stages of production — crude goods (raw materials), intermediate goods (work in process) and finished goods, according to the U.S. Department of Labor, which oversees the BLS.[30] The PPI publishes over 600 industry price indexes in combination with over 5,000 specific product line and product category sub-indexes based on NAICS (North American Industry Classification System); they are the first price measures released each month.

The U.S. Bureau of Labor Statistics calculates unadjusted indexes for all product groups using actual sales dollars. These indexes typically are used by supply management to predict price trends, determine whether supplier price increases for purchased inputs are equitable, and as a basis for contract negotiations. For example, if Pulte Homes, Inc., a large U.S. residential home builder, buys preassembled roof frames and the supplier is attempting to raise prices, supply management personnel could review the cost growth of lumber using the PPI to determine if the increase is legitimate. Supply management professionals and their suppliers also use the PPI to predict price inflation and negotiate price escalation clauses.

The PPI for commodities also may be seasonally adjusted when there is some economic rationale for doing so, and when statistical tests indicate that there is seasonality present. The ISM *Glossary* (2014) defines seasonality as "a repetitive pattern of demand from year to year that indicates quantitative differences based on regular time periods (seasons)." Adjustments may be made for the normally occurring and repeatable effects such as weather, regular marketing and production cycles, model changeovers, seasonal discounts and holidays.[31] These seasonally adjusted indexes are used to analyze general price trends in the economy. Figure 4-1 illustrates the change in the U.S. PPI for truck transportation.

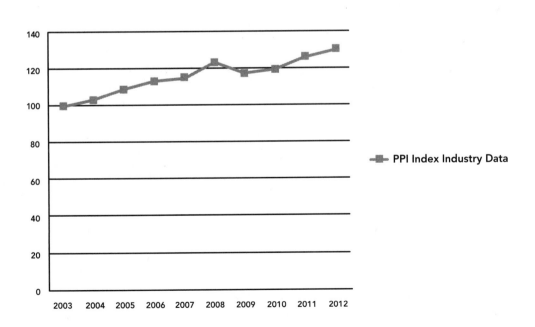

Figure 4-1: Annual Percent Changes for Truck Transportation, Unadjusted

The disadvantage of the PPIs is that they are less understood and more volatile than the CPI. PPIs also are calculated on a national rather than a regional basis, which limits their applicability for supply management professionals. Lastly, they have been limited in usefulness relative to services — although this is changing.

Consumer Price Index (CPI). In contrast to the PPI, the consumer price index (CPI) is one of the most popular measures of price inflation for retail goods and services. The CPI also is published monthly by the U.S. Department of Labor and other national agencies. The CPI measures the average change in retail prices over time for a basket of eight major groups with more than 200 categories of various goods and services. Figure 4-2 provides the weightings assigned to each group.

Figure 4-2: Sample CPI Weights

GROUP	WEIGHT

1. Housing
    Shelter (29.8%)
    Fuel and utilities (5.6%)
    Household furnishings and operations (3.8%)
	39.2%

2. Food and Beverages	16.4%

3. Transportation
    Private transportation (18.6%)
        New and used vehicles (6.9%)
        Motor fuel (6.5%)
        Parts & equipment (.48%)
        Maintenance and repairs (1.2%)
        Insurance (3.1%)
        Vehicle fees (.51%)
    Public transportation (.79%)
	19.4%

4. Medical Care	5.3%
5. Apparel	3.7%
6. Recreation	5.9%
7. Education and Communication	6.1%
8. Other Goods and Services	3.9%

Source: Price Indexes, U.S. City Average, December 2010, www.bls.gov.

The rate of price inflation is important because it affects everyone and (1) determines how much consumers must pay for goods and services, (2) the cost of doing business, (3) the cost of making personal and corporate investments, and (4) the quality of life for retirees. It also helps businesses negotiate labor contracts and governments establish fiscal policy. However, it only represents consumer purchases, does not reflect product or service substitutions consumers might make because of price, and is not particularly useful in forecasting. Thus, the CPI should not be used to predict swings in the economy because it is really a lagging indicator.

Relationship Between the PPI and the CPI. Supply management professionals also are interested in the relationship between the PPI and the CPI to evaluate their own position of strength relative to that of the supplier. Understanding the changes in these indicators is a good way to evaluate that power relationship and is shown in the following example of a fictitious auto manufacturer, ABC Motor Corp. ABC is renegotiating the contract for door panels for one of its midsize models. Steel is a major component of these door panels, so the team reviews the CPI for steel products and the PPI for new cars over the past three years. Figure 4-3 illustrates a comparison between the CPI and the PPI.

Figure 4-3: PPI to CPI Comparison

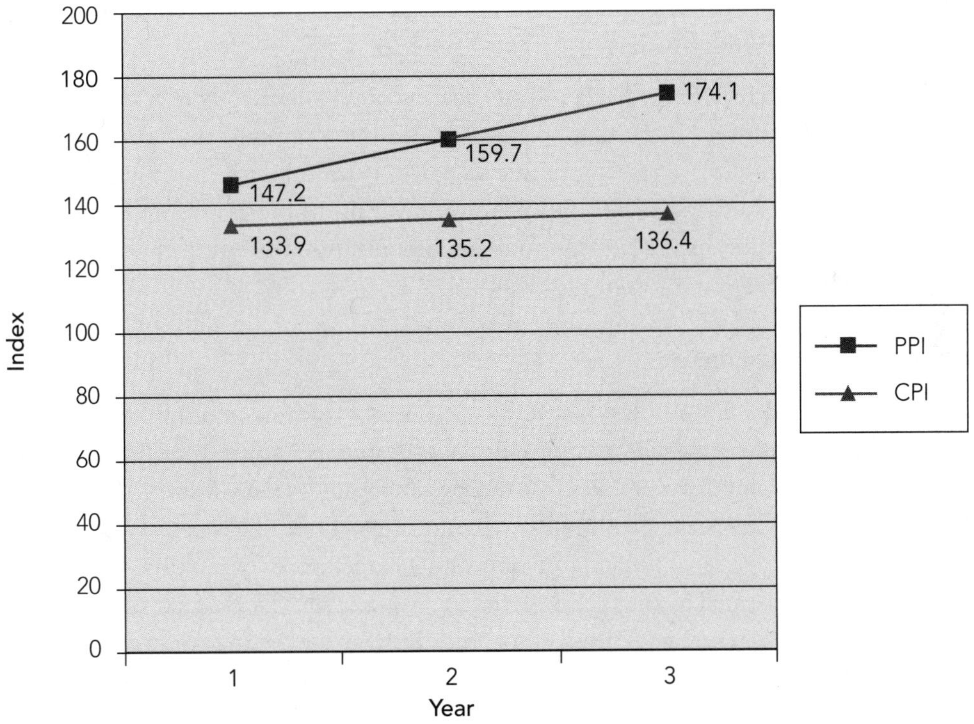

Source: Bureau of Labor Statistics.

Assume the PPI for steel products has increased significantly over the past three years, but the CPI for new automobiles has remained relatively flat. The team could use the table shown in Figure 4-4 as a rule of thumb to determine its negotiating power.

Figure 4-4: PPI to CPI Comparison 2

PPI	CPI	BUYING POWER	SUPPLIER POWER
Decreasing	Increasing	Higher	Lower
Decreasing	Flat	Higher	Lower
Decreasing	Decreasing	Lower	Lower
Increasing	Increasing	Lower	Higher
Increasing	Flat	Lower	Higher
Increasing	Decreasing	Lower	Lower

Source: Adapted from *Supplier Management & Negotiation, Module 1, Research Methods*, developed by Larry Smeltzer for Arizona State University.

Based on the table, the supply team will likely have less power at the negotiating table. Thus, the team decides to collect more recent price data and develop a cost analysis before entering into negotiations with its door panel supplier.

In the example, the PPI for steel products has increased significantly over the past three years (producer prices are increasing), while the CPI for new automobiles is relatively flat (prices to the consumer are stable). In this scenario, it will be easier for the door panel suppliers to support an argument for price increases because industry prices for steel products have risen significantly. Thus, the sourcing organization has relatively lower power in a negotiation situation for door panels.

Implicit Price Deflator

A *deflator* is a value that allows data to be measured over time in terms of some base period. An *implicit price deflator*, a measure of inflation, is "a factor used to eliminate price changes in computing a nation's real changes in output" (ISM *Glossary* 2014). Thus, it is an index of prices for everything that a country produces, making it different from the CPI — which considers consumption only and includes prices of imports. The implicit price deflator was created by the U.S. Department of Commerce and compares the average level of prices in a given year to those of a base year by using the following calculation:

$$\text{Implicit price deflator} = \frac{\text{Current-dollar GDP}}{\text{Inflation-adjusted GDP}}$$

Using economic data generated by the St. Louis Federal Reserve to compare pricing from period to period, the implicit price deflator for the third quarter of 2013 in the United Kingdom was 106.23 and the implicit price deflator for the third quarter of 2012 was 104.86. The difference indicates that prices in the economy went up 1.37 percent

(106.23 – 104.86) during that time.[32] Supply management professionals, therefore, need to consider the impact of inflation/deflation in the negotiation process.

Custom Indexes

Custom indexing is a professional tool that organizations use to measure, investigate and control price and cost changes within their own organizations. If a supply management professional forecasts an expected upswing in prices for a particular commodity, he or she may be able to find a substitute that meets requirements but is less expensive. Custom indexes are especially useful for commodities that represent a large percentage of total purchases. The supply management professional, however, also should be sure to identify any assumptions used to create the index.

A simple price index would be the price of a good or service for a given year divided by the price of that good or service for a base year. The base price is given as 100, and then later comparisons are expressed as a ratio of the later period over the base period multiplied by 100. For example, if the 2013 statistic for wheat was 130 and the base year 2000 statistic is 100, the index would be (130/100) × 100 = 130, and the percentage difference would be (130/100 – 1) × 100 = 30%. In other words, prices were up 30 percent over the base year. It is always important to report the index periodically and to use the base year for comparison. Often, supply management professionals will create a supplier price index and use it to compare against the producer price index to determine if the supplier is asking for equitable price increases. For instance, if the supplier price index has increased an average of 10 percent annually over the past two years, but the industry producer price index has increased only an average of 3 percent annually, this information can be used in the next round of negotiations to argue for lower prices or for a cost savings clause to be built into the contract.

While indexes are important to the forecasting process, organizations use other nationally published figures to aid them. Two of these are described in the following sections.

Balance of Merchandise Trade

The *balance of merchandise trade* is the difference between the value of a nation's exports to all other countries and the value of all imports from all other countries over a given time period. If exports are greater than imports, the country's balance of merchandise trade is defined as "favorable"; when imports exceed exports, the balance of merchandise trade is considered "unfavorable." Some nations, such as Great Britain, also create separate categories for goods and services trade balances, defining each, respectively, as "visible" and "invisible." A significantly large trade deficit may result in higher interest rates, depressed stock prices and lower currency exchange rates because that country will search for foreign capital to finance the deficit; these outcomes, however, can also be influenced by other factors. The United States is a good example. As of Q1 2013, the U.S. had a trade deficit of US$179.14 billion and experienced consistent trade deficits since the 1980s. This is due to the high level of oil and consumer goods imports.[33] Due to government intervention, however, interest rates were at an all-time low and, due to an improvement in the economy, stock prices were on the rise.

Balance of Payments

The *balance of payments* is "a measure for the difference in the flow of funds across a nation's boundaries" (ISM *Glossary* 2014). It is an accounting record of a nation's transactions with all other nations during a specific time period, usually one year. The account compares the amount of international currency that is taken into the economy from exports and international investments, and the amount of domestic currency that is taken out to pay for imports or investments.[34] The difference between the value of a country's exports and imports is the *balance of trade*.

The account, however, must be in balance. Thus, if a particular nation shows a trade deficit, it must export some of its gold reserves or send some of its currency reserves to those nations with a surplus. If, on the other hand, there is a surplus, that nation must receive an inflow of either or both currency and gold reserves from those nations with a deficit. In the long term, persistent deficits might be corrected through increasing interest rates (making it more difficult to borrow money), lower export prices from the international supplier, an increase in the home country's price of imports through weakening the home country's currency (taking more of the home country's currency to purchase the foreign goods), or adding tariffs or taxes (making these goods and services less attractive). Countries with a surplus also may take steps to maintain healthy global economic conditions. China, for example, experienced a trade deficit in 2012 of more than US$270 billion. However, that was expected to change with global demand slowing and an increase in commodity imports for major infrastructure projects.[35] Supply management professionals must consider all these issues when making international outsourcing decisions.

Sources of Data Used in Forecasting

A number of other popular data sources are used to create forecasts, some of which are described in the following sections.

ISM *Report On Business*® — Manufacturing and Non-Manufacturing

ISM publishes two monthly reports that provide a good overall barometer of current macroeconomic conditions. Macrodata is useful when organizations are forecasting the effects of economic trends on national or worldwide supply and demand. For example, because cotton and polyester are two common textile fibers, any indications of a low worldwide yield for cotton would suggest possible shortages of cotton and thus a shift in demand from cotton to polyester. As a result, cotton shortages might imply an increasing demand for polyester fiber if they are interchangeable, which would cause an increase in demand for the raw materials used to make polyester. This information would be used by the supply management professional to create a microforecast or an organization-specific forecast.[36]

The Manufacturing ISM *Report On Business*® is based on data collected monthly from manufacturers. As shown in the sample report summary in Figure 4-5, the Manufacturing ISM *Report On Business*® includes a number of factors that affect forecasts, including changes in new orders, production, employment, supplier deliveries, backlogs of orders, customers' inventories, exports, imports and prices. The *PMI*® is a composite index published monthly for the manufacturing sector that can be used to predict future growth or contraction.

Figure 4-5: Sample Manufacturing ISM *Report on Business*®

Manufacturing at a Glance

INDEX	Apr Index	Mar Index	% Point Change	Direction	Rate of Change	Trend* (months)
PMI®	54.9	53.7	+1.2	Growing	Faster	11
New Orders	55.1	55.1	0.0	Growing	Same	11
Production	55.7	55.9	-0.2	Growing	Slower	2
Employment	54.7	51.1	+3.6	Growing	Faster	10
Supplier Deliveries	55.9	54.0	+1.9	Slowing	Faster	11
Inventories	53.0	52.5	+0.5	Growing	Faster	3
Customers' Inventories	42.0	42.0	0.0	Too Low	Same	29
Prices	56.5	59.0	-2.5	Increasing	Slower	9
Backlog of Orders	55.5	57.5	-2.0	Growing	Slower	3
Exports	57.0	55.5	+1.5	Growing	Faster	17
Imports	58.0	54.5	+3.5	Growing	Faster	15
Overall Economy				Growing	Faster	59
Manufacturing Sector				Growing	Faster	11

*Number of months moving in current direction.
Manufacturing ISM® *Report On Business*® data is seasonally adjusted for the New Orders, Production, Employment and Supplier Deliveries Indexes.

Source: Manufacturing ISM *Report On Business*® (April 2014 data) Media Release, May 1, 2014.

A similar monthly report is issued for the non-manufacturing sector, the Non-Manufacturing ISM *Report On Business®*, and includes factors such as business activity, new orders, employment, supplier deliveries, inventories, prices, backlog of orders, exports, imports, inventory sentiment and customers' inventories, as shown in Figure 4-6. The *NMI®* (Non-Manufacturing Index), a composite index for the non-manufacturing sector, was established in January 2008.

Figure 4-6: Sample Non-Manufacturing ISM *Report on Business®*

Non-Manufacturing at a Glance

INDEX	Apr Index	Mar Index	% Point Change	Direction	Rate of Change	Trend* (months)
NMI®	55.2	53.1	+2.1	Growing	Faster	51
Business Activity	60.9	53.4	+7.5	Growing	Faster	57
New Orders	58.2	53.4	+4.8	Growing	Faster	57
Employment	51.3	53.6	-2.3	Growing	Slower	2
Supplier Deliveries	50.5	52.0	-1.5	Slowing	Slower	6
Inventories	55.5	48.0	+7.5	Growing	From Contracting	1
Prices	60.8	58.3	+2.5	Increasing	Faster	55
Backlog of Orders	49.0	51.5	-2.5	Contracting	From Growing	1
New Export Orders	57.0	49.5	+7.5	Growing	From Contracting	1
Imports	55.5	50.5	+5.0	Growing	Faster	2
Inventory Sentiment	65.0	60.5	+4.5	Too High	Faster	203

*Number of months moving in current direction.
Non-Manufacturing ISM® *Report On Business®* data is seasonally adjusted for the Business Activity, New Orders, Prices and Employment Indexes.

Source: Manufacturing ISM *Report On Business®* (April 2014 data) Media Release, May 5, 2014.

Each individual factor is reported as a *diffusion index*. A diffusion index measures the degree to which a change in something is dispersed, spread out or "diffused" in a particular group. If all members of a group of people (the sample population) are asked if something has changed and in which direction, they will answer in one of three ways: It has not changed, it has increased or it has decreased. The diffusion index is calculated by taking the percentage of those reporting "increased" added to half of the percentage of those reporting "no change." Economists and statisticians have determined that the farther the index is away from the amount that would indicate "no change" (50 percent), the greater the rate of change. Therefore, an index of 60 percent indicates a faster rate of increase than an index of 55 percent.

To achieve a valid, weighted sample, survey participants for both the Manufacturing *Report On Business*® and the Non-Manufacturing *Report On Business*® are selected based on each industry's contribution to the U.S. gross domestic product (GDP). As a result, there is a correlation between the ISM indexes and the real GDP as shown in Figure 4-7.[37]

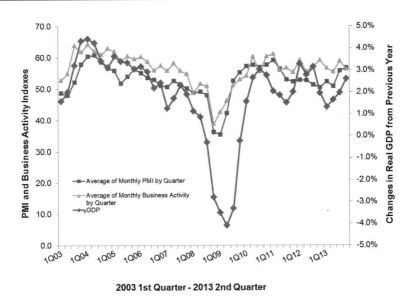

Figure 4-7: Correlation Between Institute for Supply Management® Indexes and the Real GDP

Source: Institute for Supply Management®

Each month, survey participants from both the manufacturing and non-manufacturing sectors are asked to assess their organization's performance based on a comparison of the current month to the previous month. Bradley Holcomb, CPSM, CPSD, chair of the ISM Manufacturing Business Survey Committee, notes, "The power of the PMI® is in the fact that it is based on pure data representing exactly what is happening within and across manufacturing each month, relative to the prior month. A consistent and timely data collection process allows the PMI® to be one of the first significant economic indexes published each month, and as such, provides an important leading economic indicator used by economists, investors, government agencies and companies worldwide."[38]

Application. The supply management group at a Houston, Texas company uses the ISM *Report On Business*® extensively in its forecasting efforts, project planning and ongoing communication with both suppliers and customers. According to a supply management professional at the company, "Data points are also quite useful in comparing actual versus target pricing levels, and in establishing acceptable ranges and/or controls in contracts.

"Regarding forecasting and project planning, a working knowledge of the market and its tendencies is a key to successful project management. [Supply management professionals] record the monthly ISM *Report On Business*® indexes on a spreadsheet, convert the indexes to charts and distribute this information to [the] supply management team on a worldwide basis. This data is often used in projecting and validating escalations and lead times during long-term projects.

"Regarding communication, the monthly indexes and charts are included as a segment in one of [its] management reports that indicates currency exchange rates, escalations, lead times and production cycle time applicable to major equipment items. Sharing this information with suppliers and customers provides an opportunity to work together to achieve more effective cost management in [the] supply chain network."[39]

Many countries around the world have adopted the survey methodology used by ISM and publish their own reports. Information from other countries' reports may be helpful if the supply management professional is pursuing sourcing internationally. Data from several countries currently is combined in a monthly global report as well.

U.S. Government Publications

Besides indexes, the U.S. government provides a number of publications that provide useful input in creating a forecast. For example, the Bureau of Economic Analysis publishes the *Survey of Current Business*, which is available in pdf format at www.bea.gov/scb/index.htm. This survey reports the monthly GDP and any reasons behind the change from the previous month(s), with supporting data including consumer spending, expenditures on imports and exports, business investment in inventories, government spending, and fixed investments in nonresidential property. The BEA also publishes a monthly report on U.S. exports and imports of goods and services, which is based on figures from two months prior. These numbers are used to calculate the net export figure that is used in the GDP account. Another BEA report is *International Transactions*, released quarterly, which reports trade in goods and services, foreign investment that enters the United States and capital that flows out for investment in other countries. This report is important because exports reflect the United States' ability to compete in world trade, improve corporate profitability and create jobs. Imports reflect the strength of demand from U.S. consumers: When demand is increasing, the economy is expanding, although it takes away from GDP growth.

The *Federal Reserve Bulletin*, first introduced in 1914, is a publication designed to present the U.S. Federal Reserve Board's policy issues. Contributors to the *Bulletin* include the Federal Reserve Board's Research and Statistics, Monetary Affairs, International Finance, Banking Supervision and Regulation, Consumer and Community Affairs, Reserve Bank Operations and Legal divisions. The *Bulletin* includes topical research articles, legal developments, a report on the condition of the U.S. banking industry, and other general information. As of 2013, the *Bulletin* is published on the board's website on a continuing basis and offers an email notification service to alert subscribers as it becomes available. The board also prints an annual compendium.[39]

The U.S. Department of Agriculture (USDA) reports on global trading conditions and pricing for various commodities. For example, its July 2013 *Amber Waves* online publication provided an analysis of the factors that affect worldwide sugar prices.[40] Other countries and regions also issue their own national statistics. For example, the Canadian government publishes the *Annual Survey of Manufactures* based on a collection of Canadian financial data and production data. The main financial data are the value of shipments, employment data (the number of employees, salaries and wages), the cost of raw materials, and energy consumption. Commodity data (such as materials and components, and goods shipped) also are collected for establishments that are sent long-form questionnaires. The European Union, comprised of 28 member nations (as of 2013), publishes statistics on key economic indicators such as gross national income, balance of imports and exports, and gross domestic product (GDP).[41]

International Publications

Given the nature of commerce today, supply management professionals also must examine international conditions in the marketplace.

Three international organizations that provide extensive statistical data include the United Nations (UN), the Organisation for Economic Co-Operation and Development (OECD) and the International Monetary Fund (IMF). The United Nations provides international trade statistics and a world economic survey, among other publications. *UN Comtrade*, for example, is a report on global commodity trade statistics for 174 countries. Updated monthly and available online, options for exploration, data mining and visualization through graphics are available.[42] The *World Economic Situation and Prospects* is published annually by the U.N. and provides economic growth trends, international trade issues, a projection of international uncertainties and risks, and a report on capital flows. The *World Economic and Social Survey* reports annually on issues related to developing countries such as savings, investment and growth; trade; international flows of private cash into developing nations; and systemic issues.[43] The Food and Agricultural Organization of the United Nations also publishes statistical reports regarding agricultural, nutritional, forestry and fishery products.[44]

The Organisation for Economic Co-Operation and Development is a group of 34 countries that have a mission "to promote policies that will improve the economic and social well-being of people around the world." Outside of Paris the OECD has centers in Berlin, Mexico City, Tokyo and Washington. Member governments work together to share experiences and seek solutions to common problems; work to understand what drives economic, social and environmental change; measure productivity and global flows of trade and investment; analyze and compare data to predict future trends; and set international standards on a wide range of things, from agriculture and tax to the safety of chemicals.

OECD databases cover national accounts, economic indicators, trade, employment, migration, education, energy and other areas; most of these databases are published.[45]

The International Monetary Fund (IMF) is an international organization with 188 member countries. The organization "works to foster global monetary cooperation, secure financial stability, facilitate international trade, promote high employment and sustainable economic growth, and reduce poverty around the world."

One of its publications, the *World Economic Outlook*, contains data on IMF lending, exchange rates, GDP growth, inflation, unemployment, payments balances, exports, imports, external debt, capital flows, commodity prices and more. Published twice a year, the report can be downloaded at the IMF website.[46] For instance, according to the IMF's April 2013 *World Economic Outlook*, global growth was forecast at about 3 percent, similar to 2012. This information suggests that economic conditions will remain the same. Thus, it is likely that global suppliers will continue to be less inclined to make significant capital investments through 2013 and wage increases are unlikely in the near term, so prices should not increase based on that factor.

Private Publications

Trade magazines and research reports are other good sources of information. *Mortgage Banking* and the *Journal of Business Forecasting* provide a monthly outlook on U.S. and international business and economic conditions.

Organizations also create and sell reports and research studies that can provide valuable input to a forecast. One such organization is Business Monitor International, which offers a number of services including *Business Monitor Online* with customizable email alerts from a treasuries and capital markets team; comparative risk ratings; macroeconomic analyses, forecasts and industry profiles from a team of country economists; research on global emerging markets and 24 industry verticals with five to ten-year forecasts on a number of industry indicators; and specific organization research reports.[47]

Kiplinger Washington Editors, Inc. also provides input to forecasts in the form of several publications, including *The Kiplinger Letter* and *The Kiplinger Tax Letter*, which discuss a number of topics such as interest rates, the economy, international issues, costs and employees.

Commercial Forecasts

Certain organizations also provide forecasts for specific industries. Connecticut-based Forecast International, Inc., for example, provides market intelligence and analyses in the aerospace, defense, electronics and power systems industries. Their products are designed to help corporate executives, military leaders and top government personnel in the strategic planning process and the gathering of market intelligence.[48]

Regional Surveys

Local and state governments provide forecast information as well. A good example is the website provided by the Metropolitan Council, a regional planning agency for the Minneapolis-St. Paul, Minnesota area.[49] New Zealand's Ministry of Tourism posts forecasts by region with an explanation of its methodology that is useful for local hotels, restaurants and tour operators.[50] Some university researchers survey regional conditions for a specific industry. For example, the Center for Real Estate Theory and Practice at Arizona State University publishes a monthly report on the housing market for the greater Phoenix, Arizona area.[51]

Internal Historical Data

Organizations often will develop forecasts based on their own internal data. Past forecasts of sales, standard costs, order or production lead times, the seasonality of demand for products and services, current employment levels and turnover rates, specific financial requirements or constraints, among others, may be used as a basis to create a new forecast.

Industry Sources

A number of industry-specific groups, such as the American Petroleum Institute (API), the International Cotton Advisory Council (ICAC) and the Association of International Automobile Manufacturers (AIAM), provide current and upcoming legislation that will have an impact on the industry and the economic forecast. A number of nonprofit organizations also serve specific industry groups, including APICS, the Association for Operations Management (www.apics.org), the Institute for Supply Management® (ISM; www.ism.ws), the National Association of Manufacturers (NAM; www.nam.org/) and the National Institute of Governmental Purchasing (NIGP; www.nigp.org). The United Kingdom's Chartered Institute of Purchasing and Supply (CIPS; www.cips.org), the Danish Purchasing and Logistics Forum (DILF; www.dilf.dk), India's Indian Institute of Materials Management (IIMM; www.iimm.org) and Germany's Association Materials Management Purchasing and Logistics (AMMPL; http://www.bme.de/) are just some of the other organizations worldwide that provide valuable information for their members. Their overall goal is education, but they also provide reports covering the topics of economic conditions and pricing, among others.

Online Indexes and Search Engines

Lastly, a number of other online resources are available to supply management professionals that have not already been mentioned, which are listed in Figure 4-8. The U.S. Census Bureau, for example, provides statistics on the trade deficit, construction data and median income. The Energy Information Administration website includes forecasts and analyses of the worldwide energy supply, demand and prices.

Figure 4-8: Online Resources

RESOURCE	WEBSITE
Securities and Exchange Commission's EDGAR (Electronic Data Gathering, Analysis and Retrieval) database	www.sec.gov/edgarhp.htm
Annual Energy Outlook	www.eia.gov/
Bureau of Labor statistics	www.bls.gov/
U.S. Geological Survey (Department of Minerals)	http://minerals.usgs.gov/
U.S. Census Bureau	www.census.gov/
Institute of Business Forecasting and Planning	www.ibf.org/
American Institute for Economic Research	www.aier.org/
The Forecast Institute, Inc.	www.tfiforecast.com/
CME Group	www.cmegroup.com/
U.S. Energy Information Administration	www.eia.doe.gov/
Chicago Board Options Exchange	www.cboe.com/
U.S. Department of Agriculture	www.usda.gov/
Library of Congress databases and e-resources	www.lcweb.loc.gov/
Asian Development Bank	www.adb.org/
Inter-American Development Bank (South America)	www.iadb.org/
Official Statistics on the Web (OFFSTATS)	www.offstats.auckland.ac.nz/
United Kingdom National Statistics	www.statistics.gov.uk/

Using the Data

If an organization has not had extensive experience in tracking data, it is best to begin by selecting and watching a few key indicators. It also is important to consider the significance of a given product or service that will be purchased. If a good or service is not important to an organization's competitiveness, predictions of economic growth for the next quarter or following year may be enough to make forecasts about price increases and whether it is a buyer's or seller's market. If the purchase is more important to an organization's profitability, more detailed information may be acquired, culled from some of the sources mentioned previously. This information then can be used to develop any forecasting assumptions, thus reducing risk and developing a more accurate prediction.

Global food products manufacturers such as ConAgra Foods draw from a number of sources to make their forecasts. ConAgra provides brand-name foods and ingredients to retailers, major food establishments and commercial customers worldwide. Its forecasters begin by evaluating several economic indicators to predict the marketplace, such as GDP growth, CPI, PPI, commodity prices, currency exchange rates, the ISM *Report On Business*®, job growth, productivity changes and restaurant spending. Volatility in commodity prices is a primary concern for ConAgra because commodities make up a large portion of the organization's product spend, making the negotiation process more difficult for supply management professionals as this volatility naturally affects product pricing. Thus, commodity prices for dairy, wheat, soybeans, corn, soymeal, meat, pork and poultry are tracked on a regular basis. Another concern is the price of crude oil because it affects production, packaging and transportation costs. ConAgra closely watches both crude oil futures and natural gas futures (natural gas futures pricing tends to follow crude oil).[52]

Summary

To fully understand the forecasting process, supply management professionals need a good background in the economics of forecasting, the global environment in which they work today and sources of information that can help begin the forecasting process. Because international sourcing is common, understanding the generic types of economies in operation is important. From there, understanding country-specific differences that can affect the forecast and the trading process is also essential. A number of resources, including economic indicators, government indexes, surveys and other publications, can provide a wealth of information to support the forecasting process. The key is to find the most relevant information that will result in an accurate forecast. Chapter 5 will provide more specific information on developing a forecast using key information and forecast models.

Key Points

1. Business decisions typically are based on forecasts — a prediction of the future. The overall purpose of the forecast is to minimize uncertainty in the decision-making process.
2. The world operates with a combination of economic markets — free, closed and mixed. Given the global mix of free and mixed economies, trade is relatively open today. While trade barriers have decreased, tariffs and other forms of protectionism such as trading quotas still exist.
3. The issue of local buying preferences has changed over the past decade with the advent of advanced communication technologies and a changing political climate. In general, organizations take a two-pronged approach: standardize where possible, while considering local needs.

4. To manage supplier relationships in different cultures it is first necessary to understand and value some general difference in industrial histories, relationships to technology, natural resources, religions and geography.
5. International currency fluctuations and the additional costs and legal issues associated with international sourcing can impact the ability of organizations to compete effectively, thus affecting a forecast.
6. Every economy experiences swings in the business cycle. Five possible scenarios include (1) the highest point of output before a downturn; (2) recession, or shrinking of the economy; (3) recession trough, or lowest point in economic activity; (4) recovery, or resuming growth path; and (5) expansion, beyond previous high point.
7. Organizations use leading economic indicators to predict economic change, coincident economic indicators to understand current economic conditions, and lagging indicators to respond to the economic environment once a given economic point in an economic cycle has been reached.
8. Good forecasters use a number of resources to help create a forecast, including regional and international publications, industry sources, the ISM *Report On Business*®, private publications, internal historical data, online indices and search engines.

CHAPTER 5

Forecasting Models and Methods

A pilot would never take off without filing a flight plan showing the planned route and destination, but organizations often operate without planning demand for the upcoming fiscal year. Demand planning helps ensure a product or service is available when the customer wants it and is the first step of *demand management*. Demand management, according to the ISM *Glossary* (2014), is "the proactive compilation of requirements information regarding demand (from customers, sales, marketing, finance) and the organization's capabilities from the supply side (for example, supply, operations and logistics management); the development of a consensus regarding the ability to match the requirements and capabilities; and the agreement upon a synthesized plan that can most effectively meet the customer requirements within the constraints imposed by supply chain capabilities." As the definition suggests, demand management is the basis for decision-making within the Strategic Supply Management Concept. (See Figure S-1 in the "Series Overview" at the beginning of this book.)

Demand forecasts provide estimates for demand planning. A good forecast will help improve customer service, reduce unnecessary inventories and thus working capital needs, and lower costs. Although the statement is commonly made that "all forecasts are wrong," a fairly precise forecast is still possible if calculated correctly. This requires a certain degree of analytical skills. This chapter will begin by covering some of the reasons organizations forecast and discuss several factors that affect the demand forecast. The forecasting process then is described, followed by a discussion of the types of forecasting methods typically used by organizations. The important topic of minimizing forecast error is discussed later in the chapter. Finally, sharing forecast information with suppliers is described.

Chapter Objectives

- Explain why organizations forecast.
- Discuss the factors that affect the demand forecast.
- Describe the qualitative and quantitative methods used in the forecasting process.
- Explain the methods used to detect forecast errors.
- Discuss the value of sharing forecast results with suppliers.

Why Forecast?

Supply management professionals use forecasts, with other information sources described in Chapter 4, to assist in their planning processes. Good forecasts can be used as a basis to improve a supply management professional's sourcing methods, better identify key suppliers for strategic materials and supplies, improve quality, and increase supplier performance levels. The following paragraphs describe in more detail the reasons for forecasting, beginning with the overall purposes of forecasting for organizations, followed by the reasons supply management professionals develop forecasts.

To Estimate Demand

In general, forecasting is a useful planning tool to facilitate future-oriented decisions. More specifically, however, accurate forecasts are needed to help optimize profit levels by tapping into the most lucrative revenue streams. Thus, organizations seek to forecast the sources of those revenue streams to determine where to invest their resources most wisely. For instance, businesses need to predict sales quantities for new and existing products and services, so they develop demand forecasts. While estimating expected sales dollars is common, demand must be predicted in terms of quantity and is needed for operational planning purposes. For example, organizations need to estimate material, labor, transportation, distribution and space requirements for the upcoming year.

Within this context, considering the impact of a *product life cycle* on demand is also important. The concept of the product life cycle is essentially that each product or service goes through several stages, from development to introduction to a growth stage — where sales steadily increase, to a maturity stage — where sales are relatively flat, to a decline in sales, until finally the product is discontinued. Thus, demand will vary depending on where the product or service is in the product life cycle. For instance, demand for new products to be introduced to the marketplace most likely will be fairly uncertain and therefore difficult to predict, while demand for services in the maturity phase should be relatively easy to estimate because demand for those services is stable.

A forecast also should incorporate the effect of marketing actions on the product's life cycle and on the organization's future share of the market. For example, to temporarily boost sales of a product sliding from the growth phase to the mature phase, an organization may offer a special 10 percent price decrease for sales booked in a specific month or hire a celebrity spokesperson for advertising in the upcoming selling season which, if effective, may cause a spike in demand.

To Determine If Supply Can Meet Demand

An organization also must determine whether its demand forecasts are realistic; if there will be enough, too much or not enough industry capacity to meet overall customer demand; and whether it will have the capacity to meet its share of the market. Thus, organizations first create industry *capacity forecasts* by estimating or forecasting the amount of industry capacity and availability.

To create a capacity forecast, an organization evaluates the competition in terms of overlapping product lines and market coverage, and the expected effect on the marketplace. It then estimates capacity for its own organization. For example, a bank might consider offering a new type of credit card. To determine if it has the capacity to meet customer demand, the bank must first consider any advertising campaigns that will be offered along with whether the existing hardware, software and human resources will be able to handle the expected demand.

To Predict Technology Trends

Organizations also need to forecast *technology trends* and breakthroughs that can impact demand as products and services evolve. In some industries, technological advances have significantly cut product life-cycle times. For example, the personal tablet PC industry is driven by the rapid pace of technological improvements in dual processors, operating systems and cameras, and the product life cycle for these components is less than a year.[1] If an organization is not ready for those changes, a competitor most likely will be. Senior executives, therefore, must be aware of any technology gaps that may exist within their own organization and the potential threats to revenue or market share if their competitors adopt this new technology.

Forecasting technology trends is typically carried on in an environment of uncertainty. For example, in 2012 a number of trends and changes were predicted to happen by 2014 including cloud computing, social networking, mobile devices, data management, analytics, business intelligence and compliance. According to researchers Clare Walker and Martha Coacher, "For adoption of these technologies to successfully take hold, a number of key factors need to be evaluated and planned for: changes to the business process, responsiveness and acceptance by internal and external stakeholders, and impact to corporate or regulatory compliance. Ignoring these could spell disaster and undermine customer and investor trust." [2]

To Predict Prices

Supply management also is responsible for performing *price forecasting*. Price forecasting is most commonly used for commodities such as crude oil, metals and other raw materials. For example, appliance manufacturer Maytag, now a part of Whirlpool Corp., predicts the price of cold-rolled steel — a major component of washers, dryers and dishwashers — for the upcoming year to determine product cost. This type of forecasting is important when an organization is a supplier to another industry, especially one that is changing quickly; when the goods used to make a finished product or deliver a service experience volatility in price or availability; or if international conditions have an impact on price or availability of goods or services used. Prices also can be affected by seasonality in demand patterns. For example, whole turkeys are priced lower for the Thanksgiving holiday and hams go on sale prior to Easter.

To Predict Dependent Demand

Supply management professionals in a manufacturing environment and in certain service industries (restaurants, for example) also are interested in the need for components that will be used to create their offerings. The demand for these components — which may include raw materials, ingredients, supplies, parts and subassemblies — is known as *dependent demand* because their demand depends on the demand for the finished product or service. For example, McDonald's Corp. estimates the number of Big Macs that will be sold in the upcoming year and uses that forecast to predict dependent demand for the beef patties, buns and "special sauce." A travel agency predicts the number of all-inclusive vacation packages it will sell to estimate the dependent demand for airline tickets, hotel accommodations, cruises and tours. Uncertainty in predicting material needs naturally lies in whether the demand forecast is overly optimistic, a reasonable assumption or overly pessimistic.

As a rule, material specialists will begin with the demand forecast for each finished product as a basis to create these material forecasts. Many manufacturers use a *materials resource plan* (MRP), a software program developed in the 1960s, or *manufacturing resource planning* (MRP II), which links MRP to an organization's financial system and other processes, to calculate demand for these components.[3] An MRP system helps ensure that sufficient quantities of materials are available when needed for production. Coca-Cola implemented MRP II in nine facilities around the world, beginning in 1987 at a Puerto Rico manufacturing plant. As a result, weeks of inventory went down 50 percent to 75 percent in at least two facilities, productivity increased 85 percent to 100 percent at all sites, and supplier on-time performance rose to 95 percent from 50 percent to 75 percent.[4]

The inputs to an MRP system include a *bill of materials*, a *master production schedule* and an *inventory record database*. A bill of materials is "a list containing the quantity and description of all materials required to produce one unit of a finished product" (ISM *Glossary* 2014). It will also record the relationships between each component and the number of each component that will be used (this number will be taken from the engineering and process designs created during the product design stage). The master production schedule provides the details of the quantity of each finished product that will be produced for each time period (an hour, day, week or month) within the planning horizon. The inventory records are the compilation of all inventory transactions such as the release of any new orders, the receipt of orders, inventory withdrawals or order cancellations. The MRP system then uses information from independent demand forecasts for replacement parts and maintenance items, as well as the master production schedule, inventory records that show the amount of inventory on hand and the bill of materials; this information is used to estimate the need for all materials, components and subassemblies at various specific times during the planning period. Figure 5-1 provides an illustration of a hypothetical MRP system.

Figure 5-1: Hypothetical MRP System

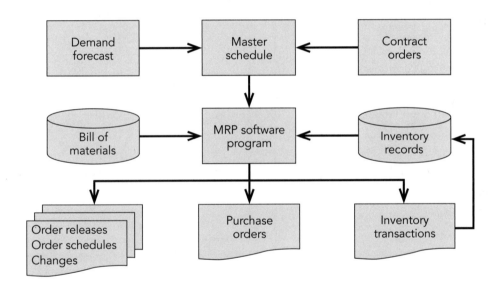

Supply management professionals then can use the results to check component availabilities, estimate price trends and generate purchase orders. Based on this data, inventory policies can be set. For example, if prices are trending down and availability is high, the supply management professional may decide to keep inventory levels to a minimum. Another important part of the process is learning the supplier's expected *order lead times*. Order lead time is measured as the span of time between placing an order with a supplier and receiving the goods. If the organization uses an MRP system, it will use dependent demand figures generated from the MRP system, expected supplier order lead times for each component, and expected supplier quality to plan when to place orders. The MRP system then will use this information provided by the supply management professional to create the materials requirements planning record, which indicates when components should be ordered and when they are expected to be received. The following example illustrates how a hypothetical organization uses the MRP record to plan deliveries.

Cox Global Manufacturing, Ltd. makes a product that uses Component A. In its planning session, the manufacturing team calculates its weekly need for Component A based on independent demand forecasts and standing contract orders. The supply management professional has told the team that the expected order lead time is two weeks and lot sizes must be in multiples of 50. The team creates a material requirements planning record based on ordering 150 units every other week and 100 on alternating weeks.

Item: Component A						
Lead time: 2 weeks				Week		
	1	2	3	4	5	6
Gross requirements	160	110	150	180	130	140
Scheduled receipts	150	100	150	100	150	100
Projected on-hand inventory (Beginning inventory = 100 units)	90	80	80	0	20	(20)
Planned receipts			150	100	150	100
Planned order releases	150	100	150	100		

The record indicates it will run out of Component A in week 6, resulting in a stop in production. As a result, they increase the order for week 4 by 50 units, as shown in the following table.

Item: Component A						
Lead time: 2 weeks				Week		
	1	2	3	4	5	6
Gross requirements	160	110	150	180	130	140
Scheduled receipts	150	100	150	100	150	150
Projected on-hand inventory (Beginning inventory = 100 units)	90	80	80	0	20	30
Planned receipts			150	100	150	150
Planned order releases	150	100	150	150		

To Estimate the Supply Management Budget

Supply management professionals must develop a forecast of any actions that need to be taken or resources required to meet their goals over the planning horizon. The forecast will be used as a basis to develop the *supply management budget*. Budgets, in a sense, are forecasts of all monies required to run the supply management organization for the upcoming year. Budgeting also is used to examine and control costs. For example, in 2013 the Finnish government cut its procurement budget in an effort to increase cost savings and manage internal cost pressures.[5]

The supply management budget generally includes four specific types of budgets:

1. *Purchased materials/operations budget* — An estimate of projected operational costs and funds expected to be spent on material and service purchases, which is based on the demand forecast.
2. *Maintenance repairs and operating (MRO) budget* — A budget tied to the expected changes in inventory levels, operating schedules and price levels.
3. *Capital budget* — A budget that covers a multiple-year horizon and is based on expected production or service delivery needs, planned equipment replacements and special projects, and expansion plans; and is tied to the strategic plan for any new mergers/acquisitions, expansion plans, new product or service lines, or other capital investments.
4. *Administrative budget* — A budget that identifies all expenses for the supply management function.

While there are many distinct needs for forecasting, the remainder of this chapter will focus on demand forecasting because it has the biggest impact on supply management decisions. The following section begins with a description of some of the factors that affect demand forecasts.

Factors That Affect Demand Forecasts

It is important to think of the demand forecast as a "living document" and to be prepared to adjust the forecast as conditions change. A forecast provides a snapshot of expected future conditions. These conditions, however, can and will change. Some issues that affect economic conditions, such as changes in the money market, geopolitical factors and global trading conditions, are discussed in Chapter 4. Five other factors that directly impact operations are summarized in Figure 5-2 and are described in the following sections.

Figure 5-2: Conditions Affecting a Forecast

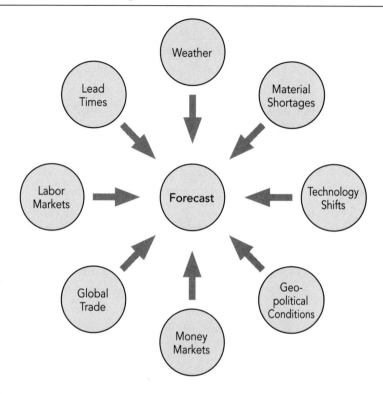

Lead Time

Lead time as defined in the ISM *Glossary* (2014) is "the time that elapses from placement of an order until receipt of the order, including time for order transmittal, processing, preparation and shipping." Unexpected changes in lead times for order deliveries can adversely affect the forecast. Ideally, customer organizations plan to receive materials as promised, but this is not always the case. Late deliveries can negatively affect an operation, slowing down the conversion and delivery process. Thus, once the forecast has initially been developed, some rethinking and modification will be needed as lead times change. An airline, for example, in anticipation of greater than originally projected expected growth, attempted to place an order for two more airplanes in addition to its original order of 80 planes. However, the manufacturer could not accept the airline's order for the additional planes, saying delivery was not possible in the near future because of capacity limitations. As a result, the airline had to adjust its forecast.[6]

Labor Markets

Labor markets also can affect the forecast. If an organization is experiencing labor shortages, for example, it will be difficult to meet the forecast. The state of Montana in the U.S., with an unemployment rate of 3 percent, faced severe labor shortages in the fast-food industry during 2006. One A&W Restaurant owner found that employees were leaving for higher-paying jobs in the oil and gas industry; he was forced to close the restaurant during the Wednesday rush hour for two weeks, losing valuable business.[7] New labor contracts or strikes also can have an impact on the forecast. In 2013 the National Union of Metalworkers of South Africa (NUMSA), with approximately 30,000 members, went on strike over wages. The strike stopped production for major car manufacturers such as Ford, General Motors and Toyota, resulting in lost car sales.[8]

Material Shortages

As manufacturers move to just-in-time and lean production and service environments (these strategies are discussed in Chapter 1), the chance for supply shortages increases and must be managed effectively. Unexpected events, such as labor shortages or delivery problems, or even natural disasters, can suddenly create material shortages that impede the ability of an organization to meet demand. In 2011, for example, GM and Peugeot-Citroen had to deal with shortages of airflow sensors after Hitachi Ltd. was forced to shut down its factory north of Tokyo due to an earthquake and tsunami (Hitachi Ltd. produces 60 percent of the world's supply). GM had to close a factory in Louisiana while Peugeot-Citroen was forced to reduce production in almost all its European plants.[9]

Shifts in Technology

Shifts in technology also impact the forecast, although generally in the long term. As mentioned previously, organizations often will create a separate technology forecast to address these issues. Deloitte releases an annual report on technology trends. For example, in 2012 it predicted that sales of personal computers (PCs) will continue to be strong in the foreseeable future because, although sales of tablets and smart phones almost tripled from 2010 to 2012, PC sales remained steady. Deloitte found that users have a preference for the large screen, like full- or mid-size keyboards with a mouse or touchpad, often need to create content rather than just watch it, and find PCs easy to use for common tasks.[10]

Weather Conditions

Climactic conditions, while out of the control of the forecaster, can have an impact on the forecast. In 2012, Hurricane Sandy affected the Northeast U.S. for about a week. The primary challenges were "disruption to logistics and transportation of product and the lack of power — first electrical and then fuel."[11] However, technology has improved response times. According to Thomas Derry, CEO, Institute for Supply Management®, "Some firms are making huge investments in new technological capabilities to ensure they have the data they need in real time to make critical business decisions. The information available to supply chain leaders in some companies is so impressive I wouldn't be surprised to learn that it surpasses the information available even to U.S. government agencies." The availability of real-time data on weather, political events and other risk factors has greatly improved response time to disasters. Also, more organizations have developed plans for how to handle operations in the event of a disaster.[12] Real-time forecasts help organizations set inventory levels, create sourcing and replenishment strategies, and are even used to notify downstream suppliers when to start production of a particular product.

Keeping in mind that these conditions certainly can alter a forecast, and it is essential that an organization have business continuity plans for disasters, organizations should still go through the forecasting process. An effective forecasting framework is essential to minimizing waste. The following section provides a general framework for developing a demand forecast.

Demand Forecasting Process

In general, organizations go through a five-step process, as illustrated in Figure 5-3, to create a forecast, beginning with the planning process (Step 1 — selecting what will be forecasted, choosing the forecast time horizon and deciding which forecasting model[s] will be used). At this point, it is time to gather any data necessary to create the forecast (Step 2). Once the data is collected and organized, the forecast is created (Step 3). The last steps are to validate the forecast (Step 4) and then implement the results (Step 5).

Figure 5-3: Forecasting Process

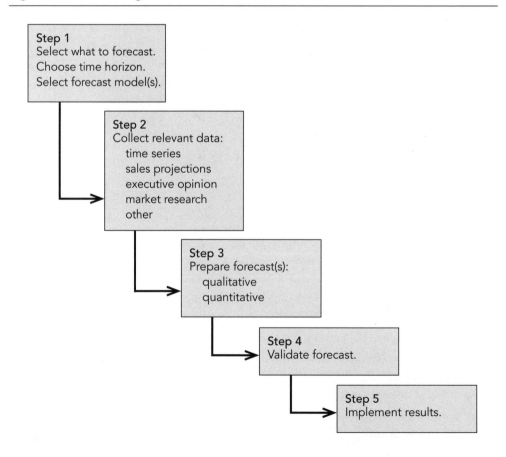

Brooks Sports, Inc., a U.S. designer of high-performance running footwear, apparel and accessories, changed its forecasting process in 2001 when the organization shifted from selling a broader product line to promoting a set of high-performance products aimed at serious runners. It implemented a collaborative forecasting process that would support the new strategic direction of the organization. Brooks first develops monthly statistical forecasts at the stock-keeping unit (SKU) level based on any trends and seasonal patterns. On a quarterly basis, the sales staff and management prepare a demand forecast for the next 12 months using data collected via the Internet, with a focus on major accounts. Lastly, forecasters compare the statistical forecasts with the sales forecasts, make any necessary adjustments, and prepare the final monthly forecast. The organization has found that forecast accuracy has improved by approximately 40 percent since the new process was implemented.[13]

Length of Forecast

Forecasts typically can be broken down into *long-term*, *medium-term* and *short-term* time frames. While there is some argument about the time span that should encompass each of these forecasts, long-term demand forecasts usually are developed for more than one year and are used as a basis for capacity planning, and making location decisions and process changes. Medium-term forecasts, varying from three months to one year, help organizations make decisions regarding staffing, production or service delivery, purchasing and distribution. Lastly, short-term forecasts (less than three months) are used as the basis to schedule the workforce, manage inventory, plan production and develop schedules for final product assembly. Senior managers normally will be involved in longer-term demand forecasting; midlevel marketing, supply management, logistics and operations personnel will contribute to medium-term forecasts; and frontline employees will be involved in forecasting shorter-term needs for labor, materials and production.

DNATA, one of the world's largest air services providers originally located in the Middle East and is in 38 countries with more than 20,000 employees, has used SAS software since 1993 for forecasting. Annually, volume forecasts are created to help plan for expected revenues and expenses. On a daily basis, shop floor managers use forecasting to manage the deployment of resources in their operational areas. Long-term forecasting is used to plan for future facilities and the expansion of current cargo terminal operations. Since formalizing the process, DNATA has reduced forecasting inaccuracies to less than 10 percent. According to Jean-Pierre DePauw, divisional senior vice president, "This [fewer forecasting inaccuracies] has led to a considerable improvement in the decision-making process, particularly in regard to facility expansion and new projects."[14]

The planning horizon for short-term forecasting can vary considerably depending on the type of organization. For example, while DNATA uses daily forecasts, the head nurses at a hospital may forecast in one-hour increments for surgeries, a fast-food franchise manager might create weekly forecasts for workforce needs, a retailer could forecast demand based on the season, and a manufacturer might forecast quarterly labor needs.

Top-Down and Bottom-Up Forecasting

Organizations typically create an annual forecast for planning purposes. They generally begin at the macrolevel with an aggregate forecast for all products and services offered, which is an easier prediction, followed by product lines and then individual items or SKUs. Organizations then generally use either a *top-down* or *bottom-up* approach to allocate demand by location. The top-down approach also is known as the *decomposition approach* because an organization forecasts demand for each product or service and then allocates a percentage of that demand for each retail site, distribution center or manufacturing plant. For example, if a retail clothing chain of 60 stores forecasts overall sales of a particular sweater to be 20,000 units, the forecaster allocates demand by store and provides that information to the chain's distribution centers. The bottom-up approach takes a reverse approach, forecasting demand by store or region, and rolling up those forecasts into an *aggregate forecast*. The demand forecast for all products and services then is used to create an *aggregate plan*, which breaks down all labor and material requirements, usually by quarter.

The top-down approach has been found to be more accurate at the top level and is used for developing strategic plans and budgets. However, forecasting at the lower levels does not tend to be accurate because actual demand fluctuations are not considered. For instance, many retailers have difficulty forecasting the popularity of specific colors or sizes store-to-store. The top-down approach also will miss current stock position of the stores compared with the desired stock position and store lead times, "which can lead to too much or too little stock arriving too early or too late — the result being excess inventory holding or missed sales," according to GRA, a consulting firm.[15]

Conversely, the bottom-up approach is recommended for tactical planning and scheduling.[16] It generally results in smaller forecast errors and less bias at the lower levels because it reflects the actual changes in demand. However, higher-level forecasts are generally poorer.

Canadian retailer Northern Group Retail, Ltd. uses the top-down approach and has overcome some of its lower-level forecasting problems by adopting software tools. The software helps the organization "forecast items down to the store and item level" and as a result, it can customize its merchandise store-by-store. Inventory levels have dropped significantly, stores are more productive, and gross margins are higher than the industry average.[17]

A leading producer of canned and bottled juice drinks used both the top-down and bottom-up approach to its advantage. The first week of each month, demand planners use a bottom-up approach, working with the field sales managers to develop a rolling six-month forecast for the top 75 customers (they account for 70 percent of the producer's revenues), which then are aggregated. The second week, a top-down approach is used in which a series of consensus-building meetings are conducted among managers and directors of sales, marketing and trade marketing. The team reviews forecast error rates and makes adjustments for any upcoming sales promotions. With additional input from demand planning, the final forecast is prepared.[18]

The types of forecasts an organization uses are related to the time period covered by the forecast, which may be developed using a mix of *qualitative* and *quantitative* methods. Common forecast methods and their applicability are summarized in Figure 5-4 and discussed further in the following section, beginning with a description of qualitative forecasting techniques.

Figure 5-4: Forecasting Methods

FORECAST METHOD		TIME FRAME		
Qualitative	Description	Long Term	Medium Term	Short Term
Sales force composite	A manager reviews each salesperson's best estimate of the expected level of customer demand for his or her region. Forecast then is compiled at the district and national levels for an overall forecast.	X	X	X
Market research	Surveys are collected from consumers to estimate the degree of interest in a product or service.	X	X	X
Jury of executive opinion	Executive opinion is based on the experience, knowledge and opinions of employees from key areas within an organization and external parties such as customers and suppliers.	X	X	X
Delphi method	Moderator collects results from survey sent to panel of experts and then creates a new survey that is sent to the group. This process continues until consensus is reached.	X		
Quantitative	Description	Long Term	Medium Term	Short Term
Naive forecast	The upcoming forecast is set equal to the most recent period's demand.			X
Simple moving average	The mean of at least two recent periods of demand data is the basis for the next period's demand forecast.		X	X
Weighted moving average	Weights are used on each past demand period to place more emphasis on certain periods based on experience.		X	X

FORECAST METHOD		TIME FRAME		
Quantitative	Description	Long Term	Medium Term	Short Term
Exponential smoothing	Each forecast is weighted by a given fraction, known as the smoothing constant, of the difference between the most recent actual demand and forecast.		X	X
Multiplicative seasonality	Seasonality is expressed in terms of a percentage of the average demand using an indexing method.		X	
Trend-adjusted exponential smoothing	An exponentially smoothed forecast is adjusted by incorporating a trend value.		X	
Regression analysis	A straight line is fitted to past data using a fitting technique known as the least squares method.	X	X	
Box-Jenkins	Complicated yet accurate method estimates a mathematical formula that will approximately generate the historical demand patterns in a time series.		X	
Winter's model	Simultaneously considers the effects of trend and seasonal factors using the exponential smoothing technique.		X	
Single-period model	Past demand data is used to determine how much stock to order based on probability analysis.		X	X

Qualitative Forecasts

Qualitative, or judgmental, forecasts are known as such because they are developed based on the opinions of others such as managers or other experts, estimates from the sales staff, or the results of market research. They are used most often when an organization has no background in quantitative forecasting or when no quantitative data is available for analysis. Qualitative forecasts also are valuable when quantitative forecasts are not particularly accurate and the decision-maker (CEO, president or other senior executive) has a high level of experiential knowledge that is difficult to incorporate into the quantitative forecast. This is often the case when organizations are performing long-range planning or predicting technology trends. Qualitative forecasts also are useful in adjusting for specific events that will take place in the future, such as competitive actions, special promotions, and domestic or international political events. Some examples of qualitative forecasts are provided in the next section.

Sales Force Composite

In one commonly used method, each salesperson provides a best estimate of the expected level of customer demand for his or her region. A manager then reviews each forecast to make sure it is realistic. Based on this information, the forecast is compiled at the district and national levels for an overall forecast.

This approach offers several advantages because the sales force likely has the most knowledge on what customers will be buying and in what quantities; regional sales information can be used to manage inventories, distribution and sales staffing; and regional sales can be rolled up into one overall forecast. Marketing organizations frequently share sales force composites with supply management professionals to improve forecast accuracy, negotiation capabilities, and service to internal and external customers.[19] The downside is that salespeople tend to have their own biases that can adversely affect the forecast. For instance, salespeople may not always be particularly astute in determining what customers will actually buy. Additionally, if performance is based on the forecast, the salesperson may provide an underestimate, working diligently only until he or she has reached his or her projection. Conversely, the salesperson may strive to exceed the projection to look good. Companies today can use forecasting software to help make sales more predictable and overcome inaccurate predictions.

To overcome these problems, Sport Obermeyer, a U.S. manufacturer of fashion skiwear, uses independent sales forecasts from a panel of experts for each product as one component in its strategy to improve customer responsiveness and reduce risk. Where forecasts differed significantly, the organization concluded that demand was unpredictable and adjusted production downward. Sport Obermeyer was able to reduce markdowns and increase profitability by two-thirds the first year after implementation.[20]

Market Research

Market research uses surveys collected from consumers to estimate the degree of interest in a product or service. Surveys may be administered in a number of ways, including by telephone, email, online or personal interviews. Organizations also use customer relationship management (CRM) software to track buying behavior. Marketing personnel attempt to select a sample representing a specific population and then analyze the data using both statistical tools and their own judgment. While market research is used as the basis for short-term, medium-term and long-term forecasting, its accuracy is best for the short term.

Several disadvantages are associated with using surveys in market research. For example, the wording used in survey questions may not always result in learning the true feelings of the consumer. Without actually seeing the product, consumers also may have a difficult time imagining a new product's usefulness. Moreover, if people do respond to a survey, the fact that they say they will buy or use a product or service is no guarantee that they will actually do so. To resolve some of these issues, organizations use online or email surveys that can be completed quickly and easily. Vermont Teddy Bear Co., a gift delivery service, used online surveys that included photographs of product concepts to help develop its demand forecast for new items. This form of market research has worked so well that the results are used to help the organization decide which designs go into production and the production quantities. Organizations also are collecting and organizing customer data by using CRM software applications to support the forecasting process. Purchasing and returns transactions, demographic information and responses to marketing promotions can help marketing estimate the future needs of existing and potential customers.

Jury of Executive Opinion

A forecast employing executive opinion uses the experience, knowledge and opinions of employees from key areas within an organization and external parties such as customers and suppliers. This type of forecast typically is used when past data does not exist, when causal relationships have not been identified, when a forecast is completely out of line with competitors, national or world events are changing, or an executive has some information that is not available to the forecaster. For example, executives may adjust a sales forecast for a newly developed sales promotion that has not yet been released. Senior management also may be aware of a new trade agreement that has been signed or a war developing that will open up new selling opportunities. The makers of Tylenol, for instance, had to use a jury of executive opinion to forecast sales for 1983 after a tampering scare in 1982 because demand was highly uncertain. Executive opinion also may be used to develop a forecast for a new product or service without a previous track record. These managers normally hold two or three forecast meetings, perhaps starting with the sales forecast, and work toward consensus.

The advantage of this method is its simplicity and relative ease of use. However, it is subject to a high degree of judgmental bias. These biases often occur because of the dominant positions of some persons such as senior managers, an individual's personal charisma that can sway people, someone who tends to dominate the conversation, or the "alleged expertise" of one individual.

The Delphi Method

The Delphi Method is used to lessen the potential biases commonly found using a jury of executive opinion. A structured approach is used to derive consensus from a panel of experts — usually five to ten — who maintain anonymity. Anonymity is important because it allows each participant to express his or her opinion freely. The Delphi Method also eliminates the need for group meetings. However, it can take multiple iterations to reach consensus, and participants may opt to drop out of the process.

A coordinator sends the panel an initial survey, usually asking questions regarding sales revenue estimates including a minimum and maximum, the likelihood that these estimates will materialize, and the reasoning behind each participant's estimates. The coordinator then tabulates the results and sends them back along with any anonymous statements.

Each participant reviews the results with an option to adjust his or her original estimates based on the opinions of the other respondents, and submits any changes along with the reasons for diverging from the original estimates. This process continues until consensus is reached.

Other uses for the Delphi Method besides sales revenues include long-range forecasting for product and service demand, developing projections for new product demand, pricing, and predicting technological developments. CMM International, for example, used the Delphi Method to predict the prices of products from food additives.[21] The results from forecasting societal changes, scientific advances, the competitive environment or government regulation also can be used to help direct the organization's research and development personnel. While qualitative forecasts are valuable, quantitative methods based on mathematics have their rightful place. If a product has been on the market a long time and demand is relatively predictable, only quantitative forecasts may be necessary. Campbell Soup Co., for instance, has little trouble forecasting demand for its tomato and chicken noodle condensed soups, which have been around for more than 100 years. With current computer capabilities and software, quantitative forecasting also is much less tedious, allowing forecasters to focus on interpreting the results rather than on assembling the information.[22] The following two sections provide a discussion of two categories of quantitative models: *time series* and *causal analysis*.

Time Series Forecasting

Time series models use time-based data, which is a set of observations collected at regular intervals over a given time horizon. A clothing retailer might review daily or weekly sales data for each store over the past five years. The data points would be related to specific points in time; thus, the data could be used for time series analysis. The underlying assumption is that a forecast can be created based on patterns observed within the time series data.

Four main patterns may be present separately or in combination:

1. *Horizontal or flat.* Demand data values tend to fluctuate around a mean that does not vary. This pattern is the easiest to predict because of its simplicity. Some examples of horizontal demand include products or services found in the mature stage of their life cycles, such as bread or legal services.
2. *Seasonality.* Any pattern that is observed regularly occurs for a constant length of time and is influenced by given seasonal factors such as day of the week, or a given month or quarter, is considered seasonal. For example, hospitals experience certain peaks in demand for their services during the day. Demand for banking services typically spike on paydays such as Fridays, and on the 15th and 30th day of each month.
3. *Trend.* An increasing or decreasing pattern of demand over time is considered a trend. For example, demand for CDs continues to decline because customers can easily download music to their portable devices.

4. *Cycle*. A cycle is longer than a season, often a multiyear phenomenon, and is tied to economic fluctuations, such as recessions or inflation. A cycle is probably the most difficult pattern to predict. Economic indicators and indexes generally are used to predict cycles, and are discussed in Chapter 4.

A time series is made up of a demand pattern comprised of some combination of these four patterns plus some random variation, which is unexplainable and cannot be predicted. Thus, it can be difficult to make a forecast given the number of patterns that may be present. However, several forecasting models are useful in keeping the amount of random variation to a minimum. Models used to predict relatively flat or horizontal demand are discussed in the following section.

Naive Approach

One of the simplest forecasting methods used is to set the upcoming forecast equal to the most recent period's demand. For example, if Walgreen Co., a U.S. drugstore chain, sells 1,000 bottles of 100-count vitamin C in September, the forecast for October also would be 1,000 bottles. Organizations often use this method as a starting point and then make adjustments based on past experience. This method can be used as a basis of comparison against more sophisticated models. It is the least expensive, easiest and most efficient method.

Moving Averages

The *simple moving average* "calculates the average of the most current 'n' periods. In each recalculation, the most current period's data is added and the oldest data is removed" (ISM *Glossary* 2014). The forecast typically is based on a calculation of the mean for at least two recent periods of demand data. The data is summed and then divided by the number of time periods used in the calculation. For example, if a forecaster at German retailer Metro Group wants to predict demand for a size 40 (U.S. size 10) woman's dress in a specific style for April using a three-month simple moving average, the calculation would be the average of actual demand for January, February and March. The formula to calculate the moving average is:

$$\text{Moving average} = \frac{\sum \text{demand for past } n \text{ periods}}{n}$$

$\sum$ = a symbol that represents the sum of

n = number for periods included in the moving average.

Using the Metro example, if actual demand for January, February and March was 2,500, 3,200 and 2,750 dresses, respectively, the forecast for April would be

April forecast = (2,500 + 3,200 + 2,750)/3 = 2,816.7 ≈ 2,817 dresses

As data from a new time period is added, data from the earliest time period is dropped from the average calculation. Again, using the Metro example, when the forecaster wants to predict demand for May, he or she would use actual demand from February, March and April. This method is fairly reliable if the forecaster can assume that demand will remain relatively flat over time.

If a noticeable demand pattern is observed, the forecaster can apply individual weights to each past demand period to place more emphasis on certain periods. For example, an office supply organization might notice that within a three-month period, the most accurate forecast for computer printers is calculated by weighting the most recent month by 50 percent, the second most recent month by 30 percent and the third most recent month by 20 percent. Weights usually are determined based on the forecaster's past experience; there is no set formula. The forecaster often experiments with past demand data to determine the weightings that will provide the most accurate forecast. However, the sum of the weights must be equal to 1. The calculation of the weighted moving average is as follows:

Weighted moving average = $\sum$ [(weight for period n)(demand for period n)]

In the following example of an office supply organization such as OfficeMax or Staples, the forecaster collects data on demand for boxes of private-label inkjet paper from April (5,500), May (5,700) and June (5,950). Applying the weighted moving average method, and weights of 20 percent, 30 percent and 50 percent, respectively, the forecast for July would be:

July forecast = (5,500 × 20%) + (5,700 × 30%) + (5,950 × 50%) = 5,785 boxes

The advantage of the simple and weighted moving average methods is the ability to smooth out any unexpected fluctuations in demand so that stable estimates can be made. However, as the number of periods averaged increases, the smoothing effect of the simple moving average method also increases, making these methods less sensitive to actual changes in the data. Another disadvantage of either method is the inability to effectively forecast trends because of the smoothing effect. In the previous example, for instance, although there appears to be an upward trend in demand, the forecast for July is less than the demand for June. Moreover, the simple and weighted moving average methods cannot predict unprecedented events because they are based on historical data. Lastly, both methods require a significant amount of past data to be effective.

Exponential Smoothing

While the simple and weighted moving average methods require a large amount of past data, the *exponential smoothing method* requires relatively little data and is useful when demand is relatively flat or horizontal. The methodology "weights the demand for the most recent period and the forecast for the previous period as a basis for the current forecast" (ISM *Glossary* 2014). This method is fairly accurate, and few calculations are required. However, exponential smoothing is a more sophisticated method than the simple or weighted moving averages, and a qualitative method such as the Delphi Method or managerial experience must be used to set the initial forecast. Exponential smoothing is widely used in wholesale organizations, service organizations and retailing.

Each forecast is weighted by a given decimal value, known as the *smoothing constant*, which is the difference between the most recent actual demand and the forecast. The smoothing constant will range between 0 and 1, and is determined by the forecaster. The formula to calculate the forecast is as follows:

$$\text{Forecast}_{t+1} = \text{Forecast}_t + \alpha(\text{Actual Demand}_t - \text{Forecast}_t)$$

where

t = current time period

t+1 = following time period

α = alpha = smoothing constant ($0 \leq \alpha \leq 1$)

The following example illustrates the exponential smoothing method.

JJ International sells patio furniture to retailers in Australia. Susan, the organization's forecaster, has collected the following demand data for one of its tables, as is shown in the following table:

Month	Demand
May	450
June	440
July	420
August	460
September	485
October	435

Susan decides to use the exponential smoothing method to calculate the forecast for June, July and August using the exponential smoothing method and a smoothing constant of $\alpha = 0.3$ based on her past experience. She assumes the forecast for May (F_{May}) is 450 tables. Given:

$F_{May} = 450$, $\alpha = 0.3$

Susan first calculates the forecast for June:
$F_{June} = F_{May} + 0.3(A_{May} - F_{May}) = 450 + 0.3(450 - 450) = 450$ tables

She then calculates the forecast for July:
$F_{July} = F_{June} + 0.3(A_{June} - F_{June}) = 450 + 0.3(440 - 450) = 447$ tables

Lastly, Susan calculates the forecast for August:
$F_{August} = F_{July} + 0.3(A_{July} - F_{July}) = 447 + 0.3(420 - 447) = 438.9 \approx 439$ tables.

Although any smoothing constant α between 0 and 1 can be used, values closer to 1 more heavily weight the previous period's demand, increasing the responsiveness of the forecast to changes in actual demand. Conversely, an α value closer to 0 weights the previous period's demand less heavily, resulting in a forecast that is less responsive to demand fluctuations. The next example illustrates the effect of different alpha values. Note that while the forecast is most responsive when the alpha value is 0.8, it may not be the most accurate. A comparison of the errors also would be needed to determine which alpha value results in the most *accurate* forecast. More on forecast accuracy is found later in this chapter.

Susan, the forecaster at JJ International, wants to compare forecasts using the exponential smoothing method and different alpha values. She calculates the monthly forecast using alpha values of 0.2, 0.4, 0.6 and 0.8.

An Excel spreadsheet was used for the forecast example using Tools, Data Analysis and Exponential Smoothing for each alpha value. The following three spreadsheets illustrate how to set up the calculations based on $\alpha = 0.2$ (complete results are already shown in each example). (In the second spreadsheet, Excel requires the user to enter a *damping factor* rather than a smoothing constant. A damping factor provides the same function as a smoothing constant but is the inverse, $1 - \alpha$. Thus, the damping factor that should be used for calculating the forecast is $1 - 0.2 = 0.8$.) The software also assumes that the first period forecast is equal to the actual demand.

Step 1. *Create a table of the raw data. Select "Data," then "Data Analysis."* (Note that Data Analysis is freely available in Microsoft Excel but is not enabled by default. To enable it, go to FILE, then OPTIONS. Select ADD-INs, ANALYSIS TOOLPAK and click GO to install it. Then, follow the instructions above to work with Data Analysis.)

Step 2. *Select "Exponential Smoothing" and "OK."*

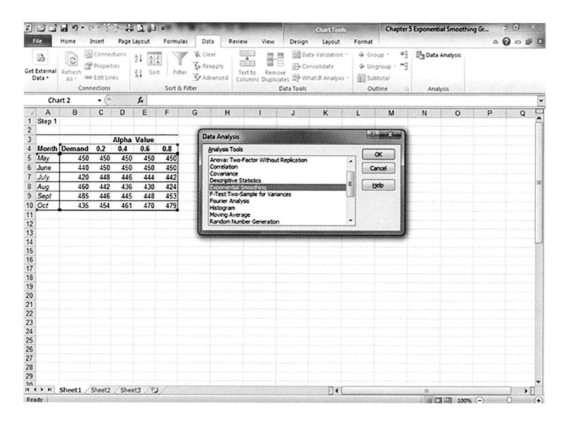

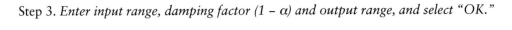

Step 3. *Enter input range, damping factor (1 − α) and output range, and select "OK."*

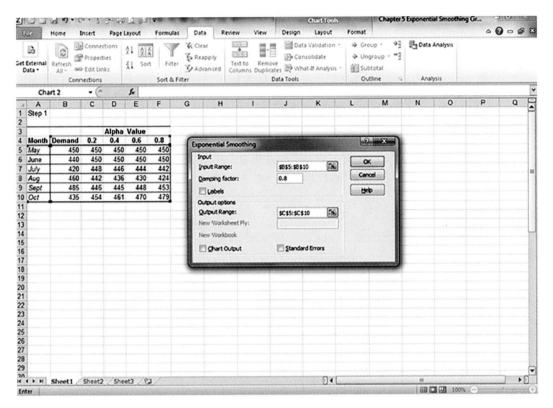

Step 4. *Repeat Steps 1 through 3 to develop the other forecasts. A graph then can be created using the spreadsheet results and graphing function.*

Susan notices that the forecast for $\alpha = 0.2$ is flatter and less responsive to the actual demand, that the forecast is more responsive as the alpha value increases, and that the forecasts for $\alpha = 0.8$ is the most responsive to the actual demand. However, all forecasts trail the actual demand. For example, note that the actual demand in July was 420. The forecasts for July are all higher than the demand but closer to the actual demand for June. In August, the actual demand was 460, while all forecasts were less than the actual demand of 460 and closer to the actual demand for July. Similarly, in September the forecasts were all less than the actual demand of 485 but closer to the actual demand for August.

While moving average and exponential smoothing models are good for relatively flat demand, seasonality is common for many organizations, requiring a different forecasting method. The following section provides a discussion of one method commonly used — the seasonal index.

Forecasting Seasonality

Most organizations will experience some type of seasonal pattern for one or more of their products or services. The goal is to recognize not only when those seasons occur, but how each season's demand exceeds or falls below average demand. While several methods are used to calculate measures to reflect seasonality, this chapter will present one method known as *multiplicative seasonality*, where seasonality is expressed in terms of a percentage of the average demand. This percentage above or below the average is known as the *seasonal index*. For instance, if demand for snow skis in the fall months is 1.5 times the average annual demand, fall demand is 50 percent above the average annual demand.

The steps to calculate a seasonal index are illustrated in the following example. Notice the variation in forecasted demand is based on the season.

Premium Pools builds swimming pools in Arizona and other states. Pat, the owner, has noticed a seasonal pattern in demand each year and would like to use this information to make better supply decisions for the organization's materials. Historically, procurement policies have been based on obtaining volume discounts; as a result, inventory costs have risen significantly in the past year. Following is demand data for the past two years:

Season	2011	2012
Spring	200	220
Summer	450	465
Fall	150	155
Winter	90	92
Total	890	932

CHAPTER 5: Forecasting Models and Methods

To calculate the seasonal index, Pat uses the multiplicative seasonal index method:

Step 1. Pat calculates the average demand for each quarter by dividing the total annual demand for each year by 4:

Year 1: 890/4 = 222.5
Year 2: 932/4 = 233

Step 2. He then calculates the seasonal index for every season for the past two years by dividing the actual demand for each season by the average demand per season (rounding to three decimal points):

Season	2011	2012
Spring	200/222.5 = 0.899	220/233 = 0.944
Summer	450/222.5 = 2.022	465/233 = 1.996
Fall	150/222.5 = 0.674	155/233 = 0.665
Winter	90/222.5 = 0.404	92/233 = 0.395

Step 3. The average seasonal index then is calculated:

Season	Average Seasonal Index
Spring	(0.899 + 0.944)/2 = 0.922
Summer	(2.022 + 1.996)/2 = 2.009
Fall	(0.674 + 0.665)/2 = 0.670
Winter	(0.404 + 0.395)/2 = 0.400

Step 4. Pat expects to build 975 pools in 2013 based on a sales force composite; he calculates the average expected quarterly demand to be 975/4 or 243.75 pools, rounded to 244 pools.

Step 5. With this information, Pat forecasts the demand for each season for 2013 (rounded to the nearest whole pool):

Season	Seasonal Forecast (Pools)
Spring	244(0.922) = 225
Summer	244(2.009) = 490
Fall	244(0.670) = 163
Winter	244(0.400) = 98
Total	976

Note: Because of rounding, the sum of the seasonal forecasts is slightly higher than the expected demand of 975 pools.

Organizations also may also experience demand trends, either up or down. For example, the demand for cloud computing solutions has experienced an upward trend.[23] Armed with this knowledge and a good forecast, supply management professionals can plan and negotiate with suppliers more effectively. The following section provides a description of two commonly used methods to forecast trends.

Forecasting a Trend

Organizations generally need several periods of data to recognize a trend. Creating a graph of past demand is helpful in providing a visual representation of any demand patterns. When a trend is observed, it is best to adopt a forecasting method that will accurately reflect that trend. Following are two commonly used methods to forecast trends.

Trend-Adjusted Exponential Smoothing Method. As described earlier in this chapter, a trend is a consistent upward or downward movement in demand over time. Exponentially smoothed forecasts are not particularly useful when trends are apparent because they always lag reality. However, an exponentially smoothed forecast can be adjusted, to a certain extent, by incorporating a trend component; this is known as *trend-adjusted exponential smoothing*. This method uses two smoothing constants, α and β. The α value smooths the initial forecast using the exponential smoothing method, while the β value smooths the trend. β, similar to α, *must* be between 0 and 1. Higher values of β (closer to 1) mean the forecaster has placed more emphasis on changes in recent trends, while a small weight (closer to 0) lessens the effect of a current trend. Forecasters generally set the values for the first-period smoothed forecast and trend based on past experience and trial and error. The more periods of demand data that are available to the forecaster, the easier it will be to estimate those values. There are three equations for this method:

1. **Smoothing the initial forecast:** $F_{t+1} = \alpha A_t + (1 - \alpha)(F_t + T_t)$

2. **Smoothing the trend:** $T_{t+1} = \beta(F_{t+1} - F_t) + (1 - \beta)T_t$

3. **Trend-adjusted forecast:** $TAF_{t+1} = F_{t+1} + T_{t+1}$

    Where:

    F_t = exponentially smoothed average in period t

    A_t = actual demand in period t

    T_t = exponentially smoothed trend in period t

    α = smoothing constant ($0 \leq \alpha \leq 1$)

    β = smoothing constant for trend ($0 \leq \beta \leq 1$).

This method, while useful, is best used with the help of forecasting software because of the extensive calculations required. The next example provides an application of trend-adjusted exponential smoothing using both manual calculations and an Excel spreadsheet.

An upscale restaurant in Calgary, Alberta, Canada has experienced an upward trend in the sales of one of its menu items, bread pudding. The restaurant's forecaster, Ben, has collected demand data from the past ten weeks to create a forecast using trend-adjusted exponential smoothing, as shown in the following chart:

Week	Demand	Week	Demand
1	51	6	56
2	54	7	58
3	53	8	60
4	55	9	60
5	57	10	62

Ben decides, based on past experience, to use the following values to calculate the forecast:

Initial forecast (week 1) = F_1 = 50
Initial trend (week 1) = T_1 = 1
Alpha (α) = 0.30
Beta (β) = 0.20

Ben could manually calculate the forecast for week 11. To create the forecast, he must first start by calculating the forecast for week 2 and then progress consecutively through each week until he reaches week 11. Using the initial forecast and trend values for week 1, Ben calculates the forecast for week 2:

1. **Smoothing the initial forecast:**
   $F_{t+1} = \alpha A_t + (1 - \alpha)(F_t + T_t)$
   = 0.3(51) + (1 − 0.30)(50 + 1) = 15.3 + 35.7 = 51

2. **Smoothing the trend:**
   $T_{t+1} = \beta(F_{t+1} - F_t) + (1 - \beta)T_t$
   = 0.20 (51 − 50) + (1 − 0.20)(1) = 1

3. **Trend-adjusted forecast:**
   $TAF_{t+1} = F_{t+1} + T_{t+1}$
   = 51 + 1 = 52

The forecast for week 3 is:

1. *Smoothing the initial forecast:*
   $F_{t+1} = \alpha A_t + (1 - \alpha)(F_t + T_t)$
   $= 0.30(54) + (1 - 0.30)(51 + 1)$
   $= 16.2 + 36.4 = 52.6$

2. *Smoothing the trend:*
   $T_{t+1} = \beta(F_{t+1} - F_t) + (1 - \beta)T_t$
   $= 0.20(52.6 - 51) + (1 - 0.20)(1)$
   $= 0.32 + 0.8 = 1.12$

3. *Trend-adjusted forecast:*
   $TAF_{t+1} = F_{t+1} + T_{t+1}$
   $= 52.6 + 1.12 = 53.72 \approx 54$

Ben continues these calculations until he reaches week 11. The forecast for week 11 is based week 10's forecast of 60.4 and week 10's trend of 1.1:

1. *Smoothing the initial forecast:*
   $F_{t+1} = \alpha A_t + (1 - \alpha)(F_t + T_t)$
   $= 0.30(62) + (1 - 0.30)(60.4 + 1.1)$
   $18.6 + 43.05 = 61.65$

2. *Smoothing the trend:*
   $T_{t+1} = \beta(F_{t+1} - F_t) + (1 - \beta)T_t$
   $0.20(61.65 - 60.4) + (1 - 0.20)(1.1)$
   $= 0.25 + 0.88 = 1.13$

3. *Trend-adjusted forecast:*
   $TAF_{t+1} = F_{t+1} + T_{t+1}$
   $= 61.65 + 1.13 = 62.78 \approx 63$

Alternatively, Ben could use forecasting software. Figure 5-5 provides a graph of the results. Notice that Ben is correct in using trend adjusted exponential smoothing because demand and the forecast closely track.

Figure 5-5: Trend-Adjusted Exponential Smoothing

Week	Actual Demand	Smoothed Forecast	Trend	Trend-Adjusted Forecast
1	51.0	50.0	1.0	51.0
2	54.0	51.0	1.0	52.0
3	53.0	52.6	1.1	53.7
4	55.0	53.5	1.1	54.6
5	57.0	54.7	1.1	55.8
6	56.0	56.2	1.2	57.3
7	58.0	56.9	1.1	58.0
8	60.0	58.0	1.1	59.1
9	60.0	59.4	1.1	60.5
10	62.0	60.4	1.1	61.5
11		61.6	1.1	62.8

Alpha 0.3
Beta 0.2

To calculate the forecast, enter the initial adjusted demand, smoothed forecast, and trend for Week 1 in cells B10, C10, and D10, respectively; in Cell E10 take the sum of Cells C10 and D10 (=c10+d10). To calculate the smoothed forecast for Week 2, enter =$B$21*B10+(1- $B$21) *(C10+D10) in Cell C11; copy and paste this formula into Cells C12 through C20. To calculate the trend, enter =$B$22*(C11-C10)+(1-$B$22)*D10 in Cell D11; copy and paste this formula into Cells D12 through D20. To calculate the trend-adjusted forecast, enter =C11+D11 in Cell E11; copy and paste this formula into Cells E12 through E20.

Plot graph using Insert, Chart, Line.

Linear Regression. When demand exhibits a clear linear trend either upward or downward, linear regression can be used with a time series of historical data. *Linear regression* has been defined as "a causal method in which one variable (the dependent variable) is related to one or more independent variables by a linear equation."[24] The dependent variable is the one that will be forecast, while the independent variable is one that is expected to have a significant effect on the dependent variable. Using linear regression, a straight line is fitted to past data based on a fitting technique known as the *least squares method*. In trend analysis, the dependent variable — demand or price — is expected to change linearly as the independent variable — time or quantity purchased — changes. Supply management professionals may use linear regression, for example, to predict price trends for specific goods or materials based on quantities purchased. The equation used to generate the forecast is:

$Y = a + bX$

Where Y = forecast for period i

X = time or quantity variable

a = intercept of Y at $X = 0$

b = slope of the line.

The coefficients a and b are calculated (notice that b must be computed first) using the least squares method as follows:

$$b = n \frac{\sum(xy) - \sum x \sum y}{n \sum x^2 - (\sum x)^2}$$

$$a = \frac{\sum y - b \sum x}{n}$$

where

x = independent variable values

y = dependent variable values

n = number of observations.

Rather than performing calculations by hand, which can be tedious and subject to error, forecasting software is an easier alternative. However, Excel spreadsheets may be used as the following example illustrates this method.

Sunshine Shades, a Chinese manufacturer of window shades for automobiles, has been experiencing an upward trend in prices for one of its raw materials. The organization's supply management professional creates a trend line using Excel or other software to predict the next month's price based on past prices.

Figure 5-6 illustrates the results in graph form and shows that use of linear regression is appropriate for Sunshine Shades because demand and the forecast track closely.

Figure 5-6: Linear Trend Line

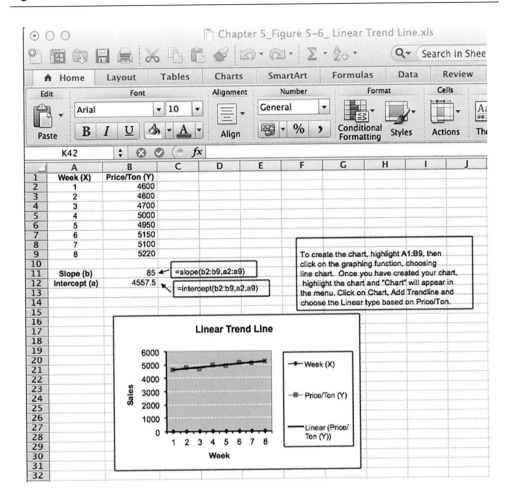

The supply management professional then calculates the forecast for weeks 9, 10 and 11, using the slope and intercept coefficients:

Forecast$_{Week\ 9}$ = $a + bX$ = US$4,557.5 + US$85(9) = US$5,322.50/ton

Forecast$_{Week\ 10}$ = $4,557.5 + $85(10) = S$5,407.50/ton

Forecast$_{Week\ 11}$ = $4,557.5 + $85(11) = $5,492.50/ton

Simultaneously Considering Trends and Seasonal Patterns

Organizations may realize not only a consistent upward or downward trend in a time series, but also seasonality for a particular item. Hospitals, for example, have always experienced seasonality in demand for emergency room care but in recent years also have noticed a significant upward trend.[25] The data presented in Figure 5-7 provides an illustration where both seasonality and an upward trend are evident. Note that demand in quarter 1 has steadily increased year after year. The same is true for quarters 2, 3 and 4. However, there also appears to be evidence of seasonality each year. The *Winter's Model*, otherwise known as *triple exponential smoothing* or *seasonal exponential smoothing*, is commonly applied in this situation. It uses the trend-adjusted exponential method discussed earlier but adds a third parameter, gamma (g), to adjust for seasonal factors. As with other more complex methods, Winter's Model should be performed using the appropriate forecasting software. Further discussion of this method is beyond the scope of this text but good forecasting textbooks are available, such as Business Forecasting by Wilson and Keating and Forecasting: Methods & Applications by Makridakis, et al.

Figure 5-7: Time Series Illustrates Both a Trend and Seasonality

	DEMAND		
Week	2010	2011	2012
Quarter 1	148	194	276
Quarter 2	94	129	158
Quarter 3	57	77	96
Quarter 4	135	188	221

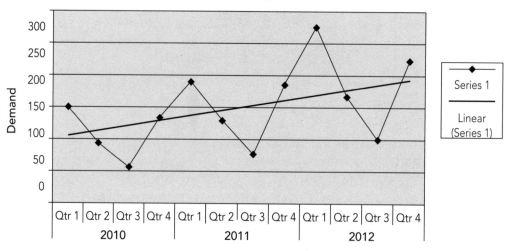

Box-Jenkins Method

The goal of the Box-Jenkins Method is to find a mathematical formula that will approximately generate the historical demand patterns in a time series. Today there are software packages with algorithms to both decide when to use Box-Jenkins models and to automatically decide on the form to be used. For example, this method has been used to estimate demand for hospital emergency room services, to predict foreign exchange rates and to forecast demand for international tourism services.[26] The advantage of the method is that it can be applied to a variety of modeling situations. However, a large amount of data is required and computer software support is required.

The Box-Jenkins Method is a heuristic, which means a few steps are repeated as necessary to develop an accurate forecast. The process involves first identifying the appropriate *ARIMA* process, which then is fitted to the time series data. ARIMA is an acronym that represents an integration of autoregressive (the use of historical data to predict the future) and moving average models. *Fitting the data* means to adjust the data so the time series is relatively flat by removing trends and seasonality through *differencing* (taking the difference between consecutive values that makes modeling easier) and *transformation* (taking the square root or log of each value that helps stabilize the variation when demand changes to a different level) methods.

Graphs of the transformed and differenced data then are used to identify the ARIMA processes that could be a good fit to the data. This analysis is used for *parameter estimation*, or finding the values of the model coefficients that will provide the best fit for the data. The assumptions of the model then are tested; if the model is not satisfactory, the forecaster must go back and review the graphs again for a more appropriate model. The fitted model then is used as a basis for the forecast.

In some instances, an organization may experience special circumstances that require a different type of modeling process. The single-period model is one method that can be used; it is discussed further in the following section.

The Single-Period Model

This model is of special importance to businesses that accumulate inventory with a relatively short selling season such as a one-time special event. Past demand data is used to determine how much stock to order based on probability analysis. The assumption is that demand is highly variable but follows a known probability distribution. The goal is to maximize profit, minimize lost sales and avoid an overstocking situation. The following example provides an illustration of the single-period model.

Jeff Jones owns a small Christmas tree lot in Woodland, California. Each year he purchases trees from a local tree farm, but he must place his order in July to have enough trees for sale to his customers. Jeff plans to sell each tree for US$45. He pays his supplier US$20 per tree, for a net profit of US$25. Any trees not sold by December 23 will be sold for US$15 (he expects that any trees remaining after December 23 will be sold for the lower price). Jeff usually sells between 50 and 90 trees each year.

He must place his order in multiples of 10. Based on past years' sales, Jeff has estimated the probability of selling the six-foot blue spruce, which is one of his more popular trees:

Demand (Blue Spruce)	Probability
50	.10
60	.15
70	.35
80	.30
90	.10

There are three possible outcomes in this scenario: (1) Jeff will sell the exact number of trees he ordered, (2) the number of trees he orders will be greater than the number of trees that will be demanded, or (3) the number of trees he orders will be less than the number of trees that will be demanded.

The following payoff table summarizes Jeff's calculations

	Payoff Table				
Probability of Occurrence	.10	.15	.35	.30	.10
Customer Demand (trees)	50	60	70	80	90

Number of Trees Ordered	Expected Profit in US$					
50	$1,250	$1,250	$1,250	$1,250	$1,250	$1,250
60	$1,200	$1,500	$1,500	$1,500	$1,500	$1,470
70	$1,150	$1,450	$1,750	$1,750	$1,750	$1,645
80	$1,100	$1,400	$1,700	$2,000	$2,000	$1,715
90	$1,050	$1,350	$1,650	$1,950	$2,250	$1,695

Jeff starts by calculating the payoff when supply equals demand:

Payoff = trees demanded (selling price − unit cost)

For example, when 60 trees are purchased and 60 trees are sold, the payoff is 60 trees × ($45 − 20) = US$1,500.

He also calculates the payoff when the number of trees ordered is greater than demand:

Payoff =
[(number of trees demanded) × (net profit) − (trees ordered − trees demanded) × (net profit)]

Thus, if Jeff orders 70 trees but only 60 are sold before December 24th, the payoff is

(60 × $25) − (10 × $5) = $1,450.

Lastly, Jeff calculates the payoff if the number of trees ordered is less than demand:

Payoff = trees ordered (selling price − unit cost)

For example, if Jeff orders 60 trees but demand that year was for 70 trees, he still can sell only 60 trees and the payoff is:

60 × $25 = $1,500

He then calculates the expected total payoff by multiplying the expected profit for each order quantity by the probability that he will sell that quantity, and then takes the sum of those values. For example, the expected profit for ordering 50 trees is:

($1,250 × 0.30) +
($1,250 × 0.10) = $1,250

The expected profit for ordering 80 trees is:

($1,100 × 0.10) + ($1,400 × 0.15) + ($1,700 × 0.35) + ($2,000 × 0.30) + ($2,000 × 0.10) = $1,715

Jeff reviews the results and decides to order 80 blue spruce trees because the expected profit is the highest.

There are also circumstances when the forecaster is able to identify relationships among demand and other variables. In these situations, causal modeling is commonly used and is described in the following section.

Causal Modeling

In *causal* or *associative models*, the dependent variable in the forecast is assumed to be related in some way to other independent variables within the environment. Utility companies, for example, typically forecast sales to commercial customers (the dependent variable) based on the weather, inflation rates, number of customers, electric/gas prices and employment levels.[27] Least squares regression models have been proven to be the best forecasting method when causal linear relationships are evident and thus are discussed further in the following section.

Least Squares Regression Models

The goal of least squares regression models is to find one or more independent variables that are good predictors of the dependent variable. If there is only one independent variable, the model is known as *simple regression*. When the forecaster finds two or more variables to be good predictors, this is known as *multiple regression*. The parameters a and b are calculated using the same formulas described in the section for trend analysis. These parameters define a straight line that minimizes the sum of the squared errors, or deviations. In the case of simple regression, the formula is $Y = a + bX$, while the multiple regression model is $Yi = a + b_1X_1 + b_2X_2 + b_3X_3 \ldots + b_zX_z$. These formulas then are used to make future predictions based on the expected value of the independent variable(s).

Four assumptions or conditions are required to use linear regression:

1. The independent and dependent variables are linearly related.
2. The errors are independent of each other or, in other words, there is no serial correlation.
3. There is constant variance of the errors, or homoscedasticity, versus the prediction.
4. The errors are normally distributed.

To further understand linear regression, consider the following example:

John and Joan have been mortgage brokers for the past five years. They arrange for home financing using funds from local investors. John and Joan have found that interest rates have an impact on the amount of business they generate each year. They collected the following data for the past five years:

Year	Average Interest Rate	Loan Value (y)
1	5.5	$1,150
2	5.75	$1,040
3	6.0	$1,000
4	6.5	$950
5	6.0	$990

The projected interest rate for year 6 is 5.75 percent.

With forecasting software or an Excel spreadsheet (illustrated below), John and Joan use regression analysis and calculate the slope and the intercept, to estimate their expected loan volume. The slope is 188,181.82 and the intercept is 2,145,681.82.

Figure 5-8: Least Squares Regression

Year	Average Interest Rate	Loan Value (y)
1	5.5	$1,150,000
2	5.75	$1,040,000
3	6.0	$1,000,000
4	6.5	$950,000
5	6.0	$990,000
Slope (a)	(188,181.82)	=slope (c2:c6, b2:b6)
Intercept (b)	2,145,681.82	=intercept (c2:c6, b2:b6)

To forecast their expected loan value for year 6, they use the linear regression equation:

Loan value = a + bx = $2,145,681.82 − $188,181.82(5.75) = $1,063,636 (rounded)
Thus, John and Joan expect to generate US$1,063,636 in loans in year 6.

Several forecast models have been described in the previous sections of this chapter. How does one know, however, which of these models will be the best predictor given a particular business environment? The given model will be useful only if the forecasting method is accurate and unbiased. The following section discusses forecast accuracy.

Forecast Accuracy

A large chemical company was experiencing a higher than expected error rate in its forecasts even though it had implemented an ERP system that included a forecasting module. Forecast accuracy was better with the module but there were still disruptions in some of its manufacturing lines because of uneven demand patterns. After a continuous improvement process project was implemented, the team determined that the statistically generated forecasts needed to be reviewed and adjusted as necessary by the sales engineer. The team found that "the biggest obstacle was the lack of understanding of the costs of forecast accuracy," so a major education and training program was implemented to help the sales engineers understand the impact to the bottom line. Six months after the new process was implemented, forecast accuracy increased from 77 percent to 94 percent and on-time performance and customer service satisfaction improved from 83 percent to 93 percent.[28]

The previous example suggests that forecast errors can be costly, and forecasters need some measures to estimate and improve forecast accuracy. Forecasters can begin by examining the amount of *forecast error*, defined as the difference between the forecast and the actual demand, for a specified period. In statistics, these errors are known as *residuals*. For any given period:

Forecast error = Actual demand − Forecast demand.

Forecast errors may be either random or biased. *Random errors* are those that cannot be explained by the forecast method. *Bias errors* occur because some type of consistent error is made in the forecast, such as selecting the wrong variables in a regression analysis, using an incorrect trend line or shifting the seasonal demand from where it actually occurs. As a result, purchasing, stocking and labor problems — as well as other issues related to forecast errors — can occur.

Examining forecast errors for a specified time period, such as for a week or a month, for example, does not provide a complete picture. Rather, the forecaster needs to examine forecast error over several past time periods and, as a further step, use this information to select the "best" forecast by comparing the forecast error between two or more forecasting models.

A second point is that while looking at errors over several time periods is good, errors tend to cancel each other out because some will be negative while others will be positive. For example, if the forecast errors using the exponential smoothing method over the past six months were +1, +6, −2, −6, +2 and −1, the running sum of the errors is 0. At face value, the forecast method appears to be a good one, but in reality, each monthly forecast was inaccurate. Thus, forecasters generally transform each error into an *absolute value* (a positive number) to better understand the magnitude of the errors. Using this same example, and transforming each error to an absolute value, the sum of the errors is now 18 (1 + 6 + 2 + 6 + 2 + 1 = 18).

Forecasters then use the absolute value of each error to create a measure that will be used to evaluate two or more forecasting methods. The *mean absolute deviation* (MAD), the *mean absolute percentage error* (MAPE) and the *mean squared error* (MSE) are three commonly used measures. The MAD is the average of the absolute values over a given number of time periods, and is calculated as follows:

$$MAD = \frac{\sum_{i=1}^{n} |A_t - F_t|}{n}$$

where

A_t = Actual demand for given time period t

F_t = Forecast for given time period t

n = number of time periods included in analysis

$|\ |$ = a symbol that indicates the absolute value.

Some forecasters calculate the standard error, which is the standard deviation of the sampling distribution of the mean. The standard error offers a simple measure of the uncertainty of a given forecast and can be used to create confidence intervals, which provide a range in which the forecaster feels confident that the forecast is accurate. The formula to calculate the standard error is:

SE = s/√n

where:

s = sample standard deviation

n = number of observations in the sample.

The MAPE is calculated by dividing the absolute forecast error by the actual demand for each time period. The advantage of this method is that the forecaster has a better idea of the true magnitude of the forecast error. For example, if the error is 20 for a given month, the magnitude is much smaller if the actual demand is 4,000 (0.005) rather than 400 (0.05). The values then are summed, averaged and multiplied by 100. The formula to calculate MAPE is illustrated below:

$$MAPE = \frac{1}{n} \sum_{i=1}^{n} \left| \frac{A_t - F_t}{A_t} \right| (100)$$

Tracking Signal

While the measure of forecast error provides a snapshot of forecast accuracy, the forecaster also needs some assurance that his or her predictions are unbiased over time. One method used to control forecast bias is through the use of a *tracking signal*, which measures how well the forecast is tracking actual upward or downward fluctuations in demand over time. The tracking signal is the running sum of the forecast errors (RSFE) divided by the MAD, calculated as:

$$\text{Tracking signal} = \frac{\sum_{i=1}^{n}(A_t - F_t)}{MAD}$$

The tracking signal is checked each time period to determine whether it falls outside some preset control limits. If the tracking signal is equal to 0, the forecast is equal to the actual demand. A tracking signal greater than 0 indicates the actual demand exceeds the forecast, while a tracking signal less than 1 indicates the actual demand is less than the forecast. A rule of thumb is to use a tracking signal of ±4 for inventory items that are carried in higher volumes (or more critical to operations) and ±8 for lower volume (or less critical) inventories. Forecasters generally plot the tracking signal on a graph to detect any drift, or gradual changes. The following example illustrates how to calculate the MAD and MAPE, and includes a calculation of the tracking signal.

Chris, a supply management professional for C&G Supplies, reviews monthly forecasted demand for copy paper. (C&G's forecaster uses the three-period moving average method.) Chris also reviews the calculated MAD, MAPE and tracking signal (see Figure 5-9 for a graph of the tracking signal).

CHAPTER 5: Forecasting Models and Methods

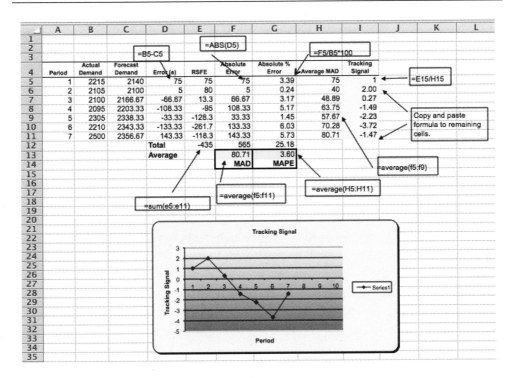

Figure 5-9: Tracking Signal

The MAD is helpful when used to compare the MAD for another forecasting method (the smaller the value of the MAD, the more accurate the forecast). However, the MAPE is useful to Chris because it is an indicator of the absolute percentage error. Based on his calculations, forecast errors are averaging 3.6 percent, which is relatively small. The tracking signal indicates that the three-period moving average was initially under-forecasting and then was over-forecasting. More data is needed for further interpretation, but at this point in time, there does not appear to be any bias present. The tracking signal also falls between ±4 MADs, which is acceptable for less critical items. Thus, Chris feels comfortable using the three-period moving average to order supplies, although he will continue to monitor the performance indicators closely.

The *mean squared error* is an average of the squared errors. Taking the square of each error prevents positive and negative errors from canceling out each other, and it amplifies the effect of large errors. Thus, this method is useful when large errors are costly or damaging to the organization, such as for an organization that makes expensive surgical replacement parts (hip sockets, pacemakers, etc.). The formula to calculate the MSE is:

$$\text{MSE} = \frac{\sum_{i=1}^{n}(A_t - F_t)^2}{n}$$

Managing Forecast Data With Suppliers

Historically, organizations have created and monitored their own forecasts, using the information to create schedules for manufacturing or service providers, estimate labor needs, and place orders with suppliers. A typical scenario might be a manufacturing organization that prepares a forecast to make 50,000 bath towels in several colors, based on past sales data. A schedule then would be sent to the production facility, materials and dyes would be purchased, and the towels would be created. However, if customer orders came in and did not match the forecast — perhaps all the orders were for a single color — then more materials and dyes would have to be purchased to meet demand for that one color, and kits with the mix of colors would either sit idle or be "robbed" for parts.

Research has shown that decisions made based on customers' orders only, rather than on actual real-time data, results in the *bullwhip effect*. The bullwhip effect occurs when small changes in customer demand increasingly become exaggerated as that demand is communicated upstream in the supply chain, from retailers to wholesalers and distributors, all the way back to the manufacturer. Thus, supply management organizations must find a manageable way to share forecast data with their suppliers to minimize inventories and related costs for both parties. From a supply management perspective, suppliers need to be able to forecast demand accurately to deliver the items ordered by their customers in the right quantities at the right times. Information sharing also helps reduce inventory costs, and is essential for those organizations operating in just-in-time or lean environments.

However, some lessons can be learned from Walmart's pioneer efforts in information sharing. First, "collaboration drives innovation, where (supply management) and suppliers all benefit from a central point of truth." Second, innovation happens when suppliers compete in a healthy manner. And third, with healthy competition and shared real-time forecast data, both supply management professionals and suppliers can reduce costs and increase supply chain efficiency.[29]

Many supply management professionals advocate sharing projections and forecasts with suppliers. Mitchell Millstein, CFPIM, president and chief quantitative office of Supply Velocity, Inc., a consulting organization based in St. Louis, Missouri, says that if an organization wants to reduce order quantities and on-hand inventory, it must give suppliers forecast information and be responsible for the parts that suppliers build based on the forecast. "Any other method is sticking suppliers with inventory which has to be paid for sooner or later," he says.[30]

Collaborative Planning, Forecasting and Replenishment (CPFR) is a term commonly used to describe the information-sharing process. CPFR is "a collaborative process between buyer and seller involving the exchange of jointly developed sales forecasts, inventory replenishment schedules and promotion plans. Both parties benefit from these co-managed processes and shared information" (ISM *Glossary* 2014). Organizations also may jointly develop production plans, forecasting models and replenishment schedules in an effort to reduce supply chain costs.

Organizations have adopted CPFR to varying degrees. A division of Baxter Healthcare, a medical products and service provider, works with the American Red Cross to obtain forecasts of blood collection products so it can increase its efficiency in inventory planning to meet its customers' needs.[31]

In another example, a leading sports accessories supplier had very little visibility into demand and therefore could not accurately predict how much product each retailer needed to have in stock. This was further complicated by the need to sell to large mass retailers as well as smaller specialty retailers. The company first implemented a software solution that included the type of forecasting needed, inventory optimization, replenishment planning, and CPFR. As a result, forecast error was reduced and supply chain visibility increased. With better visibility, other problems became evident. For example, a monthly review of the forecast revealed some buying irregularities with a key retailer that also was using CPRF. This discovery led to a collaborative relationship, and together they uncovered and resolved the problems. As a result, the supplier's sales improved, inventories were reduced, and members of the supply chain became proactive in planning and category management.[32]

A large Spanish regional retailer, a German-based international consumer goods manufacturer, and a packaging supplier partnered to fully implement CPFR. Their joint objectives were many: to improve sales growth; reduce costs through a reduction in returns, rush orders, inventory levels, production changes and lead times; improve service levels; reduce stockouts; improve relationships with trading partners; increase the reliability and stability of processes; and improve supply chain visibility. The consumer goods manufacturer initially provided its sales and order forecasts to jointly develop a shared forecast with the retailer. Using point-of-sale (POS) data, together they tackled the out-of-stock problems that were occurring by redefining the processes from the regional distribution centers to the POS. The consumer goods manufacturer then worked to develop closer relationships with its packaging suppliers for critical items — increasing visibility and efficiency — which enabled suppliers to improve their production planning process. As a result, they saw a significant improvement in forecast accuracy, particularly for promotional products. The manufacturer improved its service level and also improved on-time deliveries and deliveries-in-full.

Overcoming Difficulties

The cited benefits of collaboration include improved forecast accuracy, a decrease in inventory levels and improved service levels.[33] As stated by Timothy Oleson, Chief Supply Chain Officer for Bonneville Power Administration, "Collaboration ensures an aligned, diverse and innovative solution for many of the issues and challenges faced by supply management organizations today. If you build your problem-solving and opportunity-building processes on a foundation of collaboration, your team and internal partners can't help but be more successful in creating sustainable value."[34] However, there may be difficulties in implementing the sharing process. Both supply management and supplier must see the advantages of collaboration, and the relationship must be supported by senior management on both sides. Oftentimes the benefits will have to be proven. To be successful the two organizations also must be in alignment in their goals, and technological infrastructures must be compatible so data can be shared and visible.[35]

Maintaining confidentiality to protect any access to sensitive information from competitors is also a factor. Organizations are working to mitigate this barrier through a process of developing long-term partnerships with key suppliers, using controlled access with firewalled computer software systems and incorporating confidentiality agreements into their contracts.

Lastly, supply management professionals must consider the legal implications of sharing forecast information. Terms and conditions should be specifically included in the contract because they may affect the customer organization's responsibilities. However, they can be stated in many ways. For example, forecasting terms may state that supply chain members should meet at given intervals to share information informally. Conversely, the terms may require some type of materials management system with sharing of sophisticated forecasts.

Summary

If conducted properly, demand management and forecasting can result in better use of resources and, as a result, a more competitive organization. These processes should be used as a basis for budget development, the allocation of resources, labor decisions, technology adoption and work scheduling, among other areas. Moreover, a demand management and forecasting process is most effective when there is a collaborative effort among senior management and multiple functions within an organization, including marketing, operations, finance and supply management.

The starting point for the demand management process is forecasting. Many methods are available to improve forecasting, including both qualitative and quantitative techniques. Qualitative techniques are used when management's insight and experience are required, while quantitative techniques are valuable in their objectivity. However, the best organizations seek a balance between qualitative and quantitative techniques to develop the most accurate forecast. Forecasts are also dynamic documents that must be revised when conditions change, or when the chosen forecast methods no longer produce effective predictions. Tracking forecast errors to determine if the chosen forecast methods still are accurate and viable is important to effective forecasting.

Key Points

1. Organizations prepare forecasts to (1) estimate demand, (2) determine if supply can meet demand, (3) predict technology trends, (4) predict prices, (5) predict dependent demand, and (5) estimate supply management budget.
2. A number of factors can alter a forecaster's original predictions, including (1) lead time changes, (2) changing labor conditions, (3) material shortages, (4) technological shifts, and (5) the weather.
3. Organizations generally go through a five-step process to create a forecast, beginning with selecting what will be forecasted, picking the time horizon for the forecast and choosing the forecasting model(s) that will be used. Data then is gathered, the forecast is prepared, the forecast model is validated and the results are implemented.
4. Qualitative, or judgmental, forecasts are developed based on the opinions of others, such as managers or other experts, estimates from the sales staff, or the results of consumer surveys. A number of qualitative forecast methods are available, including sales force composite, jury of executive opinion, market research and the Delphi Method.
5. Time series models use a time series, which is a set of observations collected at regular intervals over a given time horizon. A time series may provide evidence of a flat or horizontal demand pattern, seasonality, trends or cycles.
6. Three common and relatively easy to use time series models are simple moving average, weighted moving average and exponential smoothing.
7. Seasonality can be forecast using a multiplicative model to create a seasonal index.
8. Trends can be forecast using a linear regression model or trend-adjusted exponential smoothing.
9. The Box-Jenkins Method is a heuristic, where the goal is to find a mathematical formula that will approximately generate the historical demand patterns in a time series.
10. Winter's Model simultaneously considers the effects of time-varying demand levels and seasonal factors, and is otherwise known as triple exponential smoothing or seasonal exponential smoothing because it incorporates exponential smoothing.
11. The single-period model uses probabilities to estimate demand for items with a relatively short selling season such as a one-time special event.
12. Forecasters need some measures to determine forecast accuracy and begin by examining the amount of forecast error, defined as the difference between the forecast and the actual demand, for a specified period.

13. Three methods to estimate forecast error are the mean absolute deviation (MAD), the mean absolute percentage error (MAPE) and the mean square error (MSE). Forecasters also estimate bias by using a tracking signal, which is a ratio of the running sum of forecast errors to the cumulative MAD.
14. Organizations are adopting collaboration initiatives to varying degrees. Collaborative Planning, Forecasting and Replenishment is one collaboration process by which supply chain trading partners jointly plan key supply chain activities from production and delivery of raw materials to production and delivery of final products to end customers.

CHAPTER

6

Warehouse Management and Materials Handling

In a perfect world, organizations would be able to precisely predict demand for goods and supplies, and products would be instantly replenished to meet that demand. As a result, there would be no need for storage facilities because inventories would never be held. As pointed out in Chapters 4 and 5, however, demand is subject to a number of uncontrollable factors, and even a good forecasting process will not result in perfect predictions. Even if the forecasting process was perfect, organizations still would need perfectly responsive production and absolutely reliable, instant transportation delivery.

In practice, organizations use inventory to improve their ability to coordinate supply with demand, and keep transportation and supply costs reasonable. With inventory, effective and efficient warehouses and materials handling systems are needed to facilitate the storage and movement of these materials, goods and supplies to support production and service delivery. See the Supporting Foundation element of the Strategic Supply Management Concept (see Figure S-1 in the "Series Overview" at the beginning of this book).

This chapter will focus on warehouse management and materials handling, beginning with some fundamentals including definitions and warehouse types. Next, a description of factors that must be made with respect to locating warehouses and creating a network is provided. A discussion of the need to plan the design of the actual warehouse to meet an organization's needs follows. The chapter concludes with a discussion on current trends in warehousing.

Chapter Objectives
- Define the role of warehousing in the supply management process.
- Discuss how warehouses can help meet organizational needs.
- Explore the considerations involved with locating a warehouse.
- Identify various warehouse designs and tracking systems.
- Discuss current trends in warehousing.

Warehousing Basics

Historically, warehousing has been viewed as a way to meet internal and external customer needs by holding inventory while at the same time avoiding losses that could occur through waste, obsolescence and deterioration. Today's thinking is much more focused on balancing the trade-offs between higher customer service, lower inventory levels and lower operating costs, with international sourcing adding even more complexity. Organizations also realize that value is not created unless inventory is moving toward the customer. Thus, inventory is not sitting in warehouses as long as it used to. Technology is being used to provide real-time information on the location, status and amount of inventory held within a warehouse, which helps facilitate movement. Moreover, business practices such as lean and just-in-time (JIT) production (discussed in Chapter 1) are providing impetus to improve warehousing activities to meet faster delivery times.[1]

A *warehouse* is a "facility used for receiving, storing and shipping to and from production or distribution locations" (ISM *Glossary* 2014). Goods such as those purchased for resale, raw materials, work-in-progress goods, consumable items and finished goods are all held in warehouses.[2] Materials handling equipment is used for sorting and placing inventory into the correct location within the warehouse, as well as selecting, picking and moving inventory to the loading areas for shipment.

Types of Warehouses

Warehouses are used to meet specific organizational needs, and can be broken down into the following types:

1. *Commodity warehouses* limit their services to storing and handling certain commodities, such as lumber, cotton, tobacco, grain and other products that spoil easily.
2. *Bulk storage warehouses* offer storage and handling of products in bulk, such as liquid chemicals, oil, highway salts and syrups. They also mix products and break bulk as part of their services.

3. *Temperature-controlled warehouses* control the storage environment so that both temperature and humidity are regulated. Perishables such as fruits, vegetables and frozen foods, as well as some chemicals and drugs, require this type of storage. Retailers and distributors also may have a warehouse that contains a temperature-controlled area along with areas for nonperishables.
4. *Household goods warehouses* store and handle household items and furniture as their specialty. Though furniture manufacturers may use these warehouses, the major users are household moving organizations.
5. *General merchandise warehouses* are the most common type and handle a broad range of merchandise. The merchandise stored in this type of warehouse usually does not require the special facilities or the special handling as noted previously.
6. *Miniwarehouses* are small warehouses with unit space varying from 20 to 200 square feet and often are grouped together in clusters. They are designed to provide extra space, and few services are provided. Convenient location to renters is an attraction, but security may be a problem.[3]

Distribution Center Versus Warehouse

It is important to differentiate between warehouses and distribution centers. The term *warehouse* is broader, referring to a building or structure used to store materials for security, protection and distribution. Materials, such as quarried rock or fermenting wine, may in many instances be stored for long periods of time in a warehouse. Conversely, according to the ISM *Glossary* (2014), a *distribution center* is "a warehouse for storing and shipping material, usually finished goods, often located at a distance from the manufacturing site." A distribution center's main function is specifically to provide a quick throughput of goods to support operations within a region.[4] Organizations may have warehouses that provide both short-term and long-term storage solutions, although it is more common today to physically separate them.

Another difference is that a warehouse normally holds inventory for a single organization or location such as a manufacturing site, while a distribution center typically supports many locations. For example, Walmart manages a large distribution network with its own fleet of trucks to deliver product to its more than 10,000 retail stores in 27 countries. Its distribution centers are specialized and include import, fashion, grocery and perishables, and general merchandise.[5]

Retailers in particular greatly benefit from the use of distribution centers. They allow a store location to stock a large number of products without having to incur high transportation costs. Suppliers deliver in bulk to distribution centers, where they are stored until broken down into smaller quantities and delivered to retail locations. They also may opt to incorporate *cross-docking*, a distribution system in which freight moves in and out of a distribution center or point without ever being stored there. More on cross-docking can be found later in this chapter. Trucking is the most common mode of transportation to move goods in and out of a distribution center, although rail, air or ship combined with short-haul trucking may be used for long-distance or international shipments.

Whether dealing with a warehouse or a distribution center, location is an important decision organizations must make.

Warehouse Location

For new organizations, the warehouse location decision arises as they determine the number and location of warehouses that will be needed to support production and/or distribution. Essentially, they are designing a new network of warehouses and distribution centers that will support operations. If an organization covers a wide geographic region, it may consider multiple locations for its inventory to save on the cost of transportation. On the other hand, existing organizations that are expanding operations typically face the decision of whether to expand a current facility or add another warehouse to their logistics network. This often occurs because existing facilities do not have enough capacity, or customer service is being negatively affected.

Overall, warehouses should be geographically located within an organization's supply and distribution channels so that they support the organizational strategies, maintain business continuity and minimize the total cost of receiving, storing and transporting inventory. The inventory must move from suppliers to existing or future production sites (in the case of a manufacturer), and from the organization to distribution centers, retailers and customers. This is not an easy task. If an organization has the wrong number of warehouses and distribution centers, they are in the wrong locations and/or do not serve the intended function, the supply chain will have a suboptimal cost structure and customer service will suffer. A public organization also is likely to consider issues such as service to the general public and location convenience, while a private organization will focus on market position, competition within the region and potential profitability. Regardless of organization type, once an organization determines that it does need at least one new warehouse, several factors should be weighed.

Financial Considerations

An important consideration is whether the space should be leased or owned. If existing warehouse space is available and affordable, leasing may be the best option, at least in the short term. A *lease* is a contract in which one party obtains use of another party's asset.[6] The immediate ability to have storage capability without a capital investment is an advantage. The purchase of land and buildings can be a substantial investment, particularly for a start-up organization. Many organizations, however, opt to own their own structures because of the offsetting benefits of more control and flexibility, lower costs over the long run, and tax benefits because of depreciation allowances.

The Japanese considered the costs of land when developing the practice of JIT systems, which minimized waste in the supply chain via direct shipments by suppliers. When JIT was being implemented by Toyota, Japan was a poor country that could not afford waste in its manufacturing. High land prices also were a reason for implementing JIT, for many organizations could not afford property for an elaborate warehouse system. As land prices became more affordable in Japan during the 1990s, more organizations began considering warehouse expansions as ways to reduce their transportation costs.[7] By considering various aspects of cost, the Japanese were better able to develop an effective logistics system. They were so successful, in fact, that JIT now is used throughout the world, not just in Japan.

Other major cost considerations are energy, labor and transportation. As energy costs continue to rise, increased local utility costs are an important factor. (Labor and transportation are discussed in more detail in the following paragraphs.) Organizations also need to consider the strategic role of their distribution centers(s), how the asset will look to investors, whether they can manage the distribution center(s) better than a third party can, and if this is the best use of their money.[8]

Labor Costs and Availability. Labor costs are less important today because of the increase in automation, but organizations must take into consideration worker productivity, quality, work ethic and, most important, location. Labor statistics for the areas being considered are readily available, and can indicate unemployment rates and regional wages.

Based on the laws of supply and demand, an organization can locate in a high unemployment area and usually have an ample supply of workers available even for modest pay. However, locations where there is a strong union presence, such as in many developed countries, generally means workers will likely vote for representation, resulting in higher wage and benefit costs.

Labor costs can be significant for any organization. To stay competitive, an organization must effectively manage this area. Increased labor costs within the United States, for example, have led many organizations to outsource functions that have been traditionally performed by their own workforces. Supply management professionals should be aware of such trends and their potential impacts on warehousing.

The level of staffing required is another consideration, and naturally will vary from one organization to the next. Depending on the type, size and complexity of an operation, positions such as warehouse worker, truck driver and materials manager may be necessary. With the use of various software systems for office and floor operations, support staff that is knowledgeable in technology is essential. The type and number of personnel required to effectively operate a warehouse must be a prominent part of a warehouse management system plan, for these costs will be ongoing.

Transportation Costs and Requirements. Transportation is probably the largest variable cost component in the location decision. For example, if an organization locates a warehouse outside a major metropolitan area because property is inexpensive, it must consider the costs of transporting goods back into the city if that is where the customer base resides.

Planners should begin by determining what modes of transportation will be most practical for the area and will benefit the organization the most. However, they also must consider the available transportation options. Not all transportation providers may serve a location that is under consideration. Thus, supply management professionals can provide the research needed in this area. For example, if an organization ships low-value commodities such as coal or wheat, rail or water transportation is the best option. However, this will require the organization to locate its warehouse near or even at a seaport or rail station. In North America, Kansas City is strategically located in practically the center of the United States. With excellent connections to the highways and rail service that is superior to other locations, this city serves as a distribution center hub for many organizations. Transportation challenges in developing countries require careful consideration and knowledge about the country's infrastructure, transportation providers and schedules. For example, locating a manufacturing facility in a developing country may be attractive because of lower construction and labor costs, but a lack of developed roads can make shipping finished goods a problem. More on the advantages and disadvantages of the different modes of transportation available can be found in Chapter 7.

For example, Ranger Steel, a privately owned steel plate distributor, had shipped from one distribution center at the Port of Houston to all its U.S. customers. With fuel prices spiking and new insurance requirements for truck drivers, however, shipping became very expensive. By adding distribution centers in various locations around the country, delivery times were cut to an average of 24 hours because inventory was closer to the customer. Ranger Steel actually cut its transportation costs and improved customer service.[9]

Environmental Considerations

An organization also should take environmental issues into consideration in its warehouse location decision. In the early 1990s, environmental concerns came to the forefront, as consumers demanded the organizations they bought from provide environmentally friendly products and practices. As a result, organizations across the world are making the commitment to be environmentally responsible for products throughout the supply chain, including the specification that products are environmentally friendly.[10]

Supply management should be proactive in the environmental areas of logistics, including packaging, remanufacturing, disposal and reuse. In fact, the term *green purchasing* has been coined and refers to "making environmentally conscious decisions throughout the purchasing process beginning with product and process design through product disposal" (ISM *Glossary* 2014). *Green logistics* also is used and refers to an organization's efforts to measure and minimize the environmental impact of logistics activities. Some environmental issues an organization may consider when deciding on a location include the availability of local recycling programs, and cleanup and disposal requirements for hazardous materials as well as obsolete or out-of-date inventory.

Governmental Considerations

Local, state, federal and individual country laws and regulations also will likely play a role in locating a warehouse. These often are tied to the goal of keeping the community or region environmentally safe. Zoning ordinances in the United States are also a consideration, for an organization may have to request rezoning — a potentially lengthy process. Building regulations and restrictions vary greatly in other countries. Obviously, an organization must be aware of such restrictions when looking to locate a warehouse in a certain part of the world. For example, in Germany, building and land-use regulations established by the Federal Ministry of Transport, Building and Urban Development must be adhered to.[11]

Political Considerations

To bring new industry and new jobs into their areas, some governmental entities are willing to offer tax breaks and other financial incentives. Some of these incentives may include corporate income tax credits, ad valorem tax abatements, sales or use-tax exemptions, financial help with land acquisition or site improvements, financing of the facility, and assistance with relocation and hiring.[12] Depending on the local politics, officials may be eager to attract new industry, particularly when the economy is declining. Others may not be inclined to do so, however, for they may represent constituents who do not wish to see changes in their region.

Warehouse and Materials Handling Design Factors

In conjunction with the location decision, organizations also must plan and design the warehouse or distribution center in terms of layout and equipment needs that will support their business model, increase productivity and minimize the total cost of operations.

Facility Design

The design and layout of the warehouse must be orderly so that materials flow efficiently, locations are clearly identified and space utilization is optimal. According to the Chartered Institute of Transport and Logistics in the United Kingdom, the four principal types of warehouse layouts (depicted in Figure 6-1) are shown below:

Figure 6-1: Warehouse Designs

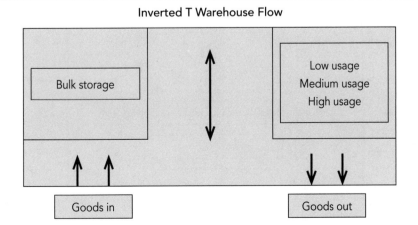

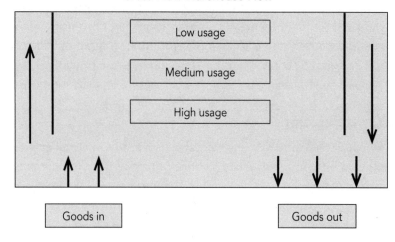

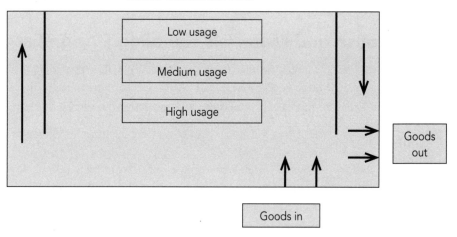

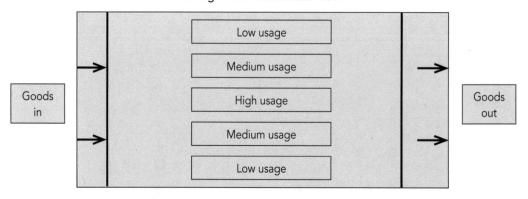

1. *Inverted T warehouse flow.* Goods going in and out are located on the same side of the warehouse, with designated areas for bulk storage. Low-use items are placed furthest away from the exit and high-use items nearest. This saves time and minimizes distances traveled for fast-moving stocks.
2. *Cross-flow warehouse.* This is a one-way system with incoming goods flowing to the left of the entry and into one of three storage areas, depending on usage. This design retains the main advantages of the T system, but removes central aisle congestion.
3. *Corner warehouse flow.* This design has the incoming and outgoing goods at adjacent sides of the same corner of the warehouse. This layout reduces congestion during times of high throughput activity.
4. *Through-flow warehouse.* This warehouse design has the advantage of being a flow system with entry and exit points on opposite sides. It achieves good, wide aisle space, but there are some disadvantages: (1) all materials have to travel the full length of the building between receipt and issuance; (2) materials coming in and going out on different sides of the building increase security risks and surveillance; and (3) if the warehouse is to be expanded it can only happen on two sides unless the bays are moved.[13]

If an organization already owns a facility and wants to increase capacity, it may choose to expand a facility vertically — otherwise known as *build up*, or horizontally — referred to as *build out*. The height of the building will dictate how high shelving can be assembled, which is a key consideration in warehouse design. The higher the shelf racking, the better the space utilization; therefore, in addition to square footage or square meters, it is important to consider cubic footage or cubic meters. Vertical capacity requirements relate directly to the type of equipment that will be needed (discussed below).

Today warehouse and distribution center designs can be created and customized with software to address the organization's needs. Some of these issues are discussed in the following sections.

Space Requirements

As mentioned throughout this chapter, when designing the facility, the amount of warehousing and storage space must be determined based on the needs of the organization. For example, overestimating the amount of space needed can result in unnecessary costs in the way of unused space, energy and maintenance. Building services costs represent a significant portion of annual building costs. On the other hand, underestimating space may result in an overcrowded and inefficient warehouse operation. The objectives should be to efficiently use space with the building's cubic footage and achieve balanced traffic flows. If stock movements can be minimized, both in number and distance, then an organization can avoid double handling (a costly practice).

Specifically, the space required for each type of stock needs to be determined, along with the characteristics of the space. Size, shape, weight and the perishable nature of stocks will factor in as well. Lastly, space must be designed to accommodate material handling equipment and personnel requirements. Figure 6-2 lists some reasons why warehouse space requirements may vary.[14]

Figure 6-2: Reasons for Fluctuations in Warehouse Space Required

LESS SPACE REQUIRED	MORE SPACE REQUIRED
Decreased production	Growth of market or market share
Decrease in number of SKUs	Shorter product life cycles
Less volatile demand	Increase in number of SKUs
Longer product life cycles	Direct store delivery to customer
Customer takes control of deliveries	Elimination of distributors
Smaller manufacturing quantities	Expansion into specialized markets
Higher inventory turns	Imported and exported items
Smaller purchase quantities (JIT)	Longer production increases
Quick response suppliers	Increases in manufacturing quantities
Cross-docking	Customer wants fast response times
Carriers perform consolidation	Forward-buying

Source: Adapted from T. Hines, *Supply Chain Strategies* (London: Elsevier Butterworth-Heinemann, 2004).

Fluctuations in Warehouse Space Required

Two types of storage systems typically are used — fixed and random. A *fixed location* system is one that stores the inventory item in a set physical location. For example, if a certain electrical transformer is stored on aisle 12, shelf A, it can always be found there. This method of storage usually has lower space utilization and higher accuracy. Conversely, *random location* systems store inventory in any available space. As a rule, the use of random locations results in a higher utilization of space, but lower accuracy. In either system, the warehouse location of material should be identified in the inventory records. And, ultimately, organizations must ensure that the needed materials get to the customer. Therefore, they must be aware of how materials can be stored and how they can be accessed quickly. This requires determining specific needs for materials handling equipment.

Materials Handling Equipment Requirements

Warehousing has its own "tools of the trade," which include various types of equipment to lift and transport materials. Equipment requirements will depend on the type of materials that will be moved. For example, materials such as steel and piping require overhead single and double girder cranes. In the petroleum and chemical industry, drum lifts are commonly used along with forklifts and dollies. A warehouse operation will not typically use any one piece of equipment exclusively, but rather combine a set of manual and automated tools that best fit its operational needs.

A variety of equipment options are available for warehouse operations. These include manual equipment, power-assisted equipment, and fully automated and mechanized systems and robotics. Manual equipment is flexible, can be used to move a variety of materials, and represents a fairly modest investment. It makes sense to use manual equipment when the warehouse holds a variety of different goods. There are some limitations to this equipment, however, including the limited capabilities of the operator with regard to load size and speed. Two examples of manual equipment are two-wheeled and four-wheeled hand trucks and pallet jacks. Pallet jacks, used to manually transport palletized materials, also may be needed, as well as scissor lifts and rolling ladders.

The output of the warehouse can be increased by using power-assisted equipment. Power-assisted equipment increases the lifting capacity for an operator and allows loads to be stacked. The most common types are forklifts and high lifts. Forklifts are considered standard equipment and can accommodate just about any type of palletized load. While this equipment costs more than manual lifts do, the investment still is quite reasonable and therefore popular. Multi-story warehouses with multi-tiered racking systems will require pneumatic lifts to safely retrieve high-placed items.

Some warehouse and distribution systems have improved product movement through the use of robotics. For example, Johnson Controls, a producer of batteries for automobiles and hybrid electric vehicles, wanted to improve the battery handling process at its Middletown, Delaware facility. The company implemented a robotic palletizing system, which eliminated manual handling and exceeded its throughput requirements.[15] Other warehouses are fully automated, using *automated storage and retrieval systems* (AS/RS). With the availability of computer-controlled equipment, bar coding and scanning technology, organizations can operate these systems with minimal staffing. Product orders can be filled by using automated picking systems that retrieve products off the warehouse shelf and place them on a conveyer system to transport them to a loading dock, and then on to the customers. These systems are justified when an operation has a substantial and constant flow of goods into and out of the warehouse. Operating costs are lower with automated systems, but the initial investment is high. Failure of automation is always a risk, so ongoing system maintenance is important. Suncup Juice, maker of frozen juice products, uses an AS/RS in its deep freeze warehouses. According to Ned Gregory, president of the company, "By bringing the frozen product to the worker, it significantly reduces travel time by workers, wrong picks and product and facility damage, which are prevalent in contemporary deep-freeze warehouses using forklifts."[16]

Order Picking System. Orders also must be picked; this may be performed manually or through an automated process. *Manual order picking* involves warehouse personnel physically retrieving an item from the shelf and bringing it to a staging, distribution or will-call area. Some materials do not require picking equipment, while others will require a forklift or pallet jack. Smaller warehouses with lower volume may be best suited to continue using manual systems and traditional materials handling equipment.

Larger warehouses typically use *mechanized systems* that are automated order fulfillment systems that use advanced design storage and distribution structures. A *pick module* is a type of mechanized system used in many busy distribution centers. It is designed to pick both bulk items (such as cases of goods) and single items (referred to as "eaches"). The system is constructed of various racking components such as uprights and beams, and includes decking, controls, lighting and conveyor belts. A fully mechanized picking system may be the best choice for a high-volume distribution center. It can create efficiencies as well as improve order throughput time and customer service.

A leading picking technology in the warehouse industry is *voice recognition* devices. An August 2013 survey entitled "The Motorola Solutions Future of Warehousing" polled warehouse IT and operations professionals in the manufacturing, retail, wholesale and third-party logistics (3PL) markets on the state of warehousing today and their vision for warehousing and distribution in the future. One of the findings from the survey indicated that "as the industry moves to reduce order fulfillment costs and increase worker efficiency and productivity, the picking and replenishment solutions of the next five years (by 2018) will shift more toward true multimodal operation, with a 142 percent increase in the integration of voice-directed and screen-directed picking on flexible mobile devices along with a 113 percent increase for voice-, scan- and keyed-response workflows."[17]

For example, U.S. Foods, Inc., a wholesale distributor with Chili's, Damon's and Pizzeria Uno among its customers, has adopted voice recognition devices. Because of a problem with mispicks in its distribution centers, it incorporated voice recognition technology within its existing warehouse management system. This resulted in a 75 percent reduction in mispicks and incorrect orders.[18]

In summary, the right level of automation to use in the warehouse takes careful consideration. An organization should consider whether to continue to use the traditional manual system of order picking — which is quite labor-intensive, or look at an automated system that usually requires a sizable initial investment but reduces labor costs and improves accuracy — or a combination of both. The same Motorola Solutions survey found "warehouse professionals expect a significant shift away from pen and paper-based processes (71 percent decrease) to handheld mobile computers and tablets (100 percent increase) for cycle counting and inventory validation by 2018."[19]

Docks. Part of the warehouse design includes the dock configuration. The dock needs to be accessible for both internal and external users, and also have the capacity to meet the traffic needs of each. A *single dock* may be appropriate for a smaller facility with low to moderate shipping activity, while a *two-dock* system can handle a higher-use operation where shipping and receiving are going on simultaneously.

Cross-docking is a distribution system popularized by Walmart. Cross-docking is "a distribution technique used to minimize or eliminate warehousing by unloading incoming materials and loading the materials in outbound trailers or rail cars, without storing the items in a warehouse. Cross-docking is used to change the type of conveyance, to sort material intended for different destinations or to combine material from different origins while minimizing or eliminating warehousing" (ISM *Glossary* 2014). For example, a global consumer products organization such as Procter & Gamble Co. will deliver finished goods from its manufacturing plants to Walmart's distribution centers, where they are unloaded and placed into a number of waiting Walmart trailers and immediately redistributed to retail locations. This eliminates unnecessary storage and handling, and reduces costs.[20]

Security Needs. Another consideration in designing a warehouse is security. Efforts must be taken by an organization to secure its investment in parts, supplies and equipment through appropriate means. The goal is to adequately protect an organization's fiscal, physical and human resources from theft or harm. All inventories represent a significant investment that must be kept safe and secure.

Proper equipment must be in place to protect the inventory from theft and fire. Fire codes or other regulations usually dictate alarm and extinguishing equipment that is appropriate for an industrial warehouse. Security systems with television monitors and badge entry also can be good investments in ensuring warehouse security. For specialized inventory, additional considerations are necessary. Chemical storage, for instance, requires a proper environment and often its own storage room. Perishable items, such as food, may need refrigerated storage to adequately protect it. Businesses such as convenience stores, grocery retailers and pizza chains rely heavily on refrigerated storage. Of the top 25 public refrigerated warehouses within North America, four organizations (AmeriCold Logistics, Lineage Logistics, Millard Refrigerated Services, and Preferred Freezer Services) account for approximately 62 percent of the cubic feet available.[21]

Physical Tracking Systems. Numerous tracking systems are available for today's warehouse manager. The use of *bar coding*, an inventory control system that employs machine-readable bar codes to identify an organization's inventory, is common today. The bar codes are attached to or imprinted on each box or item, and are a pattern of parallel bars and spaces that actually represent specific characters and numbers. The device used for reading the bar code and sending that information to the software system is called a *bar code scanner*. The Motorola Solutions survey indicated while "only 67 percent of items received at a warehouse are bar coded today, survey respondents expected supplier management initiatives and trading partner compliance requirements to drive higher utilization in the coming years — reaching an estimated 84 percent by 2018."[22]

Bar codes can be used in countless applications because they interface with software, possess decoding logic, and can be easily printed. Bar coding allows for the easy identification of an organization's inventory and interfaces with computerized records. It is highly accurate and can help the warehouse operate more efficiently. Besides assisting with material inventories, bar coding also is useful for keeping track of equipment, furniture and other assets. The use of bar codes in the retail grocery industry has been common for many years. It reduces data entry errors, which improve processing speed and inventory accuracy. One common application is using a bar code as an *intelligent shipping label*. Within a very small face, information can be stored and accessed, including purchase information, carrier code and freight sort code. Figure 6-3 provides an example of an intelligent mail label.

Figure 6-3: Intelligent Mail Shipping Label

Source: Art Avery and Associates. Reprinted with permission, available from www.elogistics101.com/Article/Barcode% 20Secrets.htm.

Radio frequency identification (RFID), which involves a radio chip attached to an inventory product that allows it to be tracked, has had a variety of uses within the supply chain, such as identifying tractors and trailers at a distribution facility and communicating with mobile personnel (drivers). The purpose of an RFID system is to allow data to be transmitted via a mobile device (a tag) that is read and processed according to the needs of the application. Used in the 1930s to identify friendly and unfriendly aircrafts, RFID continues to prove its value. While the total market was worth about US$7.9 billion in 2013, according to a 2013 report, "Full deployment by retailers and other industries is expected to drive the RFID market to a US$30 billion industry by 2024."[23]

The DOD also uses a *unique identification devices* (UID) system to distinguish one asset from another; UIDs can be used with RFID bar codes. All DOD suppliers must affix

UID labels on items with an acquisition cost of at least US$5,000, classified or sensitive items, items that are serially managed, or property that is furnished to third parties such as contractors.[24]

Safety Considerations. Warehouses and distribution centers must maintain a safe work environment. With the increased use of automated equipment (rollers, conveyors, and so on), if proper precautions are not taken, a hazardous environment can result. Clear policies and procedures must be developed to ensure worker safety, including machinery guards, eye protection, chemical storage and protection from falls. Government regulations will guide a supply management professional on minimally accepted procedures, but those should be considered a starting point to develop a specific safety program for an organization's own warehouse. Accident and hazard reporting, equipment operations training and scheduled safety meetings are all part of such a program. A safe and accident-free workplace is obviously a plus for workers, but it also can pay off for the organization as well; claims caused by on-the-job injuries are reduced, workers' compensation insurance rates are lower with a sound safety record, and an organization increases its goodwill and reputation.

Security Issues. Ever since the events of September 11, 2001, both public and private organizations are aware of the threats surrounding terrorism and are employing additional security measures at their storage facilities.[25] Prior to that time, supply management professionals may not have perceived much risk, at least in certain regions — but the world is now a different place. An example of materials that should warrant increased attention during transportation and storage include fertilizer, ammunition and water chemicals.

The *Customs-Trade Partnership Against Terrorism* (C-TPAT) program is a "joint U.S. government-business initiative to build cooperative relationships that strengthen overall supply chain and border security. Through the initiative, businesses ensure the integrity of their security practices and communicate their security guidelines to their business partners (importers, carriers, brokers, warehouse operators, manufacturers and so on) within the supply chain" (ISM *Glossary* 2014). As of July 2013 the voluntary program had nearly 10,572 certified partners and 7 mutual recognition agreements with New Zealand, Canada, Jordan, Japan, Korea, the European Union and Taiwan.[26] Among its many security initiatives is the practice of inspecting empty trailers, including measuring interiors and exteriors to ensure they are not carrying any hidden items that could disrupt the supply chain. It is certainly a good practice for organizations to embrace the C-TPAT certification program; it is widely recognized as one of the most effective means of providing the highest level of cargo security.[27]

Throughout the world, government agencies are working with industry to ensure safe working environments, including warehousing and distribution. Within the United States, for example, the Occupational Safety and Health Administration (OSHA) oversees workplace safety, while in China, the State Administration of Work Safety (SAWS) handles this.

Software Support. A *warehouse management system* (WMS) is a computer software program designed specifically for managing the movement and storage of materials throughout the warehouse (ISM *Glossary* 2014). These systems are readily available today and are used by large and small organizations alike. Off-the-shelf packages can be highly effective, but many organizations choose to make modifications and customizations to better fit their needs. The adoption of this technology is required to keep pace in today's global markets, as a WMS can provide new levels of efficiency and throughput. Although the term warehouse still is commonly used, some industry leaders feel the model should be more of a "high-velocity distribution center," with the dominant principle being that products in motion add value.[28] Warehouse management systems can operate on a Microsoft or other platform and include products such as those from SAP and Oracle, whose enterprise systems contain a materials management module, as well as more specialized packages like a WMS offered by AFS Technologies. AFS's WMS is modular and fully integratable, can serve single or multiple sites, and is available with a dedicated server or cloud technology.[29]

Organizations in all industries have benefited from the use of a WMS. Core capabilities of these systems (see Figure 6-4) include delivery management, inspection, labor management, picking and shipping. Many also include enhanced functionality such as labor management, parcel shipping and yard management. ITS Logistics, a 3PL specializing in the outdoor sports market, implemented a new WMS to better meet its needs. The old system involved too many steps and couldn't manage the layout of two of its facilities. The new system, in contrast, can serve the needs of multiple clients with diverse needs. ITS Logistics uses a basic WMS platform with added modules to handle reports and alerts; the system provides a 3-D view of each warehouse and a self-service portal so that customers can remotely see their inventories. The WMS helps ITS better meet its customers' assembly, labeling and packing requirements, and provides better knowledge of what product is in the warehouse at any given time. The pick, pack and shipping process has also become more streamlined with the use of RFID technology. As a result, shipping accuracy has improved to 99.95 percent and inventory data accuracy is at 99 percent.[30]

Figure 6-4: Warehouse Management System (WMS) Core Applications

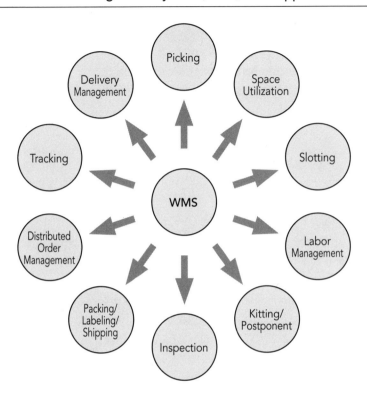

In summary, the design and layout of a warehouse facility is critical if the facility is to have effective, efficient flows of inventory. Spending adequate time and resources on planning a warehouse, based on an organization's projected needs, is certain to pay dividends. Once location and design planning are complete, it is time for implementation.

Implementation

The final step of any planning process is the implementation of the project. Doing so requires that the business continue to operate effectively during the transition. Test runs or pilot testing of the new warehouse often are performed to ensure there are no disruptions in supply. Experienced workers from existing warehouses also may be brought in to ensure continuity.

Similar to any project, the following questions should be considered to successfully add and construct a new warehouse or a set of warehouses:
- Who will be responsible for implementation?
- What are the goals of the implementation, and how are specific actions aligned with goals?

- What is the time line for meeting the implementation goals?
- Who is responsible for achieving milestones on the time lines?
- How will business continuity be assured during implementation?
- How will effectiveness be monitored and evaluated?
- What training and development strategies will be used?
- How will rapid changes in technology be dealt with?
- How will funding be provided over the life of the plan?

As with any project, there are some basic rules to successfully implement and achieve long-range objectives. These can be easily applied to any industry, including materials management and warehouse planning.

1. *Successful efforts involve stakeholders and gain their support.* Planning requires consideration of values and priorities, and should reflect the views of all those involved in the process. Inclusion of stakeholders takes time, but is essential to the success of the effort.
2. *Prioritizing goals is an essential step.* Plans should reflect the priorities of an organization. The most useful plans are succinct and easily translate into effective measures.
3. *Commitment from the top.* The leaders of an organization must commit to the planning effort up front. There also must be a commitment to implement strategies recommended by the committee.
4. *Broad representation.* The planning committee should have representatives from several, if not all, areas of the organization. This ensures the needs of all areas are addressed and will help foster buy-in.
5. *Communication.* All parts of the organization must be made aware of the goals and strategies developed. A committee may have made the recommendations, but it is up to every program area to implement change and also be accountable.

Warehouse Trends

With the advent of mobile technology, life has become more complicated for supply chains of brick-and-mortar stores. Smartphone apps allow the consumer to quickly scan an item's bar codes at a local store and search for that item for less. A few more clicks, and the item is on its way to the consumer's home by the next day. As a result, e-commerce is increasing a larger segment of shipping volume, and the concept of multi-channel or omni-channel order fulfillment has emerged. Today warehouses and distribution centers are more flexible, handling "direct-to-consumer order fulfillment, store replenishment, wholesale distribution, and global distribution" from one facility.[31]

According to a 2012 survey of warehousing trends, "The role of technology in warehouses has shifted from purely reducing costs and has increasingly expanded into adjacent benefits that can drive differentiation and profitable growth for their businesses." Management increasingly is viewing the warehouse function as an asset with the potential to increase profitability. As a result, more organizations are implementing WMSs that contain all the available features. Organizations are also equipping workers with handheld computers or tablets. With these changes people will be equipped with more technology solutions such as voice- or screen-directed picking using mobile devices.[32]

Because operating a warehouse can be a costly venture, however, an organization should consider all aspects of warehouse management before making a decision that best fits its needs. Many organizations are seeing the value of *outsourcing* the warehouse function, which continues to be a viable option within supply management as e-tailing takes off. Many professional organizations specialize in managing inventories for a variety of clients. Often this decision comes down to *value analysis*, which is a systematic evaluation of the value of a good or service. This provides insight into the inherent worth of the service (in this case, warehousing) with the objective being to maintain functional suitability while reducing cost. This type of approach to business decision-making is all part of strategic outsourcing, a foundation of supply management.

Some good questions to ask when making the outsourcing decision include those listed below:

1. Is the function strategic to the organization?
2. Does the process provide the organization with a competitive edge?
3. Is a performance upgrade needed in the area to separate it from the competition?

When the answer to any of the questions is "No," an organization should then consider outsourcing the process.

Virtual warehouses are also more commonplace, and provide a level of connectedness that allows an organization to maintain a high level of confidence in its distribution system.[33] Actual buildings and real inventory still exist, as at least some inventory is stored and managed by an organization's suppliers. Through the use of the Internet, multiple computer systems are communicating and sharing product information in real time with the supplier network. Orders then are shipped directly from the supplier to the customer, ideally in a seamless and timely manner. The Internet can provide the ideal vehicle for establishing a virtual supply chain.[34]

For example, ByBox, a parts storage and distribution company, uses an electronic locker service to move parts between engineers at Minolta Konica. Previously, parts needed by an engineer would be sent to a central location for collection. Now, using the ByBox2Box system, an engineer can address a ByBox2Box label to the recipient engineer, place the item in a secure locker, and it will be picked up and delivered directly.[35] Robert's Sysco Foods, Inc., a US$45 million distributor headquartered in Springfield, Illinois, expanded its product line of 5,500 items through virtual warehousing. Sales representatives determine each customer's needs; if a product is not carried in their own warehouse, they link directly to their partner's (Dot Foods, Inc.) virtual warehouse program. Dot Foods, a large redistributor with more than 20,000 products, has distribution centers located across the United States. This partnership has eliminated the need for expanding Robert's Foods' existing warehouse while significantly increasing its offerings. Orders from Dot are packed and shipped to Robert's Foods' distribution center, which then are cross-docked and delivered to the customers the following day. As a result, sales have increased more than 16 percent, Robert's has been able to reduce its inventory of slow-moving and special items previously carried in its warehouse, and the organization has improved its competitive position.[36]

Sustainability has come to the forefront as organizations work to reduce waste. A 2011 survey found that almost half of the respondents had sustainability initiatives in place. Some changes are as simple as installing fans to circulate temperature-controlled air, changing out lighting fixtures to energy-conserving fluorescent lights, and replacing or repairing dock doors so they are tightly sealed. Another initiative is running or charging equipment during off-peak hours. Some organizations have invested in rooftop solar displays.[37] Staples was facing the problem of excessive packaging. The company used five standard box sizes for shipments which, many times, resulted in over-packaging and higher shipping costs. Staples purchased "smart-size packaging," an on-demand packaging technology from the Swedish firm, Packsize International. The technology is integrated with Staples' warehouse management system (WMS) to produce the correct size box.[38]

Summary

Many considerations go into creating a network of warehouses. Supply management professionals must be aware of the strategic objectives of their organizations, as well as the choices to be made with warehousing facilities. Cost is always an issue, both the initial investment and ongoing costs such as labor and equipment maintenance. It should not be surprising that technology plays a key role in warehousing and logistics. Understanding these technologies and trends and knowing when to incorporate them into an organization will remain a challenge for organizations.

Key Points

1. Warehouses are facilities used for receiving, storing and distributing materials in support of organizational strategies. They house goods purchased for resale, raw materials, consumable items and finished goods.
2. The basic types of warehouses can be classified as commodity, bulk storage, temperature-controlled, household goods, general merchandise and mini-warehouses.
3. A distribution center provides for a quick throughput of goods to support operations within a region.
4. Materials handling equipment is used for sorting and placing inventory into the correct locations within the warehouse and for selecting, picking and moving inventory to the loading areas for shipment.

5. When designing a warehouse network, there are trade-offs to consider between higher customer service, lower inventory levels and lower operating costs.
6. When adding warehouse capacity, the organization must determine where to locate a new warehouse.
7. The factors that determine the location of a new warehouse include whether to lease or buy transportation costs, labor costs, supply, environmental issues, governmental restrictions and political incentives.
8. The four principle types of warehouse layouts are inverted T, cross-flow, corner and through-flow.
9. Physical tracking technology, which is common today, includes bar coding, intelligent shipping labels, RFID and UID.

CHAPTER

7

Logistics Management and International Transportation

The supply management professional must be aware of the flow and storage of materials throughout the acquisition process, otherwise known as logistics. *Logistics* is part of one of the supporting structures of the Strategic Supply Management Concept. (See Series Overview, Figure S-1.) It "is the process of planning, implementing and controlling the efficient, cost-effective flow and storage of raw materials, in-process inventory, finished goods and related information from point of origin to point of consumption for the purpose of conforming to customer requirements" (ISM *Glossary* 2014). Typical logistics activities include inbound and outbound transportation, warehousing, fleet management, materials handling, order fulfillment, demand planning and management of third-party logistics providers. Other activities that take place after a product is finished and approved for shipment are logistics, including selecting distribution outlets, responding to product orders, managing the transportation between downstream parties and overseeing the return of goods. Logistics is one of the key components of supply management, as well as a contributor to the economy.

Logistics management, in its broadest form, includes the "management of all activities that take place after a product is finished and approved for shipping, including finished goods inventory, selection of distribution outlets, response to product orders and all transportation between downstream parties, including returned goods" (ISM *Glossary* 2014). In a 2011 study of 249 manufacturing and service firms, close to 55 percent of the respondents stated that logistics was a substantial or extensive part of supply management's responsibilities.[1] Supply management professionals work on a variety of logistics activities, including managing the activities associated with selecting inbound and outbound transportation, and third-party (3PL) or fourth-party (4PL) logistics providers; estimating logistics costs; inventory classification, managing information systems between suppliers, carriers and supply management; and *reverse logistics* (RL). Supply management professionals are increasingly concerned with reverse logistics activities, "which include product returns, packaging reuse, minimization of waste and repairs that flow back into an outbound supply chain. The objectives of RL are cost reduction, environmental benefits and source reductions" (ISM *Glossary* 2014). Logistics activities also must be effectively integrated with other key business functions of the organization — marketing, sales, manufacturing, finance, information technology, and possibly others — to enhance organizational performance.

For a manufacturer, both inbound and outbound logistics are of concern; not only are raw materials coming into the production facility, but finished goods can simultaneously be going out the other door. Service sectors, including health care, education and hospitality services, also have important needs in the area of logistics because they have inventory that supports their operations. Regardless of the organization involved, one organization's outbound logistics is another's inbound.

Many facets of logistics management will be addressed in this chapter: the various modes of transportation, the role of shipping organizations and freight forwarders, along with traffic patterns, will be discussed, as will international transportation and international commercial terms (Incoterms® Rules). Whether working in logistics domestically or internationally, the technology impacts are significant. Supply management professionals must be aware of the technology tools available to them, and the associated costs and risks. Thorough policies and procedures are important parts of logistics, and transportation restrictions and carrier performance auditing are certainly a part of such policies. Freight claims and damaged shipments also fall in the area of logistics, and supply management professionals must be prepared to resolve these situations. Finally, performance measures and cost savings initiatives will be discussed.

Chapter Objectives
- Discuss the various functions involved in logistics management.
- Identify the basic modes of transportation along with their respective advantages and disadvantages.
- Explore the issues involved with global transportation including the use of international commercial terms.

- Discuss the options available for supply management professionals to resolve delivery problems.
- Identify ways to measure performance within logistics management.

History of Logistics

The term *logistics* originated from the Greek word *logistikos* and was used by the Roman armies who identified the military administrative officials as *Logists*.[2] According to S. Tzu and G. Gagliardi, the importance of logistics was noted as far back as 500 B.C. in a book about war strategies.[3] The field of logistics has evolved globally over the years. In the 1970s and beyond, organizations focused on managing logistics costs to stay competitive. Today, logistics is considered an essential operational activity for cost reduction and improved customer service.[4]

Supply chain management (SCM) evolved in the 1980s and 1990s. This concept included the management of all activities in the supply chain from manufacturer to final customer. With the development of SCM also came a realization that all activities must add value to the organization, including logistics.[5] The nature of the supply management profession can be further described as the identification, acquisition, access, positioning and management of resources and related capabilities the organization needs or potentially needs in the attainment of its strategic objectives.[6] The components of supply management include disposition/investment recovery, distribution, inventory control, logistics, materials management, operations, packaging, procurement/purchasing, product/service development, quality, receiving, strategic sourcing transportation/traffic/shipping, and warehousing/stores.

Supply management plays a vital role within an organization, and often lends its expertise in areas such as logistics. All supply management professionals must have a good working relationship with their colleagues who work in the logistics segment of their function, and must understand the limitations and trade-offs present in logistical decision-making.

Transportation Modes and Roles

Modes of Transportation

The five basic modes (or types) of transportation are motor carriage, rail, air, water and pipeline. Each of these modes is unique and comes with its own set of advantages and disadvantages. *Motor carriage* is the primary mode of transportation in the United States, with annual operating revenues of more than US$266 billion.[7] Also known as trucking or highway transportation, this industry consists of both small and large carriers, resulting in a very competitive market. Advantages of motor carriage include a high availability of carriers, prompt transit times and generally reliable service. A disadvantage of using this mode is the geographic limitations of driving on the roadways. For instance, the use of trucking is not feasible for an organization shipping its products from Hawaii to the mainland.

Another important mode is movement by *rail*, which transports materials such as stone, clay and grain. According to the Association of American Railroads (AAR), rail accounts for about 40 percent of intercity freight volume.[8] During 2012, the railroad industry shipped 1.713 trillion ton-miles of freight in the United States.[9] Rail transportation is considered dependable because the railways are less subject to weather delays, unlike other modes. However, there is a greater chance of damage. Container shipping, also referred to as COFC (container on freight car), is a form of multimodal transportation and is used by shippers because there is less damage, goods can easily be transferred from ships at port and less labor is involved. Another prime disadvantage to rail transport is the need for another mode to complete the movement, which is usually trucking.

Movement by *water* is the oldest form of transportation, but still plays a key role in today's global marketplace. This mode includes oceangoing ships as well as barges used on inland waterways. When organizations use ocean shipping, they have the option of using liner service with published rates and schedules or chartering a ship on a contract basis. Some organizations, such as ExxonMobil, own their own vessels. United States water transportation providers alone ship approximately 2.0 billion metric tons of products each year, both domestic and foreign.[10] Shipping by water often is used in strategic areas, such as China, to move low-value bulk materials and heavy items. Water transportation promotes international trade and is essential to industries such as automotive, electronics and heavy equipment, to name just a few. However, it often takes much longer (weeks versus days by truck or hours by air) to ship products by this mode (a noted disadvantage). An important maritime law supply management professionals should be aware of is known as the General Average. In brief, should any cargo be thrown overboard or any expenses incurred because of an emergency situation while en route, all losses will be split proportionally between the parties that hold a financial interest in the voyage. This principle is often referred to as the York-Antwerp Rules, which provide the details for applying the General Average.[11]

Billions of dollars are spent each year on another mode — domestic and international *air transportation* — making it a major component of an organization's logistics program. For example, in 2012, international cargo carried by U.S. air carriers totaled more than 17 billion ton-miles. Since 2004, however, demand for world air cargo has steadily decreased, with back-to-back declines in 2011 and 2012. The decline has been due to the Great Recession of 2007-2008 and rising fuel prices.[12]

Transport by air includes all material shipments made by air cargo carriers devoted to freight only, and passenger airlines that carry freight in the belly of the airplane. While the cost of an air shipment is much higher than shipment by truck, a major advantage is that delivery times can be significantly reduced over long distances, and the need for trucking is minimal. An overnight cross-country shipment of a component that keeps operations running is well worth the increase in freight costs. Saks Fifth Avenue, for example, contracts some of its merchandise for overnight air delivery to improve customer service.[13] Using air freight can help organizations reduce their inventories and related carrying costs.

Pipelines, which have been around since the mid-1800s, are considered the hidden giant of American transportation.[14] This transportation mode is used extensively in the petroleum industry, but also is used to move materials such as coal slurry and natural gas. Pipelines are available throughout the world, and in 2013 close to 117,000 miles of pipelines were in the planning or construction phases.[15] In the United States, the Federal Energy Regulatory Commission (FERC) regulates the pipeline industry, which includes more than 100 regulated pipelines within the U.S. alone. With close to 150,000 miles of pipeline, operating revenues in 2014 were US$9.987 billion.[16] With its resistance to inclement weather, this mode boasts tremendous dependability. One disadvantage to pipelines is the high initial investment to construct the line, and the cost of related equipment.

More often than not, shipments will travel by two or more modes. For example, goods might be shipped via container to the United States on an ocean liner, then later be transferred to a railcar for transport to a train depot, with the final movement made by truck. This is known as a *multimodal shipment*. As a result, supply management professionals often rely on their supplier or a third party to coordinate the transportation of these more complex shipments. More on the use of third parties is discussed later in this chapter.

Trade-Offs Among Modes

Supply management professionals have a number of choices for transporting materials. No single mode of transportation is best for all deliveries. Each mode has its own characteristics concerning cost, delivery speed, potential for damage en route and reliability (see Figure 7-1 for a comparison). Air freight is usually the quickest way to transport goods, but is also the most costly. Rail and ocean are the slowest modes of transportation but the least costly; rail and ocean can also move freight types that cannot be moved by air. A supply management professional must consider whether faster delivery warrants the additional cost. In many cases, it does. However, it is also a good idea to look for cost savings solutions that do not significantly affect shipping times. Del Monte, for example, initially thought it would sacrifice on-time performance by switching from trucking to COFC. The corporation operates two pet food production plants in Pennsylvania and Alabama, which ship finished product to a distribution center in Atlanta. However, by improving coordination and scheduling, Del Monte was able to make deliveries within a half day of the trucking option and save money.[17]

Figure 7-1: Mode Advantages/Disadvantages

MODE	ADVANTAGES	DISADVANTAGES
Motor Carriage	High availability Ease of accessibility Reliable service	Impacted by weather Limited international use
Air Freight	Faster shipments International use Handle sensitive cargo	Higher shipping costs Requires other modes
Rail	Move large volumes Low cost structure	Limited accessibility
Water	International use Transport heavy, bulk items	Limited accessibility
Pipeline	High dependability Ideal for liquid products	Equipment investment Maintenance costs

Source: Adapted from Stanley and Matthews, *Logistics and Transportation* (Herndon, VA: National Institute of Governmental Purchasing, 2007), 24.

Roles of Third-Party Providers

Supply management is responsible for the on-time delivery of incoming goods; thus, it must ensure a high level of performance from its transportation providers, whether they are internal (also known as private carriers) or external (public or for-hire carriers). The negotiation for, management of and coordination with these third parties often is the responsibility of supply management. As mentioned previously, independent organizations that design and manage some or all of an organization's logistical needs are known as *third-party logistics* (3PL) providers, and often are used because of their specialized expertise and experience. The term *third party*, or 3PL, originated because these entities facilitate each transportation movement between a procurement organization and its suppliers without actually taking ownership of a shipment.

While some 3PLs are simply transportation providers or public warehouses, others offer an array of other services, including information systems, freight bill auditing, inventory management, and control and consulting. Organizations such as FedEx Supply Chain®, UPS Supply Chain Solutions and Menlo Worldwide Logistics consider themselves solutions providers. A few of these services are described in the following paragraphs.

Freight forwarders play an important role in logistics because they provide a transportation service to smaller organizations that want to ship at a competitive rate. The freight forwarder combines these shipments from multiple shippers to make a full carload (CL) or truckload (TL) at a lower freight rate than the shipper could negotiate on its own. Less than carload (LCL) and less than truckload (LTL) rates are logically higher. The rates charged by freight forwarders can be very competitive, particularly when moving goods a long distance. *Air freight forwarders* specialize in the small shipments of air cargo,[18] while *ocean freight forwarders* typically consolidate smaller ocean shipments into containers.

Third parties that act as intermediaries between buyer and seller are known as *brokers*. They represent a carrier as its sales agents and a shipper as its traffic managers. Brokers solicit business from shippers based on the known availability of the carriers they represent. A broker typically will charge the carrier's published rates to the shipper, deducting a certain percentage as its commission (typically 7 percent to 10 percent) and remit the remainder to the carrier.

Shippers also often organize into *shippers' associations*, which are nonprofit cooperatives that negotiate lower rates for their members based on large volumes. They can save their members money by leveraging combined shipments that avoid markups.

A *fourth-party logistics* provider (4PL) is essentially an integrator that brings together the resources and capabilities of its own organization and others to design and operate a comprehensive supply chain solution. It provides the "management of both inbound and outbound materials, parts, supplies and finished good for other organizations. A 4PL is often a separate entity established as a joint venture, or a long-term contract between a primary client and one or more partners that act as a single interface between the client and multiple logistics service providers" (ISM *Glossary* 2014). Many service providers may fit within this category, including consultants, IT providers, private organizations and logistics professionals traditionally known for 3PL services. Based on an organization's specific supply chain initiatives, a 4PL can build a set of activities for its client. Areas such as invoice management, call centers and warehousing facilities are commonly associated with 4PLs.[19]

Understanding the various modes of transportation is important for supply management professionals. Knowing which mode to employ for a particular shipment, the ability to track shipments and when to use third-party support is invaluable. Equally important is an understanding of the role globalization plays in today's markets. Key issues involved with international transportation are covered in the following section.

International Transportation Issues

Global Logistics

Globalization is common today for industrialized nations and a growing trend for developing nations, making it a key issue in supply management. Therefore, many organizations have developed international supply strategies. Global supply chains can provide products that are not available locally or can provide a competitive advantage. Although similar goods may be sourced locally, sources in other parts of the world may offer them at more competitive costs, higher levels of quality or with more features.

P.F. Johnson and colleagues suggest many reasons to do business with global suppliers. These include the following:
- Lower pricing;
- Improved quality;
- Better availability;
- Reduced cycle time;
- Better technical standards; and
- Advanced technology.[20]

However, there also are challenges when negotiating for international logistics services. These include language barriers, quality control differences, foreign laws and political instability.[21]

Trends in Global Logistics and World Trade

Several trends are emerging throughout the world that greatly impact supply management. From 2011 to 2012, world trade growth declined from 5.2 percent to 2.0 percent, and was expected to hover around 3.3 percent in 2013. This was due to sluggish economies in the European Union and uncertainty about the euro, although the United States and Chinese economies were growing in 2013. Exports for Japan decreased by three percent in 2012, while developing Asia experienced an upturn.[22]

However, world trade has increased faster than world production, which indicates the growing importance of supply chain management. According to a recent study, customers are more demanding but they also expect lower costs.[23] Logistics costs typically account for four percent to six percent of total costs and are on the rise, presently exceeding eight percent for manufacturers. At the same time, globalization continues to expand to emerging countries, where transportation infrastructures are poor. This wrinkle has increased logistics complexity and, as a result, logistics performance has deteriorated. Also, transportation costs continue to increase and are viewed as more of a barrier to trade than tariffs.

Companies are also experiencing an increase in disruptions to the supply chain and are looking for ways to mitigate this risk by increasing the transparency of tier-two suppliers and the visibility of inventory in the pipeline. Lastly, the focus on sustainability initiatives in logistics is increasing, although there is still uncertainty surrounding how to develop goals and strategies, and how to measure and evaluate these efforts.[24]

In 2012, the global trade fleet was comprised of more than 1.5 million ships, with a combined tonnage of nearly 598 million gross tons. The fleet is made up of general cargo ships, oil tankers, bulk carriers, container ships and other ships. Bulk carriers account for nearly 41 percent of the fleet, while tankers make up 33 percent[25] (See Figure 7-2). Some of these ships are technically sophisticated and represent a significant investment, with larger container ships and oil tankers costing more than US$100 million to build.

CHAPTER 7: Logistics Management and International Transportation

Figure 7-2: World Merchant Fleet

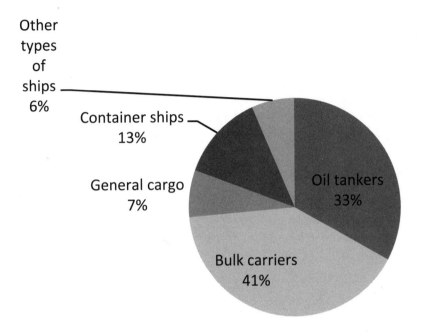

Source: United Nations Conference on Trade & Development (UNCTAD), available from http://unctadstat.unctad.org/TableViewer/tableView.aspx?ReportId=93, accessed October 14, 2013.

Global Third Parties

Like domestic transportation, a number of third parties play active roles in international shipping. *Foreign freight forwarders* retain experts in global shipping to assist smaller organizations that do not have the necessary experience or expertise. Along with combining smaller loads into containers that can fill a ship, they ensure that all legal obligations are met.

Two examples of third parties specifically related to ocean shipping are ship brokers and ship agents. Sales representatives that work for charter vessel owners, acting as middlemen between the shippers and ship owners, are known as *ship brokers*. *Ship agents* represent a ship operator while the ship is docked in port, and manage its arrival, berthing, loading, unloading and customs clearance. They also arrange for the payment of any fees that are due while the ship is in port. Shipping agents can provide the shipper with information on the arrival of the ship that contains its goods and arrange for pickup or delivery.

Customs house brokers are licensed to enter and clear goods through customs. They make sure that the documentation necessary for a shipment to clear customs is accurate and complete. The shipper gives a customs house broker power of attorney to pay any import duties that are due with the shipment. The transfer of information for shipment clearance is now performed electronically, reducing overall shipment times. The custom broker's expertise on import regulations or the specific requirements of certain products can be valuable to an organization, especially those with large or unique international shipping requirements.

A shipper may also require the expertise of an *export packer*. Because of country-specific rules and regulations on packaging, an export packer can hasten the movement of goods through customs. Also, because duties often are based on the weight of the package, an export packer will know what materials and methods will be the least costly to the shipper. Lastly, the export packer will ensure that the shipment receives the right level of protection against climate changes and rough handling.

Import and Export Documentation

Proper documentation plays a key role for both buyers and sellers involved in international trade. Various documents are used to address issues such as taxation, accounting, bookkeeping and payment. According to E.G. Hinkelman, the most common trade documents fall into these categories:

- *Export documents* are required by the customs office of the exporting country and can vary greatly between countries. License, permits, declarations and inspection certificates are all a part of export documentation.
- Documents issued by a shipping line, air cargo carrier or trucking organization that spell out the terms of the transport are known as *transport documents*. The bill of lading is the most important transport document.
- *Inspection documents* are issued at the request of the buyer to certify the quality and quantity of the materials. These documents also satisfy import and export requirements.
- *Insurance documents* are normally in the form of a policy or a certificate, and verify insurance coverage of the goods being shipped.
- *Payment documents* include letters of credit, advices and commercial invoices that address how the payment process will occur.
- Documents that are required by the customs authority of import are known as *import documents*. Minimal documentation includes an entry form and bill of lading, but may include other documents depending on the country of origin and the type of goods being shipped.[26]

International Commercial Terms (Incoterms® Rules)

The Incoterms® Rules are a set of standard delivery terms developed by the International Chamber of Commerce (ICC), primarily for use in international shipping. The ICC approved the newest version of the terms, designated Incoterms® Rules 2010, which became effective January 1, 2011.

For some time the Incoterms® Rules have consisted of 13 terms. Incoterms® Rules 2010 eliminate four of the previously-existing terms (DDU, DES, DEQ and DAF) and add two new terms (DAT and DAP), resulting in a total of 11 terms. The new version is made available for both domestic and international use; contracting parties should, however, review the applicability of these terms to the domestic environment prior to applying them.

The terms have been structured to increase incrementally the obligations (control, risk and cost) on one party while decreasing the obligations of the other, depending on the specific term chosen. Each term clarifies which party is responsible for the following items:

- Inland freight (transportation within the origination country);
- Forwarder selection;
- Export clearance;
- Carrier selection and scheduling;
- International freight;
- Import clearance; and
- On-carriage (transportation within the destination country).

Delivery occurs (and *risk of loss* transfers) at the point designated by the term selected. Transfer of *title* is NOT covered by any of the Incoterms® Rules and must be separately specified by the parties.

The Incoterms® Rules can be divided into two groups — multimodal (available for multiple forms of transport, including land, air and waterway transportation) and single mode (applicable only to waterway transportation).

The multimodal terms are listed below:

- Ex works (EXW) named place (seller's premises);
- Free Carrier At (FCA) point in seller's country;
- Carriage Paid (CPT) destination point named;
- Carriage Insurance Paid (CIP) destination point named;
- Delivered at Terminal (DAT) port, airport, terminal — this term is *added* by Incoterms® Rules 2010;
- Delivered at Place (DAP) destination point named — this term is *added* by Incoterms® Rules 2010; and
- Delivered Duty Paid (DDP) destination point named.

The single mode terms (which can only be used with waterway transportation) are those listed below:

- Free Alongside Ship (FAS) named vessel at loading port;
- Free On Board (FOB) named vessel at loading port;
- Carriage & Freight (CFR) named ocean or river port of destination; and
- Carriage, Insurance & Freight (CIF) named ocean or river port of destination.

The terms in each group are listed above in order of increasing responsibility for the seller (and correspondingly decreasing responsibility for the buyer). For example, using the term EXW makes the seller responsible only for making the goods available at its own premises; delivery occurs and risk of loss transfers at that point. When the term DDP is used, the seller becomes responsible for everything except on-carriage where the location for delivery is not the buyer's actual location. DDP is the only Incoterm® Rule that makes the seller responsible for import clearance.

Buyers in the United States who are likely to be familiar with delivery terms defined within the Article 2 and 2A of the Uniform Commercial Code (UCC) should pay particular attention to the overlap in the use of certain terms/abbreviations between the Incoterms® Rules and the UCC. "Free on board" (FOB), "free alongside" (FAS) and "Carriage, Insurance & Freight" (CIF) are all used in the UCC, but their definitions there are much different from the definition of the same terms in the Incoterms® Rules. Under the Incoterms® Rules, all three of the overlapping terms (FOB, FAS and CIF) fall into the "single mode" group, meaning they can only be used for waterway transportation. Under the UCC only FAS is limited to use with a vessel.

Although the new Incoterms® Rules 2010 became available for use as of January 1, 2011, Incoterms® Rules 2000 will continue to be available. It is incumbent upon contracting parties to determine which term they want to use and to designate the version being applied.

Numerous publications and seminars are available through the International Chamber of Commerce (http://store.iccbooksusa.net/) as well as from other organizations explaining in depth the application of both Incoterms® Rules 2000 and Incoterms® Rules 2010.[27]

Figure 7-3 describes these groups in more detail.

Figure 7-3: International Commercial Terms (Incoterms® Rules)

Term	Incoterms® Rules Definition
The multimodal (available for multiple forms of transport, including land, air and waterway transportation) terms are:	
Ex works (EXW) named place (seller's location)	The price that the seller quotes applies only at the point of origin. The buyer takes possession of the shipment at the point of origin and bears all costs and risks associated with transporting the goods to the destination. This Incoterms® rule is regarded as the most open-ended. There is generally nothing specific regarding delivery and a mutually convenient pickup time for exporter and importer is agreed upon. Used for any mode of transport.
Free Carrier At (FCA) named place (seller's country)	Seller delivers goods, cleared for export, to the buyer-designated carrier at a named location. Used for any mode of transport. Seller must load goods onto the buyer's carrier. The key document signifying transfer of responsibility is receipt by carrier to exporter.

Term	Incoterms® Rules Definition
Carriage Paid To (CPT) named place of destination	Used for any mode of transportation. Buyer assumes title and risk of loss when goods are delivered to the carrier. Seller pays shipping to destination. CPT delivery takes place when the exporter hands over goods to the carrier. The exporter is given bill of lading or equivalent document (air waybill, sea waybill, multimodal bill of lading).
Carriage Insurance Paid (CIP) named place of destination	An Incoterms® rule under which seller delivers goods to seller-designated carrier, pays cost of carriage to named destination and must obtain insurance to cover buyer's risk of loss in transit. Buyer bears risk of loss and any additional costs after seller's delivery to carrier, protected by seller's insurance. Used for any mode of transportation; same as CPT, but seller pays for insurance and names buyer as beneficiary.
Delivered at Terminal (DAT) named place of destination	Seller delivers goods to a named terminal in the destination country. Buyer is responsible for import clearance and any further in-country carriage. This term is one of two terms considered to be replacement terms for Delivered Duty Unpaid (DDU), which is eliminated from Incoterms® 2010.
Delivered at Place (DAP) named place of destination	Seller delivers goods to the buyer's facility or another named location (other than a terminal) in the destination country. Buyer is responsible for import clearance and any further in-country carriage. This term is one of two terms considered to be replacement terms for Delivered Duty Unpaid (DDU), which is eliminated from Incoterms® Rules 2010.
Delivered Duty Paid (DDP) named place of destination	Seller (exporter) is responsible for all costs involved in delivering the goods to a named place of destination and for clearing customs in the country of import. Seller provides literally door-to-door delivery, including customs clearance in the port of export and the port of destination. Thus, seller bears the entire risk of loss until goods are delivered to the buyer's premises. Full term is "DDP named place of destination." Delivery takes place when exporter places goods at disposal of importer in city of delivery. There is no corresponding transportation document, although bill of lading is usually used. Used for any mode of transportation. Seller bears all risk and customs responsibilities until the goods are delivered to a specified location and clear import customs. Buyer assumes risk and title when the goods are delivered to the buyer's specified location.
The single mode terms (which can only be used with waterway transportation) are:	
Free Alongside Ship (FAS) named vessel at loading port	Used only for maritime trade (transport by vessel). Under this arrangement, the supplier agrees to deliver the goods in proper condition alongside the vessel. The buyer assumes all subsequent risks and expenses after delivery to the pier. *This term can only be used for waterway transportation.*
Free On Board (FOB) named vessel at loading port	Used only for maritime trade (transport by vessel) under which responsibility for the shipment transfers from exporter to importer when shipment is loaded aboard the vessel. Seller must load the goods onto the ship. Centuries of maritime tradition say that the FOB point is the Ship's Rail. This is also referred to as "Freight on Board," which is the older maritime term of trade. If the freight falls while loading, however, it is the exporter's responsibility if it lands on quay, but it is the importer's responsibility if it lands on ship. The documentation of delivery is the ocean bill of lading or sea waybill. *This term can only be used for waterway transportation.*

Term	Incoterms® Rules Definition
Cost & Freight (CFR) named port of destination	Goods are considered to be "delivered" (and buyer assumes risk of loss) when they pass the ship's rail in the port of shipment. The seller is responsible for clearing the goods for export and for costs and freight to bring the goods to the destination port. *This term can only be used for waterway transportation.*
Cost, Insurance & Freight (CIF) named port of destination	Similar to Cost & Freight (CFR) where goods are considered to be "delivered" (and buyer assumes risk of loss) when they pass the ship's rail in the port of shipment. The seller is responsible for clearing the goods for export and for costs and freight to bring the goods to the destination port. Under CIF the seller must also obtain marine insurance against buyer's risk of loss or damage in transit. *This term can only be used for waterway transportation.*

Source: ISM *Guide to the Incoterms® Rules*, Summary from International Chamber of Commerce, www.iccwbo.org/products-and-services/trade-facilitation/Incoterms-2010/, June 2013.

An example of applying Incoterms® Rules 2010 might include a German organization manufacturing goods in a Brazilian plant. If an order of goods was set to be delivered to New Jersey in the U.S., then the contract between the German organization and the U.S. customer would need to address the specific terms of the transaction. Assuming EXW (Ex Works) Brazil was specified in the transaction, the goods would be made available for pickup at the German organization's Brazilian facility and delivery would be considered to take place when the goods were released to the customer's transportation provider. At this point the customer is responsible for all transportation costs and incurs all risk.

Security Considerations

Given the heightened awareness of security in the supply since 2001, two major initiatives have been implemented to ensure the safe transportation of goods globally.

Customs-Trade Partnership Against Terrorism (C-TPAT). A voluntary security initiative through the U.S. Customs and Border Protection (CBP) is the Customs-Trade Partnership Against Terrorism (C-TPAT). This partnership was designed to encourage importers, manufacturers, brokers, carriers, freight consolidators, non-vessel-owning operators and terminal operators to strengthen security practices and improve the integrity of the supply chain. There are over 10,000 certified partners that account for fifty percent of the value of what is imported into the United States.

For individual organizations to participate in C-TPAT, they must apply to the CBP. Participants must commit to the following actions:
- Comprehensive self-assessment of their supply chains based on C-TPAT guidelines;
- Completed supply chain security profile questionnaire;
- Development of a program to enhance their security; and
- Communication of C-TPAT strategies to other organizations in their supply chains.

Once an organization becomes a partner, it signs an agreement to (1) protect the supply chain, (2) identify any security gaps, and (3) implement security measures and best practices.[28]

C-TPAT provides organizations an opportunity to actively combat terrorism. Hopefully, the supply chain will be safer for customers, employees and suppliers. The other potential benefits of C-TPAT include the expedited release of shipments, a reduced number of inspections and an emphasis on self-policing.

Container Security Initiative. Another effective approach to security in global logistics is the Container Security Initiative (CSI), which was developed in the aftermath of the terrorist attacks on the U.S. on September 11, 2001. The purpose of CSI is to protect the global trading system as well as the trade lanes between ports by identifying high-risk containers and implementing a prescreening process using technology.[29] This initiative was rolled out in 2002, beginning with the international ports that shipped the greatest volume of containers to the United States. A list of the CSI ports currently operating can be found at https://www.dhs.gov/container-security-initiative-ports.

Transportation Policies and Procedures

Transportation Restrictions

Throughout the world, many rules and restrictions surround transportation. Carriers in the trucking industry, for example, must comply with size and weight restrictions. Because trucks must travel under bridges and overpasses, they are restricted to 13.5 feet in height by the U.S. Department of Transportation. Width and length must comply with appropriate regulations to ensure a safe environment on the roadways. Depending on what country or state the truck is traveling in, it may or may not be able to haul multiple trailers. Two trailers being pulled is referred to as a double (and three trailers are known as a triple). The latter is prohibited in some U.S. states. Australia, however, allows "road trains" — semi-trucks pulling up to four trailers — in certain regional areas.[30]

There are also restrictions regarding the movement of hazardous and regulated materials, which include but are not limited to explosives, gases, flammable liquids and solids, poisons, and corrosive metals. Supply management professionals have the greatest influence on what should be purchased because of their knowledge of the products, materials and services that are on the market. Thus, they should look for non-hazardous products as replacements for hazardous ones when possible. If a switch is not possible, however, it is important to comply with any laws and regulations regarding the movement and disposal of hazardous and regulated materials.

For example, the federal regulations in Canada are comprehensive in their requirements for transporting dangerous goods (otherwise known as hazardous materials in the United States). These regulations are enforced by a variety of inspectors, including the Royal Canadian Mounted Police.[31] Singapore has adopted several international rules and regulations regarding the movement of dangerous goods. Additional initiatives that support these rules and regulations have been implemented by the country's Dangerous Goods agencies such as the National Environmental Agency (NEA) and the Singapore Civil Defense Force.[32]

The U.S. Environmental Protection Agency (EPA) and the European Union also have strict regulations, including documentation and audit requirements. To make sure hazardous materials are moved safely and comply with country and U.S. federal, state, and local laws, supply management professionals should receive systematic and recurrent training.

Freight Classifications and Rates

Carriers charge line haul rates (or prices) to move goods between two points that are not in the same local pickup and delivery area. With the advent of deregulation, most rates today are negotiated between the shipper and its carriers, and set into contract form. The economic basis for setting rates stems from former regulatory standards such as classes and distance. The class system categorizes goods with similar characteristics such as value, density and susceptibility to damage and theft. Most of the less-than-truckload (LTL) carriers that are party to the National Motor Freight Classification™ (NMFC) system publish their own class rates, which are based on the NMFC classifications.[33]

Today, a carrier commonly evaluates a shipper's goods according to its published rates and then applies a distance cost/rate to them. In many cases, the carrier's published rates are the starting point for negotiating better rates based on other mitigating factors such as total volume with the carrier, favorable directional or seasonal flows, better packaging, and faster loading and unloading capabilities.

When setting rates, carriers consider two factors: *cost of service* and the *value of the service*. The first assesses the actual cost of providing the service, while the latter considers the value of the service to the shipper. The intent of the carrier in setting a particular rate is to cover the fixed and variable costs, as well as include a profit margin. *Fixed costs* are not subject to change even if the level of activity changes. Fuel and labor are examples of *variable costs*, for they change based on the level of activity (or output). Higher-value goods often impact the rates charged. The potential of damaging high-cost goods in transit tends to increase insurance costs to protect against the loss. Other factors affecting rates include product weight and density, specialized handling such as refrigeration, and various government regulations.

Freight Terms

Within the area of logistics and transportation, there is a unique language. Some of the freight terms that supply management professionals must be familiar with are found in the appendix, "Transportation Terminology," at the end of this chapter. Becoming familiar with the terminology used within the transportation and logistics industry will be of significant benefit to supply management professionals.

Resolving Delivery Problems

There always will be instances where deliveries are late, goods are damaged, or the shipper has shorted or over-shipped an order. Poor performance on the part of the shipper or carrier can result in poorly performing customer operations and, as a result, poor customer service. The following sections describe some of the ways these issues often are averted or resolved.

Delivery Tracking and Tracing Systems

To prevent delivery problems, organizations use tracking and tracing systems for their shipments. This allows users to access real-time information on their products in transit, as well as provide information to customers via online access to organization websites. These systems increase operational efficiency with the quality and accuracy of the data provided. International organizations such as United Parcel Service (UPS), DHL, FedEx and AIT Worldwide Logistics use such systems for their package tracking.

The Retailer Owned Food Distributors & Associates (ROFDA) adopted track-and-trace software in 2013. The web-based technology allows the cooperative of independent food wholesalers to identify "where backward sources and forward recipients of product" are located in the supply chain in close to real time. The software also allows ROFDA to manage any documents related to receiving, storing, sharing and regulations. The expected benefits are an increased ability to offer fresher products, quickly meet changing federal food safety requirements, and reduce costs by decreasing the occurrences of products that can't be sold.[34]

Visible Versus Latent Damage

As mentioned earlier, damage or loss can occur during the shipment of goods, even with the best efforts of the carrier. Lost goods are items that are missing from a shipment or simply cannot be found while in transit. If the goods actually do arrive at the intended destination but are not in an acceptable condition, they are considered damaged. Damage can be either visible or latent. *Visible damages* are easy to detect during routine inspection. An automobile delivered with a cracked windshield is an example of visible damage. Latent defects, on the other hand, are not easy to detect. A *latent defect* is one that is hidden and is therefore unnoticeable during inspection. An air compressor that looked fine when delivered but was later found to have a faulty electrical switch would be an example of latent damage.

The buyer of the goods has protection in cases of both visible and latent damage. Goods that are visibly damaged can be refused for delivery or can be replaced at no additional cost to the buyer. Latent damages can be a bit more challenging, particularly if the defect is discovered after a lot of time has passed. The buyer, however, still may invoke its warranty rights to replace or repair the item.

The proper receipt of purchased materials is a basic yet important part of supply management. The following determinations should be made for all incoming shipments:
- Whether the goods were actually ordered by the organization;
- If any visible damage occurred in transit;
- That the quantities received are correct; and
- That the shipping documentation is complete.[35]

Freight Claims

A *freight claim* is "a claim against a carrier due to loss of, or damage to, goods transported by the carrier." It could also be filed for "erroneous rates and weights in assessment of freight charges" (ISM *Glossary* 2014). Operational error is one of the most common causes of freight claims. The error can be made by the shipper, carrier or buyer in areas such as order processing, packaging, loading or bracing. Damage in transit can occur when materials being shipped are not handled in a safe and reasonable manner or when the proper equipment is not used. Proactive carriers will work to satisfy the shipper's issues immediately. In many instances, however, a freight claim will be necessary.

A freight claim can be filed when any one of the following three conditions exist:
1. A party has the legal right to file;
2. The time limit for filing has not expired; or
3. There is clear evidence that the carrier was the cause of the loss.

A claim is based on a party's ability to file a proper freight claim that clearly demonstrates it has suffered a loss because of the fault of the carrier. Only after such a claim is presented can the carrier begin to consider the claim. For motor carriage shipments, the governing regulations can be found in the U.S. Code of Federal Regulations (49 CFR Part 370) entitled *Principles and Practices for the Investigation and Voluntary Disposition of Loss and Damage Claims and Processing Salvage*.[36] Although most claims are filed much earlier, a claimant actually has up to nine months from the date of delivery (or the date on which delivery should have occurred) to file a written claim. The carrier then has up to 30 days to acknowledge the claim and assign it a claim number. Within 120 days, the carrier must resolve the claim by paying the amount requested, negotiating a fair compromise or proving it was not liable. The CFR regulations apply within the United States only. Globally, loss and damage claims often are negotiated between the parties involved. For example, a European organization might negotiate lower freight rates by agreeing to limit claims for loss and damage during transit.

Resolution Process

Logistical conflicts undoubtedly will arise between supply management professionals, suppliers and the logistics providers. Whether the conflicts involve damaged goods, late deliveries or disputed freight rate charges, to name a few, the parties involved must settle the disputes. In the event a freight claim is not settled amicably, the supply management professional may use other means to resolve the issue.

A typical resolution process begins with an escalation process to settle the dispute. The supply management professional should first make contact with the shipper or carrier to resolve the situation. In the event the shipper or carrier is unable to satisfactorily rectify the matter, the next step is for the supply management professional to file a claim. Based on inspection records kept by receiving, it can be determined whether responsibility lies with the shipper or the carrier. For example, damaged boxes are likely due to the carrier while a short order is the responsibility of the shipper.

Some negotiation may be required to resolve the claim, and is a skill that is critical for supply management professionals. Narrowing the differences in a dispute can allow both parties to give a little and arrive at a mutually agreeable resolution. When both parties end a negotiation feeling satisfied with the outcome, it is a win-win proposition. However, this is not always possible; in the event a claim cannot be settled amicably, litigation may be necessary. Litigation can be costly and time-consuming for all involved. Although the judicial system is available to all, it is often preferable to resolve differences outside of the courts.

The carrier or shipper may opt to take corrective action before a claim is filed and avoid the escalation process. For example, in the event the supply management professional's organization does not receive an order, the carrier would convey this information to the shipper and the supply management professional's organization that the goods have been lost in transit. The carrier would then seek to retrieve the goods. In the event the goods cannot be found, the supply management professional's organization would immediately file a claim. Another situation can occur when an over-shipment has been made. The buying organization can either keep the additional goods and pay for them, or return them to the shipper for a refund. A third scenario could occur where goods arrived damaged. The responsible party might offer to replace or repair them, or the receiving organization may do the repairs and charge the party responsible for the damage.[37]

Freight Bill Auditing

A *freight bill audit* is "a critical review of an organization's freight bills to determine if the assessed charges were correct." An audit "checks the classification, rating, or extension, either by a third party or an inside auditor" (ISM *Glossary* 2014). Many mistakes in billing occur as a result of human error, which can include variances in rates, descriptions, weights and routing. According to a 2011 study by Logica (now AFS), a parcel and freight audit company, shippers were overcharged an average of 13 percent on their freight bills.[38]

While the auditing function can be performed internally or externally, many organizations find it beneficial to contract out this service. A small organization can find it particularly advantageous to do so, for it likely does not have a staff person for this function.

Auditing companies normally provide service on a percentage of the dollars recovered. Larger organizations often have a computerized transportation management system that can perform freight bill audits automatically.

Carrier Performance Auditing

Management within the supply chain extends beyond the internal operations of an organization. The performance of suppliers and carriers must be optimal to ensure value to the customer. Monitoring, auditing and benchmarking performance can help secure a competitive edge within an industry. It is important to remember, however, that auditing should be carried out in a constructive manner, focusing on improvement rather than taking a punitive approach.

General issues that may need to be addressed include those listed below:
- Willingness to work as a partner;
- Commitment to continuous improvement;
- Access to innovation;
- Flexibility in logistics systems design; and
- Degree of common core values with the customer.[39]

Specific areas of performance that can be audited with a carrier include on-time deliveries, reduction in throughput times, delivery quality, billing accuracy and cost reduction.

Logistics Performance Measures and Strategies

Up to this point, the focus has been on the planning and implementation of logistics plans. Organizations, however, must periodically review logistical activities to determine if expected goals are being met. Thus, measurement and control are important for continuous improvement. The following section begins with several common logistics measures and concludes with some general approaches and strategies to manage the measurement process.

Logistics Metrics

Three areas of concern to logistics are (1) inventory, (2) transportation, and (3) customer service. A description of metrics commonly used to evaluate each of these activity areas follows.

Inventory Turns. Calculating inventory turns is a key method for determining best-in-class performance in logistics and supply management. *Inventory turnover* is "a measure of the velocity of total inventory movement through the organization, found by dividing annual sales (at cost) by the average aggregate inventory value maintained during the year. The higher the turnover, generally, the more favorable the measure" (ISM *Glossary* 2014). It acts as an overall indicator of material movement within an organization. An item that has old inventory and turns over once a year has a higher holding cost than one that turns over two or three times a year.

Transportation Costs. Measuring transportation costs will force an organization to closely look at its actual costs for receiving raw materials and for shipping its products. Therefore, supply management professionals should consider the following questions:

- What are the customer requirements?
- How much time will be taken in transportation?
- What are the costs and benefits of various modes of transportation?
- What are the security or other risk factors?
- What are the storage requirements?
- How well do the transport supplier's systems and standards such as packing, labeling and documentation integrate with your organization?[40]

Customer Service Measurements. Several areas that must be measured directly impact customer service. These include on-time delivery, product assortment availability and accuracy of orders. As an organization's service levels increase, so do the costs of storing, processing and transporting orders. So while supply management wants customer service at a high level, there also should be a concern about what this is costing. This is certainly an area to strive for, as balance and service level are things that are always subject to adjustment. Overall customer service measurements also are useful. Many organizations use short surveys to gauge customer satisfaction, including web-based surveys linked to online ordering systems.

Caterpillar Inc. Example

Caterpillar Inc., manufactures mining and construction equipment, diesel and natural gas engines, industrial turbines and diesel locomotives. The company also provides more than 620,000 individual service repair parts to its global customers through its service parts supply chain. A high level of customer service is critical to meet the customer's high expectations. Any interruptions in Caterpillar's supply chain can jeopardize a customer's operations. In a process improvement initiative, Caterpillar was able to reduce its inventory levels by over fifty percent while, at the same time, significantly improve customer service levels. Orders are now shipped in less than 24 hours 99 percent of the time. This was accomplished by incorporating new technology, outsourcing some warehouse facilities, and adding regional distribution centers closer to major customers. In all, Caterpillar saves greater than US$460 million annually through these initiatives.[41]

Logistics As a Profit Center

A progressive approach to controlling logistics is to view it as a potential profit center. Like other areas of an organization, logistics will have capital expenditures and will incur labor and material costs, but it has the potential to add value through its inbound and distribution center activities. These two particular activities can generate both revenue and sales.[42]

Thus, the costs of logistics services should be determined; these costs plus an added value or markup becomes the *transfer price*. The transfer price is added to the transfer prices from operations and marketing to estimate the total product price. Once the transfer price for logistics is established, the supply management professional can look for ways to improve profitability of his or her profit center.[43] Organizations also need to ensure that logistics does not profit at the expense of the departments they are serving. As with most things, there is a balance that supply management professionals must strive for.

A supply management professional also must have accurate and timely information about performance to effectively control logistics. This can be accomplished through periodic reviews of logistics activities, also known as *logistics audits*. These audits are necessary to establish reference points for report generation, and also to correct errors and misinformation.[44] Logistics audits also can be used as bases to improve an organization's distribution network, customer service and packaging design; reduce inventory requirements; or benchmark against other organizations considered best-in-class.

Productivity Reports

While audits may be conducted on an irregular basis, some routine reporting on logistics must be performed to control the function. For example, productivity reports typically are used to measure the efficiency of the various logistical activities. The goal is to put activity performance in relative perspective. Specifically, the output — performance — is treated as the numerator and the input — resources — as the denominator, creating a performance ratio. Productivity reporting is particularly useful for those companies looking to lower supply chain and distribution costs. Warehouse management systems (WMSs) provide basic reporting capabilities, while there are productivity management systems that provide a broad range of discrete measures as well as training in best methods, supervisor engagement, and employee feedback and counseling.[45] For example, a warehouse manager would be interested in the following measures:

- Inventory levels;
- Inventory turnover;
- Operating costs;
- Operations productivity; and
- Warehouse cost/unit.[46]

Some of the top evaluation ratios in logistics include the following:
- Logistics cost to sales;
- Activity cost to total logistics cost;

- Logistics cost to industry standard or average;
- Logistics cost to budget; and
- Logistics resources budgeted to actual cost.

Using Scorecards

A *scorecard* is simply a form of "performance measurement and management that records the ratings from a performance evaluation process" (ISM *Glossary* 2014). For an organization to improve its performance in supply management, it must first know where it stands relative to activities and outputs. Once this baseline data is established, supply management professionals can set benchmarks for targeted performance. Often, best practices with other comparable organizations are considered when setting these performance goals. Over a set period of time (quarterly, for example), performance in various supply areas is measured and documented. This information then is used to assess performance in the past and to develop strategies for improved future performance.

The *Supply Chain Operations Reference* (SCOR) model is a "supply chain mapping model from the Supply Chain Council that offers definitions, mapping conventions, metrics and a methodology for constructing the map. It also includes all flows: information, goods and money" (ISM *Glossary* 2014). It was developed by the Supply Chain Council as a cross-industry standard diagnostic for supply chain management. The model integrates processes, metrics and best practices. This model is further discussed in Chapter 9.

Summary

Logistics management remains a key area for supply management professionals, both today and in the future. Having a working knowledge of the modes of transportation as well as the advantages of using external resources such as freight forwarders is important. Globalization continues to play a role in all sectors, with international trade having a language all its own. The use of Incoterms® Rules will ensure that both buyers and sellers are on the same page. Ensuring top performance in logistics includes monitoring the work of transportation carriers, as well as measuring the ongoing effectiveness of logistics functions. A number of tools and reports are available to help senior management assess organization performance within the supply chain. By being aware of best practices in their industry, supply management professionals can assist their organizations in making sound decisions.

Key Points

1. Logistics management includes all activities that occur after a product is finished, including distribution selection, product order response and the return of goods.
2. The five basic modes of transportation are (1) motor carriage, (2) rail, (3) water, (4) air, and (5) pipeline, with each having its own advantages, disadvantages and cost trade-offs.
3. Third-party logistics providers (3PL) and fourth-party logistics providers (4PL) provide information, knowledge and valuable services to an organization. Third-party options include freight forwarders, brokers and multichannel merchants.
4. Global logistics is a key issue in supply management because international trade will continue to increase in the years to come. There are many benefits to using global suppliers.
5. The most common freight classifications are class rates and commodity rates, which can take the form of carload (CL) or less-than-carload (LCL).
6. Logistics and transportation has a language all its own, so the supply management professional must be aware of terms such as *cartage*, *demurrage*, *dunnage* and *incentive rates*.
7. Damaged and lost shipments can occur, so knowing how to file freight claims and who is responsible for damage are important.
8. Logistics measurements commonly used by organizations include cost to sales, cost to budget, inventory turns and customer service.
9. Productivity reports and scorecards are two means to measure logistics performance.

Appendix: Transportation Terminology

- **Basing point:** a point at which rates to another destination are computed.
- **Cartage:** local hauling between locations in the same town or city.
- **Charge-backs:** costs assumed by the carrier for independent contractors with the understanding that these costs will be charged back later.
- **Classification:** a publication containing a list of articles and the classes to which they are assigned for the purpose of applying rates.
- **Consignee:** the person named in a freight contract that the goods have been shipped or turned over to for care.
- **Demurrage:** the extra charges paid for detaining a freight car or ship beyond the permitted time for loading or unloading.
- **Differential rate:** the amount added to or deducted from a through rate to establish a rate.
- **Distance rate:** a charge made on the basis of miles traveled.
- **Dunnage:** the material used to protect or support truck freight and its weight, listed separately on the bill of lading.
- **FAK:** "freight all kinds"; usually refers to full container loads of shipments containing mixed types of freight.
- **Free astray:** shipment that is miscarried or unloaded at the wrong location and then forwarded to the correct location at no charge.
- **Incentive rates:** lower than usual tariff rates assessed because a rail shipper offers a greater volume than specified in the tariff.
- **Joint rate:** a rate for hauling a single shipment over two or more transportation lines (the lines involved cooperate to offer the service).
- **Multiple care rates:** rates established for shippers transporting large quantities of goods that fill up several rail freight cars.
- **Rate basis:** the formula that includes specific factors or elements that control the making of a rate.
- **Released rate:** a lower rate charged if the shipper releases the carrier from loss and damage liability during shipment.
- **Standard rates:** rates established for direct routes from one point to another. Rates by other routes between the same points are set in relation to the standard rate.
- **Through rates:** applicable for transportation all the way from point of origin to destination. A through rate may be either a joint rate or a combination of two or more rates.
- **Volume rates:** used in the trucking industry to refer to a low rate offered to shippers who agree to ship a large quantity of freight over a specified time period.

CHAPTER

8

Asset and Inventory Management

To meet today's goals of speed, competitiveness, customer service and responsiveness requires that organizations address productivity issues and work to eliminate nonvalue-adding activities. Inventory management, in particular, has been a target for improvement because of its impact on quality and delivery. Finding ways to improve inventory velocity and increase the frequency of deliveries has been a hot topic in recent years. Just-in-time and lean production, supplier-managed inventories and inventory consolidation techniques are some of the methods organizations are using to add value.

Supply management professionals also are concerned with the management of long-term assets for many reasons, although perhaps the most important one is that assets represent a major investment for any organization. Long-term assets generate income for an organization for longer than one operating cycle and include property, equipment and other assets. Obviously, these assets require proper attention.

This chapter discusses a number of issues related to asset and inventory management, beginning with an introduction to some terms. A brief overview of asset management then is provided, followed by a more extensive discussion of inventory management. The importance of inventory accuracy is addressed and covers areas such as inventory counting, shrinkage and material returns. Replenishment tools are important, for they allow the depleted inventory to be replaced and ready to issue when next needed. This section also covers inventory classification systems and order quantities, and how to address slow-moving stocks.

Chapter Objectives
- Define assets and their role in supply management.
- Discuss the importance of asset management and asset recovery.
- Discuss how inventory can be classified, tracked and reconciled.
- Identify inventory replenishment and priority tools available to supply management professionals.
- Explore current trends in inventory replenishment.
- Identify the types of surplus materials and various methods for disposition.

Assets Defined

Assets are anything of economic value. "A *tangible asset*, such as real estate, a building, equipment or cash, can be touched." An *intangible asset*, "such as a brand name, goodwill or reputation, that has value, (but) cannot be physically seen or touched" (ISM *Glossary* 2014). On the balance sheet, real estate, equipment and buildings generally are considered long-term tangible assets, while inventory, cash and receivables fall under short-term assets. *Inventory* is "any material, component or product that is held for use at a later time" (ISM *Glossary* 2014) and is a special category of assets. As noted earlier in this book, each item in inventory is typically referred to as a *stock-keeping unit* (SKU). A unique number or bar code differentiates each SKU. For example, a shirt style sold at a department store would require a different SKU for each size. All organizations must determine which SKUs are to be stocked. This determination generally is made based on a number of factors, including but not limited to customer preferences, industry trends, product cost, demand forecasts, profitability and storage capacity. More on-demand forecasting is found in Chapter 5, and Chapter 6 discusses storage capacity issues.

Cash and receivables are also important to the liquidity of an organization, but are not the topic of this chapter. Briefly, when supply management can shorten product cycle times, an invoice can be issued more quickly, resulting in improved cash flow. Additionally, by keeping order quantities and inventories low, an organization can improve its position with current liabilities. These are just two examples of the dividends resulting from greater integration between supply management and operations.[1] In some organizations, supply management may play a support role within the organization, yet it still can effectively reduce costs within the supply chain. A 2011 study of 249 manufacturing and service firms found that inventory control was an extensive or substantial part of supply management's responsibilities in slightly over 46 percent of those surveyed.[2] Figure 8-1 illustrates how the major elements of an organization's balance sheet are linked to supply management.

Figure 8-1: How Supply Management Links to the Balance Sheet

Balance Sheet Link	Supply Management
ASSETS	
Short-Term	
Cash	
Receivables	Order cycle time
	Order completion rate
	Invoice accuracy
Inventories	Inventory policies
	Service levels
Long-Term	
Property, plant and equipment	Distribution facilities
	Transportation equipment
LIABILITIES	
Current liabilities	Procurement policies
Debt	Financing options for inventory
	Financing for plant, equipment
Equity	

Source: Adapted from M. Christopher, *Logistics and Supply Chain Management* (London: Prentice-Hall, 2005).

Asset management, also known as property management, equipment management and sometimes even inventory control, involves maintaining an accurate accounting of assets, properly identifying each asset and asset recovery.[3] As described in Chapter 6, these fixed assets are used to support the management of inventory. The accuracy of the data used for this process is critical. To determine the financial health of an organization, the net value of its assets is measured and reported. Capital assets are typically assigned to a schedule in which their value is depreciated for a predetermined period of time. Asset recovery is "the re-employment, reuse, recycling or regeneration of something of value (property, equipment, goods and so on) that no longer is necessary for the original intent; the return of environmental conditions to the state they were prior to an action" (ISM *Glossary* 2014).

Inventory management is a subset of asset management and is defined as the "business function concerned strictly with planning and controlling *inventory*" (ISM *Glossary* 2014). Managing an inventory of expendable goods is very different from other assets because inventory is (or should be) transformed (for example, components into finished goods into sold merchandise) or temporarily stored before transformation. Assets, on the other hand, are used to facilitate the transformation. For example, a restaurant's building and equipment help facilitate the transformation of raw ingredients into meals for sale to patrons. Forecasting inventory needs also takes place more frequently (monthly or even daily), inventory models are used to determine order quantities, and the amount of control varies based on usage and value.

While some may not consider asset and inventory management glamorous, it remains a key function within the supply management profession. It includes many elements considered critical to supply management, such as data management and analysis, and cost analysis and management, which are key areas within the Strategic Supply Management Concept (see Figure S-1 in the "Series Overview" at the beginning of this book). The following sections provide an overview of asset management, beginning with the classification of assets.

Asset Management

Fixed assets, also referred to as *property, plant and equipment*, are long-term assets (see Figure 8-2). The ISM *Glossary* (2014) defines *fixed assets* as "assets that last more than a year, with an impact on shareholder value, and are considered by management to be worth controlling." *Property*, often referred to as *real property*, can be the most significant investment because it includes land and rights to the land, ground improvements, utility distribution systems and physical building structures such as warehouses and distribution centers that support the management of inventory. Permanent fixtures to an organization's facilities also are considered real property; they include items such as the warehouse itself, delivery dock and parking lot. *Plant* refers to the operational components such as shelving, conveyors and picking systems that make up the warehouse network. Technically, these may not be part of the real property; however, they can be considered semi-permanent as they will likely stay in place if the facility is sold and used for a similar purpose. *Equipment* also represents a significant investment and includes items such as delivery vehicles, railcars, technology hardware, office furniture and lift equipment. These articles would be considered portable and are likely to stay with an organization and not with the structure.

Figure 8-2: Fixed-Asset Classifications

PROPERTY	PLANT	EQUIPMENT	OTHER
Land and rights Ground improvements Utility systems Buildings, structures	Shelving units Conveyor systems Picking systems	Delivery vehicles Forklifts and other lift equipment Computers Bar code readers Office equipment	Software Trademarks Literary Works Customer Lists Patented Technology

Source: M. Christopher, *Logistics and Supply Chain Management* (London: Prentice-Hall, 2011); and Accounting Tools®, http://www.accountingtools.com/questions-and-answers/what-is-the-proper-classification-of-fixed-assets.html, accessed October 15, 2013.

Effective Asset Management Programs

A sound fixed asset management program involves several elements, including a current listing of all assets, a record of their value and a clear delineation of the responsibility for asset management activities. Effective and efficient use of these assets is possible when such a program is in place. The responsibility and accountability of asset management is something that each organization needs to decide for itself. Because supply management is experienced in the acquisition and disposition of assets, and may already participate in the management of expendable inventory, it may oversee this responsibility. In small organizations, supply management often wears many hats, including asset management. A larger organization may have a specialized program for this function within the supply management department. Figure 8-3 shows an example of how an organization might be structured.

Figure 8-3: Typical Supply Management Organization

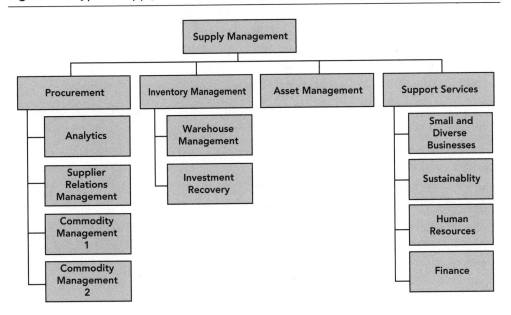

Many software programs are available today that deal specifically with asset management; these can be a sound investment for any size organization. These systems include modules for both the physical tracking and accounting of fixed assets, as well as help desk functions and preventive maintenance. An example of a successful system implementation is University Hospital of Tübingen, Germany. The University wanted to improve maintenance for its 360 buildings to prevent malfunctions and minimize costs. Using an IBM® software solution, the organization can better monitor the campus. Its database stores inventory information on 70,000 pieces of equipment, facilities and systems including location, asset number, manufacturer and technical specifications. The University's support team is alerted to any outages, broken phones and stalled elevators, among other problems. A performance dashboard helps to improve day-to-day operations.[4]

Tax policy on assets. Tax policies can vary from country to country. In the United States, for example, certain assets may qualify for the IRS Section 179 deduction for depreciation. This deduction allows organizations to deduct a portion of the total cost of the asset over its useful life. Ideally, the useful life of the asset is more than five years. Qualifying assets must be tangible, purchased for business use, and on the IRS eligibility list. Some examples of qualifying assets include machinery, software and supplies. The IRS sets a maximum on the allowed dollar exemption each year depending on the type of business (for example, partnership, S Corporation, or other type of corporation) and business income. Each year that the deduction for depreciation is taken reduces the asset's adjusted cost basis.[5]

Asset Recovery

Finding a new use for existing assets is a good business practice. It can minimize environmental impacts and reduce an organization's disposal costs. As explained earlier in this chapter, asset management is a broader term representing a comprehensive approach to acquiring, tracking, managing and reporting on assets. Therefore, asset recovery is an important component of asset management.

Asset recovery applies primarily to an organization's management of its surplus (or idle) equipment. When executed well, it will have a positive impact on return on assets, capital spending and cash flow.[6] Surplus assets can be written off the books for accounting purposes, and when this occurs organizations often look to equipment scrap dealers or an asset recovery organization for any kind of return. It is in this type of instance, however, when a supply management professional can bring tremendous value to the organization. Finding a new use for existing assets is good business practice and minimizes environmental impacts. By coordinating acquisition efforts throughout the organization and maintaining an accurate asset listing, purchases of new equipment can be avoided. This use of an asset is ideal, but when the equipment is not needed within the organization, supply management should seek to get top value on the open market as a way to maximize the return on invested capital.

Several key factors to success can be found in best-in-class asset recovery programs, and are listed below:

- An accurate and up-to-date database reflecting all idle or surplus plant, equipment and property with detailed descriptions, asset history and photos;
- Access to the database for all internal users;
- A responsible person at each major location who is designated the asset recovery point person and who functions within the internal network for asset management;
- A professional who is responsible for overseeing the program, the database and the network of internal contacts;

- Internal policies that facilitate the fair value transfer of idle equipment among organization locations;
- Access to market expertise for used equipment or idle real estate through use of a master agreement with an appropriate service provider; and
- Use of the master agreement service provider to determine fair value for internal transfers and to monetize the asset when no internal transfers are appropriate.[7]

As noted earlier, assets represent a significant investment for an organization. They need to be classified, tracked and monitored during their life cycle and, when appropriate, need to be disposed of in a manner that results in maximum return. Technology tools and systems that provide the necessary information in an efficient manner must be employed. Involving supply management professionals in the asset classification and disposition process will reap rewards for an organization.

Along with managing an organization's assets, supply management professionals also must handle inventory, which is another area that needs consistent and effective control. The following sections cover this topic in greater detail.

Importance of Inventory Management

As first mentioned in Chapter 5, the *bullwhip effect* refers to the fact that minor changes in customer demand can become exaggerated as that demand is communicated up the supply chain (retailers, wholesalers, distributors, manufacturers, and so on). These exaggerations, along with the tendency to accumulate safety stock at each point in the supply chain, amplify or intensify for three reasons. First, the bullwhip effect is exaggerated when an organization places the responsibility for meeting demand on the supplier's shoulders, regardless of actual demand fluctuations. Second, carrying too much inventory results when organizations continue with a functional silo mentality, in which each business function optimizes solutions based on its own needs rather than on those of the supply chain. Lastly, when supply management professionals take advantage of pricing discounts, the bullwhip effect is worse because organizations are carrying excess inventory in the system and as a result are increasing the need for warehouse space.

The problem worsens because of the means used to transfer demand and activity data through the supply chain. Typically, demand data is communicated function-to-function or organization-to-organization, but not necessarily in an accurate manner or with regularity. Activity data, which contains production quantities and the number of product movements within an organization and between supply chain members, also can contain errors. The combination of errors from these two data sources only compounds the problem. The bullwhip effect is essentially wasteful, occurs because of a lack of information across the supply chain, and results in unnecessarily high inventory levels.[8]

Poor inventory policies, along with data inaccuracies, can lead to difficulty in responding to changes in demand and thus trouble scheduling production. As a result, production managers find it hard to manage labor requirements because of the variability in demand. The result is an increase in production costs attributed to overtime and "undertime." Data mistakes also result in problems controlling inventory levels and managing warehouse requirements. Additionally, the bullwhip effect can result in customer dissatisfaction because of late or shorted orders. When ordering problems occur, operations spends more time and money to "put out fires" — in terms of expediting costs, additional safety stock and more expensive shipping methods — to satisfy the customer. To improve materials scheduling and customer service and reduce overall supply chain costs, organizations need to minimize the bullwhip effect through more effective inventory management practices and more collaboration with suppliers, as discussed throughout this book. Developing and maintaining relationships with suppliers and internal stakeholders should be viewed as a key to success for supply management professionals.[9]

The following sections discuss the various elements of inventory management, beginning with inventory classification techniques.

Classifying Inventory

There is an old saying that all inventories are not created equally. This simply means that certain priority items in an inventory warrant closer attention and control by the supply management professional. For example, supply management professionals might classify SKUs as indirect purchases — those that will be used internally by some process or management system, and direct purchases — those items that will be used in production or service delivery and sold to an external customer. Another approach is to classify SKUs by their physical characteristics. Retailers, for example, use category management to classify items as dairy, fresh fruits and vegetables, meat, drugs and so on. Category specialists then oversee the purchase and management of their group. Alternatively, the policy at a given warehouse could be that expensive or critical items are tracked more frequently than other materials. Because these items often represent a large annual expenditure for an organization, this only makes sense. Health care distributors, for example, track hip or knee replacement parts more closely than bandages. Another system that might be used is based on the scarcity of the materials and the lead time necessary to obtain the goods. This type of classification helps in reducing the lead time required, at least in the case of vital and essential items.

ABC Classification

Organizations may opt to use an *ABC classification* method, based on the Pareto analysis — or 80/20 rule. In other words, a small percentage of SKUs should account for a majority of the purchases made. SKUs are divided into three classes, A, B and C. A total value is calculated for each SKU based on annual usage and total purchase dollars spent.

For example, if an organization uses 1,000 of a SKU each year and spends US$20/unit, the total value equals 1,000 units × US$20 = US$20,000/year. The SKUs then are ranked high to low.

According to the *Supply Management Handbook*, one of the most useful ways to develop an ABC classification is to begin with an inventory report listing all items in descending order of dollars spent. This will indicate at a glance where the bulk of the dollars reside in an inventory. Normally, the higher-value items are considered "A," medium value as "B" and low-value items as "C." The smaller percentage items that represent the majority of the dollars (class A) should receive close oversight to maintain scheduled deliveries and minimal inventory. Class B items are reviewed periodically with a normal amount of oversight and only given high priority when the need is critical. The lowest priority of items, class C, would receive minimal attention and could even be ordered in bulk so there is plenty on hand. Procurement cards also are used for C items. Class C items represent only a small percentage of dollars spent.[10] Figure 8-4 provides an example of a typical ABC classification.

Figure 8-4   ABC Classification

Class	Percentage of Total Items Purchased	Percentage of Value of Total Purchases
A	10 - 20	70 - 80
B	15 - 25	10 - 20
C	65 - 75	5 - 10

Source: Adapted from ISM *Glossary of Key Supply Management Terms*, Institute for Supply Management®, 2014.

As shown in Figure 8-4, the class A items represent just 10 percent to 20 percent of the total items, but account for 70 percent to 80 percent of the dollars spent. This general rule can be applied to any inventory, even if more than three categories are established. While it may not be an exact science, ABC classification does allow the supply management professional to focus on what is most important.

Slow-moving stocks can be a challenge for any supply management professional. These items have low inventory turns and relatively low demand, which may or may not have been anticipated. These stocks should be carefully considered. The first reaction to slow-moving items is often to think they are not profitable and should be disposed of. This may or may not be accurate. Even if an item has only two turns in a year's time, it may be important to keeping a customer's business. Technische Unie (TNU), a Netherlands-based wholesaler, distributes electrical equipment, heating and climate technology, plumbing, and sanitary and consumer goods. The company needed a solution to improving inventory turnover. Of its 350,000 line items, 72,000 were considered slow-moving products. TNU faced problems with forecast accuracy, particularly with its slow-moving items.

As a result, it implemented a demand, inventory and replenishment planning solution to support forecasting of slow-moving items. At first, overall inventory levels went up due to rebalancing of inventory and sell-out of lower demand items. Once this was accomplished, however, inventory turns and order fill rates improved and forecasts were more accurate for all parts, including those identified as slow moving.[11] There can be many reasons for slow-moving stocks, including changes in customer preferences and advancements in technology. In these cases, it may be wise to phase out an item or at least not carry as much in inventory. At some point, a slow-moving item may become obsolete and will need to be dealt with as such.

Inventory Accuracy and Integrity

While inventory is a short-term asset, it usually represents a major investment for any organization. Depending on the type and size of the organization, the investment in inventory could easily be in the millions of dollars. Thus, it is incumbent on those who oversee these inventories to ensure that they are well managed. This includes knowing the exact quantity of the materials on hand, as well as the dollar value of the inventory. When inventory records are not accurate, there is an increased chance for unfilled orders, resulting in customer dissatisfaction, obsolescence and theft. Also, if inventory records indicate an item is in stock when in fact it either is not or it has been misplaced, production delays and additional costs to track and expedite shipments can result. Technology is an important means to effectively and efficiently track and control inventory.

Tracking Issues and Returns

The terms *issue* and *return* simply refer to inventory either going out of or coming into the warehouse. The steps normally involved with issuing inventory are picking, staging and delivery. Upon a request from an internal user, such as from the sales department, an electronic *pick ticket* is generated in the warehouse identifying the materials needed. The item is then retrieved, or picked, from wherever it resides in the warehouse and then staged for the customer. Staging can be a separate area of the warehouse where materials are housed until they are either delivered or picked up.

Returns can occur for a variety of reasons. Perhaps more material was received than was needed, or an incorrect item was received. If a customer does return material to the warehouse, proper procedures must be in place to inspect the item to ensure its condition and adjust the inventory count. Because a return generates additional costs in labor time and handling, many organizations require a *restocking fee*. It is not unusual for a customer to pay 20 percent of the original purchase price to return an item.

Verifying Inventory Levels

While virtually all organizations today use computer software that can accurately track what should be in inventory, physically verifying those records still is necessary. This is known as *taking a physical inventory* and refers to the actual counting of the materials on hand in the warehouse. Often warehouse personnel do the counting or, in some cases, a third-party inventory service is brought in under contract. Count sheets or handheld devices are used to record the actual amount of inventory on hand. Organizations will commonly conduct a physical count at a set period of time, usually at the end of the business year, to match actual inventory levels against the electronic records. An annual physical count is a method that many supply management professionals are familiar with, for this inventory ties into an annual income statement and balance sheet. Arizona State University, for example, requires any departments with an inventory in excess of US$100,000 to conduct an annual physical count, and includes this policy in its Financial Services Manual.[12]

Cycle Counting. Many organizations in the United States and abroad also verify their inventory through the use of *cycle counting*, which is performed throughout the year. Cycle counting, as defined in the ISM *Glossary* (2014), is "a physical stock-checking system in which the inventory is divided into groups that are physically counted at predetermined intervals, depending on their ABC classification. Thus, the physical inventory counting goes on continuously without interrupting operations or storeroom activities." This is also referred to as *continuous inventory*. Cycle counting represents a proactive approach to inventory management, since inventory records are verified on a frequent basis and not just during a one-time event that "cleans up" an inventory that is inaccurate the rest of the year. It is a best practice that makes inventory accuracy a priority, and something to strive for on an ongoing basis. An Oklahoma City, Oklahoma, U.S. retailer with 19 stores manually counts its inventory 51 times per year. According to its operations vice president, conducting cycle counts make the difference between what's real and what's not. The method improves inventory accuracy for the retailer, which means less inventory is carried and the retail chain can respond to customer sales trends faster.

Counting a portion of warehouse items monthly or quarterly is a wise business practice for supply management professionals. It allows for the counting process to be spread out over time by dividing the effort into smaller and more manageable tasks. Cycle counting continues to be the preferred method for ensuring inventory accuracy, as it results in lower inventory write-offs as a percentage of inventory investment.[13]

Inventory Reporting Measures. Although any measurement of inventory starts with cycle counting, the reporting format is typically presented in three ways: weeks of supply, average aggregate inventory value and inventory turnover. The *weeks of supply* is calculated by dividing the average aggregate inventory value by sales per week (at cost). The *average aggregate inventory value* is the sum of the dollar values of all items that are held in inventory. *Inventory turnover* measures the velocity of total inventory movement through an organization. As a rule, a higher rate of turnover is better. The formula to calculate inventory turnover is:

$$\text{Inventory turnover} = \frac{\text{Annual sales (at cost)}}{\text{Average aggregate inventory value}}$$

Ideally, inventory will be sold or turned over multiple times in a year. High inventory turns are desirable because they increase cash flow and reduce the possibility of obsolescence. How many inventory turns are ideal? There is no single best rate for inventory turns, but some industry averages are useful. The inventory turnover is calculated by dividing an organization's cost of goods sold by its average of cost of inventory during the year. Figure 8-5 provides a list of inventory turnover ratios in various industries.

Figure 8-5: Inventory Turnover Ratios by Industry Corporations, Q1 2013

Industry	Inventory Turnover Ratio
Forestry and Wood Products	10.82
Restaurants	21.15
Grocery stores	13.96
Furniture and Fixtures	6.66
Chemical Manufacturing	4.65
Tires	4.87
Construction Services	1.79
Computer Software	20.06
Railroads	15.64

Source: CSIMarket.com, Financial Intelligence Company, www.csimarket.com, accessed October 15, 2013.

Reconciliation

Once an inventory item has been counted and compared against the perpetual records, discrepancies may appear. Less inventory on hand than is expected is referred to as *shrinkage* — a reduction in the amount of inventory on hand for reasons other than issuance or a sale. This can be the result of materials being lost, stolen or misplaced, and also through natural causes such as evaporation and deterioration. Certain materials are more prone to experience shrinkage, such as batteries, drill bits or computer components. If specific items repeatedly experience shrinkage, then policy changes may be warranted. Additional security measures or relocation of the items can help address the problem and reduce theft and pilferage in the future.

These variances normally are noted on discrepancy reports. Significant variances that are noted will warrant attention and often result in a recheck of the item and its actual quantity. To settle or resolve these variances is known as reconciliation. To reconcile the inventory records, an adjustment will be required. These reports also will serve as an audit trail for the warehouse.

Measuring Accuracy

Inventory accuracy is an important performance measurement because it indicates whether the actual inventory on hand matches the inventory records. Inventory management specialists typically divide the number of SKUs with an accurate count by the total number selected for counting. For example, if 96 SKUs were found to be accurate out of 100 counted, the inventory accuracy would be 0.96, or 96 percent. Making these results known to key warehouse staff on a regular basis can help identify problem areas, as well as keep staff informed when accuracy benchmarks are met.

Because accuracy is so important, it is imperative that a physical inventory is taken periodically and that it is conducted correctly. This allows for the inventory system to be updated so that it accurately reflects materials available in the warehouse. When a discrepancy occurs, meaning the quantity on hand is different than what the inventory system indicates, a correction then is made through an *inventory adjustment*. The World Health Organization (WHO), for example, provides written guidelines to its employees for taking physical counts. It recommends that each product be counted at least once per year, but fast-moving items are to be counted more frequently. A key to accurate counts is an organized storeroom. Products must be counted by the units by which they were issued. For example, a prescription drug would be counted by the tablet rather than by the box. Stock-keeping records must be updated at the time of the physical count, and identified by the date in a new color of ink. Any damaged or expired product is disposed of at the time of the count. Lastly, corrective actions are taken as needed.[14]

Excess material can result when warehouse inventories are not managed accurately and effectively. In many cases, this excess will need to be disposed of, usually at a loss. Later in the chapter, multichannel disposition plans will be explored, including various methods of disposal or reclamation.

Inventory Policies and Procedures

The efficient and effective operation of any business function requires sound policies and procedures. Inventory management is no exception. The supply management professional must play a key role in the development of an organization's inventory policies, which also must have the support and buy-in of senior management. Policies should be easily understood by both customers and staff, and should be reviewed and updated periodically. For example, certain inventory issues must be addressed in a warehouse policies and procedures manual. Figure 8-6 provides a list of items that warrant consideration.

Figure 8-6: Warehouse Policy Issues

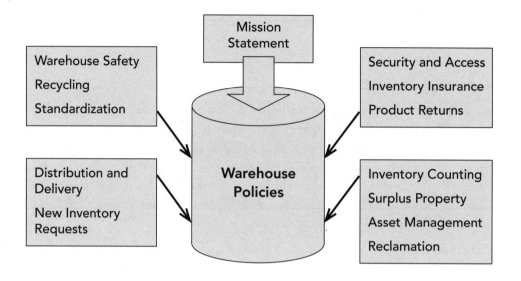

The importance of a well-developed policy manual for the warehouse should not be underestimated. It provides a blueprint for the entire organization of its supply management practices and reflects the value of the warehouse operation. Best-in-class organizations inevitably will have sound policies and procedures regarding inventory management, as well as policies on inventory valuation. More on managing the warehouse can be found in Chapter 6.

Inventory Valuation

The three basic methods used to valuate inventory are LIFO, FIFO and average costing. *Inventory valuation* determines the dollar value of inventory on hand at a given point in time.

LIFO stands for last in, first out, and assumes that items purchased last are sold first. Because these items are likely higher in value in times of inflation or asset appreciation, the remaining inventory is valued at an older price, which gives the organization a lower value for remaining inventory on its balance sheet. *FIFO* means first in, first out, and assumes that items purchased first are also sold first. For instance, an electrical component sold out of inventory would be issued at the oldest or first price.

Average costing assigns an inventory value for an item at the average cost paid. If two air compressors were in inventory, one purchased for US$750 and the other for US$850, the average inventory value for each would be US$800 ((US$750 + US$850)/2).

Organizations also must determine reordering polices, which are discussed in the following section.

Replenishment and Priority Tools

Knowing when and how much to purchase of a particular item will always serve as a challenge to supply management professionals. To begin this discussion, it is important to understand the costs incurred from owning inventory.

Inventory Holding Costs

Also referred to as *inventory carrying costs, inventory holding costs* represent what it costs an organization to keep "inventory on hand, including the opportunity cost of invested funds (finance costs); storage and handling costs (overhead costs); taxes and insurance (ownership costs); and shrinkage, damage and obsolescence (risk costs). Holding costs typically are stated as a percentage of an inventory item's value over a period of time" (ISM *Glossary* 2014).

The cost of maintaining an inventory can be substantial for an organization. Surprisingly, inventory holding costs can run between 20 percent and 40 percent, which is considered a conservative range. Some industry experts calculate this number to be even higher. One estimate indicates that when all capital, labor, investment, variable and tracking costs are summed, inventory holding costs can reach 35 percent to 50 percent per year.[15] To assess the true cost of inventory, supply management professionals must look beyond just the cost of the inventory itself. Also, even though public sector warehouses typically avoid taxes, the holding costs still are considerable.

Following are the components used to calculate the inventory holding costs:

- *Invested funds.* The capital used to purchase the inventory must be considered, whether it is financed through a third party or through the organization's cash flow. This includes lost opportunity costs of capital invested elsewhere.
- *Storage.* The cost for the physical storage of the goods can include rent, utilities, equipment and maintenance costs.
- *Handling.* The cost to handle the inventory, including receiving and picking costs, can be substantial when wages, benefits and other personnel costs are considered.
- *Taxes.* Taxes paid on the value of the inventory on hand, as well as property taxes.
- *Insurance.* Insurance premiums for properly protecting the inventory investment and warehouse facility.
- *Shrinkage.* The loss or shrinkage of inventory, which can be caused by human error or pilferage.
- *Obsolescence.* The losses because of materials becoming out of date.

To assess the true cost of carrying inventory, consider all the costs that go into owning or leasing a warehouse as well as inventory. Only then can the inventory holding costs for an organization be determined. Supply management also should be aware of these costs when placing large orders. The negotiated purchase price may reflect a deep discount, but after factoring in holding costs, the price may not be so attractive. More organizations are moving toward maintaining the smallest amount of inventory possible to meet customer service goals. However, international sourcing adds complexity to inventory management. Because of some of the risks associated with international sourcing and the need to maintain the continuity of business, many organizations are adding inventory. Global sourcing also can add between 20 days and 50 days to lead times.[16] As a result, companies tend to add inventory in the pipeline and at the receiving site. Researchers found that an increase from domestic to global sourcing of 10 percent resulted in a higher level of inventory investment by 8.8 percent. However, moving from single to dual sourcing mitigated or reduced the increased investment by 11 percent.[17]

Inventory Ordering Costs

Each time supply management places an order, *inventory ordering costs* are incurred. For the identical item, the costs associated with each order should be the same, no matter what the order size because the same activities will occur.

Some of the costs specifically tied to processing an order include the following:
- Preparing a material requisition, including phone, fax and email;
- Request for quote process, including quote analysis;
- Price negotiation and order issuance;
- Administrative, expediting and receiving costs; and
- Invoice processing and payables cost.

Once an organization has collected this cost information, it can begin the process of calculating the order size for each item.

Determining the Order Size

What is the optimum amount of material to order? Some inventory management systems employ a *fixed order quantity* approach in which the amount of material ordered does not vary; only the frequency and timing of the order varies. For instance, a printing shop may order a certain paper only by the pallet. The order size is always one pallet, but depending on actual demand, the order could be placed monthly or quarterly.

If the fixed quantity is large, then the organization will benefit from a lower purchase price. This also makes the acquisition process more straightforward, as the material and quantity are always the same. A potential disadvantage to fixed order quantity is the tendency for higher inventory levels. As previously mentioned, an organization can obtain lower pricing for larger orders, but there is always a cost to handle and store the material. Inventory holding costs are significant and were discussed earlier in this chapter.

For many years, the *economic order quantity* (EOQ) has been used to assist supply management professionals as a starting point to estimate the fixed order quantity. The EOQ formula balances the cost of holding inventory with the cost to order it. The generally accepted formula for calculating the most basic EOQ is:

$$EOQ = \sqrt{\frac{2(\text{Annual usage in units})(\text{Order Cost})}{(\text{Carrying Cost})}}$$

Notice that annual usage is expressed in units and is based on the forecasted usage. As previously noted, the order cost is the sum of all fixed costs incurred when an item is ordered, and the annual holding cost is the cost associated with having inventory on hand.

The EOQ is a viable tool for the supply management field; often it is a built-in function of stand-alone inventory management software products and materials management modules. The formula gives the supply professional valuable information prior to order placement. The EOQ value often is adjusted to accommodate such issues as factory packaging, shipping requirements and quantity discounts.

Figure 8-7 provides an example of total annual inventory costs based on the frequency and size of the order. For purposes of this example, the ordering cost is US$33.33/order, the order size annual demand is 5,000, and the carrying costs are at 12 percent. The formula to calculate total annual costs is:

Total Annual Cost = Carrying Costs + Ordering Costs = (Order Size/2)(Carrying Cost) + (AnnualDemand/Order Size)(Ordering Costs)

Based on this information, the optimum value is reached with three orders per year. At that frequency, the carrying and acquisition costs are balanced.

Deciding When to Reorder. Once the EOQ has been determined, inventory levels are monitored. When inventory levels reach the reorder point, an order for the EOQ is triggered. "A reorder point is a predetermined inventory level that triggers an order. This level provides adequate inventory to meet anticipated demand during the time it takes to receive the order" (ISM *Glossary* 2014). Where should the reorder point be set? Generally, the supply management professional will set this so that enough material is on hand to meet the demand until the new order is received. A number of factors are considered when determining the reorder point. These include the importance of the item (will it stop production or provision of service?), the anticipated demand (how much is needed?), and the supplier lead time (how long will it take?).

Figure 8-7   Total Annual Inventory Costs Example in US$

	NUMBER OF ORDERS PER YEAR				
	1	2	3	6	10
Order Size	5,000	2,500	1,667	834	500
Average Inventory (Order Size/2)	2,500	1,250	883	417	250
Carrying Costs (Order Size/2 * 12%)	$300	$150	$100	$50	$30
Ordering Costs (Annual Demand/ Order Size * $33)	$33	$67	$100	$200	$333
Total Annual Inventory Cost	$333	$217	$200	$250	$363

Source: S.H. Corwin, *Intermediate Public Procurement*, 2nd ed. (Herndon, VA: National Institute of Governmental Purchasing, 2000).

Variable Order Systems

Organizations also may opt to preset a maximum inventory level needed to run operations efficiently as well as a reorder point, and then review inventory levels periodically. When inventory reaches the reorder point, enough inventory is ordered to bring levels back up to the maximum. This type of system is common when review and ordering costs are relatively high.

Safety Stock

Whether a fixed or variable order system is used, *safety stock* is always a consideration. Safety stock is sometimes referred to as *buffer stock* because additional inventory is held as a safeguard against fluctuations in either the supply or demand of an item or delivery risk, such as with the use of international suppliers. In the event of a spike in demand, safety stock can become quite valuable as it prevents a stockout or a total depletion of material on hand. Depending on the importance of the item in question, the safety stock literally can save the day and keep a production line running, ensure valuable goods are ready for delivery to the final customer, or maintain an optimal level of service.

The challenge with this concept is carrying an ample amount of safety stock without stockpiling it unnecessarily. The latter can be costly. Normally, the level of adequate safety stock can be determined by knowing the supplier's lead time to acquire an item.

For example, if three days are required to secure the materials, then having an average of three days' usage of safety stock in the warehouse makes sense. An experienced supply management professional will use this information, along with his or her experience, to determine an appropriate safety stock level.

Another important consideration is the type of control system that should be adopted.

Inventory Control Systems

Inventory managers monitor and control inventory in two common ways. With a perpetual inventory control system, an organization's inventory values are kept continuously in line with its actual inventory on hand. After each purchase, withdrawal and sales transaction, the inventory records are updated. If inventory levels for an item have fallen below a set amount, more will be ordered. The ability to maintain continuously updated records is possible with inventory management software. A perpetual inventory management system still requires an organization to periodically take a physical count to ensure that the computer records are accurate. The EOQ model typically is used in perpetual inventory management systems. Walmart uses a perpetual inventory system. Through the use of bar code scanners, RFID and computerized inventory systems, it can tell how many items are in stock currently, how many were sold last week or even how many are on hand at individual stores. A 2007 study revealed that the use of RFID significantly improved inventory accuracy at Walmart.[18]

This differs from a *periodic inventory* system, where transactions are recorded in an account as purchases, withdrawals and sales are made. However, inventory is only reviewed on a periodic basis (for example, weekly, monthly or quarterly) to determine if more should be ordered from the supplier. A periodic inventory system generally is used by smaller organizations or those where inventory withdrawals are infrequent. A variable order system is commonly used with a periodic inventory control system. For example, a building supply company would purchase supplies and materials throughout the year to perform its work, but the inventory account is updated only at the end of each quarter to reflect actual inventory on hand.

Other inventory control considerations may include those listed below:
- Should the inventory be held in-house or by a supplier?
- What inventory items receive top priority and attention?
- How can one ensure that inventory levels remain relatively low?

There is no single correct answer for any of these questions, but by becoming aware of the tools available, supply professionals can best position themselves and their organizations for success. The next section begins with a discussion of inventory costs.

Trends in Inventory Replenishment

A supply management professional may save acquisition costs because of negotiated volume discounts, which at first glance may seem attractive. A retailer such as Home Depot, for example, could decide to place one large order for a particular style of refrigerator to realize a savings on the total purchase cost. However, carrying and handling costs will be high and probably will not offset the savings. Organizations are increasingly finding ways to reduce the amount of inventory carried. Retailers, for example, allow customers to use their smart phones to place orders. They can then search for the item(s) systemwide and ship from the nearest store or distribution center directly to the customer.

Inventory Consolidation

Private and public organizations alike work toward maintaining a leaner inventory. This includes reducing the amount and types of inventory on hand, as well as consolidating inventories at multiple locations. By reducing the number of locations, organizations are experiencing cost savings in several areas. Operational costs can be reduced with fewer sites, and inventory levels also are reduced. One of the other prime areas where organizations see savings is in the reduction of their safety stock. Inventory usage may be consistent, but fewer sites mean less overall safety stock.

With multiple locations, lead times for each facility can vary, even for the same product. This type of decentralization can make forecasting requirements quite challenging. When selecting the appropriate facility for consolidating inventory, key considerations include which sites have the lowest lead time and the best operational efficiency.[19] Deere & Company revamped its Worldwide Commercial and Consumer Equipment (C&CE) division in an effort to reduce inventory costs by 28 percent. At the time of the initiative, about 70 percent of C&CE's finished product was located on the premises of its 2,500 dealers, including seasonal items such as lawn mowers. The dealers wanted enough product on hand to assure they met demand, and initially were uncomfortable with reducing inventory levels. In response, C&CE decided to reduce dealer inventory by 25 percent each year for four years. C&CE also improved its manufacturing planning process to create production schedules that could easily adjust to demand changes. Forecasts were revisited monthly to make any needed adjustments. C&CE moved from a batch process to an assembly line that had readily available parts to build any model any time of the day based on current demand. To improve cycle time, an extra layer of five regional distribution, or "temporary merge," centers were added to aid in the flow from production sites to the dealers. Multiple orders are now shipped by truck so the trucks typically leave full. Although the change resulted in slightly more inventory in the factory warehouses, overall inventory levels decreased by half and order lead time was reduced from 10 days to 5 days.[20]

Just-in-Time Inventory Management

The Japanese have held that excess inventory equates to waste and is not a good use of an organization's resources. Perhaps as a result of the scarcity of industrial space in their country, the Japanese developed the *kanban system* to ensure low levels of inventory.[21] The word *kanban* is Japanese for the type of card that originally was used in manufacturing environments. Kanban is defined in the ISM *Glossary* (2014) as "a printed card that contains specific information such as part name, description, quantity and so on that signals a cycle of replenishment for production and materials. It is an order release mechanism and one of the primary tools of a just-in-time (JIT) manufacturing system." Toyota has successfully employed kanban in its production scheduling system. By requesting a predefined standard quantity of a component or subassembly, Toyota work centers can better ensure low setup costs and short lead times.[22] Production personnel use the kanban to convey to supply management that additional inventory is needed. Placed in the bin, the kanban card is removed when the inventory is depleted, and the card then is given to the supply management professional. This action prompts a replenishment order for the item and helps keep inventory levels low. The kanban system is most effective for small lot sizes of high volume/low value items that are regularly used.[23]

For instance, if a quantity of roller bearings is used up on the production floor, kanban will ensure it is replenished only at the time it is needed and not before. This prevents a build-up of inventory which, in turn, reduces costs. This is consistent with the philosophy behind kanban, which is to maintain a well-balanced supply chain.

Inventory Scheduling

Flow manufacturing, or flow production, is a "demand-based manufacturing strategy where items are pulled through a coordinated manufacturing process based on the ongoing monitoring of customer demand (for example, product is made based on customer demand in daily schedules)" (ISM *Glossary* 2014). Contrary to traditional manufacturing methods, individual units of production "flow" directly through the manufacturing process without the time delays associated with batching. Traditional manufacturing practices include batching of partially completed parts into lots, waiting in front of another manufacturing process for further processing. Traditional factories also move in-process inventories extensive distances from one manufacturing process to another. By reducing or eliminating batching and unnecessary routing, lead times can be reduced, and the cost of work-in-process and finished goods is reduced. Because there are fewer materials on the shop floor, material control is simplified in terms of tracking and management activities. A manufacturer also can move from a build-to-stock to a build-to-order environment.

Founded in Japanese manufacturing principles, and specifically the pulling of materials through production based on actual customer demand, organizations using a flow manufacturing strategy typically create manufacturing cells, which are u-shaped physical layouts of manufacturing equipment to manage the flow of materials. Within the cells, all manufacturing steps are carried on for similar parts, and workers are trained to operate all equipment within the cell. The u-shaped design eliminates much of the waste in production because workers travel less between unfinished and finished product, and virtually all work-in-process is eliminated.

Part of flow manufacturing is *level scheduling* of production, defined as a technique to balance production throughput at each workstation to meet expected *cycle times*. The cycle time is a measure of how frequently each unit will be produced. Important to the success of flow manufacturing is converting suppliers to the same business strategy.

DemandPoint, for example, offers flow manufacturing training, consulting and software products. The organization developed the Demand Flow™ Factory model, which is a mathematical set of tools used to design flow lines and processes to lessen manufacturing lead times by reducing waste. Ultimately, the goals are to increase manufacturing speed, responsiveness and flexibility.[24]

Supplier-Managed Inventory

The traditional method for replenishing inventory was to simply place an order with a supplier when materials were depleted as needed. Suppliers were given no advance knowledge of the customer's requirements, often resulting in rush orders, increased freight costs and delays in production.

Supplier-managed inventory (SMI) is a progressive approach to controlling inventory. Also referred to as vendor-managed inventory, this concept gained ground in the 1990s as organizations focused on reducing supply chain costs. The ISM *Glossary* (2014) states, "a supplier is responsible for ensuring that stock is maintained at appropriate levels in the supply professional's facility and for replenishing items when these levels drop." With SMI, the supplier receives information about the needs of the customer, including historical usage, current inventory levels, material forecasts and promotional products. This information then allows the supplier to assume responsibility for inventory management. Suppliers assume the risks of having the necessary levels of inventory on hand. Upper-stock and lower-stock levels are conveyed by the customer, but the task of inventory replenishment falls to the supplier. In many cases, the supplier owns the inventory being managed until the product is issued.

There are many benefits to a well-run supplier-managed inventory program. These may include some or all of these:
- Partnership is formed between the parties.
- Communications are improved.
- Order processing speed is improved.
- Purchases are generated on a predefined basis.
- Fill rates improve.
- Stockouts decrease.

- Inventory turns improve.
- Planning and order costs decrease.
- Overall service levels improve.

SMI does have its limitations, however. Some organizations may hesitate to implement such a program for fear they are losing control of their inventories. An increased dependence on the supplier also may be perceived as a disadvantage of SMI. Thus, it is important to take precautions to assure success. First, be sure that everyone involved understands the process. Second, test the inventory data and stocking limits to assure an accurate ordering process. Third, make sure suppliers are notified in the event of an upcoming promotion or special event that could impact demand. And last, include in the agreement the steps that should be taken in the event of an overstock.[25] Still, SMI offers numerous advantages to both the supplier and the customer. Both may have their own reasons for embarking on the partnership, but ultimately SMI must be beneficial for all.

An example of a company that successfully redesigned its SMI program is The Dannon Company (Dannon), which sells several million cups of yogurt each day in close to 100 flavors. In 2010, SMI was identified as a key enabler of Dannon's ability to improve supply chain visibility and product flow to retailers' shelves, and to reduce supply chain waste. While Dannon had success with its SMI program over the previous 10 years, it realized that SMI was "narrowly focused and considered to be a supply chain process only." Also, the company had only initiated SMI with a few large retail partners and wanted to expand the program. Dannon's new objectives were to increase sales, decrease costs and improve customer satisfaction. By adopting a new generation SMI platform, the company realized significant productivity gains including higher inventory turnover, an increase in the number of SMI partners to over 20 locations, and an average service level of 97 percent where SMI has been in place for at least six months.[26]

Inventory Disposition

While it is easy to see the value in concentrating on the "front end" of inventory management, such as material forecasts and order quantities, it also is important to properly deal with obsolete and damaged stocks at the "back end." Leading organizations have begun to pay more attention not only to their procurement practices but also to the disposal of surplus material, which can turn the idle equipment into value.[27]

Investment Recovery Principles

Investment recovery is defined in the ISM *Glossary* (2014) as a "systematic, centralized organizational effort to manage the surplus/obsolete equipment/material and scrap recovery/marketing/disposition activities in a manner that recovers as much of the original capital investment as possible." An organization's inventory and assets continue to have value when they reach the end of their useful lives. Very often it falls to the supply management professional to properly dispose of these assets — and to do so with maximum investment recovery in mind. Supply management is most knowledgeable of the markets an organization buys in, as well as the supplier base of potential interested parties. The following should be kept in mind when disposing of an organization's assets:

- Items must be disposed of in a timely manner since there is a cost to keeping them on hand.
- Whatever disposal method is employed, it should attempt to maximize proceeds for the organization.
- When unneeded assets are converted to cash, they should be used to offset the cost of operations or invested in new assets.[28]

This chapter covers the area of asset disposition related to inventory. Assets also can include capital equipment and computer hardware, which are covered in Chapter 7. Reverse logistics is a broad and evolving field. *Reverse logistics* is defined by the Reverse Logistics Association as "all activity associated with a product/service *after* the point of sale, the ultimate goal to optimize or make more efficient aftermarket activity, thus saving money and environmental resources.[29] As described in the ISM *Glossary* (2014), "The objectives of RL are cost reduction, environmental benefits and source reductions."

Supply management professionals are rightfully concerned with the cost of reverse logistics activities. This concern is supported by a recent study by Accenture, a management consulting, technology and outsourcing firm, which found that returns were costing consumer electronics companies alone about US$16.7 billion per year. The study also revealed that these companies did not understand their full landed costs.[30]

However, successful reverse logistics programs have improved customer service as well as financial performance. Lexmark, for example, owns a parts distribution center in Louisville, Kentucky, which receives returned parts as part of its operation. After reviewing the process, the company found that the documentation received with the returned parts made it difficult to determine whether the part was good or defective. Parts thought to be defective were sent to the supplier for testing so it could determine the cause of the defect and possibly rework it for future use. However, not all parts shipped to the supplier were defective, costing Lexmark money in unnecessary testing. The process was improved by creating a label with defective part information and a bar code containing the claim number, part and service required. The bar code could then be scanned, linking the part to the service order. Also, using new Lexmark software, orders now contain accurate shipping information. As a result, parts returned to stock improved by 54 percent, and savings were expected to be US$900,000 the first year of the new process because good parts would no longer be tested.[31] An example that further demonstrates commitment on a global scale is Hewlett-Packard (HP), which provides recycling services for computer equipment, printing supplies, batteries and cell phones. Since 1987, "HP has recovered over 3.2 billion pounds of products for reuse and recycling."[32] Members of the supply chain, along with logistics service providers, must be committed to establishing good reverse logistics programs. Therefore, it should be a part of an organization's current and future supply strategies.

A *multichannel disposition plan* will allow an organization to use a variety of approaches to dispose of its excess inventory — and even finished goods if they become damaged. Such a plan will consider a number of factors to ensure that a disposition method is appropriate for the material at hand. These factors include market demand, the condition of the item, marketing opportunities and market trends.

One method fits all circumstances — a multichannel disposition plan. Products such as bicycles may have a high consumer demand and be sold off through online systems like eBay or Craigslist. Raw materials would likely be more specialized, so a negotiated sale to another manufacturer may be more appropriate. For instance, a mechanical contractor with a large quantity of steel plate left over from a completed project may be able to sell the material to a railcar manufacturer that uses the same material in its processes.

Surplus Material Categories

Surplus materials can come in many shapes, sizes and varieties. *Surplus property* is a term used to describe materials and assets that no longer are needed by an organization. They can include inventory items as well as noninventory assets that may fall under the control of supply management. These items may become available for many reasons and fall into the following general categories.

Damaged stock is material that has suffered some type of damage or neglect and is therefore not fit for its intended use. This damage can occur because of defective manufacturing, improper handling or inadequate packaging. Material that arrives at the warehouse damaged should be refused or returned to the supplier. However, if the damage is not apparent and only discovered at a later time, the buying organization may have to take responsibility. To avoid damaging goods during handling, warehouse personnel should be well trained in proper materials handling procedures. "Residue from operations and off-spec production items that cannot be reworked or used for the originally intended purposes" is considered *scrap material* (ISM *Glossary* 2014). Scrap can be generated by an organization and can include material left over from special projects or from normal production. Often scrap includes nonferrous metals such as copper, aluminum and brass. In recent years, the recycling of scrap metals has grown. Because of tight markets, increased values and organizational commitment to sustainability, the U.S. recycled 82 million tons of materials in 2009.[33]

Inventory items subject to *spoilage* are those that deteriorate or rot over time. These items include food products, chemicals or rubber products that have limited shelf lives. Spoiled items do not normally have any value. Local bakery outlets, however, can offer discounted breads and pastries to consumers. They still are within their product expiration dates but usually are closer to that date than the same products on shelves of major grocery retailers.

Obsolete stocks are inventory items that no longer can serve their intended purpose because of market or operational changes.[34] As technology advances in every industry and market, products can become obsolete quickly. This can be a challenge faced by supply management professionals, whether their inventory consists of ship repair parts or high-tech computer equipment. These stocks have outlived their useful lives to the current owner and are not likely to be sold at their full value. However, every effort should be made to get as much value out of the inventory as possible. In some cases, such as with the government, ownership is transferred from one agency to another. For example, the Federal Excess Property Program (FEPP) allows for the loan of United States Department of Agriculture (USDA) Forest Service-owned property to State Foresters for the purposes of fighting wildland and rural fires. The Forest Service acquires most of this excess property (defined as unneeded by an agency) from the Department of Defense (DoD).[35]

Disposal Marketplace

An important part of an organization's disposition process is a sound knowledge of the disposal marketplace. Many options are available for the supply management professional to dispose of surplus property. More than likely an organization will use experts in a given industry that provide disposition services and are neither the buyer nor the seller — otherwise referred to as *third-party specialists*. One type of third-party specialist is the *broker*, an intermediary that brings the buyer and the seller together. They do not take ownership of the goods, but provide brokerage services for a fee. Payment arrangements are handled between the buyer and the seller. Another option is the *dealer* who specializes in buying and selling, but actually takes ownership of the goods and resells them at a profit. Supply management professionals, again, must be knowledgeable about, and connected in, the industries in which they work, and be able to employ the services of an outside party that is most beneficial to their organization. Public Surplus is an organization that sells all types of equipment on behalf of government agencies (www.publicsurplus.com), while Surplus Record serves as a directory of surplus electrical equipment (www.surplusrecord.com). Both use the Internet as a prime marketing tool to provide disposition services to their clients.

Other organizations in the marketplace serve as a resource for disposition of assets and for developing sustainable strategies that can be considered at the start of the acquisition process. Interface® offers sustainable floor covering and interior fabrics for the commercial market. The organization is committed to sustainable business practices that minimize the impact on our environment. For Interface®, these types of practices are not just sound business practices, but rather a corporate philosophy that resonates from the chief executive and throughout the entire organization.[36]

Disposition Methods

Numerous avenues are available for disposing of surplus property. If other departments in the organization do not have a need for the item (reuse within the organization generally is preferable), then the following methods should be considered.

An *auction* is a type of public sale where the goods are sold to the highest bidder. Heavy equipment and motor vehicles often are sold online through an auction process. Commercial sites exist, such as Liquidation.com, that specialize in the sale of surplus inventory from retailers; and PoliceAuctions.com, that auction government surplus, cars and antiques. The advantage of an online sale is that more potential buyers will see the wares, which often results in higher sale prices. Applying the value of existing equipment against the purchase of new is referred to as a *trade-in*. An organization is in a better position to leverage a higher price from a buyer when a potential new sale is on the line. Disposing of equipment separately can result in a lower financial return.

Similar to the method of procuring a new item, a bid process also can be used to dispose of property. Interested buyers submit written bids to the organization, which then selects the most advantageous offer. This method often is employed in the public sector. *Retail sales* can be a viable means of disposal if the value and quantity of the equipment are high enough. Because retail space is required to display the sale items, this can be relatively costly. When surplus equipment is offered to an organization's staff through an *employee sale*, other benefits can be realized. For example, when Brigham Young University is ready to "retire" any of its fleet of vehicles, it first offers them to employees at wholesale prices.[37] This is a great deal for the employees and saves the organization significant transaction costs associated with disposal in the marketplace. Preset prices can ensure that the organization gets a fair market value, and it avoids the time and expense of dealing with outside parties. This is a common private sector practice that also is used by some public agencies.

Donation and discard are methods that will not realize revenue for an organization. A *donation* is the transferring of property to another party at no cost to the party. Often, not-for-profit organizations are the recipients of these donations. A lack of revenue does not necessarily mean there is no value or return for the donating organization. The demonstration of goodwill through a community donation certainly can be beneficial, and is tax deductible in many cases. *Discard* refers to literally throwing away an item of no value. This is a last resort and should be used only if there is truly no value in the item and no demand for it.

A prime objective when disposing of surplus property of any type is to obtain maximum value. Hard-earned capital was used to purchase the inventory item, so naturally an organization wants to recoup as much of the original investment as possible.

One of the first steps is to establish a baseline value for the item. In some industries, published guides can be used to assist with this value determination. The automotive and RV industries use such guides, including books and websites to gauge current value. Since 1926 the *Kelley Blue Book* has provided market pricing for all types of motor vehicles, and is used extensively in the automobile industry (www.kbb.com). Additionally, the National Automotive Dealers Association began publishing the *NADA Guide* in 2000, which serves as an appraisal guide for autos, motorcycles and recreational vehicles (www.nadaguides.com). The book value of an asset is calculated on its original value less the accumulated depreciation to date. Past or current sales figures also can be used as a resource. The price an item can command on the open market is referred to as its *fair market value*. While simplistic, Figure 8-8 can serve as a general guideline or a method for establishing an item's potential value, with the factor serving as the multiplier against its original cost.

Figure 8-8: Value of Surplus Material

TYPE	CONDITION	FACTOR
New	In original container	1.0
Excellent	Like new condition	.90
Good	Solid working condition	.85
Fair	Needs refurbishing	.50
Poor	Needs complete rebuilding	.40
Scrap	Appropriate for salvage	.30

Source: Chandrashekar, A. and Dougless, T. "Asset Recovery: New Dynamics for Purchasing Organizations," *International Journal of Purchasing and Materials Management,* (September 22, 1997).

Disposition methods of surplus materials are important, but the area of physical storage cannot be overlooked. The following section deals with issues related to establishing a physical warehouse to house materials, including surplus.

Equipment Lending

A special form of disposition is equipment lending. Organizations loan equipment to others for a variety of reasons. For example, an organization might lend a potential buyer a copy machine to determine if the equipment will function as required before purchase or lease. The lending of the equipment also might help facilitate the relationship between buyer and seller. Lastly, if a disaster has occurred, such as Hurricane Sandy, one organization might lend another organization equipment to assist it with returning to full operating capacity.

Value Stream Mapping

Value stream mapping (VSM) was originally "a lean manufacturing technique in which the transformation of materials is traced from beginning to end to determine if there is waste in the process either in the form of a step where no value is added or a point of 'wait time' when material is being stored to await further value-adding transformation. This concept may also be applied to services" (ISM *Glossary* 2014). Value stream mapping, which is similar to flow charting or process mapping, objectively looks at a process to determine value-added and nonvalue-added components. This technique can be useful in many areas of supply management, including warehousing or services purchasing. J. Womack and D. Jones define the value stream as "a set of all actions, both value- and nonvalue-added, required to bring a specific product (whether a good, a service or some combination of the two) through the (critical) main flows."[38] Organizations can have several value streams, including investment recovery for surplus materials. When this or any other business process is mapped, an organization can determine what steps do not add value and consider eliminating them. VSM is an effective tool that provides material processing steps with information flow, and allows an organization to make the best use of its resources.

One of the easiest ways to create a VSM is to create a cross-functional team from managers and non-managers throughout the organization. For supply management processes, this team likely would include operations, procurement and customer service groups. An ideal size team includes between seven and ten members. The first step for the VSM team is called a *kaizen*, which is Japanese for "change for the better." With an experienced facilitator, the group can work through the steps of VSM; these are listed below:

1. Determine the process family.
2. Draw the current state map.
3. Identify wasteful activities and root cause.
4. Determine and draw the future state map.
5. Draft a plan to arrive at the future state.[39]

The VSM process can help organizations build improvements and efficiencies in their processes. It requires a dedicated team of professionals who are willing to think beyond their current practices.

Summary

Asset and inventory management continues to play a valuable role within the supply management field. Whether in the areas of supplier relationship management, cost management or social responsibility, the supply management professional certainly contributes toward organizational success. The importance of inventory management was addressed in this chapter, as well as what it takes to maintain an accurate inventory.

Today's warehouses rely on various third parties for both inventory management and distribution support, as outsourcing continues to face all areas of an organization. Being aware of industry trends, disposition channels and virtual warehouses will ensure the inventory function continues to add value

Key Points

1. Assets are property that retain their value over a period of time. These can include vehicles, building structures and equipment, for each has an economic life along with a residual value. The management of these items is known as asset management, which is a segment of materials management. The three categories of fixed assets are property, plant and equipment.
2. The three ways to valuate inventory are LIFO, FIFO and average costing.
3. Supplier-managed inventory (SMI) is a growing trend and can offer many benefits to both the customer and the supplier.
4. A small portion of the items in an inventory represent the largest investment, and should therefore be monitored more closely through the use of ABC classification.
5. Because inventory holding costs are high, organizations should attempt to balance their acquisition and holding costs by applying the EOQ formula.
6. Inventory turnover measures the velocity of total inventory movement through an organization.
7. Flow manufacturing is a term used to describe a "one-piece flow" business strategy that allows an organization to establish a continuous sequencing of product that is replenished either from external suppliers or other internal processes based on actual customer demand.
8. Manual order picking involves the use of warehouse personnel to physically retrieve an item, while mechanized systems automate the order fulfillment process.
9. Value stream mapping is a technique that evaluates a process and identifies both value-added and nonvalue-added activities.
10. Organizations should consider a number of factors when developing a multichannel disposition plan, including market demand, item condition and marketing opportunities.
11. When disposing of surplus materials and inventory, the supply management professional should attempt to obtain the maximum value for the organization.

CHAPTER

9

Quality in Supply Management

The issue of quality has evolved greatly within the field of supply management, and its importance has not waned. As stated in a 2013 *Quality* magazine editorial, "Companies are still being dogged by high-profile quality defects. The list is long and getting longer, and crosses every industry."[1] Supply management professionals can't afford not to rank quality at the top of their priority lists, and quality should be viewed as a critical factor in the sourcing decision.

Earlier in this book, the Strategic Supply Management Concept was depicted (see Figure S-1), and it is evident that quality impacts many areas of supply management. When considering supply chain linkages and supplier relationship management, it is critical to maintain a high standard of quality.

This chapter will reflect on the importance of quality by first looking at several key definitions (see Figure 9-1) and their applications to the supply management profession. Also covered in this chapter will be various quality programs and tools that can be used to make a positive impact on poorly performing processes. Improving supply management also is important, so appraisal processes are discussed. Lastly, given the amount of outsourcing today, techniques and methods to improve supplier performance are covered.

Chapter Objectives

- Discuss supply management's role in assuring quality.
- Identify the quality improvement models that can help improve the competitiveness of organizations.
- Explore how the use of quality tools can be used within supply management.

- Explore the processes that can help improve performance within supply management.
- Discuss how supplier performance can be measured and improved.

Defining Quality and Its Role in Supply Management

Quality can be described as a precise and measurable variable that is inherently present in the characteristics of a product or service. It also has been defined as synonymous with "innate excellence." A high-quality product or service should be superior to other like items. *Quality management* is "the function of planning, organizing, controlling and improving the quality of products and processes" (ISM *Glossary* 2014).

Quality assurance is "a management function that includes establishing specifications that can be met by suppliers; using suppliers that have the capability to provide adequate quality within those specifications; applying control processes that assure high-quality products and services; and developing the means for measuring the product, service and cost performance of suppliers, and comparing it with requirements" (ISM *Glossary* 2014). A function of quality assurance is quality control. *Quality control* "is responsible for measuring quality performance and comparing it with specification requirements as a basis for controlling output quality levels" (ISM *Glossary* 2014). Another related term is *quality improvement*, which is "enhancements that increase value or decrease time requirements of processes, activities, performance, products and other areas" (ISM *Glossary* 2014).

Supply Management's Role in Quality Assurance

The role of supply management in assuring quality is to ensure that the goods and services acquired meet quality expectations and that they support the strategic objectives of the organization. This includes identifying products, determining customer needs, identifying the right suppliers and establishing metrics to verify the quality of services and products.[2] A product that simply conforms to a specification or standard may be minimally acceptable, but that does not mean it is quality.

Whether it is hiring a consultant to support a service provider's operations or acquiring raw materials to be used in the manufacture of finished goods, the supply professional plays a key role in ensuring quality. For many U.S. manufacturers, 50 percent or more of the final price of a finished product can be attributed to the cost of the purchased goods, and the services spend ranges between 30 percent and 70 percent.[3] Thus, when supply management improves the level of quality through its suppliers, an organization's competitiveness is improved.

Research indicates that organizations will rely even more on supply management in the future. Thus, supply management professionals must continue to play active roles for their organizations in securing quality goods and services. By developing and executing value acquisitions, supply management can ensure maximum return for their organizations.[4] In a 2011 study of 344 manufacturing and service organizations, respondents rated the importance of a best-in-class supplier base as above average, but were somewhat below

Figure 9-1: Quality Terminology

TERM	DEFINITION
Quality	A precise and measurable variable which is inherently present in the characteristics of a product or service.
Quality Management	The function of planning, organizing, controlling and improving the quality of products and processes.
Quality Assurance	Management function that includes establishing specifications that can be met by suppliers; using suppliers that have the capability to provide adequate quality within those specifications; applying control processes that assure high-quality products and services; and developing the means for measuring the product, service, and cost performance of suppliers and comparing it with requirements.
Quality Control	Measures quality performance and compares it with specification requirements as a basis for controlling output quality levels.
Quality Improvement	Enhancements that increase value or decrease time requirements of processes, activities, performance, products and other areas
Quality Circle	A group of workers doing similar work, who voluntarily meet regularly during normal working hours to identify, analyze and implement improvement opportunities.
Quality Function Deployment (QFD)	A structured method for translating user requirements into detailed design specifications using a continual stream of "what/how" matrices. QFD links the needs of the customer (end user) with design, development, engineering, manufacturing and service functions. It helps organizations seek out both spoken and unspoken needs, translate these into actions and designs, and focus various business functions toward achieving this common goal.
Quality Gate	A system of strategically placed quality inspection steps to ensure discrepant parts are not passed to the next operation and that processing error feedback is quickly provided to the station which produced the defect.

Source: Cavinato, J.L., A.E. Flynn, M.L. Harding, C.S. Lallatin, M.L. Peck, H.M. Pohlig, S.R. Sturzl and V. Tucker (Eds.). ISM *Glossary of Key Supply Management Terms*, 6th edition, Institute for Supply Management®, Tempe, AZ, 2014.

average in implementation, revealing an opportunity for improvement.[5] Because it may interact with any part of an organization on a given project, supply management has the chance to make a positive impact on a daily basis. By assuming a leadership role and employing the tools discussed in this chapter, supply management professionals can best add value to their organizations. This new, advanced responsibility means that supply management must take responsibility not only for negotiating the equipment purchase, but also for the performance of the equipment and the supplier throughout the entire life cycle. To achieve this, supply management must monitor and improve the performance of its suppliers.

Supply management, however, also must realize the risks of over-specifying quality parameters. Developing product requirements that are excessive can result in additional costs and delays. To ensure an appropriate level of quality, a *performance specification* should be considered. This approach simply "details the performance criteria required for a particular material or service" (ISM *Glossary* 2014). For example, Skidmore, Owings & Merrill LLP (SOM), the designer of Chicago's 100-story Trump Tower, wrote performance specifications detailing the requirements for concrete mix. Prairie Materials, the supplier and concrete producer, then developed a high performance concrete mix. Stan Korista of SOM states that the result was successful, with efficient "concrete pumps and placing booms, and the development of forming systems that can be erected safely and quickly then moved to the next location."[6]

Quality Models

A number of improvement models and programs are being used by organizations today to increase quality and competitiveness; several have proved to be tried-and-true by some leading organizations such as Toyota, Bank of America, Deere & Company and Target. The following section will address current processes that can increase quality, beginning with Six Sigma.

Six Sigma

A leading quality improvement model for many organizations today is *Six Sigma*. As briefly discussed in Chapter 1, this is a disciplined methodology that uses relevant data to eliminate defects in a process. The objective of Six Sigma is the implementation of a measurement-based strategy aimed at reducing variances and improving processes. Organizations that implement Six Sigma are striving for a level of quality that is near perfection. For a process to achieve Six Sigma status, it must produce no more than 3.4 defects per million opportunities.[7]

DMAIC and DMADV are two Six Sigma processes that organizations commonly use to improve performance. DMAIC (define, measure, analyze, improve, control) is used for existing processes in need of incremental improvement, while DMADV (define, measure, analyze, design, verify) applies to either new or existing processes requiring more than just incremental improvements (see Figure 9-2).[8]

Six Sigma programs have been used to develop new processes for manufacturing and service sectors, as well as to improve existing processes in need of improvement. When General Electric's former CEO Jack Welch needed a methodology to benchmark business performance, he implemented Six Sigma; in one year alone, the bottom line improved by US$600 million.[9]

Services organizations, such as Bank of America Corp., adopted Six Sigma to improve their supply management process. Bank of America managed more than US$7 billion

Figure 9-2: DMAIC Versus DMADV

DMAIC Improve existing processes incrementally	DMADV New processes or improve existing processes more than incrementally
D – Define project deliverables and customer goals.	D – Define project deliverables and customer goals.
M – Measure the process to determine current performance.	M – Measure and determine customer's needs and specifications.
A – Analyze and determine the root causes of any defects.	A – Analyze process options that will meet the customer's needs.
I – Improve the process by eliminating defects.	D – Define the process in detail to meet the customer's needs.
C – Control future process performance.	V – Verify design performance and ability to meet customer's needs.

Source: Adapted from SixSigma, www.isixsigma.com/dictionary/DMAIC-57.htm.

annually in services, which accounts for 60 percent of its overall spend. Using the DMAIC process, the financial services provider improved an established sourcing process to convey clear expectations to, and share its business objectives with, service providers. Using a supplier relationship management (SRM) system, Bank of America appointed trained professionals to oversee supplier performance. The key objective with its outsourced services was to establish key relationships that result in cost savings and faster service deliveries.[10]

In addition to improving quality in the supply management processes, Six Sigma can be effectively applied to project management. As supply management professionals continue to lead projects for their organizations, this can be an extremely effective tool. The project management process was covered in more detail in Chapter 2.

Some organizations have matched Six Sigma with lean thinking which is known as *lean six sigma*. As discussed in Chapter 1, the goal of *lean thinking* is to "eliminate waste and achieve major cost, inventory and lead time reductions in less than a year" (ISM *Glossary* 2014). When combined with Six Sigma, quality not only improves due to process controls but also improves because there's a smaller chance the product will be damaged with a shortened process. The key elements of a Lean Six Sigma program include the following:

- Using a project approach to identify significant process problems;
- Linking strategy, goals and performance indicators to the selection of projects;
- Training those involved in project management, Six Sigma and lean thinking; and
- Standardizing new processes and deploying process controls.[11]

Standardization Programs

When an organization has a recurring need for the same or similar parts, products and services over time, it can benefit greatly from a standardization program. *Standardization*, "the process of agreeing on a common specification," improves quality and leads to efficiencies and cost savings (ISM *Glossary* 2014). A *specification* is "a description of the technical requirements for a material, product or service" (ISM *Glossary* 2014). Service providers use a statement of work to identify their specifications. "The standardization process can take place at different levels: across an organization, throughout an industry, across a nation and around the world" (ISM *Glossary* 2014). Such efforts, at least at the organizational level, must involve supply management. For example, instead of acquiring similar parts with the same or slightly different specifications, the supply management professional's goal is to standardize by ordering from one or two suppliers. Standardization is a driving factor for organizations that operate in a just-in-time (JIT) environment.

Standardization has several advantages. First, fewer varieties of products are being acquired — which means they can be purchased in volume — and that usually results in supplier discounts. As a result, the cost of inventory is reduced. Second, organizations that seek standardization are generally moving away from custom parts — which are bought at a premium — and looking for off-the-shelf parts when possible. Third, supply chain costs can be reduced because, as variety decreases, fewer parts need to be ordered and tracked. Also, fewer parts are stored in warehouses, reducing inventory carrying costs. With fewer suppliers there is less variability, which means a consistent quality experience for the customer. As well, with common parts across products, product completion time is shorter. Lastly, common parts and components can be reused on future models, reducing product design time.[12] Volkswagen was the first to use the same parts across its models, allowing the auto manufacturer to design cars with small variations that can sell in multiple markets around the world.[13] However, the reliance on fewer suppliers is often perceived as reducing competition, thereby increasing costs. A focus on standardization can also result in missed new product or service opportunities because innovative ideas are not encouraged. As well, customers may feel limited in their choices and seek out the competition, resulting in lost sales.[14]

A well-conceived *standardization program* can result in cost reduction for an organization, as well as lead to efficiencies in procurement, inventory control, training and maintenance. Proper testing methods must be established to ensure that products provided are of acceptable quality. The use of a standardization committee is key to such a program. Besides supply management, which often assumes a leadership role with standardization, other departments to involve include engineering, operations, maintenance, sales and production. For example, the State of Wisconsin states in its procurement manual: "Standards committees may be formed by the State Bureau of Procurement for the purpose of drafting standard specifications or acceptable products lists, establishing standardized policies or procedures affecting a specific commodity or procurement technique, resolving disputes or rectifying unusual situations, or conducting pilot projects." Other activities could include seeking supplier input and setting up criteria for a benchmarking program.[15]

What areas are prime candidates for standardization? Just about any good or service that an organization buys can benefit. This certainly includes high-volume items that can result in leveraged pricing from a single supplier. For example, if several thousand light fixtures are purchased in a given year, selecting a standard fixture type for quality and appearance could be a very attractive opportunity for a lighting distributor. The opportunity for reduced pricing based on exclusive use could benefit both buyer and seller. Other areas, including the procurement of facilities and maintenance/repair/operating (MRO) supplies, should also be considered.

Standardization can include the designation of specific brand names, such as Hewlett Packard printers. It also can result in generic requirements that include product features which may open up the purchase to any manufacturer that can meet those requirements. The other outcome could be the establishment of a *qualified products list* (QPL), which is "a list of preapproved products of acceptable specifications for use by the organization" (ISM *Glossary* 2014).

In addition to effects within an organization, standardization can have an impact on both national and international fronts. As markets continue to globalize, the need for universal standards becomes even more important because, when non-harmonized standards exist in various countries or regions, trade barriers result. Developing nations are particularly aware of this challenge. As a result, the Slovenian Institute for Standardization, for example, has set national standards for Slovenia that are compatible with European and other international standards so it can attract business.[16]

Standardization also can prompt communication among designers, assisting with increasing the ratio of products to parts. For instance, an organization may have 50 products that are created from 500 unique parts, which results in a products-to-parts ratio of 0.1. If the same 50 products are created from 400 parts, then the ratio is improved to 0.125 and results in a higher standardization. This type of product standardization is a key part of just-in-time (JIT) inventory systems.[17]

A key component of a material standardization program is the cost/benefit analysis. This can help in "selling" the effort to senior management as well as justifying the decisions made by the standards committee. A *cost/benefit analysis* is a thorough "examination of both the costs and benefits of alternative courses of action in determining whether a course of action should be pursued" (ISM *Glossary* 2014). This will assist an organization in determining whether or not to pursue such action. In the case of a standardization program, the benefits described earlier in this chapter would be included, as well as the projected cost savings from reduced inventory and standardized training. When product standards are implemented, then only those subcomponents that support the particular product are necessary to have on hand in inventory. Logically, this saves time and money when fewer items are stocked. With a reduced need for training internal staff on maintaining multiple products or systems, additional efficiencies and savings are gained. Material standardization is likely to cost an organization up front for time and resources committed, but in the long run it can pay dividends with the efficiencies created.

When Deere & Company recognized that up to 70 percent of the manufactured product costs occurred externally, it aggressively pursued material standardization. This effort included the reduction of its standard shipping containers from 43 to 3. By taking aggressive steps early on in the process, it was able to reduce its supply chain costs significantly. By employing this and other lean supply strategies, Deere moved closer to one of its overall goals: to design products that delight its customers at the lowest total cost.[18]

While standardization certainly can result in holding fewer items, it differs from simplification. "*Simplification* is a reduction in the number of sizes and designs of an item that an organization uses" (ISM *Glossary* 2014). A good example of simplification is the 3M™ Wheel Weight System, which was designed to meet precision wheel balancing requirements. This allows organizations to reduce their costs by eliminating traditional wheel weight inventories of various sizes.[19]

Numerous international and professional standards groups develop and maintain standards such as the International Organization for Standardization (ISO), or help facilitate the creation and promotion of standards including the United Nations Standard Products and Services Committee (UNSPSC), the American National Standards Institute (ANSI) and the Institute for Electric and Electronic Engineers (IEEE). The following sections provide further discussion of these standards groups.

International Organization for Standardization (ISO)

ISO is the International Organization for Standardization, a network of the national standards institutes in more than 160 countries worldwide. A nongovernmental organization, ISO is based in Geneva, Switzerland, and offers one membership per country. In the United States, this member organization is the American National Standards Institute (ANSI). It acts as a bridging organization for the public and private sectors, while addressing the needs of business and consumers alike. To promote and develop global standards, third-party registration and accrediting councils evaluate an organization's quality systems.

When there is an absence of standards, products can be of poor quality or incompatible with existing equipment. ISO standards contribute toward making the supply of products and services consistent, efficient and safe. ISO is the world's largest developer of standards, including but not limited to ISO 9000, 14000, 50001, and 22000 (see Figure 9-3 for a brief description of each). ISO 9000 and ISO 14000 are the oldest standards, addressing quality management and environmental management systems, respectively; ISO 50001 deals with creating an effective energy management policy, and ISO 22000 addresses food safety management.[20]

Figure 9-3: ISO Standards

ISO STANDARD	DESCRIPTION
ISO 9000	Family of standards addressing aspects of quality management system (QMS): • ISO 9000:2005 — covers basic QMS concepts and language • ISO 9001:2008 — criteria for QMS • ISO 9004:2009 — guidance on making a QMS more efficient and effective • ISO 19011:2012 — guidance on internal and external audits of a QMS
ISO 14000	Family of standards addressing environmental management: • ISO 14001:2004 — sets criteria for an environmental management system (EMS) • ISO 14001:2004 and SMEs — provides a checklist for small businesses
ISO 50001:2011	Provides framework for requirements for developing, enforcing and measuring an energy management policy
ISO 22000	Family of standards that addresses food safety management (FSM): • ISO 22000:2005 — covers overall guidelines for FSM • ISO/TS 22004:2005 — guidelines for applying ISO 22000 • ISO 22005:2007 — addresses traceability in the feed and food chain • ISO/TS 22002-1:2009 — specifies the requirements for food manufacturing • ISO/TS 22002-3:2011 — specifies the requirements for farming • ISO/TS 22003: 2007 - guidelines for audit and certification groups

Source: International Standardization Organization (ISO), www.iso.org, accessed October 24, 2013

While ISO 9001 certification has reached an overall high level of maturity in Europe, there is still significant growth in certificates issued in Italy, East Asia and the Pacific Region, and the number of certificates issued for all other standards increased from 6 percent to 12 percent between 2010 and 2011.[21] Because of the focus on sustainability, however, ISO has seen an impressive growth rate of 25,000 ISO 140001 certifications per year, with 250,000 certifications issued in 155 countries through 2010.[22] (Sustainability and social responsibility also is discussed in Volume 1 of the ISM *Professional Series: Foundation of Supply Management*.)

There are a number of benefits to attaining ISO certification, including those listed below:
- Operations and productivity improve, which reduce costs;
- Quality improves, which can increase customer satisfaction, leading to increased sales;
- Organizations can gain access to new markets; and
- The negative impact on the environment is minimized.[23]

Quality assurance is a key issue for supply management professionals, and ISO standards can assist both internally and externally. Organizations that practice processes such as production and raw materials acquisition can be registered as ISO, as can outside suppliers. With more and more organizations throughout the world focusing on quality throughout the supply chain, ISO 9000 may very well be the most important family of standards for supply management.

Other Standards Organizations

While the ISO is well known, there are other organizations that manage or facilitate standard development including the GS1 US™, the United Nations Development Programme (UNDP), the American National Standards Institute (ANSI) and IEEE. GS1 US™ and UNDP, for example, manage The United Nations Standard Products and Services Code® (UNSPSC®), which is a global, multi-sector standard created to establish an efficient and accurate classification of products and services. It aids in gaining spend analysis visibility through its classification system, and helps supply management professionals make the best use of their electronic commerce capabilities.[24]

Founded in 1918, ANSI plays an important role in setting standards, bringing together interested U.S. individuals, organizations, government agencies and other groups to voluntarily create standards agreements. ANSI also "promotes the use of U.S. standards internationally...and encourages the adoption of international standards as national standards where they meet the needs of the user community."[25] As a founding member of the ISO, ANSI leads many of ISO's committees and carries forward U.S. standards for adoption as international standards. ANSI also "accredits standards developers, certification bodies and technical advisory groups (TAGs) to both the International Organization for Standardization (ISO) and the International Electrotechnical Commission (IEC)."[26]

IEEE, a membership-based professional association, is a "leading authority on areas ranging from aerospace systems, computers and telecommunications to biomedical engineering, electric power and consumer electronics."[27] The primary purpose of IEEE is to "foster technological innovation and excellence for the benefit of humanity."[28] The Institute develops and publishes industry standards for a wide range of technologies which are available at its website. It provides a good reference point for supply management professionals as they seek out and review specifications of innovative products and materials.

Quality Tools

The enemy of quality within the supply chain is inconsistency. By applying the quality tools discussed in the following sections, supply management professionals can achieve a consistent level of quality for their organizations.

Plan-Do-Check-Act Cycle

W. Edward Deming's four-step plan for process improvement is known as the plan-do-check-act (PDCA) cycle. The improvement cycle may seem intuitive, but it nevertheless has proved to be very effective as a problem-solving tool for countless organizations. A quality team begins by selecting a process that is flawed and documents it based on collected data. Once the team has prepared a cost/benefit analysis, it creates an improvement plan. It then implements the plan and measures the effect of the changes. The results then are measured against the original goals and, if deemed successful, the new process is standardized in the organization.[29] Kaoru Ishikawa further developed Deming's plan and created the six steps for quality improvement that are illustrated in Figure 9-4.[30]

Figure 9-4: Ishikawa's Six Steps

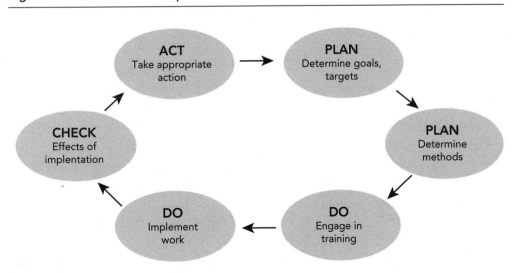

Source: K. Ishikawa, *What is Total Quality Control?: The Japanese Way*, Prentice-Hall, 1991.

Histograms

A *histogram*, as defined in the ISM *Glossary* (2014), is "a diagram of values being measured versus the frequency with which each occurs. When a process is running normally (only common causes are present), the histogram is depicted by a bell-shaped curve." A histogram is a useful tool for summarizing and displaying the distribution of a process data set. It is a simple graph that can be constructed by segmenting the range of data into equal-size groups. The vertical axis is labeled "frequency" and the horizontal access is labeled with the range of the variable being reported. A histogram conveys the most common response in the system as well as what distribution the data takes (varied, centered, and so on). For example, based on customer complaints a bank might investigate how long it takes a teller to serve the drive-up window. Figure 9-5 provides an example of a histogram based on the data the bank collected.

Figure 9-5: Service Time Frequency

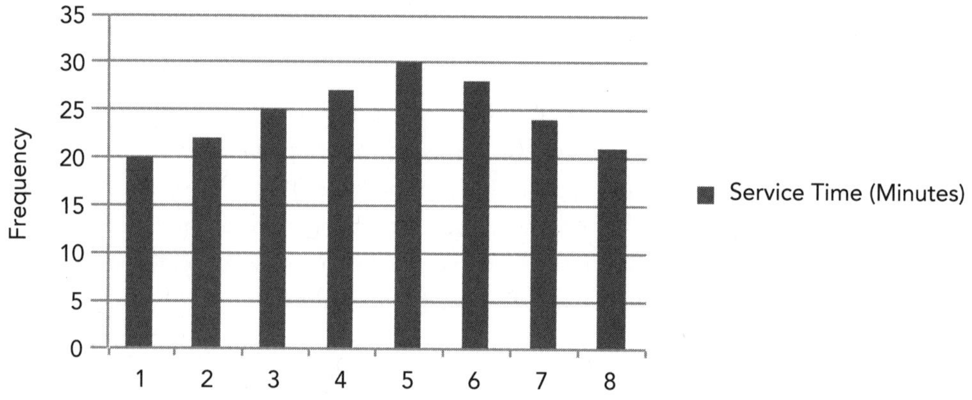

Pareto Analysis

Throughout history many have played a significant role in the development of quality management principles. Vilfredo Pareto was an Italian economist who studied the distribution of wealth. What he found was that a relatively small amount of the population (20 percent) controlled the majority of the wealth (80 percent). This has come to be known as the Pareto analysis, or the 80/20 rule. As mentioned in Chapter 8, his theory was the basis for the ABC inventory classification system, but it also played a significant role in quality management. Essentially what Pareto contended was that a vital few have the greatest impact on the whole; in other words, about 80 percent of the problems often result from only 20 percent of the potential causes. For example, most of the problems with suppliers may come from a small percentage of the supplier base, or just a few production areas can account for the largest share of defective products. As discussed in Chapter 2, Pareto analysis can also be used to identify potential process improvement projects.

In the 1930s, Dr. J. M. Juran conceptualized the Pareto analysis and the use of the Pareto chart, which allowed millions of managers to help differentiate the vital few from the useful many within the organization. His *Quality Control Handbook* still serves as a valuable reference for supply management professionals, because it provides guidance on how quality goods and services can lead to improved performance.[31] For example, if a supply management professional determined one of its suppliers was underperforming in deliveries, it might begin by searching for the underlying causes of poor performance. She would first identify the possible reasons for poor performance, go back through her records and collect data on the frequency of the possible causes over a period of time, and prepare a Pareto chart. Figure 9-6 provides a hypothetical example of the results. From there she could initiate an improvement process with her supplier.

Figure 9-6: Delivery Performance

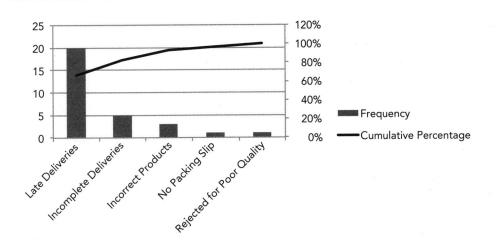

W. Edward Deming is considered one of the 20th century's leading authorities on quality. Deming contended that management actually controls 85 percent of the process while operations controls only 15 percent of the improvement. For instance, management has the ability to replace machinery if a current machine cannot consistently produce conforming products. It also has the authority to revise the acceptable tolerances within a specification.[32] An operator certainly plays a key role in the manufacturing process, but it is actually an organization's management team that has the greatest ability to improve quality. Deming's teachings stressed the need to constantly strive for improved quality and productivity. By monitoring the way a process works, rather than conducting mass inspections, an organization can improve productivity and lower its costs.

Fishbone Diagram

The *fishbone diagram* (also known as the "cause-and-effect diagram" and discussed in Chapter 2) was developed by Kaoru Ishikawa as a way to identify root causes of problems in a process that results in delays and waste. The problem itself is identified in the head of the fish, while major causes are noted at the major bones (see Figure 9-7). For each cause, the question of "Why?" is asked up to five times. These answers are the root causes that allow an organization to identify existing problems and ultimately improve quality. Ishikawa and Deming were colleagues, and both used this diagram when working with organizations to improve their management policies and practices.

Figure 9-7: Fishbone Diagram

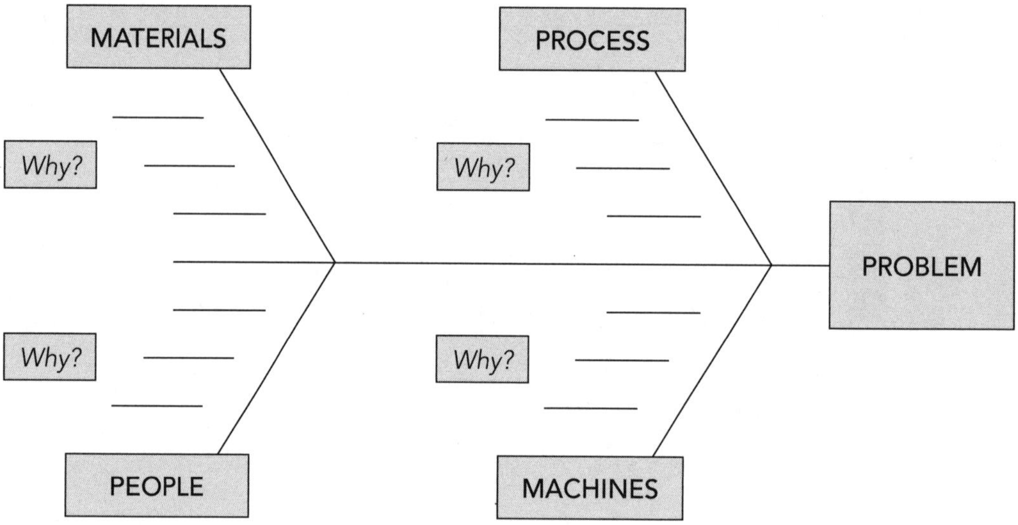

Run Charts

A *run chart* as illustrated in Figure 9-8 is a graphic representation of system performance over a period of time. "The X axis is time and the Y axis is the attribute being measured. With sufficient data, upper and lower control limits can be statistically derived that will indicate if future data points are in or out of control" (ISM *Glossary* 2014). The run chart can help determine if the system is stable, and can offer data against which to make future changes.

Figure 9-8 Sample Run Chart

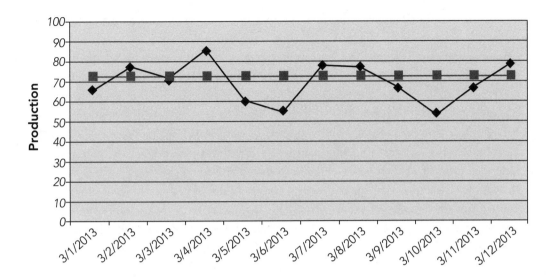

By understanding what a normal, predictable variation is, an organization can avoid under-controlling or over-controlling a process. Each improvement effort should include a team that evaluates system performance to assemble baseline data that changes can be evaluated against. The following steps are useful in constructing a run chart:

1. Plan how and where data will be obtained by writing an operational definition.
2. Complete the chart-identified information, including what is measured, dates, locations, collector and other relevant data.
3. Calculate the process average.
4. Calculate the upper and lower control limits.
5. Determine the scaling for the chart.
6. Interpret the chart.

When interpreting the run chart, an organization should look for the following results, for they can indicate an unstable process or one that is not in control:
- A point outside the limits (99.7 percent should fall within the limits);
- A run of seven points: above the center line, below the center line, going in one direction up, going in one direction down; or
- Nonrandom patterns: cycles (may indicate too many data are combined — shift, equipment, and so on), too close to average (center line), too far from average (center line).[33]

Statistical Process Control

Statistical Process Control (SPC) is a quality control method employed primarily in manufacturing that uses control charts to detect whether a process is under control. SPC uses the application of statistical control charts to measure and analyze the variation in processing operations. "The methodology monitors the process to determine whether outside influences are causing the process to go 'out of control.' The objective is to identify and correct such influences before defective products are produced, and thus keep the process 'in control' (ISM *Glossary* 2014). Service providers such as Taco Bell, Domino's and the Ritz-Carlton, however, also use SPC to improve operations. This method was originally used by Deming to assist the American war effort during World War II by improving industrial production methods. Deming introduced SPC to industry leaders in Japan after the war. He created a basis for the control chart and developed the concept of statistical control through a series of experiments. SPC is quite different than traditional quality control, where all finished products are inspected for conformance with predetermined specifications. Using statistical tools, SPC observes the performance of a production line to predict problems that can result in inferior products.

An example would be a production facility that fills plastic containers with liquid hand soap. When production is running as planned, the containers receive 10 ounces of product within certain tolerances. If the environment changes so can the inputs; if a belt pulley wears out it may dispense 10.5 ounces. Left unchecked, each overfill can result in waste and lost profits. By using statistical tools, such problems can be detected by quality personnel. When the root cause of such a variation is detected, it can be corrected before it becomes a larger problem. Many organizations require proof of SPC from suppliers, particularly for manufactured products they deem critical. Carlyle & Finch Co., a pioneer in arc searchlight technology, has discovered several benefits from using SPC software. The company makes more than 10,000 individual parts, and needed the software to meet government standards. Once fully functional, operators were able to easily enter inspection information and see any problems immediately on the chart. Part inspection time was down by 50 percent, and the percentage of rejects at final inspection was reduced by two-thirds. Best of all, customer-found defects were reduced to zero.[34]

Capability Indexes

Variations can occur in any manufacturing process, because each machine is different as is each component that is produced, even if the differences only are detectable by a microscope. The key is to ensure the variations stay within an upper and a lower specification limit. The capability of a process must be examined to see if it can produce within the required parameters on a consistent basis. Once any abnormal causes have been eliminated from the process, it is considered to be in statistical control. *Cp* and *Cpk* are two common ways to measure capability. Each of these methods compares the process spread with the specification spread, and measures the variation. Cpk measures how well-centered on the desired value the process spread is, as well as the tightness of the variation. For example, a food manufacturer might measure the exact weight of a product and compare it against the desired weight using a capability index.

Figure 9-9 illustrates the normal variation for a custom manufactured bushing, which has a specification spread of 3.030 inches +/- 0.030. This means the dimension should be 3.00 inches but can be as much as 3.03 inches or as little as 2.97 inches and still be within an acceptable tolerance. When a run of 50 bushings is produced, the results are noted, which represent normal variations.

Figure 9-9: Example of Normal Variation

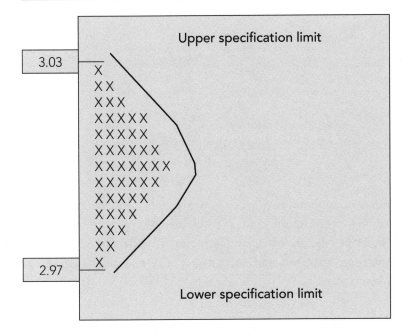

The middle of the range is known as the specification target. Ideally, these occurrences are minimized when the process spread is within the specification spread, and maximized when the process spread is outside the specification spread. When the bell curve is centered in the middle of the specification and is narrow (as shown in Figure 9-9), this indicates a quality process that is in control. When production units are not centered on the specification target, and more of the occurrences are outside of the set tolerances, that target is deemed unacceptable (see Figure 9-10). In this example, too many occurrences are falling within the upper end of the specification limit, which is why the bell curve appears higher than normal. These situations require attention, for the cause must be determined to correct production. Reasons for unacceptable production outputs can include an inexperienced operator, inferior properties of raw materials or a procedural change in methods between work shifts.

Figure 9-10: Example of Unacceptable Variation

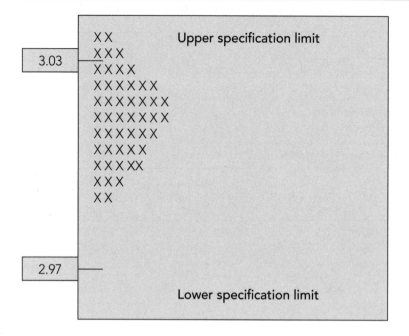

While these tools can be used to improve specific supply management activities and processes, a broader goal often is to assess and advance the supply management function. The following section describes the use of capability maturity models to appraise the current state of an organization's supply management capabilities, and use that appraisal as a baseline for such advancement.

Improving Supply Management Performance

The *capability maturity model* (CMM) is an appraisal process that was developed to measure and improve an organization's critical core capabilities. Mark Paul and a team of researchers at Carnegie Mellon University's Software Engineering Institute (SEI) developed the CMM in the 1980s to help military officers quickly assess and describe a contractor's ability to deliver the specified software on time. In 2014, the CMM model will be moved to the CMMI Institute at Carnegie Mellon (http://cmmiinstitute.com/). While the original intent was to measure the maturity level of the software development processes, several other process areas have since been added to the model. Although similar to ISO 9001, which sets a minimum standard to specify manufacturing and service industry quality levels, CMMs are more explicit in defining how to achieve continuous improvement within an organization. A CMM also confirms the progress an organization is achieving with its processes and helps make the benefits of process improvement visible to other employees.

The appraisal process is used to assess any needs within a customer-supplier relationship. It also can be used to help motivate and facilitate buy-in from various stakeholders within and outside an organization. Essentially, the capability maturity model is one tool that can help organizations determine the current maturity of their processes, identify the ones that need improvement, and then support their move to the next level of excellence through continuous improvement practices. CMMs provide a place to begin the road to improvement for a given process by bringing together the organization's past experiences. The model then allows team members to work within a structured framework to prioritize their actions and come up with a definition of what improvement means to their organization. Lastly, a maturity model can be used as a benchmark against other organizations.

Organizations generally go through five levels of process maturity:

1. *Initial.* The sourcing process is considered ad hoc, chaotic and hectic. Management understands the value of this process; it is accepted and practiced among the majority of organizations within a given industry. However, the life cycle of sourcing is not completely understood and the organization does not know any part of the process in any level of detail. Process documentation is used infrequently and on an ad hoc basis. Employees are not held accountable for using the process or following standard operating procedures.

2. *Repeatable.* The sourcing process has moved from the initial stage to where it is used more repeatedly because of external pressures. Parts of the process have been improved such as supplier assessment or contract management, but minimal improvement is evident over the initial stage for the entire sourcing process. There is no policy that requires the consistent use of the process or set standards.

3. *Defined.* The sourcing process is basically defined as a standard business process and required to be used by all levels of the organization. The sourcing activities are linked together and the process is more focused. People inside the organization now understand the effect of each activity on other activities. Formal documentation now has been created to standardize the process. Some metrics to measure performance begin to emerge.

4. *Managed.* The sourcing process is now an organized, standard business process, and management and measurement take place. The process has been fully integrated with all other core processes, and a supply management department emerges that is responsible for outsourcing. Metrics are used periodically to measure the process and make decisions.

5. *Optimized.* To remain at this stage the organization must seek process improvements and optimization in a formal continuous manner. Metrics are used systematically to measure process quality, efficiency and effectiveness. Continuous improvement practices are in place to improve the sourcing process. Process streamlining initiatives also are being implemented to improve the process.

The original CMMs have since been more fully developed into the capability maturity model integrated, which is discussed further in the following section.

Capability Maturity Model Integrated

The *capability maturity model integrated* (CMMI) is a collection of best practices that aid organizations in improving their processes. Released in 2001, CMMI integrates the CMM software used for the original capability maturity model, Electrical Industry Alliance Interim Standards, and Integrated Product Development CMM into one framework. Thus, CMMI can address several areas of improvement at the same time, rather than as separate initiatives, over the product development life cycle. The Standard CMMI Appraisal Method for Process Improvement (SCAMPI) uses oral presentations, demonstrations, surveys and databases and other instruments to rate the strengths and weaknesses of a given process based on the CMMI models. An appraisal team, which often is outsourced to third parties, makes the assessment. A CMMI product suite is available that provides a framework, models and appraisal methods, and materials.

CMMI also has been applied to the acquisition process for systems or services to improve supplier capabilities, which, in turn, can help them deliver products at a higher quality more quickly, at a lower cost, using the most suitable technology.[35] Known as CMMI-ACQ, it covers six process areas:

1. Solicitation and supplier agreement development;
2. Acquisitions management;
3. Acquisitions requirements development;
4. Acquisitions technical solutions;
5. Acquisitions validation; and
6. Acquisitions verification.

These six process areas are supplemented by 16 other process areas, including project management, organization and support.

One organization that has successfully adopted CMMI is the U.S. Navy. Its Team SPAWAR (Space and Naval Warfare Systems Command) was facing problems with one of its suppliers that was delivering software documentation on time but with multiple errors. The team decided to assess its supplier's processes using CMMI-ACQ and CMMI-DEV (which focuses on best practices to improve product and service development). Using a five-step process, the team developed an action plan for improvement. A major change was the co-location of a Navy technical specialist on the supplier's premises. This allowed for closer oversight of the supplier's processes and immediate guidance from the Navy when questions arose. Once implemented, major improvements occurred, including a 50 percent reduction in documentation errors, greater collaboration between the Navy and supplier, and the supplier's implementation of internal process training.[36]

Contract Management Maturity Model©

Effective contracts depend, to a great degree, on the processes used to create them. Thus, to award and successfully manage contracts, an organization should have processes in place that are disciplined and capable. Another tool developed in 2003 by the U.S. Department of Defense is the *contract management maturity model* (CMMM), which measures an organization's contract management process capability against the five levels described earlier, and then uses the evaluation as a guide to continuously improve process capability. The key contract management areas are (1) procurement planning, which identifies the business needs that will best be met by outsourcing; (2) solicitation planning — the preparation of documents to support the solicitation process; (3) solicitation; (4) source selection; (5) contract administration; and (6) contract closeout. These areas are all part of the Strategic Supply Management Concept identified earlier in the book (Figure S-1).[37]

There are five levels of contract management process maturity, as described in Figure 9-11. At the ad hoc level (level 1), rudimentary contract management processes exist with some informal documentation, but there is no accountability for not following the standards and processes. The better organizations transition through the second level (basic) to fully established and required processes throughout their organization as defined in the structured level (level 3). At this point, senior management is providing direction and approval for the contracting strategy, decision-making process, required documents, and the terms and conditions. The best organizations attain an integrated (level 4) or an optimized level (level 5), using performance metrics regularly to measure contract management processes. Continuous improvement efforts are in place by which the organization applies lessons learned from past experiences and establishes a set of best practices.[38]

Figure 9-11: Contract Management Maturity Levels

MATURITY LEVEL		DESCRIPTION
1	Ad hoc	Contract management processes exist and are accepted and practiced. Management understands the benefits of a contract management process. It includes some informal contract management process documentation and is used on an ad hoc basis. Managers and personnel are not held accountable for not following standards.
2	Basic	Some basic contract management processes and standards are in place but only required on complex, critical and highly visible contracts. Consistent policies and standards do not exist on other contracts. Processes and standards exist but have not been institutionalized throughout the organization.

Figure 9-11: Contract Management Maturity Levels

MATURITY LEVEL		DESCRIPTION
3	Structured	Contract management processes have been fully developed, institutionalized and mandated throughout the organization. Formal documentation has been developed, and some processes may be automated. The processes and documentation can be tailored for the unique aspects of each contract. Senior management provides guidance, direction, approval of contracting strategy, decision, documents, and terms and conditions.
4	Integrated	Contract management processes have been fully integrated with the organization's core processes and the end user or customer. Performance metrics are used periodically to measure the contract management process and make related decisions.
5	Optimized	Contract management processes are fully integrated with the organization's core processes and end user or customer. Performance metrics are used systematically to improve process quality. Contract management personnel apply lessons learned and develop best practices. Continuous improvement efforts are used to improve and streamline contract management processes.

Source: Adapted from G. A. Garrett and R. G. Rendon, *Contract Management: Organizational Assessment Tools* (Asburn, VA: National Contract Management Association, 2005).

Once some form of capability maturity model analysis is complete, organizations can engage in a two-pronged strategy: (1) continuous improvement activities, and (2) breakthrough improvement initiatives such as Six Sigma or Lean Six Sigma. Beyond performance assessment, organizations also must find ways to improve supplier performance to fulfill their missions and visions. The following section covers these issues.

Measuring and Evaluating Supplier Performance

Organizations today are relying on external suppliers more than ever, and this is expected to increase in the future. By developing strategies to align and manage supplier relationships, organizations can increase their ability to stay competitive. *Supplier performance measurement* is the process of measuring, analyzing and managing supplier performance for the purpose of reducing costs, mitigating risk and driving continuous improvement. With global competition, mass customization, increased customer expectations and harsh economic conditions, organizations are counting on their suppliers to furnish larger portions of parts, materials and assemblies formerly provided internally. There is also a high cost associated with failing to adequately manage a supplier's performance. It is estimated that billions of dollars are lost as a result of poor supplier performance. While it may not be practical to closely monitor all suppliers, it is important to focus on key suppliers. Most organizations monitor the performance of suppliers that meet one or more of the following criteria:

- Represents the largest portion of total spend;
- Produces a critical product;
- Is a large supplier in the market;
- Is located in a geographically desirable location; or
- Is needed to maintain a critical supply relationship.

For example, a manufacturer of healthcare equipment may use a performance management system only on those suppliers on which it spends more than US$500,000 annually. This may represent only 25 percent of its supplier base, but it is concentrating its efforts on the relationships that have the biggest strategic and financial impact on its organization.

Improving Supplier Performance

To improve supplier performance, organizations must first develop, measure and evaluate their own quality requirements, as discussed earlier in this chapter. Only by becoming aware of internal standards for quality can an organization realistically set the mark for its suppliers.

To determine the requirements and expectations of the final customer, an organization can use customer/user surveys and interviews. A survey can be a formal instrument — either written or electronic — or a less formal means of feedback such as personal conversations or correspondence. Whatever method is employed, the important thing is to obtain accurate and relevant responses from the customer or user. Once the survey results are tallied, they can be analyzed to develop product specifications. These can include acceptable levels of performance, use, safety and reliability. The selected suppliers then will need to comply with these requirements.

Focus Groups

When individuals are brought together "for a facilitated exchange of ideas about a specific topic for purposes of getting input and gaining perspective that may influence decision-making," this is referred to as a *focus group* (ISM *Glossary* 2014). This process allows organizations to research issues related to the products and services they provide in a market and to assess the needs of their customers. Focus groups can help them better provide existing services, as well as gauge how well a new product or service will be received. For example, an organization that specializes in data storage may use a focus group to gather feedback on the direction of data storage within the healthcare sector. This can help position it to expand into a new market with new customers, but it also can assist it with serving the needs of its existing clients.

Focus groups include a series of interviews with up to a maximum of about 12 people at the same time. A great deal of information is gathered during these interview sessions. To prepare, an organization must identify the major objectives of the sessions. Carefully developing the questions that will be asked of participants is an important part of the planning process. Of course, participants must be identified and provided with information about the session. This can include sharing the agenda, the questions to be asked and how participants can obtain the results of the focus group effort. Whether provided by an internal or external source, an experienced facilitator is key to a productive process. He or she can keep participants involved and moving in the right direction. Summary results in the form of a report will come out of the process, which will be forwarded to management so that decisions can be made.

Gauge Internal Requirements

It is also important to remember that supply management plays a key role within the organization. Supply management professionals negotiate on behalf of their internal customers, so it is critical that effective relationships be built with them, and that supply management professionals clearly understand their needs and requirements. The following represent ideal organizational characteristics:

- Working closely with the immediate customer on supply chain design, cost and customer issues;
- Understanding the end customer's wants/needs;
- Understanding market trends; and
- Recognizing the importance of communicating customer needs throughout the organization.[39]

Today's markets are more competitive than ever, so organizations must take advantage of any and all opportunities to improve their competitive advantage. Because most organizations rely on their suppliers more than ever, developing performance measurements for suppliers is necessary to ensure competitiveness. One of the hardest tasks an organization faces, however, is establishing its internal requirements and determining what to measure. A measurement must be meaningful, while at the same time it must be achievable. An important issue is to establish measures today with goals and objectives that can be accomplished tomorrow. The ability of an organization to measure is a critical key to its success.

Some important tools that can assist supply management professionals include scorecards, benchmarking, and the Supply Chain Operations Reference (SCOR®) Model. Scorecards can assist an organization in determining how well internal requirements are being met. A scorecard is "a performance measurement and management document that records the ratings from an evaluation process" (ISM *Glossary* 2014). *Benchmarking* is "a process by which selected practices and results of one organization are compared to those of one or more other organizations to establish targets for improvement. Benchmarking can be performed by identifying best-in-class organizations and visiting them for information gathering and comparison; or by responding to surveys from third-party independent research organizations that collect, aggregate and disseminate the benchmark data" (ISM *Glossary* 2014). Xerox Corporation was the first organization to use *competitive benchmarking* back in 1976. (Xerox collected data from several other organizations and generated a report that compared it to the aggregated data from the other "best firms."[40]) Since then, benchmarking has been used to measure performance throughout an organization, including manufacturing, marketing and supply management. Measurement areas to gauge supplier performance include the following:

- Order cycle times;
- Delivery reliability;
- Cost management;
- Frequency of delivery;
- Stock availability;
- Documentation quality;
- Order completeness; and
- Technical support.

The Supply Chain Council's SCOR® measurement model is widely used. SCOR® "offers definitions, mapping conventions, metrics and a methodology for constructing the map. It also includes all flows: information, goods and money" (ISM *Glossary* 2014). SCOR® considers the following:

- All customer interactions, from order entry through paid invoice;
- All product transactions, from a supplier's supplier to a customer's customer, including equipment, spare parts, bulk products, software, and so on; and
- All customer interactions, from the study of aggregate demand to the fulfillment of orders.

One organization using SCOR® that has been recognized for their operational excellence is Agilent Technologies. By using the SCOR® model, the organization was able to improve supply chain visibility, increase its responsiveness to customers, and reduce inventory.[41] Figure 9-12 offers a perspective on what an organization can benchmark using the SCOR® model.

Figure 9-12: SCOR® Performance Framework

CORE PERFORMANCE ATTRIBUTE	DEFINITION	HIGH LEVEL METRICS
Supply Chain Reliability	The ability to perform tasks as promised, on time, complete, with the right documentation	Percent of orders delivered in full Delivery performance to customer commit date Documentation accuracy Perfect condition
Supply Chain Responsiveness	The speed at which processes are consistently completed	Order fulfillment cycle time Source cycle time Make cycle time Deliver cycle time Delivery retail cycle time
Supply Chain Agility	The ability to respond to unforecasted events, both internal and external	Flexibility Adaptability
Supply Chain Costs	The cost associated with operating processes	Supply chain management cost Cost of goods sold Cost to plan Cost to source Cost to make Cost to deliver Cost to return Mitigation cost
Supply Chain Asset Management	The effectiveness in the management of assets to support demand	Cash-to-cash cycle time Days sales outstanding Inventory days of supply Days payable outstanding Return on supply chain fixed assets Supply chain fixed costs Return on working capital Accounts payable (payables outstanding) Accounts receivable (receivables outstanding) Inventory

Source: Adapted from "SCOR® Quick Reference Guide, Version 11.0", 2012, accessed December 6, 2013, https://supply-chain.org/f/SCOR11QRG.pdf; and, "Our Frameworks," https://supply-chain.org/our-frameworks

Developing Supplier Measures

Organizations throughout the world are working to improve their relationships with key suppliers. One of the most important decisions for them is which concept to apply when measuring the performance of the supplier. A concept that has been successfully employed time and again is the *balanced scorecard* (BSC). Developed by Robert Kaplan and David Norton in the early 1990s, the BSC "links performance measures to each other and also to the organization's vision and strategy. The key performance categories are financial performance, customer knowledge, internal business processes and learning and growth" (ISM *Glossary* 2014).

A *supplier rating system* is "a method used to evaluate and rate suppliers' performance, which generally emphasizes quality, service, delivery and price. Rating formulas vary depending on the nature of the item being purchased, the quality required and competition within the supply industry. More formalized systems require internal stakeholders to assign a weight (often out of 100 percent) to each key performance indicator" (ISM *Glossary* 2014). A supplier rating system can be developed to evaluate performance areas such as service quality, product defects and on-time deliveries. A set amount of points are possible to earn, with deductions for occurrences such as product failures and late deliveries attributable to the supplier. Figure 9-13 represents a typical system for rating suppliers.

Figure 9-13 Supplier Rating System

Supplier Name: Ace Electrical		
INDICATOR	POSSIBLE	SCORE

Product Quality
    Fitness for purpose
    Durability
    End customer satisfaction
    Packaging
	30	26

Service Quality
    On-site service
    Installation
    Training
    Warranty response
	25	21

Delivery Reliability
    On-time deliveries
    Late shipments
    Carrier consistency
    Over/under shipments
	20	18

Figure 9-13 Supplier Rating System *continued*

Supplier Name: Ace Electrical		
INDICATOR	**POSSIBLE**	**SCORE**

Service Quality
    On-site service
    Installation
    Training
    Warranty response
	20	21

Delivery Reliability
    On-time deliveries
    Late shipments
    Carrier consistency
    Over/under shipments
	20	18

Customer Service
    Responsiveness
    Flexibility
    Designated account manager
    Problem-solving
	15	12

Financial Administration
    Price competitiveness
    Invoicing procedures
    Timely payment to subs
    Financial stability
	10	7

Overall Rating	100	84

The goal of product quality is always zero defects. A *material reject rating* (MRR) divides the total number of rejected products by the total units received, calculating a percentage of reject materials. Considerations that go into delivery performance include cycle time reduction, delivery dates kept, short lead times and quick deliveries for urgent needs. When evaluating a supplier's cost performance, the *total cost of ownership* should be evaluated, including all costs associated with the acquisition of the good or service as well as any additional costs incurred before or after product or service delivery. According to the ISM *Glossary* (2014), "costs are often grouped into pre-transaction, transaction and post-transaction costs, or into acquisition price and in-house costs. To use cost of ownership analysis as a cost reduction tool, it is necessary to identify and analyze the cost drivers to look for any avoidable costs."

Many things are involved when evaluating a supplier's performance, so there can be potential distortions. For example, the subjectivity of the end user can impact a supplier rating in the areas of product quality and customer service. The expertise and training of the internal staff also can be a factor. And as with any process, the quality and validity of the data must be sound to be of value.

Supplier Audits

When determining the capability of a supplier, many indicators must be considered. A potential supplier may have a long history of performance, operate state-of-the-art facilities, possess ISO registration and have the desire to partner on a long-term basis. These are all positive signs indicating that a supplier is considered best-in-class, but additional evaluating still may be necessary. Using *supplier audits* is another helpful tool in supplier selection and monitoring. A supplier audit is "an assessment of a supplier's capabilities against a set of established criteria to verify the economics, ease of use and functional feasibility of the product or service to be purchased" (ISM *Glossary* 2014). It can include a review of documents, processes and facilities to affirm compliance with legal and contractual requirements.

There are three basic types of supplier audits; they are outlined below:
1. *Systems audit.* Checks internal documentation of compliance audits.
2. *Process audit.* Checks the supplier's cost, quality and delivery and other critical processes for capability and improvement.
3. *Product and service audit.* Checks the supplied product or service for conformance to technical standards and performance standards.

Normally, audits are formal and highly structured, beginning with an early discussion of the purpose and scope of the audit. Based on the scope and intent of the audit, an organization may investigate the following areas:
- Quality manual, procedures and work instructions;
- Organizational structure;
- Logistics processes;
- Cost sharing;
- Technical capabilities;
- Business to business (B2B) capabilities;
- Training and certifications;
- Documentation;
- Final product test and evaluation;
- Corrective and preventive actions;
- Measuring equipment and calibration; and
- Storage and delivery.

An audit is a snapshot in time of a supplier and its performance. Efforts should be made to ensure the picture is accurate and that the audit is done in a nonthreatening manner. Strategic partnerships with key suppliers should be viewed as long-term relationships that are mutually beneficial. An audit, therefore, should not be seen by either party as anything other than an opportunity to make improvements.

At times, an audit may identify a need for supplier training. This can include remedial training on an existing process or requirement. When a remedy or corrective action is needed, *remedial training* should be used. Supplier training can be provided by an organization's staff or by qualified third parties. Depending on the nature of the training, it may make sense to conduct it at the supplier's facility.

Effect of Legal Requirements

Part of the responsibility of supply management is to be aware of the legal requirements and obligations of its suppliers. Effectively communicating and negotiating with supplier representatives is certainly of value when managing performance, but at times it is necessary for an organization to claim its legal position.

Terms that are negotiated into a supplier contract can certainly be beneficial. Provisions that offer protection with regard to set delivery times, zero-defect product guarantees and on-site services are just a few examples. By being aware of these contractual requirements, the supply management professional can better position himself or herself during discussions of supplier performance. When a term or provision is included within the contract, the supplier has a legal obligation to perform. In most instances, the supply professional can leverage these terms to prompt supplier performance. There are, of course, legal remedies available through the judicial system when other, less formal means are unsuccessful. When legal remedies are pursued, it is wise for organizations to use legal counsel. Whether an organization employs in-house attorneys or secures these services through a contract, supply management professionals must be ready to work with legal counsel when dealing with complex issues. This is especially true in disputes arising with international suppliers when differences in languages, laws and business practices can create additional challenges.

Supplier Selection Factors

Because supplier selection practices significantly impact supply chain quality, they must be given top priority by supply management. This may be the best opportunity to pursue both prevention and quality at the source. Prevention deals with taking a strategic approach to avoid defects and problems before they occur. Ideally, this can be accomplished at the same time quality is being assured. As the lead in supplier selection, supply management professionals must consult with other business areas such as engineering, manufacturing and quality assurance. By gathering input from others and diligently evaluating potential suppliers, an organization can best position itself for top supplier performance.

As organizations of all types rely on outside suppliers, it is obviously important to properly select the best ones available. Supply management professionals aim to meet organizational needs through the use of suppliers, and ensure attributes such as quality, capability, technology and service. For example, a supplier's ability to fulfill customer requirements at a high level, and do so while simultaneously working with other customers, is an indicator of its *capacity* (see Chapter 3 for additional discussion). Meeting an organization's capacity requirements moves beyond the supplier's experience and expertise, and measures its ability to take on additional clients. If a consulting organization is ranked the best in its field, but is only a two-person team with a heavy schedule of engagements throughout the U.S. and South America, it simply may not have the ability (or capacity) to fulfill the requirements of a company seeking its assistance. The issue of *capability* looks at a supplier's experience and expertise, which verifies it is qualified within its area and has performed successfully for an extended period of time for other organizations. Therefore, it is important to assess both the capacity and capability of a supplier before considering it, as both are directly related to the quality the supplier can deliver.

Today's best practices include the development of key suppliers into partnership status. *Supplier development* is "a systematic effort to create and maintain a network of competent suppliers, and to improve various supplier capabilities that are necessary for the purchasing organization to meet its competitive challenges" (ISM *Glossary* 2014). Toyota is a good example of an organization that actively works with key suppliers to ensure quality. Personnel from the automobile manufacturer went into the supplier facility to explain exactly what was needed with regard to materials. These visits helped the suppliers identify waste and inefficiencies in their own systems and gave them an opportunity to improve them. This type of on-site collaboration was a departure from traditional negotiations, which were viewed as adversarial. Toyota's approach provided benefits for both parties, and was truly viewed as a win-win situation.[42] The services and products provided by supplier partners are done so in a seamless manner, and a great deal of confidence is instilled in them. These supplier partners are capable and mature, and they have proved themselves by delivering the highest quality of services at competitive prices. Most organizations possess only a handful of these partners.

Weighted Average Method. Many factors can be involved in supplier selection, and these can vary from organization to organization. Cost and cost management, availability, technology, past performance and financial stability are some of the common issues of concern to supply management professionals. Once these factors are selected, organizations often use some form of a *weighted average method* for evaluation purposes. Each factor is assigned a weight based on its relative importance to the acquisition. The ultimate goal is to enter into an agreement with a qualified supplier that provides quality goods and services. To help ensure such quality, a review of a supplier's past practices in providing quality is a good idea. A buying organization can look at its own experience with a supplier (asking, "has it provided quality in the past?"), as well as the experience of other customers. By reviewing a supplier's quality assurance policies — and even visiting its facility, a supply professional can better determine quality practices.

This is also an area where certifications and registrations from third parties can prove beneficial. As discussed earlier in this chapter, an ISO certification is a strong indicator of a supplier's commitment to quality processes. *Good Manufacturing Practices* (GmP) was "first prepared by the World Health Organization (WHO) in 1967, and currently extended through international organizations and country-specific regulations, GmP ensures quality assurance, compliance and good product development within the therapeutic goods industry, including pharmaceutical, biotechnology and medical device industries. This concept has been extended to food packaging to ensure quality, hygiene and traceability. In the U.S., the European Union, India, Canada and other countries, these regulations have the force of law and require that manufacturers, processors and packagers of drugs, medical devices, some food, and blood take proactive steps to ensure that their products are safe, pure and effective. GmP regulations require a quality approach to manufacturing, enabling companies to minimize or eliminate instances of contamination, mix-ups and errors. In the U.S., the Food and Drug Administration (FDA) administers and monitors the standards" (ISM *Glossary* 2014). The FDA tracks problems and can inspect the operations of a manufacturer to ensure compliance with GmP.

Supplier Testing. A determination should be made about the extent of testing that will be conducted, as well as what test methodologies will be used. A competitive and widely used measurement in certain industries is *parts per million* (PPM), which refers to the average number of defective parts produced out of one million. Earlier in this chapter, the Six Sigma and Lean Six Sigma programs were discussed, which require a level of 3.4 PPM defect levels. This achievement of quality certainly is best-in-class.

Regardless of the testing method or standard, the procurement organization and the supplier must be in agreement. Lockheed Martin Missiles and Fire Control (MFC), 2012 winner of the Malcolm Baldrige award, has taken steps to ensure the quality of its suppliers and, at the same time, provide quality service to the customer. As a result, supplier delivery time and quality have been virtually 100 percent since 2006 and 2007, respectively. And, even with a growth rate of 1,000 percent since 2001, MFC has achieved an on-time performance delivery record of 99.4 percent. According to the Baldrige survey of MFC's customers, all said they would probably or definitely continue doing business with MFC.[43]

Quality often is associated with parts and components, but it is equally important when acquiring services. Many organizations ensure service quality through the use of service level agreements, which are addressed in the following section.

Service Level Agreements

The services sector represents more than half the gross domestic product (GDP)[44], and is one of increasing spend for supply management. Today, supply management develops contracts for all types of professional services including computing, janitorial, health insurance, advertising, legal services and financial advice, among others. A *service level agreement* (SLA) is a common tool used within the service sector to define the work scope, set expectations, and define the relationship of the buyer and service provider. The SLA also addresses what the provider is promising, how the services will be performed, the metrics and means of measurement, the consequences in the event of failure to perform, and any long-term aspects of the agreement (ISM *Glossary* 2014).

An SLA will assist both parties in better understanding the roles and responsibilities of each other. It can lead to increased customer satisfaction, as well as improved lead times and on-time deliveries. The agreement spells out an organization's expectations and what can happen if they are not met. If properly established, it can greatly benefit the buying organization in managing supplier performance. The quality of a service provider can be measured in a number of ways and, whichever method is employed, it should be spelled out in the SLA. Metrics that assess quality should address the following:

- Service quality performance;
- Cost management;
- Reliability performance;
- Customer satisfaction;
- Response time;
- Corrective action responsiveness;
- Parts per million levels (Six Sigma);
- Reject of service-related materials;
- Quality of performance;
- Accuracy;
- Completeness of work product;
- Technology;
- Customer service; and
- Customer availability.[45]

Inspection and Testing. When an organization contracts for services and includes an SLA, a provision for inspecting and testing quality may be included. *Inspection* is the "act of checking the quality of products and services to determine whether they meet specifications" (ISM *Glossary* 2014). In an information technology service arena, for instance, the quality of computer components may be subject to inspection on an intermittent basis. Likewise, the quality of the service could be inspected, including a key requirement for system uptime. There may even be a penalty in the SLA for downtime outside of an acceptable level. Although 100 percent uptime may be every organization's goal, the standard may vary depending on the service provided.

To truly establish a win-win relationship with SLAs, the following steps should be considered:

1. *Gather background information.* Before asking for commitments from its supplier, an organization must carefully review its needs and priorities. Also, the supplier should assess its service history and realistically determine the level of service it can provide.
2. *Ensure agreement about the agreement.* Sometimes the parties to an agreement can have very different views of what can be accomplished. Before developing the SLA, it is a good idea to have a candid discussion to ensure there is basic agreement about the SLA.

3. *Establish ground rules for working together.* The parties need to discuss and agree on the division of responsibility for tasks, scheduling and potential impediments. Identifying communication styles and preferences also can minimize conflict.
4. *Develop the agreement.* This is an important step, but certainly not the only step. With assistance from each organization, the agreement must be debated and negotiated with regard to content. This step can take several weeks or even several months. Figure 9-14 provides a template for a service level agreement.
5. *Generate buy-in.* Before finalizing the SLA, all stakeholders must weigh in and make suggestions. Besides gathering team buy-in, this step also will improve the quality of the final agreement.
6. *Complete the pre-implementation tasks.* Identify and complete the tasks that need to precede implementing the agreement. This may include developing tracking and reporting mechanisms, as well as training.
7. *Implement and manage the agreement.* A point of contact should be established for problems, maintenance of ongoing communication, service reviews and implementing modifications.[46] The management of an SLA is a key function and requires a variety of skills. One must be knowledgeable of the operational needs of its organization, but must also be familiar with the other party's business practices. Being skilled in communications and negotiations is important, as well as being able to commit the necessary time and energy to the agreement. Serving as the point of contact for any problems or concerns and regularly assessing how the relationship can be improved also is important.

McDonald's America uses SLAs when contracting with its point-of-sale information technology (IT) suppliers, and the standards are high. According to David Grooms, CIO, a supplier must "be accessible at an individual restaurant level" and strictly live up to the terms of its SLA. Once the agreement is signed, suppliers are reviewed quarterly against the SLA to assure compliance. In 2008, McDonald's selected Par Tech as its first IT Supplier of the Year from more than 100 candidates using SLAs along with supplier scorecards.[47]

Figure 9-14: Service Level Agreement Template

This template covers recommended terms and conditions to incorporate into a Service Agreement. Agreement terms and conditions should, at a minimum, include the following:

Introductory Paragraph
Introductory paragraph includes effective date, parties involved and effective date.

1. Services Provided
Contractor shall provide those services listed and described in Exhibit A attached hereto and incorporated herein by reference ("Work").

2. Compensation
During the term of this Agreement, the compensation payable by Customer to Contractor for Work shall be determined in accordance with the provisions of Exhibit B attached hereto and incorporated herein by reference.

3. Expenses
Covers who will be responsible for expenses above those addressed in Exhibit B.

4. Invoicing and Payment
Clarifies payment cycles, payment terms and details required on invoice(s).

5. Standard of Performance and Personnel
Stipulates the work must be performed according to a stated standard and by qualified personnel.

6. Inspection and Acceptance
Includes information on the organization's ability to monitor and accept the Work.

7. Warranty
Include all warranty language here.

8. Indemnification
Insert indemnification provisions.

9. Insurance
Specify the types and amounts of insurance to be required of the contractor.

10. Confidential Information
Carefully and fully detail ownership and protection of confidential information.

11. Duration of Agreement
Specify the dates the contract remains effective. Insert automatic renewal language if appropriate.

12. Cancellation for Cause
Outline what will constitute cause(s) for cancellation.

13. Termination for Convenience
Outline conditions for convenience termination.

14. Subcontracting/Assignment
Specify if work can or cannot be subcontracted or assigned.

15. Audit and Examination of Records
Reserve the right to audit and examine contractor records for a specified period of time.

Figure 9-14: Service Level Agreement Template   *continued*

16. Set-Off
Retain the right to deduct from monies due and specify conditions for the off-set.

17. Notices
Identify where notices will be communicated for the parties.

18. Compliance with Laws
Insert requirement to observe and comply with applicable laws.

19. Applicable Law and Venue
Specify the jurisdiction in which the agreement is governed.

20. Entire Agreement
Make clear the document sets forth all conditions and specifies how future modifications, if any, will be managed.

Signatures and Date
Signatures are required from both parties.

Source: Institute for Supply Management®

Minimizing Risk of Counterfeit Components

A growing risk is the use of *counterfeit components*, which are items produced by an unlicensed manufacturer that are labeled and marketed as genuine. In many cases, these components are indistinguishable from the real parts, but are of inferior quality. Depending on the application, these counterfeit components could fail and cause major problems for an organization. There has been increased use of counterfeits in the technology industry; even the U.S. government purchased new computer equipment containing these components. This is another area for ensuring quality from a supplier, particularly those that provide customers a finished product comprised of many subcomponents acquired from second-tier and third-tier suppliers. Prime suppliers should be questioned about their quality control practices in these areas, and specifically how they ensure quality from their own supplier base. Verification of policies and practices that prevent the use of counterfeit components is likely to become more common in the future. With recent increases in fake parts such as oil filters, brake pads and fuel filters in Ghana, Toyota Ghana took action in 2012 and initiated the "2012 Anti-Counterfeit Educational Campaign" using workshops, billboards and jingles to "educate customers on safety measures to avoid accidents," and condemned the use of counterfeit parts.[48] In the Middle East, BMW Group Middle East launched a regional campaign in 2013 to increase awareness and warn of the dangers of counterfeit spare parts.[49]

Summary

Ensuring quality throughout the acquisition process is an important focus for today's supply management professional. In all industries and sectors, supply management professionals must be familiar with quality processes and realize they need to play a key role in matters relating to supplier quality. As strategic outsourcing and relationship management continue to grow in use, the opportunity will continue for supply management to increase its value to its organization.

Feedback from final customers can assist with developing requirements and specifications. Supplier relationships are managed in accordance with these requirements to ensure that products and services are provided in a timely manner. Organizations must realize that markets are competitive today, and that by focusing on issues of quality they can be positioned for success.

Key Points

1. Quality management ensures that all activities to design and implement a product or service are effective and efficient.
2. Quality control compares the actual quality received with the intended goals.
3. Six Sigma is a quality process that strives for a measure of quality near perfection and uses relevant data to eliminate defects; Lean Six Sigma incorporates lean thinking to eliminate waste and improve quality.
4. ISO is the International Organization for Standardization, with the American National Standards Institute serving as the U.S. member.
5. The capability maturity model (CMM) is an appraisal process that was developed to measure and improve an organization's critical core capabilities.
6. The capability maturity model integrated (CMMI) can address several areas of improvement at the same time over the product development life cycle.
7. The Contract Management Maturity Model measures an organization's contract management process capability against five levels, and then uses the evaluation as a guide to continuously improve process capability.
8. The SCOR® model is a diagnostic tool that uses processes, metrics and best practices to benchmark an organization's performance.
9. The balanced scorecard, developed by Kaplan and Norton, links performance measures to each other and also to the organization's vision and strategy.
10. According to Deming, management has the ability to control the majority of a process improvement.
11. Service level agreements are commonly used within the service sector. An SLA defines the work scope, sets the expectations and defines the relationship between the organization and the service provider. It also addresses what the provider is promising, how the services will be performed and the means of measuring performance.

CHAPTER 10

Performance Evaluation

A challenging task for any organization is determining when, what and how to measure its performance. By focusing on particularly troublesome issues or processes, an organization can better identify what needs to be done and then fix it. Many industry leaders feel that an organization's ability to measure is a key to its success. Once measurements have been selected, then performance must be evaluated against those measurements.

Performance evaluation is key to supply management's success. This chapter starts by providing an overview of performance evaluation and measurement and why it is so important. Next, a discussion of the tools and processes that are important to measure, report and improve compliance with supply management policies and external parties is provided. To meet stakeholder needs, performance results must be evaluated and performance corrected. One of the ways to measure performance is by using key performance indicators. A corrective action process will take the results of a performance evaluation and make the necessary changes for improvement.

Supply management professionals also must be aware of various management reporting requirements, including those of the ISO, GAAP and Sarbanes-Oxley.

The final section in this chapter covers the evaluation of employees, whose objectives must be aligned with organizational goals. Criteria for their success must be determined and appropriate appraisal factors developed. Multiple sources of feedback are available for evaluating employees, including peers, customers and suppliers. With the continued advancement of the supply management profession, and the increased importance of supply management in the organization, professional development becomes more important than ever. Many opportunities exist for lifelong learning.

Chapter Objectives

- Discuss how supply management can create and employ performance measurement.
- Define performance measurement and discuss the interrelationship of measurements.
- Describe how to analyze and resolve issues raised in supply management audit reports.
- Discuss social responsibility and supplier diversity, and their roles in compliance.
- Identify the appraisal and evaluation tools that can improve employee performance.
- Discuss the importance of professional development and education for supply management professionals.

Overview

According to the ISM *Glossary* (2014), *performance evaluation* is "a comparison of actual performance to a planned level or standard to determine the degree of achievement as well as opportunities for improvement" (ISM *Glossary* 2014). *Performance measurement* is "a management technique for evaluating the performance of a particular function, person or organization, such as a supplier" (ISM *Glossary* 2014). In this chapter we will focus on the performance of the supply management professional. Measures are typically broken down into two general categories: effectiveness and efficiency. *Effectiveness measures* are outcome-focused and compare the degree that an organization or supply management professional met some previously set goal or standard, based on his or her chosen course of action. In other words, are we doing the right things? For example, the supply management organization might be measured on the success of a supplier rewards program. *Efficiency measures*, on the other hand, are output-focused and look at "relationship between planned and actual sacrifices made to realize a previously agreed-upon goal."[1] Simply put, are we doing things right? For example, an organization might develop a measure entailing the backlog of contracts that need to be renewed.

Performance measurement is important for a number of reasons. First, it helps organizations make better decisions, because measurement visibly tracks supply management's and individual performance. Visibility allows managers to spot problem areas, provide feedback and make corrections. Second, communication tends to increase and improve as the measures are discussed, coaching and mentoring take place, and plans of action are formed and implemented. Third, measurement can positively change behaviors if the right measures are used, and appropriate rewards are attached. People behave according to how they're measured, so measurement can motivate them to work toward improving their performance.[2]

When evaluating performance it is important to understand the major steps in the process. Figure 10-1 depicts the steps involved in performance evaluation.

CHAPTER 10: Performance Evaluation

Figure 10-1: Performance Measurement Steps

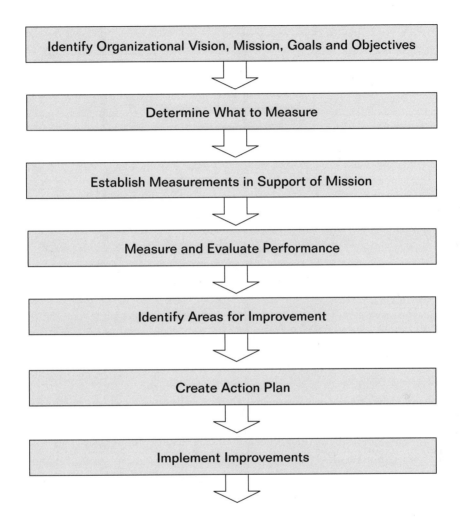

What to Measure

Numerous measurements can be considered, so the key is to find those that are meaningful for an organization, particularly as they relate to supply management. A heavy equipment manufacturer will likely have measurements that differ from those of an electronics distributor, but there are some common attributes of good performance measures. Among other things, they need to be customer-focused, credible, cost-effective and comparable. Figure 10-2 illustrates the criteria for good performance measures.

Figure 10-2: Criteria for Good Performance Measures

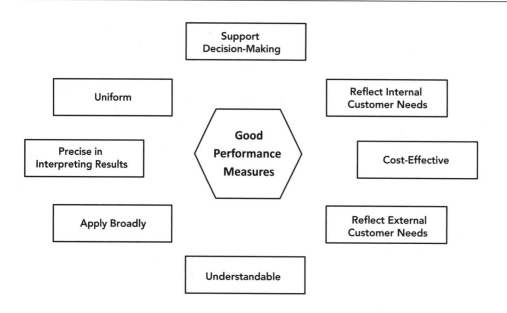

Source: Adapted from Oak Ridge Associated Universities, "Development Processes, Performance Measurement Process," accessed October 27, 2013, http://www.orau.gov/pbm/handbook/1-1.pdf.

Measurements, first and foremost, must support the strategic vision, mission, objectives and goals of the organization. Just as supply management serves to achieve the organization's mission, so do the performance measurements that are put in place. This is a direction that top leaders must both set and support. Leading organizations successful in measuring performance have created a culture of participation and continuous improvement.

Sodexo, a provider of quality of life solutions to individuals and organizations in 80 countries, has designed its measurements with its mission and objectives in mind. According to Ann Oka, senior vice president of supply management, a balanced scorecard is used to support key objectives such as "to create sustainable value, grow its business, develop its people, enhance execution and live company values. This scorecard aligns our goals, keeps our focus and communicates our progress to team members."

Oka continues, "Within supply management, we monitor employee training programs, the robustness of our succession planning process, and the actual (versus planned) delivery of our employee development plans. We formally survey internal customers annually, which is critical as we make year-over-year delivery improvements. We also use an anonymous third-party survey to gauge if our team members have the appropriate information, direction, tools and interactions to execute effectively. At the senior level, 360-degree performance evaluations are used. Sodexo also uses select metrics to gauge performance, spot opportunities for improvement and determine how best to apply resources. Because organizations focus on what they measure, those measurements must drive action."[3]

Interrelation of Measurements

Measurements also must be interrelated, so that they contribute to the flow of smooth operations within supply management. For example, actual price compared to plan, actual prices versus market index, and target prices achieved are examples of interrelated price performance measures. When measurements interface and complement each other, it is certainly an ideal situation. If the accuracy of a sales forecast can assist production by adjusting inventory on hand, for instance, this is an indication that the right measurements are in place.

Measurement Creation

Traditional measurements focused heavily on labor productivity and often overlooked true cost drivers such as product design, process complexity, quality issues and manufacturing flexibility. Measurements today need to focus on two critical areas: the customer and the competition. This typically involves measures of throughput and lead times, as well as financial measures such as asset utilization and profitability.[4] Many experts feel that if something cannot be measured, then it cannot be managed. Of course, when determining which measurements are needed, an organization must always keep in mind the needs of the customers, for they will ultimately determine the organization's success and performance, whether it offers a product or a service. Measurements must not only address the current needs of the customers, but also must be able to change as customer needs and demands change. This is why performance evaluation should be considered an evolving work in progress. Measurements and metrics that are effective today are likely to be modified or replaced in the future.

No matter the size, sector or specialization, organizations normally focus on the same general aspects of performance:
- Financial considerations;
- Customer satisfaction;
- Internal business operations;
- Employee satisfaction; and
- Community and shareholder satisfaction.[5]

For private organizations, a principle measure of success is monetary profit. While public sector agencies may not be striving for profit, they should be looking to maximize performance. They are accountable for the achievement of program goals and service delivery by legislators, suppliers and the general public. Publicly held corporations are accountable to their shareholders and public agencies to their taxpayers, but most best-in-class organizations place customer service at the top of their measurements.[6]

Results Evaluation

Once performance has been evaluated, the results must be acted on. The performance information first is formally reviewed and management is provided feedback on how future performance plans might be adjusted. An organization's performance information is used to perform benchmarking against its predetermined goals, as well as to run a comparative analysis against other organizations. This comparison will help identify opportunities for re-engineering and reallocation of resources. Top organizations that are industry leaders and are profitable year after year must be doing something right. Reviewing their best practices in the area of performance evaluation can serve as good indicators of how they achieve such success.

The results of performance evaluation should be reported throughout the organization. By sharing the performance data internally, management can continue to build a level of trust and a culture of continuous improvement. Sales performance for the global organization, for instance, can be shared with the organization's locations throughout the world. Technology can serve as a great communications tool, such as posting performance information on an intranet.

Performance results also must be communicated externally. Customers and shareholders will find this information quite valuable. Many organizations share performance data through annual reports that are made available to shareholders, executives, industry associations and the general public. Hopefully, sharing quality information can help enhance performance in the future. It can help set priorities and decision-making down the road, for the feedback from shareholders and customers influences strategic decision-making. Once performance is evaluated and reported for a set time period, the performance measurement process then starts again for future periods.

Key Performance Indicators

Key performance indicators (KPIs) can assist an organization in defining and measuring its progress. KPIs are quantifiable measurements of the improvement in performing an activity that is critical to business success (ISM *Glossary* 2014). A KPI needs to complement the overall targets of an organization and relate to its key activities. The KPIs will differ based on the type and size of the organization, but examples can include increases in international orders, help desk calls resolved promptly or percentage of on-time customer deliveries. Financial KPIs focus on gross sales, supply chain costs or working capital while allowing the organization to monitor and control its cash flow and profitability. Used as a performance management tool, a KPI can measure factors such as employee turnover, which can be an indicator of stability in the workforce.

Each KPI will need a title, definition, method of measurement and target. The number of KPIs should be limited and allow for the achievement of business goals. This keeps everyone focused on the key objectives and makes performance monitoring easier.

How does an organization choose the right KPIs? The indicators chosen must include the following:

- Reflect the goals of the organization;
- Be critical to its success;
- Be measurable and comparable; and
- Allow for corrective action.[7]

Figure 10-3 includes some KPIs that can be used within a supply management organization.

Figure 10-3: KPIs for Supply Management

TITLE	DEFINITION	MEASUREMENT
Customer Service	Satisfaction of final customers for services and good received	Percentage of customer responses that rate services as good or excellent
On-Time Delivery	Requested products delivered within requested time line	Percentage of orders delivered by customer requested date or earlier
Inventory Accuracy	Actual inventory on hand correctly reflected in inventory records	Percentage of inventory counted that matches computerized record
Cost Savings	Reduction in costs incurred that has tangible benefits (can be used for purposes other than originally intended)	Year-to-year cost savings Cost savings as percentage of budget Cost savings from financial audit
Quality of Goods	The quality of the goods, materials and services received	Level of quality Reject rate of materials
Total Costs	Combination of purchase or acquisition price of a good or service, and any additional costs incurred before or after delivery.	Total cost of ownership Life-cycle costs Supply chain costs
Lead Time	Time spent in the procurement process	Percentage of lead time reduced in procurement cycle
Value Beyond Cost	Non-cost benefits to the procurement process	Innovation Supply continuity/risk Revenue generated Social responsibility Assets acquired

Source: Adapted from A.J. Van Weele, *Purchasing & Supply Chain Management*, 5th ed., 2009, (CENGAGE Learning EMEA); R.M. Monczka and P.L. Carter, "Supply Management: Strategies for Success in the New Economy," presentation at the 96th Annual International Supply Management Conference, May 2011; and ISM *Glossary of Key Supply Management Terms*, Institute for Supply Management®, 2014.

Performance Management Systems

An *earned value management system* (EVMS) is used to establish a relationship between the cost, schedule and technical aspects of a project. It measures progress, accumulates actual costs, analyzes deviations from original plans and forecasts the completion of events. It also can make sure changes in a project are incorporated in a timely manner (ISM *Glossary* 2014). Advantages of using an EVMS as a project management tool include improving the definition of the work scope, preventing scope creep, communicating progress to stakeholders and keeping the project team focused on achieving progress. Essential features of any EVMS implementation include the following:

- A project plan that identifies work to be accomplished;
- A valuation of planned work, which is called plan value (PV); and
- Predefined earning rules or metrics to quantify the accomplishment of the work, which is called earned value (EV).

For large or more complex projects, the EVMS implementation may include additional features, such as indicators of cost performance (is the project over or under budget?) and schedule performance (is the project ahead of or behind schedule?). EVMSs, however, do have limitations. While indicating whether a project is on time, on budget and work scope is completed, it does not necessarily measure quality. It is, still, a valuable tool for supply management. (Additional information on EVMS can be found in Chapter 2.)

Value stream mapping can be applied to either goods or services as a technique to determine if there is waste in a process. It was originally used in manufacturing where "the transformation of materials was traced from the beginning of a process to the very end to determine if there is waste in the process, either in the form of a step where no value is added or a point of 'wait time' when material is being stored to await further value-adding transformation" (ISM *Glossary* 2014).

A method of measuring an organization's activities in terms of its vision and strategies is the *balanced scorecard* (BSC). This gives management a comprehensive view of business performance at a glance. It focuses not only on financial outcomes but also on the human issues that can drive the outcomes. Implementing the scorecard typically involves four steps:

1. Translating the vision into operational goals;
2. Communicating the vision and its link to individual performance;
3. Business planning; and
4. Providing/reviewing feedback and adjusting the strategy accordingly.

Organizations use a BSC to clarify and update their budgets, identify and align strategic initiatives, and conduct performance reviews to improve strategies.[8] This process views an organization from four different perspectives: (1) customer, (2) financial, (3) internal business processes, and (4) learning and growth. Metrics are developed, and data is collected and analyzed from each perspective. Veolia Water, a world leader in water and wastewater services to municipal and industrial customers, adopted the balanced scorecard process. The process was designed "to boost organizational performance; break down communication barriers between business units and departments; increase focus, strategy and results; budget and prioritize time and resources more effectively; and help the company better understand and react to the customer." Veolia started at the business unit level and then implemented the process down to the functional level. The end result has been a framework that supports growth initiatives, and helps Veolia measure the progress of its global facilities while maximizing its resources.[9] Figure 10-4 illustrates the balanced scorecard.

Figure 10-4: Balanced Scorecard

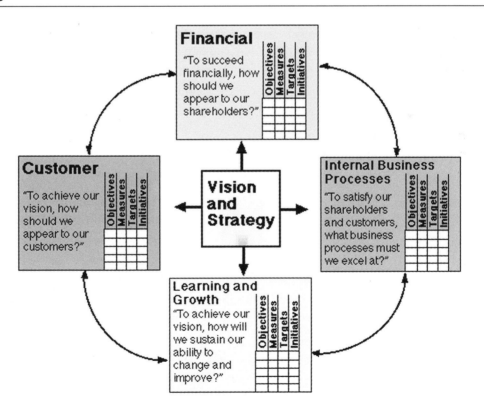

Source: 12 Manage, "Rigor and Relevance in Management," The Netherlands. Available from www.12manage.com/methods_balancedscorecard.html. Reprinted with permission.

Corrective Action Process

The performance measurement tools discussed so far in this chapter can assist supply management professionals in recognizing good performance as well as poor performance. First, a group of qualified individuals should identify potential performance problems and fully describe each one in measurable terms. The next logical step is to prioritize each problem. Prioritizing them based on factors such as criticality, importance to the customer, and cost to correct should be used to determine which problem(s) should be tackled first. A cost/benefit analysis can be very helpful in determining which problem(s) should be addressed first. Verifying the root causes of a problem is also important to finding a solution and preventing its recurrence. Once a problem has been selected as a high priority, determining the appropriate action for correcting the problem is the next step. A *corrective action process* is a means to identify, analyze and correct problems in process or performance. Conversely, a *preventive action* occurs when proactive steps are taken to avoid a problem. Often, short-term corrective actions can be put in place until a permanent solution is implemented. Once corrective action has taken place, the process should be reviewed to validate that the actions have corrected the problem. If not, the corrective action process should be repeated to continue to look for an optimal solution. The plan-do-check-act cycle described in Chapter 9 is commonly used to correct problems. As an international leader in the area of quality improvement, Federal Express Corp. (FedEx®) has identified several measurements that are key to customer satisfaction. An internal team works continually to reduce failures in areas such as damaged packages, missing proof of delivery, invoice adjustments and lost packages. These activities support FedEx®'s commitment to speed and reliability, both of which are key to staying competitive in its industry.[10]

Supply Management Audits

There's the old adage that preventive practices cost US$1, a defect caught during normal operations costs US$10, and the same defect caught after it has been sold costs US$100. The numbers aren't realistic but the point is the same: auditing is a good tool to prevent problems from occurring again. At the same time, mistakes will be missed and audits are a way to uncover those errors, make corrections, and change processes to prevent those mistakes from happening again. All audits should be viewed as opportunities to identify areas for improvement in an organization. Regardless of the reason for audits, supply management professionals can consider them as another tool to help improve performance.

Supply management professionals receive various types of reports and audits from both internal and external sources to assure compliance with corporate policies, internal and external standards, and government regulations and laws. Internal audits are designed to determine how well the supply management organization is really doing, whether established processes are actually working, and whether policies and procedures are being followed in a consistent manner. External audits consider whether an organization is complying with specific internal written policies and procedures, external standards, government regulations and/or laws. The scope of the audit can be narrow or broad. It could be as simple as determining whether invoices are being paid according to contract, or it could be as extensive as an ISO-9001:2008 audit. Figure 10-5 provides a list of possible scope issues.

Figure 10-5: Audit Scope Issues

Scope Issues
- Are the organization's internal policies and processes in place and being adhered to (monetary limits, transaction scope, responsibility and so on)?
- Are the appropriate personnel conducting their given transactions?
- Are suppliers' references and performance tracked and maintained?
- Is the supplier's capacity and financial health monitored over time?
- Are internal and external policies and practices updated, as necessary?
- Are the supplier's relationships with internal customers effective and efficient?
- Is the technology used working effectively internally, externally and across the supply chain?
- Are the supplier's innovation processes in place and used with outcomes measured?
- Are risk management policies in place and being monitored?
- Are contract administration procedures and practices in place and used?
- Are quality and inspection practices used and measured?
- Are sustainability and social responsibility initiatives embedded in procurement practices?
- Are diversity goals and objectives monitored and reported?
- Are the supplier's forecasting methods and outcomes watched and modified as required?
- Are the supplier's procurement card policies and practices being followed?
- Are purchasers responding in a timely fashion to end-user inquiries?

Source: Institute for Supply Management®.

For example, an organization that possesses ISO 9001:2008 certification has to prove via an audit process that production processes are in accordance with its quality management manual. An *ISO audit* verifies that processes such as the following are in full accordance with applicable documentation:

- Production or service processes are in compliance.
- Employees are properly informed of processes.
- Continuous quality improvement is in place.
- Process changes are handled appropriately.
- Changes are properly shared with employees.

NICE, an Israeli financial crime, risk and compliance solutions provider with clients worldwide, registered with ISO 9001:2008 in 1998 and has received and welcomed regular audits ever since. Audits cover areas such as "(1) version/product release process methodologies; (2) new service/product version plans; (3) requirements management, work flows and implementation; and (4) master plan training guidelines." Auditors have consistently commended the company for its compliance to ISO 9001:2008 standards.[11] (The ISO standardization program and its relationship to quality are discussed further in Chapter 9.)

Both internal and external audits are normally performed at set frequencies. For instance, some ISO audits are required every year and some every three years. Likewise, a financial audit may be required each year. Special audits do not have set intervals but are important nonetheless. The goal for senior management must be to establish an organization that is continually improving its policies and processes to get them in full compliance.

GAAP. GAAP stands for *generally accepted accounting principles*, which are the practices that govern financial reporting as determined by the Financial Accounting Standards Board (FASB) in the U.S. The purpose of a financial audit is to determine whether or not an organization's financial statements are prepared in accordance with GAAP. Management of an organization is ultimately responsible for preparing these financial statements, which can be prepared internally or by an outside accounting organization. When financial statements are formally audited, the auditor in charge of the process has a responsibility to issue an opinion on the accuracy and fairness of the financial statements in question.

With the increase in outsourcing, supply management professionals must also ensure that suppliers comply with GAAP. As John Shapiro and Jeffrey Mayer, partners at Freeborn and Peters LLC, state, "The company retains responsibility for compliance with GAAP by ensuring that the supplier is aware of the GAAP requirements, addressing the supplier's obligations to comply with the requirements and enforcing the penalties for the supplier's failure to comply with those requirements."[12]

Companies that outsource to suppliers in other countries also need to consider the effect of the relatively new global accounting system, International Financial Reporting Standards (IFRS), which has been adopted by more than 115 nations and 12,000 companies worldwide, including U.S. subsidiaries. Prior to IFRS, companies used GAAP as the standard. The difference between the two is that "IFRS is a philosophy on reporting financial information to give the best understanding of the company's financial situation"[13] while GAAP focuses on how financial information must be reported. For example, companies using IFRS would value inventory at current market price while GAAP values it at the acquisition price. As of 2013 the U.S. had not yet adopted IFRS, but companies working with international suppliers that have implemented IFRS will also need to comply with its standards.

Sarbanes-Oxley. The *Sarbanes-Oxley Act* (known as SOX or Sarbox) was passed in the United States in 2002. This legislation requires all publicly traded organizations to submit reports to the SEC on an annual basis, verifying the effectiveness of their internal accounting controls. These reporting requirements, as well as the penalties for noncompliance, went into effect in 2006. Based on the nature of the offense, penalties can include up to US$15 million in fines and 25 years in prison.

The SOX legislation brought about a need for corporate transparency in the area of financial reporting. It also looked to restore confidence with both investors and the general public. The six main areas of SOX are as follows:

1. *Audit committees.* Organizations must establish fully independent audit committees.
2. *Waiting period.* A minimum of one year must pass before an audit engagement member can be hired as a CEO, CFO or CAO.
3. *Loan prohibition.* Organizations may not extend loans to directors or corporate officers.
4. *Reporting.* Annual internal control reports must be produced.
5. *Disclosure.* Organizations must disclose information regarding material changes on a real-time basis.
6. *Protection.* Whistleblower protection must be provided for its employees.

Section 401 of SOX is probably one of the most important to supply management. This section states that supply management professionals must report "common business transactions, such as the receipt or payment of slotting fees or promotional allowances, supplier-managed inventories and guarantee contracts, long-term volume purchase agreements or take-or-pay commitments," according to Professors Kros and Nadler.[14] Another important section is 404, which addresses the management of internal controls. As discussed by Kros and Nadler, supply management professionals must keep "copies of documents such as purchase orders, bid and contract proposals, internal company memos, emails and the criteria used for each contract decision to ensure compliance. The quality of these internal controls must also be documented and verified during audits so that independent auditors can sign off on their effectiveness."[15]

This new level of scrutiny actually provides the supply management professional with an opportunity to work with senior management and corporate finance officers. It also serves as an opportunity for supply management professionals to demonstrate excellence and value. Some of the challenges of SOX have been the amount of labor intensiveness, a high possibility of errors and delays, and added resources required for implementation. Software solutions have made compliance much easier. Selectica, a contract management software provider, uses a contract management system with Netsuite's OpenAir project management system to meet SOX reporting requirements. Any new service work order first receives a unique identifying number in the contract management system. Once the contract is signed and the project created, this number is then entered into OpenAir, which tracks and creates reports for projects and resources, and is used for SOX reporting. Prior to using OpenAir, Selectica entered data into Excel, which was time-consuming and error-prone. The company estimates that it saves 65 percent to 75 percent of its time using OpenAir, and accuracy is significantly improved.[16]

Internationally, a growing number of corporate governance controls have been initiated. For example, Europe passed the 8th European Union Company Law Directive on Statutory Audit, which is similar to SOX, in 2006. The directive affects members of the European Union and the European Free Trade Association (EFTA). Most member countries have passed national laws in line with the directive.[17] Similarly, Japan enacted the Financial Instruments and Exchange Law in 2006 in response to a corporate scandal; this is actually stricter in its requirements than is SOX.[18]

In summary, audits should be welcome. External parties can play a valuable role in lending their expertise to an organization through an audit. The advantage to being an "outsider" is that no preconceived notions or assumptions exist. The audit needs to be conducted professionally, objectively and honestly. Audit reports inevitably will find deficiencies that an organization needs to address, and often the recommendations include the corrective action needed, the priority and the necessary time line.

Compliance with Current Policies

Every organization should have an effective set of policies — or guidelines — and evaluate them periodically to make sure they match upper management's objectives, provide a framework for making good decisions, and ensure supply management professionals have a guide to follow regarding rules and procedures. Effective policies, according to Monczka, et al., are relevant, action-oriented and current.[19] Two important policies for today's supply management professional are supplier diversity and social responsibility.

Policies regarding *supplier diversity programs* are common to both public and private sectors, and have been around in the United States for more than 30 years. They promote the use and development of small businesses including minority-owned and women-owned organizations. Ford, for example, has had its Supplier Diversity Development (SDD) for more than 24 years, and views the contributions of its minority-owned, women-owned and veteran entrepreneurs as critical to its success and growth. More than US$5.7 billion was spent with minority-owned suppliers and US$1.2 billion with women-owned businesses in 2012.[20] Supply management professionals are typically measured on the percentage of contract spend with minority-owned and women-owned businesses and with the number of subcontracts or second-tier suppliers over a given period of time.

Similar programs occur at all levels of government, including federal, state and local agencies in the United States. While set-aside programs for minorities and women have been challenged in the courts, it is still common to see the use of aspirational goals (sometimes referred to as targets) in public sector contracts. This requires large prime contractors to provide opportunities and outreach to small businesses to earn a subcontract. While not technically a requirement, the government agency will evaluate the prime contractor on its efforts and results. The diversifying of contract dollars to minority-owned, women-owned and emerging small businesses is referred to as minority, women and emerging small business (MWESB) use.

Organizations in all sectors are seeing the value of using a diverse supply pool. Senior management realizes that sourcing with minority-owned businesses makes sense, as they represent an increasing customer base. In 2009 alone, Fortune 500 organizations spent more than US$104 billion with minority-owned and women-owned businesses.[21] According to a 2012 CAPS Research benchmark report, organizations surveyed expected to increase their diversity spend by 72 percent in the next two years.[22] Developing a supplier diversity policy demonstrates an organization's awareness of local demographics, and also allows it to take a leadership position in doing the right thing. This corporate thinking expands into other parts of the world as well. Corporations in the European Union (EU), for example, have programs that positively impact the financial position of SMEs (small and medium sized enterprises), which include diverse and under-represented businesses. The benefits to the larger corporations include access to new ideas and the promotion of competition.[23]

Supplier diversity programs are commonly found in the public sector. The Port of Portland, for example, has made supplier diversity a priority since 1994. Its mission statement is "To increase local small business participation in Port of Portland projects and procurements through the integration of a Portwide process to develop and grow mutually beneficial business relationships with local small businesses." The Port runs two programs, the Disadvantaged Business Enterprise Program and its Mentor Protege Program. From 2011 to 2013, its goal was to contract eight percent of its projected spend with businesses certified as socially or economically disadvantaged. [24]

Supplier diversity is also a key strategy within the service industry. Bank of America, Turner Construction Co. and Accenture are a few of the very successful service providers that incorporate diversity as part of their mission and strategies. Hilton Hotels is also committed to providing opportunities for women-owned and minority-owned suppliers through open access to its supply management programs. Hilton pledges that the diversity of its supplier base will reflect the diversity of the communities it serves.[25]

Social responsibility (SR) (also known as corporate social responsibility or CSR) and sustainability have become common programs for organizations in all parts of the world. It is identified by the Institute for Supply Management® as a key part of the Strategic Supply Management Concept (see Figure S-1 in the "Series Overview" at the beginning of this book). So what is social responsibility? It is best defined as "a framework of measurable organization policies and procedures and resulting behavior designed to benefit the workplace, and by extension, the individual, the organization and society. The ISM *Principles of Sustainability and Social Responsibility* include the following areas: anti-corruption, diversity and inclusiveness in the workforce and supply base, environment, ethics and business conduct, financial integrity and transparency, global citizenship, health and safety, human rights, labor rights and sustainability."[26] The supplier diversity issue, discussed previously, is certainly a component of social responsibility. SR also expands to other areas of expectations for suppliers, such as commitment to human rights and their policies on environmental health and safety. Hewlett-Packard has been a leader in SR, publicly stating that one of its organizational objectives is global citizenship. As stated on its website, HP has "environmental stewards on every design team to identify design changes that may reduce environmental impact throughout the product's life cycle." HP also "reduce(d) the number and types of materials used, and standardize(d) the types of plastic resins used." These are but a few of its companywide initiatives.[27] (More information on sustainability and social responsibility can be found in the *Foundation of Supply Management*, Volume 1 of the ISM *Professional Series*.)

Evaluation of Employees

One of the primary ways of maintaining a high-performance work team within supply management is through the diligent evaluation of employee performance. The goal of employee evaluation is to ensure personal accountability to the goals of an organization. It is crucial to use a performance evaluation technique that supports achievement of organizational goals, and also to link employee expectations to its mission. When employees understand the goals of the employer, they are better able to understand their specific roles in supporting those goals. It also is important that employees understand the purpose and value of evaluations. Communication is certainly a key to such understanding. Evaluations can assess either individual or team performance, with the former being the most common. While each organization has its own evaluation technique, these techniques generally fit within two broad categories. *Summative evaluations* are intended to rate the strengths of an employee. They assess performance over a set period of time — most often the preceding year — and recognize accomplishments and successes. The tools used to diagnose weaknesses in employees' performance are referred to as *formative evaluations*. They identify areas for improvement for a specified period of time in the future.[28] For example, if supplier negotiation skills were identified as a supply management professional's weakness, and a plan was made to obtain negotiation training within six months, this is an example of formative evaluation.

An organization can use a performance evaluation system to accomplish its mission, and to improve employee performance through some type of incentive program. This can include a performance bonus that is considered on an annual basis. If an employee achieves set objectives for the year, receives high ratings from peers and consistently performs at a high level, he or she can earn additional compensation via a cash bonus. While more money always sounds good, it is not always the prime motivator for employees. Figure 10-6 offers some ideas for nonmonetary rewards.

Figure 10-6: Nonmonetary Employee Motivators

Flexible work arrangements	Allowing employees some flexibility in their work schedule or the ability to do special projects from home.
Opportunity to participate	Asking an employee to participate in a special project, such as an employee committee or budget team.
Recognition	Everyone likes a pat on the back and public acknowledgment for a job well done. This can be a formal presentation or a verbal acknowledgment.
Development opportunities	Sending employees to internal training can help them develop their skills at little or no cost.
Challenging assignments	Assignments that are new or unique can be appealing, such as new software or a design-build project.

Source: Adapted from S.S. Freyss, *Human Resource Management in Local Government*, 3rd ed. (Washington, DC: ICMA, 2009).

Part of motivating employees is valuing them as a resource within the supply management group. Every employee appreciates a pat on the back for a job well done, but this must be sincere and specific. Rather than saying "You're great," make the acknowledgment fit the accomplishment. Saying "Great job on securing that secondary supplier for electric motors" will better convey appreciation. Managers should strive to set up their employees for success and motivate them to perform at a high level. A willingness to value employees and communicate effectively will help build a positive work environment and, ultimately, a flourishing business.[29]

For each position, an organization should determine what the factors are for success in that position. To define the critical success factors of a position, a supply management professional can ask the following questions:
- What are the skills and abilities of a successful individual in this job?
- What skill weaknesses contributed to failure in the past?

- What areas of specialty or expertise are needed?
- What behavioral characteristics, such as initiative or collegiality, are ideal?[30]

Determining Appraisal Factors

The choice of the appraisal factors used in evaluating employee performance depends on the purpose of the evaluation. Most organizations aim to accomplish several objectives simultaneously. These often include improved employee performance, detection of non-performers, identification of areas for employee development and improving employee retention. Organizations also must decide whether a single appraisal system is appropriate for all employee groups, or if it should consider several parallel systems that align with the needs of each work group. There are many types of appraisal systems and factors for appraisal. They can include both quantitative and qualitative factors.

Quantitative factors are statistical in nature, resulting in a numerical answer. An example of a quantitative factor for employee performance might be the number of supplier contracts negotiated or the dollar value of inventory reduced. These results can be compared against previously determined goals, industry averages or the performance of other employees. *Qualitative factors* are subjective and are based on customer feedback and a supervisor's observations. Factors such as responsiveness to customer needs or ability to learn new tasks would be considered qualitative. Technical expertise and professional judgment are employed in qualitative evaluations, while quantitative evaluations rely on the analysis of statistical data.

Conducting Interviews

An effective manager must use his or her interview skills to gain information about employee performance. Evaluation forms and customer surveys are effective; however, sometimes personal conversations are best. An interview can give a supervisor the opportunity to gain information firsthand, either from an employee or a customer. Personal interviews can be valuable, as people tend to be more forthright in person — and even share information they may be uncomfortable putting on a survey. An interview should be open, with both sides communicating. Providing feedback also is important. This is the first step in using the information gained during the interview. For example, a major customer may convey concern to the warehouse supervisor about the level of service being provided by distribution personnel. Besides the immediate feedback given to the customer thanking him or her for the information, the supervisor should close the loop with the affected employee and discuss the matter with him or her.

There are numerous sources from which to receive feedback regarding an employee's performance. Traditionally, an employee's direct supervisor has single-handedly conducted the performance evaluation. Today, in addition to their supervisor, employees often are evaluated by their peers and coworkers. These can include members of their work team — who likely know better than anyone the level of a team member's performance, or other peers within the organization. A peer review could be from anyone else in the organization, perhaps an accounting professional holding a comparable position in the controller's office. Disadvantages of peer reviews include the difficulty in maintaining anonymity, and the fact that they are generally unpopular with employees.

Another evaluation tool that has been used is *self-assessment*. This is an opportunity for employees to evaluate their own performance against set objectives. An effective way to increase employee participation in the evaluation process, self-assessment establishes clear communication between supervisor and employee. A downside is that it can be subject to bias and inflated ratings, since the employee's own ratings tend to be higher than those of the supervisor. Self-assessment requires time and commitment from both the employee and the supervisor. (See Volume 3 of the ISM *Professional Series*, *Leadership in Supply Management*, for a discussion on skills needed in the current environment.)

Internal customers can provide valuable input on employee evaluations, particularly those who work closely with the employee. Accuracy can be less reliable if obtained from sources that are distant, or from occasional customers. For supply management staff, internal customers could include customers or end users in marketing, finance, production, maintenance or sales. This can be a form of peer review, but the supervisor gathers information specifically from individuals within the organization who receive services from supply management.

Obtaining feedback from the supplier community is not as common as a peer review, but it can still be just as effective. More than ever, supply management professionals are interacting directly with suppliers. These relationships are key to organizational success. Similar to an internal customer, a supplier can see firsthand the quality of an employee's performance. When this information is solicited in a professional manner, it can greatly aid a supervisor in evaluating an employee's performance.

Employees must be accountable for meeting their performance goals and objectives. When this does not occur, a supervisor can use certain tools to attempt to improve performance. A *performance improvement plan* is a formal document that identifies deficient areas of performance for an employee, methods to measure the needed improvement, and the repercussions if acceptable improvement is not made. This type of plan can be used when routine training, on-the-job experience and verbal instructions do not result in acceptable employee performance. This will put the employee and supervisor on the same page relative to job expectations, and can create necessary documentation for future personnel action (demotion, termination, and so on).

Staff Development

Some studies indicate significant differences in the human resources management practices by country and even by industry.

The professional development of an organization's talent is an evolving strategy, and continues to be crucial to the advancement of the supply management profession. Those new to the profession, seasoned veterans, and various economies and cultures need to hone their knowledge and expertise to increase their value. CAPS Research, in a report on *Supply Management Strategies in the New Economy*, has identified the provision of training and development for retention in all economies and cultures as a critical supply/value chain challenge in the decade ahead.[31] In-house training programs, technical seminars, online programs and college coursework all play key roles in professional development. Organizations need to incorporate new training and development approaches recognizing generational and cultural differences. Countless opportunities exist for supply management professionals to develop their portfolio of skills. Organizations of all types will need to establish a profile of supply management knowledge and skills for the development of talent in the future. A multipronged approach is necessary to develop and retain supply management professionals that may include topics including cross-cultural skills, analytical skills, business management skills and leadership skills.[32]

More and more organizations are financially supporting supply management professionals in this area. They see the value of the investment in training for their team, realizing it will pay dividends for the organization. For instance, having a certified supply management professional on staff can be just as valuable as employing a registered architect or a certified public accountant. The qualification for supply management professionals, Certified Professional in Supply Management® (CPSM®), has become a premier designation for the profession. Even when individuals within the profession pay for professional development out of their own pockets, it is money well spent. Countless times such investments have paid off in the way of promotions, upgrades and salary increases.

Finally, higher education continues to become more and more important to supply management. Today's professionals see the value of possessing a college degree, and many earn their degrees in supply management or a related field. Many schools have recognized the importance of a supply management/supply chain management curriculum. Other areas such as finance, business and project management have degree holders within the supply management ranks. In recent years, accredited college degrees have become a requirement for many supply management professionals rather than just desirable credentials. What is the value of a degree in supply management? Top-level schools such as Arizona State University, Michigan State University, Pennsylvania State University and Howard University are examples of universities offering excellent programs. Through progressive curriculum, faculty with industry experience and internship opportunities, many students have job offers in hand on graduation.

CHAPTER 10: Performance Evaluation

Summary

By establishing measurements for performance, supply management can help set the bar for an organization. This applies to internal operations, such as marketing, production and sales, as well as its extended enterprise of suppliers. There are many ways in which to measure and evaluate performance, with the key being to determine those measurements that are most appropriate. They must be realistic and achievable, and help the organization continually improve.

Effective management and evaluation of employees is important, so the techniques and skills in human resources management must be developed. Supply management professionals must be concerned with evaluating and improving staff performance, as well as how to use professional training to develop employees in their areas of improvement.

Key Points

1. Performance measurement is the process of assessing performance toward a predetermined goal; it can be qualitative or quantitative.
2. Measurements today need to focus on two critical areas: the customer and the competition.
3. The results of performance evaluation should be reported throughout the organization.
4. Key performance indicators are quantifiable measurements of the improvement in performing an activity critical to business success, and include value stream mapping and the balanced scorecard (BSC).
5. Audits that impact supply management include ISO, GAAP and SOX audits.
6. The goal of employee evaluation is to ensure personal accountability to the goals of an organization.
7. Summative evaluations are intended to rate the strengths of an employee and assess performance over a set period of time. Formative evaluations are used to diagnose weaknesses in an employee's performance and identify areas for improvement in the future.
8. Quantitative factors are statistical in nature and can be compared against previously determined goals, industry averages or the performance of other employees. Qualitative factors are subjective and based on customer feedback and a supervisor's observations.
9. Self-assessments are evaluation tools that allow employees to rate their own performance. Understandably, employees often rate their performance higher than their supervisors do.

CHAPTER

11

Knowledge Integration

It is often said that knowledge is power. Organizational knowledge is transferred through multiple mediums including face-to-face meetings, email, social media, organization newsletters and web portals, among others. Companies also rely on technology solutions to access organizational information, which increases their knowledge and helps with the decision-making process. Today's supply management professionals source internationally so they need information about "economic conditions, exchange rates, materials supply and the overall stability of countries around the world."[1] Global sourcing requires that supply management professionals have up-to-date and accurate information on country-related finances. They also rely on internally generated data and reports to gain knowledge for making important decisions. With the click of a mouse or swipe of the finger they can gain access to inventory forecasts, supplier cost proposals, purchase orders and spend analyses. Automated processes are available to optimize requisitioning and invoicing.

Even with the advances in technology, however, one of the key issues organizations still struggle with today is effectively collecting and transferring that information. For example, a large corporation with many locations may have several enterprise resource planning (ERP) systems that don't "talk" to each other. A second issue is that of information overload, while a related issue is trusting that the available information will be accurate and useful for decision-making. As author and physicist William Pollard once said, "Information is a source of learning. But unless it is organized, processed and available to the right people in a format for decision-making, it is a burden, not a benefit."[2]

Data management and analysis supports knowledge integration and is a key process in strategic supply management, as discussed in Chapter 1. This chapter more deeply covers the topics of knowledge management and knowledge integration, and the role they play in sharing information within and across organizations. Systems employed by leading organizations will be discussed, including MRP, MRP II, ERP, WMS and DRP. Other tools and processes, also covered in this chapter, include customer relationships, distribution planning and system development life cycle.

Chapter Objectives

- Explore how knowledge is transferred throughout an organization and discuss how it can be used strategically.
- Define current terminology employed within knowledge management.
- Discuss information technology systems and the various steps of system development.
- Define xRP systems and explore their role within supply management.
- Discuss how an organization can expand its technology systems to its suppliers and customers.
- Identify emerging trends in technology that impact supply management professionals.

Definitions

Knowledge can best be described as "familiarity, awareness or understanding that is gained through experience or study."[3] Employees who possess a desirable knowledge, for example in the area of contract negotiations, and are hired for their mental skills (as opposed to physical skills) are sometimes referred to as *knowledge workers*. Organizational-specific knowledge develops from combining individual knowledge into collective knowledge. Knowledge is also transferred from one subunit to another along two dimensions, technical and social. For technical information transfers to successfully occur, the source and the recipient of the information must have the necessary capabilities to recognize the value of the new information, be able to assimilate it and then apply it to a relevant business purpose, otherwise known as *absorptive capacity*. The social dimension refers to the level of knowledge sharing within the social context of an organization.[4]

The term *knowledge management* was developed in the 1990s and, according to ISM, is the "process of actively managing and leveraging internal and external information and knowledge, including methodologies for ongoing access and distribution of information and knowledge for business decision-making" (ISM *Glossary* 2014). Figure 11-1 provides the basic inputs to a knowledge management system. Knowledge is not useful unless it is applied, managed and integrated. Thus, knowledge management helps organizations use their collective knowledge to their best advantage. This is accomplished by working to improve the synergies between the data processing capabilities of their information technologies with the creativity and innovativeness of their employees. Collaboration and cooperation are critical to knowledge integration, requiring organizations to develop those necessary skills and experience that will allow for efficient and effective knowledge transfers. This is especially important when operations are in distant geographic locations. As knowledge exchanges improve, innovation has been shown to increase, making organizations more competitive.[5] Internally, companies see more system innovations and faster technical problem-solving. They also see an increase in the number of patents that result from cooperative efforts between corporate headquarters and their subsidiaries.[6]

Figure 11-1: Knowledge Management Model

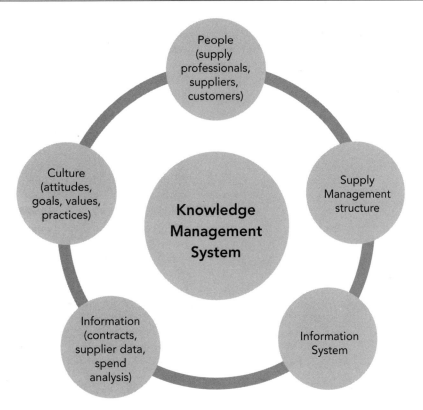

The importance of knowledge management to the supply management professional should be evident. To make sound business decisions, knowledge throughout the organization must be transferred to the decision-makers. The Strategic Supply Management Concept (see the "Series Overview" at the beginning of this book) notes that data management and analysis is a key concept for supply management professionals, who in many cases are these decision-makers. Supply management professionals must understand the concept of knowledge management and its importance to the organization, but equally important is the ability to apply the available technologies that share this knowledge. The following section covers information systems, which are the tools for collecting and transferring this data.

Information Technology Systems

The world of technology continues to reshape the supply management profession. Organizations of all sizes and sectors use technology in their daily operations. *Information technology* refers to the "set of electronic tools used by best-in-class organizations to generate, process, transfer, interpret and utilize information. These tools include state-of-the-art hardware, software, databases and networks" (ISM *Glossary* 2014). Cloud computing, big data and mobile devices are certainly affecting the way companies rethink their supply chain processes. Big data refers to the combining of data from supply chain partners to respond to changes and quickly make decisions. Complex event processing (CEP) solutions are needed to process, analyze and track the multitude of data from supply chain members. Cloud computing is a real-time, on-demand service that is managed by a third party. Using a network of remote servers, companies receive computing resources such as software applications and data centers on a subscription or pay-for-use basis. Mobile devices, such as smart phones and tablets, are commonly used in warehousing and logistics; applications are available to link supply management professionals to an ERP system.

Social media, such as LinkedIn and Facebook, also are being used to connect supply management professionals and share interests such as global sourcing and risk strategies. And, blog sites can be found which share expertise on subjects such as spend management, negotiation and sourcing in developing countries.

Information systems link business operations, such as production, supply management and logistics, with both the supplier's operation and the customer. They offer organizations the advanced tools to manage and integrate data into business processes. Organizations use this shared information for replenishing products in the workplace with their upstream operations and those of their key suppliers. For example, a retailer would use its information system to replenish store inventories as the daily information is gathered from point-of-sale terminals. Corporate headquarters would then transmit this information to the supplier, which packages individual store requirements into bar-coded parcels. These parcels are taken by a logistics service provider to a trans-shipment center, where they are sorted for store delivery. Essentially, a just-in-time (JIT) delivery is achieved that enables low levels of inventory to be carried in the stores. This replenishment system, made possible by the use of an integrated information system, is shown in Figure 11-2.

Figure 11-2: Replenishment Order System

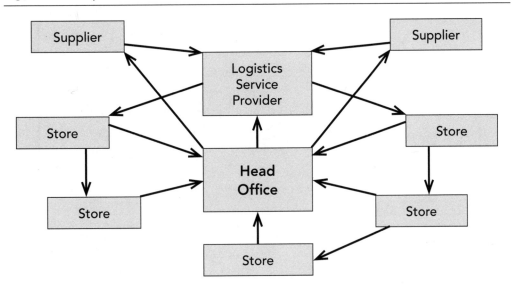

Source: Adapted from M. Christopher, *Logistics & Supply Chain Management* (London: Financial Times Prentice Hall, 2005).

The process of developing information systems through investigation, analysis, design, implementation and maintenance is known as the *system development life cycle* (SDLC). Also referred to as information systems development or application development, it covers the entire spectrum of an information system, from requirements analysis to systems maintenance. There are six phases in the SDLC, with each phase containing several steps and considerations, as shown in Figure 11-3. A description of each step follows.

Figure 11-3: System Development Life Cycle

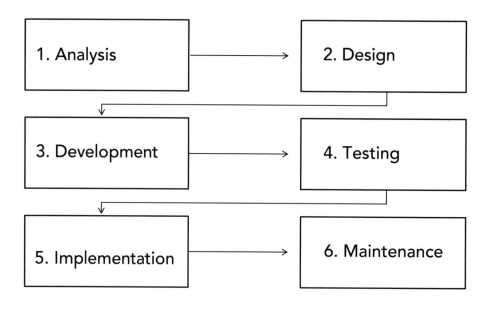

1. *Analysis*. This is the process of analyzing the informational needs of end users, the organizational environment and any present systems in use. Ultimately, the functional requirements of the system must be developed based on user needs. Requirements of the system can be documented with the use of interface storyboards or executable prototypes. This documentation will be referred to throughout the system development process to ensure the project aligns with identified needs and requirements.
2. *Design*. Once requirements have been determined, an organization can determine the specifications for hardware, software, data resources and information products that are needed. The design will serve as a system blueprint with the goal of detecting problems and errors before they are built into the final system.
3. *Development*. At this stage new components and programs are purchased and installed. The system is integrated with any existing systems (where required), and any customization based on client-specific needs is done at this time. Also, security needs should be analyzed and addressed at this stage. There could be risks to the organization, assets or individuals, so a security plan — if not already developed — is needed.
4. *Testing*. All systems must be tested to evaluate their actual functionality as compared to the intended functionality. Other issues to consider during this phase are the conversion of old data into the new system and training of employees on system use. End users are important in helping to determine whether the developed system meets the intended requirements.

5. *Implementation.* Also known as rollout, at this stage the end user takes ownership of the new or updated system and incorporates it into everyday business processes. Any security measures are enabled.
6. *Maintenance.* There will always be issues related to the data or performance. Typically, a feedback system will be available so the user can report any problems that need to be fixed. Also, IT will create and implement a regular maintenance schedule. IT will install any updates and/or upgrades that are needed to run the system more efficiently.

Other Considerations

There are other issues to consider in the SDLC process. Within supply management, there is the sourcing decision or, more specifically, a question such as, "Do we purchase an existing software product, develop our own customized system or contract with an applications service provider (ASP), which offers software as a service (SaaS)?" Regardless of the choice, the system development life cycle does not actually change; it is merely adjusted. Concepts for the software still must be considered, as well as the analysis of an organization's requirements, expertise in systems development and cost. With the availability of IT systems today, most organizations choose to outsource a stand-alone system or use SaaS. Design, development and testing are replaced with the evaluation of potential purchased products or ASPs. Compatibility of the new software with existing systems is certainly a key factor. The advantage of SaaS is lower cost, which helps small- and medium-sized businesses. The ASP also provides the expertise and performs upgrades as needed along with maintenance, security and 24/7 technical support.

The planning stages of the SDLC are of prime importance, for analysis and design must be performed properly to ensure success downstream. Good planning helps reduce errors and minimize the chances for missing production and/or service schedules.

As mentioned earlier in this chapter, several developments have reshaped the organization and changed the nature of the linkages between organizations. While information sharing has long been central to efficient supply management, the advances in technology are the driving force behind competitive strategies. Today's leading organizations use social media to create relationships and cloud computing to improve responsiveness, and the Internet has made this possible. Still, an important piece of the supply chain as it relates to the use of technology is the implementation of the tried and true xRP systems. In the acronym xRP, which stands for *extended resource planning systems*, the x may be materials, enterprise or distribution (ISM *Glossary* 2014). These systems are the backbone of any organization and will be discussed in the following sections, beginning with an overview of materials requirement planning (MRP).

Materials Resource Plan

Prior to ERP, other systems had been developed to achieve some form of integration within an organization. *Materials resource plan* (or *materials requirements planning*) (MRP) is a software program originally developed in the 1960s to define the raw material requirements needed for a specific item, component, and/or subassembly ordered by a customer or required by a business process (additional discussion of MRP is included in Chapter 5). Many MRP software applications can automatically place the raw material orders to the preferred supplier via fax, email or electronic data interchange (EDI). In 1981, MRP was extended to *manufacturing resource planning* (MRP II).

MRP II is an extension of the materials resource plan, which is a closed-loop system (it does not interface with other systems). MRP II is used by organizations to effectively plan all its resources used in a manufacturing organization. It addresses operational planning in all units and financial planning in dollars, and has a simulation capacity to address "what if" questions. MRP II (according to the ISM *Glossary* 2014) is comprised of a variety of functions that are linked together, including the following:

- Business planning;
- Sales;
- Operational planning;
- Production planning;
- Master production scheduling;
- Material requirements planning;
- Capacity requirements planning; and
- Execution of support systems for capacity and materials.

Enterprise Resource Planning (ERP)

ERP has a much broader scope than MRP or MRP II, covering basic functions of all types within an organization. The system is a demonstration of knowledge management and integration in action. Companies of all sizes, governments, nonprofits and healthcare providers are examples of organizations that use ERP systems. Essentially, an ERP system has the capability to track people, processes and technology. It "integrates various functions within an organization," creating a means of communication, and can "enable processes such as forecasting, materials management and purchasing" (ISM *Glossary* 2014). The goal for ERP adopters is to increase revenues through better customer relationship management, and improve efficiency and decision-making. Typically, these systems use multiple components of software and hardware to achieve integration within an organization and between organizations. One of the key elements of an ERP system is the use of unified databases to store data for the various modules of the system.

For a software package to be considered an ERP system, it must provide functionality in a single system that would normally be covered by two or more systems. Intuit®

QuickBooks® is an example of such a system, for it provides sales, inventory and payroll functions, an interface with the organization's bank, and other features. More commonly, ERP systems include more broad-based applications that eliminate the need for external interfaces between multiple systems.[7]

Some of these business applications include manufacturing, customer relationship management, supply chain, financials, human resources and warehouse management (see Figure 11-4). ERP systems include both *back-office systems*, that do not directly involve customers and the general public, and *front-office (or customer-facing)* systems that deal directly with customers and suppliers. The customer management module, for example, deals with customer needs. It can help an organization collect customer opinion through social media and manage its call center. The goal is to provide 24-hour access to customers, both new and existing. It allows for improved retention of customers through better relationship management and niche marketing. When operating effectively, the module can reduce the cost of sales by allowing customers to handle sales themselves. Customers can access products at any time and even configure their own orders. The ultimate goal is to secure a competitive advantage.

The supply management module of an ERP system is certainly an important tool for today's supply management professional. Depending on the system, this may be referred to as supply management or procurement, but the essential functionality should be consistent: automatic order placement and tracking, supplier pricing, master contracts, inventory replenishment and materials forecasting. A key consideration with ERP is that it is simply another tool for the supply management professional to ensure timely delivery of quality goods and services when needed and avoid shortages.

ERP can provide the following benefits:
- Operational efficiency;
- Reports for decision-making;
- Improved customer service; and
- A link to suppliers.

ACH Food Companies Inc., with 1,000 employees and US$1 billion in annual sales, implemented an ERP system in two waves: one in 2008 and the second in 2011. The new system integrated the "hodgepodge" of "poorly integrated applications." As a result, ACH benefitted considerably with visibility of all inventories across the organization, KPIs, and improved consistency of information for better decision-making. Finished goods inventories dropped by 20 percent and new product development took 75 percent less time.[8]

However, ERP as a stand-alone system is still expensive to implement, and has limitations in the ability of the software provider to customize. Companies have found it difficult to measure return on investment (ROI) because there are no tools or techniques available. And, some organizations find it difficult to adapt ERP to its business flows and processes. If they attempt to fit their organization to ERP, companies could lose a competitive advantage.

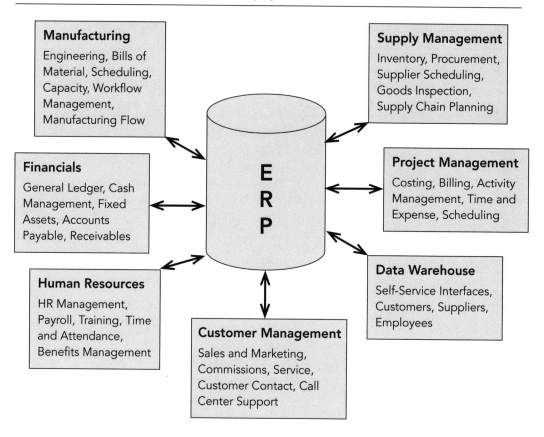

Figure 11-4: Enterprise Resource Planning Systems

There are also organizations with multiple business units or departments that operate with independent resources, missions and chain-of-command, which make consolidation into one enterprise difficult. Thus, companies need to carefully go through the software development life cycle (SDLC) process to determine if ERP is a right fit for them.

Supplier Management Software. As organizations have optimized their supply bases and created strategic relationships with key suppliers, many are employing *supplier relationship management* (SRM) software. An SRM can offer many benefits, including the ability to source and select materials quickly and to monitor supplier quality. Ariba offers an SRM application that helps an organization view supplier profiles, monitor supplier performance, manage supply risk, and identify and assess new sources of supply.[9]

Grupo Posadas, leaders in the Mexican hotel industry, needed a strategic sourcing process to improve spend visibility, create spend metrics, centralize pricing and consolidate its supply management function. It chose a sourcing solution from Ariba in 2010 and can now manage its spend categories more effectively. Grupo Posadas estimates that it has saved 18 percent and "corporate spend under contract negotiations (has increased) by 25 percent," according to Fausto Jimenez, the strategic sourcing vice president at the time. Better visibility of corporate procurement and high levels of compliance of service level agreements have enabled the company to analyze corporate spend more easily and to source more strategically. Purchase orders and processing times are tracked more easily, and suppliers can quickly confirm order availability so stockouts can be detected sooner.[10]

Warehouse Management Systems. A *warehouse management system* (WMS) is designed specifically for managing the movement, storage and shipment of materials "to and from production or distribution locations" (ISM *Glossary* 2014). A WMS can assist with receiving, picking, shipping, putaway and packing activities. (See Chapter 6, "Warehouse Management and Materials Handling.") The benefits of a WMS include an increase in the following:

- Ability to trace inventory;
- Visibility of inventory in the system;
- Inventory accuracy;
- Order fulfillment capacity, accuracy and speed;
- Speed of order pick times;
- Space utilization; and
- Labor productivity.[11]

WMS is also offered as SaaS, which minimizes implementation costs, eliminates time set aside for upgrading and can be paid for on a monthly basis.

Customer Relationship Management. *Customer relationship management* (CRM) is "an industry term for software solutions that help organizations manage customer relationships in an organized way, and which includes all aspects of interaction an organization has with its customer, whether sales or service oriented" (ISM *Glossary* 2014). These solutions can help organizations in a number of ways. One important benefit is that products and services can be provided that meet the customer's precise wants and needs, and provide better customer service. This can lead to better sales forecasting and resource management, as well as improved profitability. CRM also can improve customer retention through better relationship management and niche marketing. When operating effectively, CRM can reduce the cost of sales by allowing customers to handle sales themselves. Customers can access products at any time, and can even configure their own orders. The software also enables more effective cross-selling.[12] The ultimate goal is to secure a competitive advantage.

Distribution Requirements Planning. *Distribution requirements planning* (DRP) is "a supply chain management term for the time-based demand from the distribution center to balance the customer fill rate against inventory investment" (ISM *Glossary* 2014). This will inform the organization about what products are on hand to fulfill existing requirements and what needs to be shipped from the distribution center. *DRP II* is *distribution resource planning*, and is more sophisticated, because it accommodates replenishment for multiple warehouse sites. Planning for warehouse space, personnel requirements, transportation alternatives and financial flows are also functions of DRP II.

From ERP to ERP Cloud

A recent development has been cloud computing, which refers to access to software, computing and data storage through a network. Organizations may purchase a license to use ERP software and install it on their computers, but all access is through the Internet. Organizations may work directly with the software supplier or use SaaS on a subscription basis. While many organizations today still have a traditional ERP with an on-site license, the second most common deployment is on-demand SaaS, according to a 2011 study. Total cost of ownership, lower start-up costs and more frequent updates were primary considerations in the decision to implement SaaS.[13]

ERP and Implementation Considerations

For organizations considering a traditional ERP system or one that is subscription-based, they also must ensure that strategic thinking is a part of these implementations. Regardless of how thorough an implementation is, it must be of strategic value to be worthwhile. Where an organization is and where it wants to be in a market must first be determined before it decides the best way to get there. Technology should be considered an enabler and not a final solution. If business strategies can be defined and developed, then it is likely a technology tool can help deliver it. Organizations also need to consider the cost of either the traditional or subscription-based system, data integrity and security. An on-site solution requires the purchase of a license while SaaS, as mentioned earlier, is typically paid for through a subscription. In today's environment, organizations often run ERP along with other applications, so compatibility with other systems must be considered. Along with cost, data integrity is always an issue. Problems can occur due to human error or errors when data is transmitted from one computer to another. To avoid these issues, it is important for an ERP system to back up data regularly and include error detection and correction capability. The organization should also have processes in place to prevent the input of invalid data as well as security mechanisms in place to control access to the data. Finally, security concerns must be addressed regardless of application. On-site systems are vulnerable unless completely contained, which is unlikely. However, potential SaaS providers must be thoroughly investigated to assure their financial viability and integrity.

Technology Trends in Supply Management

The latest trends revolve around four key areas: mobile, the Internet, "big data" and security. As noted, with the broad acceptance of smartphones and tablets, procurement systems are moving away from the use of PCs and desktops. Instead, software suppliers are looking to increase the mobility of supply management professionals through the use of these tools. The ability to find suppliers, place orders and approve purchases, and perform some analytical procedures, is expected in the near future.[14]

Second, the Internet is used by virtually everyone. As a result, software providers are looking to make procurement more similar to the consumer experience for smaller transactions such as travel expenses. The procure-to-pay process can be more customized to the client's specifications.[15]

Third, there are now collaboration tools available such as Yammer and JIVE, similar to Facebook but for business enterprises. Supply management professionals now have the ability to share knowledge such as developing a category strategy, creating KPIs and designing risk assessment tools.[16]

Fourth, supply management is looking for ways to leverage "big data" to its advantage. Today, the volume, velocity and variety of data is exploding because there are so many sources. To put this into perspective, there was 500 times more data available in 2012 than in 2003. Much of the data is in an unstructured format (text and numbers, for example), making it difficult to analyze. And, it is coming so fast that organizations don't have enough time to store it before it can be used.[17]

Finally, security continues to be a major priority. As discussed earlier, with the advent of cloud computing, keeping data secure is a concern. Supply management professionals are expected to spend more time researching ASPs to assure the organization's data is safe.[18] Similarly, organizations are working to protect internal systems from security breaches both from within and without.

Summary

Supply management professionals must be aware of the importance of the proper management and analysis of data. It is imperative that the knowledge gained from this data is used to improve business practices. The knowledge also must be shared throughout the entire organization. As supply management aligns its strategies with those of the organization, it must play an active role in the sharing of data and information with other business units.

Numerous information systems are available and must be selected based on the needs and goals of the organization. Integrated systems are much more efficient than independent systems used in past years. The use of these systems is a way to efficiently manage knowledge within an organization, as well as extend knowledge to suppliers and customers. There is a life cycle for system development that supply management professionals must be familiar with, for they are an integral part of any major systems acquisition. Information technologies are commonplace in today's markets, and will only become more important in the future. Supply management professionals must pay close attention to these advancements and how they can benefit an organization. If they do not do so, they and their organizations risk being left behind.

The role of supply management continues to evolve in all business sectors. More and more, the profession is viewed as a critical and strategic player by leading organizations throughout the world. The use of technology tools that share data and knowledge across the organization will only aid this evolution. While knowledge integration is the last chapter in this book, supply management professionals should consider the concept as just the beginning. Understanding how knowledge is integrated, and how technology is used to do so, will allow supply management professionals to move forward and add even more value to the organization.

This book has covered numerous key areas of supply management, including its role in planning, product development, project management, forecasting, logistics, inventory management and quality assurance. Each of these areas is important, but combined they represent a full spectrum of knowledge for today's supply management professional.

Key Points

1. Knowledge management is the attempt to collect and make effective use of the information contained in documents, reports and plans, along with the knowledge residing in the heads of subject matter experts. Knowledge workers are employees who possess such knowledge and are hired for their mental skills.
2. Information technology refers to the set of electronic tools used to generate, process, transfer, interpret and use information. These tools include computer hardware, software, databases and networks.
3. System development life cycle (SDLC) is the process of developing information systems through analysis, design, development, testing, implementation and maintenance.
4. Materials resource plan (MRP) is a method used for defining the raw materials needed for a specific item, component or subassembly ordered by a customer or required by a business process.
5. Manufacturing resource planning (MRP II), an extension of material requirements planning, is a method used by organizations to effectively plan all its resources used in manufacturing products.
6. Enterprise Resource Planning (ERP) is a software system that integrates various functions within an organization. It can be used to enable and improve business processes, and integrates all processes of an organization into a single system.
7. A warehouse management system (WMS) manages the movement and storage of materials throughout the warehouse.
8. Customer relationship management (CRM) systems manage and deal with customer needs via the Internet.
9. Supplier relationship management (SRM) software is an application that can allow an organization to quickly source and select materials, analyze spend and monitor supplier quality.
10. Technology trends in supply management revolve around four key areas: mobile, Internet, "big data" and security.

Endnotes
Chapter 1

1. Lisa Arnseth, "Supplying Help to Those in Need," *Inside Supply Management®*, (21:12), February 2012, 28.
2. J. Goodall, "The Future of Supply Chain Management," *e-Side Supply Management* (March/April 2010).
3. Robert Monczka and Phil Carter, *Supply Management Strategies for Success in the New Economy*, CAPS Research, Tempe, AZ, 2011.
4. Ibid.
5. *The CIPSA-Hackett Group Procurement Value, Performance and Capability Study*, 2010, accessed December 13, 2013, http://www.cips.org/Documents/CIPSAWhitePapers/2011/CIPSA_Hackett.pdf.
6. Institute for Supply Management®, ISM *Principles of Sustainability and Social Responsibility with a Guide to Adoption and Implementation*, 2012, accessed December 13, 2013, http://www.ism.ws/SR/?navItemNumber=22324.
7. Peter Kraljic, "Purchasing Must Become Supply Management," *Harvard Business Review*, (September-October 1983): 109-17.
8. University of California, "Purchase Card Program, Case Study," accessed December 13, 2013, http://workingsmarter.universityofcalifornia.edu/projects/purchase-card-program/case-study/.
9. Bronson Methodist Hospital Malcolm Baldrige National Quality Award Summary, 2005, accessed December 13, 2013, www.quality.nist.gov/PDF_files/Bronson_Methodist_Hospital_Application_Summary.pdf.
10. Rochelle Rucker, "Six Sigma at Citibank," *Quality Digest*, December 1999, accessed December 13, 2013, www.qualitydigest.com/dec99/html/citibank.html.
11. C.J. McNair, "Beyond the Boundaries: Future Trends in Cost Management," *Cost Management* (January/February 2007): 15.
12. Ayon Chakrabarty and Kay Chuan Tan, "The Current State of Six Sigma Application," *Managing Service Quality* 17(2) (2007): 194–208; T.N. Goh, "A Strategic Assessment of Six Sigma," *Quality Reliability Engineering International* 18(5) (2002): 403-10.
13. Capgemini Consulting, "Waste Not Want Not — Lean Six Sigma Values for Procurement," accessed November 13, 2013, http://www.capgemini.com/blog/procurement-transformation-blog-capgemini/2012/11/waste-not-want-not-lean-six-sigma-values-for-procurement.

14. Lean Enterprise Institute, accessed December 13, 2013, http://www.lean.org/WhatsLean/Principles.cfm.
15. Lisa Arneth, "Transforming Traditional Lean Principles," *Inside Supply Management®*, (22:6), August 2011, 20.
16. S. Sengupta, "Ten Trends for the Next 10 Years," *Supply Chain Management Review*, July/August 2013, 34-39.

Chapter 2

1. Project Management Institute, "What is Project Management?," accessed December 13, 2013, http://www.pmi.org/About-Us/About-Us-What-is-Project-Management.aspx.
2. Anticlue, "Six Sigma: Defining the Problem Statement," November 27, 2006, accessed December 13, 2013, www.anticlue.net/archives/000750.htm.
3. Jerry B. Harvey, "The Abilene Paradox: The Management of Agreement," *Organizational Dynamics*, Summer 1974, 63–80.
4. Paul Evans, "Performing a SWOT Analysis of Tesco PLC," December 2006, accessed December 13, 2013, www.321books.co.uk/catalog/tesco/swot-analysis.htm.
5. Charles H. Kepner and Benjamin B. Tregoe, *The New Rational Manager* (Princeton, NJ: Princeton Research Press, 1981).
6. Kepner-Tregoe, "Interbake Foods: Integrating Two Acquisitions While Driving Bottom Line Results," 2006, accessed December 14, 2013, www.kepner-tregoe.com/PDFs/CaseStudies/InterbakeMailerKL545.pdf.
7. Jason Westland, *The Project Management Life Cycle* (London: Kogan Page, 2006), 17.
8. Samuel J. Mantel Jr., Jack R. Meredith, Scott M. Shafer and Margaret M. Sutton, *Project Management in Practice* (New York: John Wiley & Sons, 2010), 83.
9. PC World Staff, "Project Management for Modern Managers," PC World, September 9, 1999, accessed December 13, 2013, www.pcworld.com/article/id,12660/article.html; and James R. Bourk, "A New Look at Your Old Project Management Methods Can Promote Your Advantages," *Infoworld* (January 15, 2001): 52.
10. Project Management Institute, *A Guide to the Project Management Body of Knowledge*, 5th edition, 2013. Copyright and all rights reserved. Material from this publication has been reproduced with the permission of PMI.
11. Deloitte, "Core Logic — Procurement Outsourcing," 2013, accessed December 13, 2013, http://www.deloitte.com/view/en_US/us/Services/additional-services/Service-Delivery-Transformation/51a82abfb883f310VgnVCM1000003256f70aRCRD.htm.
12. James P. Lewis, *Project Planning, Scheduling and Control* (New York: McGraw-Hill, 1995), 230.

Chapter 3

1. Steven Wheelwright and Kim Clark, *Leading Product Development: The Senior Manager's Guide to Creating and Shaping the Enterprise* (New York: The Free Press, 1994), 5.
2. P. Fraser Johnson, Michiel Leenders and Anna Flynn, *Purchasing and Supply Management*, 14th ed. (New York: McGraw-Hill, 2011).
3. Lisa Arnseth, "Quantifying Commodity Spend," *Inside Supply Management®* (April 2013): 28.
4. S. Peterson, L. Webber, D. Rosselli and B. Schaefer, *2013 Chief Procurement Officer Study*, IBM Institute for Business Value, May 2013, accessed June 2013, http://public.dhe.ibm.com/common/ssi/ecm/en/gbe03561usen/GBE03561USEN.PDF.
5. Dan Dimancescu and Kemp Dwenger, *World-Class New Product Development* (New York: AMACOM, 1996), 41-42.
6. Ben Taylor, "The Top Ten Smartphones on the Market," *Time*, September 5, 2013, accessed October 7, 2013, http://techland.time.com/2013/09/05/the-top-10-smartphones-on-the-market/.
7. AppleCare Professional Support, accessed December 13, 2013, http://www.apple.com/support/products/enterprise/.
8. IDEO, "About IDEO," accessed January 13, 2014, http://www.ideo.com/about/.
9. Alger, accessed July 30, 2013, http://www.alger.com/pt/appmanager/alger/indiv?_nfpb=true&_pageLabel=alger_page_fundoverview&fundShortName=Green&fundFamily=Mutual+Funds.
10. Triodos Bank, "Socially Responsible Investment," accessed August 13, 2013, http://www.triodos.com/en/investment-management/socially-responsible-investment/.
11. Robert G. Cooper and Scott J. Edgett, "Ten Ways to Make Better Portfolio and Project Selection Decisions," *Visions* (June 2006), 11-15.
12. Joan M. Lang, "Simple Seafood Makeover," *Seafood Business* (October 3, 2007), accessed October 9, 2013, www.seafoodbusiness.com/index.asp?ItemID=3504&rcid=191&pcid=190&cid=191.
13. David Smith, "Fair Wind for World's First 5 MW Turbine," *Modern Power Systems*, (23:10), October 2003: S11-3; and "Repower 5M: Successful Offshore Premier," Repower Systems AG press release, August 24, 2006, accessed October 7, 2013, http://www.repower.de/press/press-releases/detail-press/?no_cache=1&tx_ttnews[tt_news]=1085&cHash=c6bd84a64f74d2b023b16787862bf933.
14. "Flexibility of CAD/CAM Helps Toolmaker Land Boeing 777 Tooling Project," *Mold Making Technology*, May 2011, accessed October 7, 2013, http://www.moldmakingtechnology.com/articles/flexibility-of-cadcam-helps-toolmaker-land-boeing-777-tooling-project.
15. "Dairy Fresh Farms Announces Results of New Generation Milk Test Market Launch in Western Canada," *Business Wire* (November 8, 2005), 1.

16. Jerry W. Thomas, "Product Testing," *Decision Analyst*, 1993, accessed July 30, 2013, http://www.decisionanalyst.com/Services/prodtest.dai.
17. Michael E. Porter, *Competitive Strategy*, (New York: The Free Press, 1980).
18. Stanley Holmes, "Adidas: The Machine of a New Sole," *BloombergBusinessWeek*, March 13, 2005, accessed August 14, 2013, http://www.businessweek.com/stories/2005-03-13/adidas-the-machine-of-a-new-sole; and Adidas®, "Springblade Shoes," accessed January 13, 2014, http://www.adidas.com/us/product/mens-running-springblade-m/AY699?cid=.
19. Charles O'Connor, "Wal-Mart's Top Competition Kroger Buys Harris Teeter for $2.4 Billion Cash, Adding 212 Stores in College Rich Towns," *Forbes*, July 9, 2013, accessed July 19, 2013, http://www.forbes.com/sites/clareoconnor/2013/07/09/watch-out-wal-mart-kroger-buys-harris-teeter-for-2-4-billion-cash-adding-212-stores-in-rich-college-towns/.
20. "The Global Diamond Industry," Bain & Company, 2012, accessed October 9, 2013, http://www.bain.com/Images/BAIN_REPORT_Global_diamond_industry_portrait_of_growth_.PDF; and "DeBeers Operating and Financial Review, 2012," accessed October 9, 2013, http://www.debeersgroup.com/ImageVaultFiles/id_2064/cf_5/2012_OFR.PDF.
21. EV Update, Batteries and Powertrains, "Batteries: EV Industry Looks for Rare Earth Alternatives as China Reins in Supply," accessed October 7, 2013, http://analysis.evupdate.com/batteries-power-trains/batteries-ev-industry-looks-rare-earth-alternatives-china-reins-supply.
22. Lee J. Krajewski, Larry P. Ritzman and Manoj Maholtra, *Operations Management, Processes and Supply Chains*, 12th ed., (Upper Saddle River, NJ: Prentice Hall, 2012), 334.
23. Ibid., 334.
24. Robert Picard, "Book Publishers Challenged by Distribution Problems," *Forbes*, July 27, 2011, accessed July 19, 2013, http://www.forbes.com/sites/robertpicard/2011/07/27/book-publishers-challenged-by-distribution-problems/.
25. "Look Before You Leap," *Business 2.0* (April 2005): 128.
26. Jean V. Murphy, "Logistics Plays Key Role in Success of New Product Introductions," *Global Logistics & Supply Chain Strategies* (August 2006): 58.
27. "What's the Best Way to Measure a Supply Chain? At Lexmark, Cash Is King," *Global Logistics & Supply Chain Strategies* (December 2005): 32-7.
28. "The Coca Cola Company PlantBottle™ Receives Prestigious Global Award," *Chemicals and Chemistry Business*, (June 11, 2010), 85
29. Christopher Bjork, "Zara Owner Inditex to Keep Up Expansion," *Wall Street Journal*, March 21, 2012, accessed October 7, 2013, http://online.wsj.com/article/SB10001424052702304636404577294850646407354.html.

30. Michele J. Flynn, Nancy J. Hite and Michael J. Stanly, "Identifying a Product's Raw Materials," *NAPM InfoEdge*, August 2001, accessed December 13, 2013, www.ism.ws/pubs/InfoEdge/InfoEdgearticle.cfm?ItemNumber=11862.

31. Robert B. Handfield, Gary L. Ragatz, Kenneth J. Petersen and Robert M. Monczka, "Involving Suppliers in New Product Development," *California Management Review* 42(1) (1999): 59-82.

32. Debra Leitka, "Challenges of Component Obsolescence," *Inside Supply Management®*, November 2002: 10, www.ism.ws/pubs/ISMMag/ismarticle.cfm?ItemNumber=12195.

33. Nicolette Lakemond, Ferrie van Echtelt and Finn Wynstra, "A Configuration Typology for Involving Purchasing Specialists in Product Development," *The Journal of Supply Chain Management* (Fall 2001): 11-20.

34. E.E. Scheuing, I. Wirth and D. Antos, "Early Involvement of Purchasers Saves Time and Money," *PM Network* (March 1996): 30-3.

35. J. Carbone, "Buyers Link Hands With Designers," *Purchasing Magazine* (March 16, 2006): 34-9.

36. Michael A. McGinnis and R.M. Vallopra, *Purchasing and Supplier Involvement: New Product Development and Production/Operations Process Development and Improvement* (Tempe, AZ: CAPS Research, 1999), 10.

37. Lisa M. Ellram, "Strategic Cost Management in the Supply Chain: A Purchasing and Supply Management Perspective," (Tempe, AZ: CAPS Research, 2002), 34.

38. Institute for Supply Management®, ISM *Principles of Sustainability and Social Responsibility*, 2012, accessed October 9, 2013, http://www.ism.ws/SR/content.cfm?ItemNumber=18497

39. S.V. Walton, R.B. Handfield and S.A. Melnyk, "The Green Supply Chain: Integrating Suppliers Into Environmental Management Processes," *International Journal of Purchasing and Materials Management* 34(2) (1998): 2-11; and Stephan Vachon, "Green Supply Chain Practices and the Selection of Environmental Technologies," *International Journal of Production Research* (September 2007): 4, 357-79.

Chapter 4

1. Manoj Kumar and Rajesh Kumar Singh, "Crashing Markets Spell Trouble for India's Privatization Plans," *Reuters*, August 22, 2013, accessed October 9, 2013, http://www.reuters.com/article/2013/08/22/us-india-markets-stakesales-idUSBRE97L15Y20130822.

2. I. Wakili, S. Sunday, K. Ekundayo, M. Shosonya and C. Alabi, "Nigeria: Power Firms Sold for N404 B After Gulping N3.2 Trillion," *All Africa*, October 1, 2013, accessed October 9, 2013, http://allafrica.com/stories/201310010479.html.

3. World Trade Organization (2012). "International Trade Statistics 2012," accessed June 15, 2013, https://www.wto.org/english/res_e/statis_e/its2012_e/its12_toc_e.htm.

4. World Trade Organization, "Millennium Development Goals, Trade and Development," accessed October 9, 2013, http://www.wto.org/english/thewto_e/coher_e/mdg_e/development_e.htm.
5. Ibid.
6. Brent Snavely, "Chrysler Announces Deal to Make Jeeps in China," *USA Today*, January 15, 2013, accessed July 22, 2013, http://www.usatoday.com/story/money/cars/2013/01/15/jeep-guangzhou-china/1566380/.
7. Walmart, "2013 Annual Report," accessed July 23, 2013, http://stock.walmart.com/microsites/annual-report-2013/.
8. Whirlpool Corporation, About, "Overview," accessed July 23, 2013, http://www.whirlpoolcorp.com/about/design/global_consumer_design/overview.aspx.
9. "Trendsetters: J&J's Santiago Cardenas Looks at Latin American Opportunities," *The Internationalist*, accessed October 9, 2013, http://www.internationalistmagazine.com/Trendsetter_LA/Trendsetter_LA_Cardenas_more.html.
10. Kim Ribbink, "Ola Brazil: Latin America's Biggest Market Accelerates," *PharmaVOICE*, January 2011, 50-52.
11. Charla Griffy-Brown, "Just-in-Time to Just-in-Case: Managing a Supply Chain in Uncertain Times," *Graziado Business Report* 6(2) (2003), Pepperdine University, accessed December 14, 2013, http://gbr.pepperdine.edu/2010/08/just-in-time-to-just-in-case/#return6.
12. Larry R. Smeltzer, "Managing Cultural Differences in Buyer-Supplier Relationships," *Proceedings of the 81st Annual International ISM Conference*, 1996, Chicago.
13. Heather R. Keller, "Soft Skills for Global Managers," *Inside Supply Management*® (September 2007): 26.
14. "Haier, Already a Success, Aims Higher," Interview with Zhang Ruimin, Knowledge@Wharton (April 5, 2005), accessed December 14, 2013, www.knowledgeatwharton.com.cn/index.cfm?fa=viewfeature&languageid=1&articleid=1111; and Haier, "About," accessed December 14, 2013, http://www.haieramerica.com/about.
15. "What's Ahead for 2007? Knowledge@Wharton Network Surveys the Globe" (December 13, 2006), http://knowledge.wharton.upenn.edu/article.cfm?articleid=1621; and Arthur Pinkasovitch, "What a Rising Yuan Means for You," *Forbes*, May 10, 2010, accessed July 23, 2013, http://www.forbes.com/2010/05/12/yuan-currency-investing-personal-finance-yuan-investing.html.
16. "China Yuan Ends Slightly Higher on PBOC Guidance, Recent Dollar Weakness," *Wall Street Journal*, October 8, 2013, accessed October 9, 2013, http://online.wsj.com/article/BT-CO-20131008-702908.html.
17. Gina Chon, "Global Economy: German Automakers Rev up U.S. Output; BMW and Mercedes Seek Hedge Against Weak Dollar, Giving the South an Economic Boost," *Wall Street Journal*, August 14, 2007, A-6.

ENDNOTES

18. U.S. Commodity Futures Trading Commission, *CFTC Glossary*, accessed July 25, 2013, http://www.cftc.gov/ConsumerProtection/EducationCenter/CFTCGlossary/index.htm.
19. Financial CAD Corporation, "Increasing the Effectiveness of Hedging Interest Rates and Foreign Exchange Rates: A Case Study," 2002, accessed December 14, 2013, www.comsol.ch/comsol/pub/media/pdf/fincad%20mcdonalds%20new.
20. EU Report: "Trade Protectionism Still on Rise Across the World," European Commission Press Release, September 2, 2013, accessed October 10, 2013, http://europa.eu/rapid/press-release_IP-13-807_en.htm.
21. B. Baumohl, *The Secrets of Economic Indicators*, 3rd ed. (FT Press, 2013), 21.
22. U.S. Department of Commerce, Bureau of Economic Analysis, "Measuring the Economy," September 2007, accessed December 14, 2013, www.bea.gov/national/pdf/nipa_primer.pdf.
23. Wade C. Ferguson and Jeffrey A. White, "Negotiating to Prevent Cost Increases," *NAPM InfoEdge*, May 1996, accessed December 14, 2013, www.ism.ws/pubs/InfoEdge/InfoEdgeArticle.cfm?ItemNumber=10131.
24. Daily FX, "Forex Economic Calendar," accessed October 10, 2013, http://www.dailyfx.com/calendar.
25. Parker Leavitt, "Gilbert Homebuilding Continues to Surge," The Republic/AZCentral.com, accessed July 23, 2013, http://www.azcentral.com/community/gilbert/articles/2012/07/11/20120711gilbert-homebuilding-surge-continues.html (July 14, 2012).
26. U.S. Department of Labor, Bureau of Labor Statistics, accessed July 23, 2013, http://www.bls.gov/.
27. Office of National Statistics, accessed July 23, 2013, http://www.ons.gov.uk/ons/index.html.
28. Statistics Finland, "Statistics," accessed December 14, 2013, www.stat.fi/til/index_en.html.
29. U.S. Department of Labor, Bureau of Labor Statistics, accessed December 14, 2013, www.bls.gov/.
30. U.S. Department of Labor, Bureau of Labor Statistics, "Producer Price Indexes," accessed December 14, 2013, www.bls.gov/ppi/.
31. Bureau of Labor Statistics, Producer Price Indexes, "Frequently Asked Questions," accessed January 14, 2014, http://www.bls.gov/ppi/ppifaq.htm#10.
32. Economic Research, Federal Reserve Bank of St. Louis, "GDP Implicit Price Deflator in United Kingdom," accessed October 10, 2013, http://research.stlouisfed.org/fred2/series/GBRGDPDEFQISMEI.
33. Trading Economics, United States Balance of Trade, accessed October 10, 2013, http://www.tradingeconomics.com/united-states/balance-of-trade.

34. David J. Lynch, "U.S. Trade Deficit Balloons to $805B," *USA Today*, March 14, 2006, accessed December 14, 2013, www.usatoday.com/money/economy/trade/2006-03-14-econ-usat_x.htm.
35. Trading Economics, accessed July 24, 2013, http://www.tradingeconomics.com/china/balance-of-trade.
36. H. E. Lewis, "Forecasting in the Purchasing and Supply Arena," *NAPM InfoEdge* (3:11), July 1998.
37. Current monthly reports and more detailed information can be found at www.ism.ws/.
38. Institute for Supply Management®, Bradley J. Holcomb, CPSM, CPSD, chair of the Manufacturing Business Survey Committee, September 2013.
39. Institute for Supply Management®.
40. Federal Reserve Board, Federal Reserve Bulletin, Vol. 93, 2007, accessed December 14, 2013, http://www.federalreserve.gov/pubs/bulletin/2007/07index.htm.
41. U. S. Department of Agriculture, Economic Research Service, "Amber Waves," accessed January 14, 2014, http://ers.usda.gov/amber-waves.aspx#.UtVUcvKA1pw.
42. European Commission, Eurostat, accessed October 12, 2013, http://epp.eurostat.ec.europa.eu/portal/page/portal/eurostat/home.
43. UN Comtrade, accessed August 19, 2013, http://comtrade.un.org/.
44. United Nations, Department of Economic and Social Affairs, accessed August 19, 2013, http://www.un.org/en/development/desa/index.html.
45. Food and Agricultural Organization of the United Nations, accessed August 19, 2013, http://www.fao.org/statistics/en/.
46. OECD, accessed August 19, 2013, www.oecd.org/.
47. International Monetary Fund, accessed August 19, 2013, www.imf.org/.
48. Business Monitor Online, accessed October 12, 2013, http://www.businessmonitor.com/bmo.
49. Forecast International, accessed August 19, 2013, www.forecastinternational.com/.
50. Metropolitan Council, accessed August 19, 2013, http://metrocouncil.org/
51. Ministry of Business, Innovation and Employment, New Zealand, accessed August 19, 2013, www.tourismresearch.govt.nz/Analysis/Forecasts+and+Trends/.
52. Arizona State University, W. P. Carey School of Business, accessed August 19, 2013, http://wpcarey.asu.edu/finance/real-estate/market-reports.cfm .
53. ConAgra Foods, accessed August 19, 2013, http://www.conagrafoods.com/investor-relations; and Bill Lapp, "Economic and Commodity Review," Presentation made to the ISM Foodservice Purchasing Manager's Conference, May 21, 2004, www.ism.ws/files/secure/index.cfm?FileID=3366.

Chapter 5

1. Intel, "What is a Tablet PC?," accessed December 15, 2013, http://www.intel.com/content/www/us/en/tech-tips-and-tricks/a-guide-to-tablet-pcs.html.
2. C. Walker and M. Coacher, "Building the Change-Capable Organization to Meet the Top Technology Trends of 2012 and Beyond," *CPA Practice Management* (May 2012): 16-18.
3. An MRP system also may be a module within an enterprise resource planning (ERP) system. More on ERP can be found in Chapter 11.
4. Chris Gray, "Coca Cola: 'Always' Class A MRP II," accessed December 15, 2013, http://www.partnersforexcellence.com/v2art3.htm.
5. N. deLarrinaga, "Finnish 2014 Defense Budget Slashes Procurement Spend," *James Defence Industry* (October 1, 2013).
6. Ben Mutzabaugh, "Boom Forces Boeing to Say, 'Sorry, We're Sold Out,'" *USA Today*, November 28, 2006.
7. D. Berta, "QSRs Rethink Employment Strategy During Labor Shortage," *Nation's Restaurant News*, (August 28, 2006):1.
8. Zacks Equity Research, "South Africa Auto Labor Strike Continues," *Zacks*, August 30, 2013, accessed October 12, 2013, http://www.zacks.com/stock/news/108070/South-Africa-Auto-Labor-Strike-Continues.
9. Andrew Dowell, "Japan: The Business Aftershocks; From Chips to Banks, Companies Scramble," *Wall Street Journal*, March 25, 2011, B-1.
10. Deloitte®, "Technology, Media and Telecommunications Predictions 2013," accessed October 12, 2013, http://www.deloitte.com/assets/Dcom-Shared%20Assets/Documents/TMT%20Predictions%202013%20PDFs/dttl_TMT_Predictions2013_Final.pdf.
11. Lisa Arnseth, "Superstorm Sandy Hits Home," *Inside Supply Management*®, November 2012, 9.
12. Thomas W. Derry, "Be Prepared," *Inside Supply Management*®, January 2013, 6.
13. Business Forecast Systems, "Collaborative Forecasting Running Smoothly at Brooks Sports," *Trends*, (March 2006): 5-6, accessed December 15, 2013, http://www.forecastpro.com/customers/success/brooks.htm.
14. SAS®, "A Business in Transit," accessed October 16, 2013, www.sas.com/success/dnata.html.
15. Ferret, "Top Down or Bottom Up: Making the Right Retail Demand Planning Strategy Decision with GRA," October 28, 2010, accessed October 12, 2013, http://www.ferret.com.au/c/GRA/Top-down-or-bottom-up-making-the-right-retail-demand-planning-strategy-decision-with-GRA-n900905.
16. K. B. Kahn, "Revisiting Top-Down Versus Bottom-Up Forecasting," *Journal of Business Forecasting*, 17 (Summer 1998):14.

17. Kathleen Hickey, "Retailers Starting to Get It Right — at the Store Level," *Global Logistics and Supply Chain Strategies*, April 2005, accessed December 15, 2013, http://www.jdmandassociates.com/pdfs/2005_04_Pink_Soda_%28GLandSCS%29.pdf.
18. Paul Gelly, "Managing Bottom-Up and Top-Down Approaches: Ocean Spray's Experience," *Journal of Business Forecasting* (Winter 1999/2000): 3-6.
19. Alvin Williams, Larry Giunipero and Tony Henthorne, "The Cross-Functional Imperative: The Case of Marketing and Purchasing," *International Journal of Purchasing and Materials Management* 30 (Summer 1994): 28.
20. J.H. Hammond and A. Raman, "Sport Obermeyer Ltd.," *Harvard Business Publishing* (2006): 1-19.
21. "Research and Markets Adds Report: Price Forecast for 17 Ingredients," *Professional Services Close Up* (August 31, 2012). ABI/Inform Database Complete.
22. Dave Blanchard, "Food for Thought," *Logistics Today* (June 2006): 1-2.
23. Sharon Florentine, "Demand for Cloud Skills Still Outpaces Supply of Workers," *CIO*, September 19, 2013, accessed October 13, 2013, http://www.cio.com/article/740026/Demand_for_Cloud_Skills_Still_Outpaces_Supply_of_Workers.
24. Lee J. Krajewski, Larry P. Ritzman and Manoj K. Maholtra, *Operations Management: Processes and Value Chains*, 10th ed. (Prentice Hall, 2012): 544.
25. Victoria Colliver, "Visits to Emergency Rooms Rise as Insurance Lost," *SF Gate*, October 17, 2011, accessed October 16, 2013, http://www.sfgate.com/bayarea/article/Visits-to-emergency-rooms-rise-as-insurance-lost-2326541.php.
26. R. Champion, L.D. Kinsman, G.A. Lee, K.A. Masman, E.A. May, T.M. Mills, M.D. Taylor, P.R. Thomas and R.J. Williams, "Forecasting Emergency Department Presentations," Australian Health Review, February 2007: 83-90; H. Fang and K.K. Kwong, "Forecasting Foreign Exchange Rates," *The Journal of Business Forecasting* (Winter 1991/1992): 19; and Clark Hu, "Advanced Tourism Demand Forecasting: Artificial Neural Network and Box-Jenkins Modeling, a Dissertation" (2004), Purdue University, access through ASU only, October 16, 2013, http://proquest.umi.com.ezproxy1.lib.asu.edu/pqdweb?index=0&srchmode=1&sid=1&vinst=PROD&fmt=6&startpage=-1&vname=PQD&did=764941521&scaling=FULL&pmid=66569&vtype=PQD&rqt=309&TS=1196119303&clientId clientId=25164.
27. George C.S. Wang, "Forecasting Practices in Electric and Gas Utility Companies," *The Journal of Business Forecasting* 25 (Spring 2004): 11-5.
28. J.R. Muscatello, "Forecast Accuracy Improvement with a Process Redesign: A Case Study," *The Journal of Business Forecasting* (Summer 2009): 34-35.
29. M. Waller, "How Data Sharing Drives Supply Chain Innovation," *Industry Week*, August 12, 2013, accessed October 17, 2013, http://www.industryweek.com/supplier-relationships/how-sharing-data-drives-supply-chain-innovation?page=3.
30. Email interview with Mitchell Millstein on October 14, 2013.

31. This example was adapted from Roberta J. Duffy, "The Future of Purchasing and Supply Demand-Pull Possibilities," *Purchasing Today®*, January 2000: 48.
32. R. Burnette, "CPFR: Fact, Fiction or Fantasy?," *Journal of Business Forecasting*, Winter 2010/2011: 32-35.
33. KJR Consulting, *CPFR Baseline Study, Manufacturer Profile* (Washington, DC: Grocery Manufacturers of America, 2002): 5.
34. T.J. Olesen, "Collaborating for Success," *Inside Supply Management®*, June 2012, 10.
35. Ibid.

Chapter 6

1. K. Lysons, *Purchasing and Supply Chain Management*, 8th ed. (London: FT Prentice Hall, 2012).
2. T. Hines, *Supply Chain Strategies: Demand-Driven and Customer-Focused*, 2nd edition (London: Routledge, 2013).
3. R.H. Ballou, *Business Logistics/Supply Chain Management*, 5th ed. (Upper Saddle River, NJ: Pearson Education, 2004).
4. J. Nagel, ed., *Supply Chain Management: A Procurement Perspective*, (Melbourne: Hargreen Publishing, 2003).
5. V. Govindarajan, "Tuck School of Business at Dartmouth, Case Study: Wal-Mart Stores, Inc." (2002), http://mba.tuck.dartmouth.edu/pdf/2002-2-0013.pdf; MWPVL International, Inc., "The Wal-Mart Distribution Center Network in the United States," accessed December 16, 2013, http://www.mwpvl.com/html/walmart.html; and Walmart, "Our Story," accessed December 16, 2013, http://corporate.walmart.com/our-story/.
6. L.M. Ellram and T.Y. Choi, *Supply Management for Value Enhancement* (Tempe, AZ: National Association of Purchasing Management, 2000).
7. F.A. Kuglin, *Customer-Centered Supply Chain Management* (AMACOM, 1998).
8. C. Steele, "Should I Lease or Buy? The Science of Asset Risk Strategy: Part 1," *Cargo Business News*, January 2009, accessed October 17, 2013, http://www.cargobusinessnews.com/Jan09/lease_or_buy.html.
9. Matt Hudgins, "New Hubs Arise to Serve Just-in-Case Distribution," *The New York Times*, February 12, 2013, accessed October 17, 2013, http://www.nytimes.com/2013/02/13/realestate/commercial/new-hubs-arise-to-serve-a-just-in-case-supply-chain.html?_r=0.
10. K. Babich and C. Pettijohn, *Sourcing in the Public Sector*, (Herndon, VA: National Institute of Governmental Purchasing, 2004).
11. Federal Ministry of Transport, Building and Urban Development, accessed December 16, 2013, http://www.bmvbs.de/EN/Home/home_node.html.

12. N. Bauhof, "Logistics Distribution and Warehousing 2006: Network Optimization," *Area Development Online*, 2006, accessed October 17, 2013, http://www.areadevelopment.com/specialPub/ldw06/supplyChainOptimization.shtml.
13. Hines, *Supply Chain Strategies: Demand-Driven and Customer-Focused*.
14. Hines, *Supply Chain Strategies: Customer-Driven and Customer-Focused*.
15. Bastian Solutions, "Johnson Controls: Case Study," accessed October 18, 2013, http://www.bastiansolutions.com/case-studies/manufacturing-finished-goods-industry/johnson-controls#.UmFbfxBA-8A.
16. R. Schmidt, "STORE: AS/RS Fires Up Productivity in Deep-Freeze Warehouses," *Material Handling & Logistics*, March 21, 2013, accessed October 18, 2013, http://mhlnews.com/powered-vehicles/store-asrs-fires-productivity-deep-freeze-warehouses.
17. "Study Finds 66 Percent of Warehouses Plan to Expand Technology Investments by 2018," *SupplyChain 24/7*, August 21, 2013, accessed October 18, 2013, http://www.supplychain247.com/article/study_finds_66_percent_of_warehouses_plan_to_expand_technology_investments/motorola_solutions.
18. D. Blanchard, *Supply Chain Management Best Practices* (Hoboken, NJ: John Wiley & Sons, 2010).
19. "Study Finds 66 Percent of Warehouses Plan to Expand Technology Investments by 2018," *SupplyChain 24/7*, August 21, 2013.
20. R. Schonberger, "Supply Chains: Tightening the Links," *Manufacturing Engineering* 137(3), (September 2006), 77-92.
21. Global old ChainAlliance®, "IARW North American Top 25," accessed December 16, 2013, http://www.gcca.org/resources/iarw-north-american-top-25/.
22. "Study Finds 66 Percent of Warehouses Plan to Expand Technology Investments by 2018," *SupplyChain 24/7*, August 21, 2013.
23. "RFID Market Worth $30B by 2024," RFID 24-7, October 10, 2013, accessed October 18, 2013, http://www.rfid24-7.com/2013/10/10/rfid-market-worth-30b-by-2024/.
24. L. Stanley and D. Matthews, *Logistics and Transportation* (Herndon, VA: National Institute of Governmental Purchasing, 2007).
25. Defense Procurement and Acquisition Policy (DPAP), accessed August 26, 2013, http://www.acq.osd.mil/dpap/pdi/uid/index.html.
26. C-TPAT Program Achievements, July 1, 2013, accessed October 18, 2013, http://www.cbp.gov/linkhandler/cgov/trade/cargo_security/ctpat/ctpat_news_reports/ctpat_achieve_report13.ctt/ctpat_achieve_report13.pdf.
27. Supply Chain Security International Inc., "What is C-TPAT?," accessed August 22, 2013, http://www.c-tpat.com/what-is-ctpat/ctpat-benefits/.
28. G. Gianakis and D. Matthews, *Warehousing and Inventory Control* (Herndon, VA:

National Institute of Governmental Purchasing, 2008).
29. AFS Technologies, "Warehouse Management," accessed October 18, 2013, http://www.afsi.com/afs-solutions/manufacturer-solutions/warehouse-management/.
30. R.J. Bowman, "A New Warehouse Management System," *SupplyChainBrain*, April 24, 2012, accessed October 18, 2013, http://www.supplychainbrain.com/content/index.php?id=5032&cHash=081010&tx_ttnews[tt_news]=14890.
31. Michael Levans, "Viewpoint: How Warehouse/DC Automation is Changing Logistics," *Logistics Management*, June 1, 2012, accessed October 18, 2013, http://www.logisticsmgmt.com/article/viewpoint_how_automation_is_changing_logistics; and Michael Levans, "Viewpoint: Anything, From Anytime, Anywhere," *Logistics Management*, June 1, 2013, accessed October 18, 2013, http://www.logisticsmgmt.com/article/viewpoint_anything_anytime_from_anywhere.
32. "Study Finds 66 Percent of Warehouses Plan to Expand Technology Investments by 2018," *SupplyChain* 24/7, August 21, 2013.
33. "Warehousing Goes Virtual," *Service Management* (March 2006), p. 6.
34. M. Christopher, *Logistics and Supply Chain Management* (Upper Saddle River, NJ: FT Press, 2011).
35. ByBox, "Parcel Lockers," accessed December 16, 2013, http://www.bybox.com/lockers/.
36. C. Perkins, "Robert's Foods Links Up With Virtual Warehouse," *Nation's Restaurant News* (May 24, 2004): 34.
37. L.K. Rogers, "Sustainability: Green Trends Growing in Materials Management," *Logistics Management*, November 1, 2011, accessed October 18, 2013, http://www1.logisticsmgmt.com/view/sustainability_green_trends_growing_in_materials_handling/sustainability.
38. Maida Napolitano, "Staples' Smart Packaging System Expected to Save 25,000 Metric Tons of Corrugated," *Logistics Today*, June 1, 2013, accessed October 18, 2013, http://www.logisticsmgmt.com/article/warehouse_dc_technology_and_innovation_staples_smart_packaging_happy_custom.

Chapter 7

1. P. Fraser Johnson and Michiel R. Leenders, *Supply's Organizational Roles and Responsibilities*, 2011, (Tempe, AZ: CAPS, 2012).
2. P. Cuviello, "Adapting Logistics Capabilities to National Security Requirements," 21st Annual National Logistics Conference, National Defense Industrial Association (NDIA), March 2005, www.dtic.mil/ndia/2005logistics/tuesday/cuviello.pdf.
3. S. Tzu and G. Gagliardi, *The Art of War: In Sun Tzu's Own Words* (Seattle, WA: Clearbridge Publishing, 1999).

4. Tony Hines, *Supply Chain Strategies: Demand-Driven and Customer-Focused.*
5. A.J. Van Weele, *Purchasing & Supply Chain Management*, 5th ed. (London: Thomson Learning, 2009)
6. Joe Cavinato, "Supply Management Defined, 2010," Institute for Supply Management®, accessed October 14, 2013, http://www.ism.ws/tools/content.cfm?ItemNumber=5558.
7. United States Department of Transportation, Bureau of Transportation Statistics, accessed October 14, 2013, http://www.rita.dot.gov/bts/sites/rita.dot.gov.bts/files/publications/national_transportation_statistics/index.html.
8. Association of American Railroads, "The Economic Impact of America's Freight Railroads," April 2013, accessed October 14, 2013, https://www.aar.org/keyissues/Documents/Background-papers/Economic%20Impact%20of%20US%20Freight%20RRs%20April%202013.pdf.
9. Association of American Railroads, "Class 1 Railroad Statistics," July 9, 2013, accessed October 14, 2013, https://www.aar.org/StatisticsAndPublications/Documents/AAR-Stats-2013-07-09.pdf.
10. U.S. Maritime Administration, Office of Data and Economic Analysis (2011), accessed October 14, 2013, http://www.marad.dot.gov/documents/US_Water_Transportation_Statistical_snapshot.pdf.
11. duhaime.org, Learn Law, accessed October 14, 2013, http://www.duhaime.org/LegalDictionary/G/GeneralAverage.aspx.
12. United Stated Department of Transportation, Bureau of Transportation Statistics, accessed October 14, 2013, http://www.rita.dot.gov/bts/sites/rita.dot.gov.bts/files/subject_areas/airline_information/index.html; and Boeing, "World Air Cargo Forecast: 2012-2013," accessed October 14, 2013, http://www.boeing.com/assets/pdf/commercial/cargo/wacf.pdf.
13. "Saks Incorporated 10-K," accessed October 14, 2013, https://www.saksincorporated.com/investorrelations/documents/201210Kfiling.pdf.
14. Linda Stanley and Darin Matthews, *Logistics and Transportation*, National Institute of Governmental Purchasing, Herndon, VA, 2007.
15. R. Tubb, "2013 Pipeline Construction Report," *Underground Construction*, (68:1), January 2013, accessed October 14, 2013, http://www.undergroundconstructionmagazine.com/2013-pipeline-construction-report.
16. U.S. Department of Transportation, Bureau of Transportation Statistics, "Oil Pipeline Profile," accessed December 18, 2013, https://www.rita.dot.gov/bts/sites/rita.dot.gov.bts/files/publications/national_transportation_statistics/html/table_oil_pipeline_profile.html.
17. "Del Monte Closes the Loop in Intermodal Services Program," *SupplyChainBrain Magazine*, August 4, 2009, accessed October 14, 2013, http://www.supplychainbrain.com/content/index.php?id=5032&cHash=081010&tx_ttnews[tt_news]=5937.

18. E.G. Hinkelman, *Dictionary of International Trade*, 9th ed. (Novato, CA: World Trade Press, 2010).
19. J. O'Reilly, "4PLs Take Control," *Inbound Logistics* (January 2011), accessed December 18, 2013, http://www.inboundlogistics.com/cms/article/4pls-take-control/.
20. P. Fraser Johnson, Michiel Leenders and Anna Flynn, *Purchasing and Supply Management*, 14th ed. (Boston, MA: McGraw-Hill Irwin, 2011).
21. Tony Hines, *Supply Chain Strategies: Demand-Driven and Customer-Focused*, Routledge, London, 2013.
22. WTO World Trade Report 2013, accessed October 14, 2013, http://www.wto.org/english/res_e/publications_e/wtr13_e.htm.
23. World Trade Organization, "Trade to Remain Subdued in 2013 After Sluggish Growth in 2012 as European Economies Continue to Struggle," April 10, 2013, accessed October 14, 2013, http://www.wto.org/english/news_e/pres13_e/pr688_e.htm.
24. "New Study Reveals Nine Key Trends of Global Logistics," SDCExec.com, August 9, 2013, accessed October 14, 2013, http://www.sdcexec.com/article/11080842/bvl-international-research-reveals-what-may-lie-ahead-for-supply-chain.
25. United Nations Conference on Trade and Development (UNCSTAD), accessed October 14, 2013, http://unctadstat.unctad.org/TableViewer/tableView.aspx?ReportId=93.
26. Hinkelman, *Dictionary of International Trade*.
27. ISM *Guide to the Incoterms® Rules*, Summary from International Chamber of Commerce, www.iccwbo.org/products-and-services/trade-facilitation/Incoterms-2010/, June 2013.
28. U.S. Customs and Border Protection, "C-TPAT: Program Overview," (3/14/2012), accessed October 15, 2013, http://www.cbp.gov/linkhandler/cgov/trade/cargo_security/ctpat/ctpat_program_information/what_is_ctpat/ctpat_overview.ctt/ctpat_overview.pdf.
29. P. Yang, "How Does Container Security Initiative (CSI) Affect Your Cargo?," *More Than Shipping*, January 28, 2013, accessed October 15, 2013, http://morethanshipping.com/how-does-container-security-iniative-csi-affect-your-cargo/.
30. NTC Australia, "Quick Reference Guide to National Heavy Vehicle Access Schemes and Arrangements," January 2009, accessed October 15, 2013, http://www.ntc.gov.au/filemedia/bulletins/HeavyVehicleAccessSchemesandArra.pdf.
31. Dangerous Goods Transportation Act, 2007, accessed October 13, 2013, www.assembly.nl.ca/legislation/sr/statutes/d01.htm.

32. Singapore Chemical Industry Council (SCIC), *Guidebook on Transport and Handling Dangerous Goods* (November 2009), accessed October 15, 2013, http://www.scdf.gov.sg/content/scdf_internet/en/building-professionals/fire-safety-licensing-and-enforcement/_jcr_content/par/download_6/file.res/Insert-Revision%20I%20_2009_%20SCIC.pdf.
33. National Motor Freight Association, The National Motor Freight Classification™, accessed October 15, 2013, http://www.nmfta.org/Pages/Nmfc.aspx.
34. "Food Wholesalers Adopt Track-and-Trace System," *Supermarket News*, May 16, 2013, accessed October 15, 2013, http://supermarketnews.com/food-safety/food-wholesalers-adopt-track-and-trace-system.
35. Robert M. Monczka, Robert B. Handfield, Larry C. Giunipero and James L. Patterson, *Purchasing and Supply Management*, 5th Edition (South-Western CENGAGE Learning, 2011).
36. U.S. Department of Transportation, Federal Motor Carrier Safety Administration, *Principles and Practices for the Investigation and Voluntary Disposition of Loss and Damage Claims and Processing Salvage*, as of July 16, 2013, accessed October 15, 2013, http://www.fmcsa.dot.gov/rules-regulations/administration/fmcsr/fmcsrguidedetails.aspx?menukey=370.
37. Robert M. Monczka, Robert B. Handfield, Larry C. Giunipero and James L. Patterson, *Purchasing and Supply Management*, 5th Edition (South-Western CENGAGE Learning, 2011).
38. M. Szakonyi, "US Shippers Overspent 13% in 2011, Study Says," *Journal of Commerce*, May 4, 2012, accessed October 15, 2013, http://www.joc.com/international-logistics/global-sourcing/us-shippers-overspent-13-percent-2011-study-says_20120504.html.
39. Robert M. Monczka, Robert B. Handfield, Larry C. Giunipero and James L. Patterson, *Purchasing and Supply Management*, 5th Edition (South-Western CENGAGE Learning, 2011).
40. Tony Hines, *Supply Chain Strategies: Demand-Driven and Customer-Focused*.
41. Prater and Whitehead, *An Introduction to Supply Chain Management: A Global Supply Chain Support Perspective*; Hyperformix (now CA Technologies), "Caterpillar: A Case Study," accessed October 15, 2013, http://www.ca.com/~/media/Files/SuccessStories/caterpillar-case-study.pdf.
42. K. Collison, "Massive Warehouses Built in KC's Growing Role as National Distribution Center," *Kansas City Star* (April 12, 2013), accessed October 15, 2013, http://www.mcclatchydc.com/2013/04/02/187504/massive-warehouses-built-in-kcs.html#.UiDSfT_gc44; and A.R. Partridge, "Full Circle: Reverse Logistics Keeps Products Green to the End," *Inbound Logistics*, June 2011, accessed October 15, 2013, http://www.inboundlogistics.com/cms/article/full-circle-reverse-logistics-keeps-products-green-to-the-end/.

43. T. Miller and R. de Matta, "A Global Supply Chain Profit Maximization and Transfer Pricing Model," *Journal of Business Logistics* (2008), 175-199.
44. T. Gudehus and H. Kotzab, "Time for a Checkup?," *Supply Chain Quarterly*, (October 1, 2010), accessed October 15, 2013, http://www.supplychainquarterly.com/topics/Logistics/scq201001audit/.
45. "The Ten Fallacies of Logistics Productivity Management," *Manufacturing & Logistics IT* (March 22, 2005), accessed October 15, 2013, http://www.logisticsit.com/articles/2005/03/22/829-the-10-fallacies-of-logistics-productivity.
46. A. Rushton, P. Croucher and P. Baker, editors, T*he Handbook of Logistics and Distribution Management*, 4th ed., Kogan Page (2010).

Chapter 8

1. Christopher, *Logistics and Supply Chain Management*.
2. P. Fraser Johnson and Michiel R. Leenders, *Supply's Organizational Roles and Responsibilities*, 2011, (Tempe, AZ: CAPS, 2012).
3. Brady, *Managing Fixed Assets in the Public Sector*.
4. IBM, "Smarter Maintenance at the University Hospital of Tübingen," September 4, 2013, accessed December 18, 2013, http://www-01.ibm.com/software/success/cssdb.nsf/CS/STRD-9B3FFR?OpenDocument&Site=corp&cty=en_us.
5. United States Internal Revenue Service, accessed December 18, 2013, www.irs.gov/publications/p946/ch02.html#en_US_2012_publink1000107395.
6. Rudski, et al., *Straight to the Bottom Line: An Executive's Roadmap to World Class Supply Management*, (Fort Lauderdale, FL: J. Ross Publishing, 2006).
7. Ibid.
8. J.D. Wisner and L.L. Stanley, *Process Management: Creating Value Along the Supply Chain*, (CENGAGE, 2008).
9. P. Carter, et al., *Succeeding in a Dynamic World: Supply Management in the Decade Ahead*, CAPS Research, Institute for Supply Management® and A.T. Kearney, 2007.
10. J. Cavinato, A. Flynn and R. Kauffman, *Supply Management Handbook*, 7th ed. (Tempe, AZ: Institute for Supply Management®, 2006).
11. "Unlocking Working Capital: Best Practices for Reducing Inventory," Aberdeen Group, December 2008, accessed September 2, 2013, www.aberdeen.com.
12. Arizona State University, "Inventory Policy, FIN 402: Inventory," March 1, 2005, accessed October 15, 2013, www.asu.edu/aad/manuals/fin/fin402.html.
13. T. Hurlbut, "Cycle Counting," *Inc.*, June 2005, accessed October 15, 2013, www.inc.com/resources/retail/articles/200506/counting.html.
14. World Health Organization, *Guidelines for the Storage of Essential Medicines and Other Health Commodities* (2003), last updated August 2013, accessed October 15, 2013, http://apps.who.int/medicinedocs/en/d/Js4885e/5.3.html.

15. Lee Buddress, M.E. Smith and A.R. Raedels, "Getting the Most From Your Indirect Purchasing Dollar," *Proceedings From the 2006 ISM Annual Conference* (Tempe: Institute for Supply Management®, 2006)
16. Sea-rates.com, "Transit Time/Distance Calculator," accessed October 16, 2013, http://www.searates.com/reference/portdistance/.
17. N. Jain, K. Girota and S. Netessine, "Managing Global Sourcing: Inventory Performance," *INSEAD Working Paper No. 2013/65/TOM*, July 13, 2013, accessed October 16, 2013, http://papers.ssrn.com/sol3/papers.cfm?abstract_id=1939029##.
18. B. Balchedor, "Wal-Mart-Commissioned Study Shows RFID Improves Store Inventory Accuracy," *RFID Journal*, March 13, 2008, accessed October 16, 2013, http://www.rfidjournal.com/articles/view?3969/.
19. Tony Hines, *Supply Chain Strategies: Demand-Driven and Customer-Focused*.
20. J.A. Cooke, "Running Inventory Like a Deere," *Supply Chain Quarterly*, October 4, 2007, accessed October 16, 2013, http://www.supplychainquarterly.com/topics/Finance/scq200704deere/.
21. Christopher, *Logistics and Supply Chain Management*.
22. Toyota, "Toyota Production System," accessed October 16, 2013, http://www.toyota-global.com/company/vision_philosophy/toyota_production_system/.
23. Tony Hines, *Supply Chain Strategies: Demand-Driven and Customer-Focused*.
24. DemandPoint, Inc., accessed October 16, 2013, http://www.demandpointinc.com/.
25. Vendor Managed Inventory, accessed October 16, 2013, http://www.vendormanagedinventory.com/pitfalls.php.
26. Datalliance, "A New Look at VMI: How Dannon is using VMI to Strengthen Retailer Relationships and Grow Sales," accessed October 16, 2013, http://www.datalliance.com/cgt_webinar.html.
27. Rudski, et al., *Straight to the Bottom Line*.
28. Brady, *Managing Fixed Assets in the Public Sector*.
29. Reverse Logistics Association, "What is Reverse Logistics?," accessed October 16, 2013, http://www.reverselogisticstrends.com/reverse-logistics.php.
30. D. Douthit, M. Flach and V. Agarwal, *Reducing the Quantity and Cost of Product Returns in Consumer Electronics*, Accenture, September 2, 2011, accessed October 16, 2013, http://www.accenture.com/us-en/Pages/insight-reducing-quality-cost-product-returns-consumer-electronics.aspx.
31. Lexmark, Dixie Warehouse, accessed October 16, 2013, http://www.lexmark.com/en_CA/images/vignette/vgn/images/portal/Mfg_Dixie_Warehouse_CaseStudy.pdf.
32. Hewlett-Packard, Product Return and Recycling, accessed October 16, 2013, http://www8.hp.com/us/en/hp-information/environment/product-recycling.html#.UioXyD_gc44.

33. Keep America Beautiful, Inc., Recycling Facts & Stats, accessed October 17, 2013, http://www.kab.org/site/PageServer?pagename=recycling_facts_and_stats.
34. Gianakis and Matthews, *Warehousing and Inventory Control*.
35. US Forest Service, accessed October 17, 2013, http://www.fs.fed.us/fire/partners/fepp/.
36. Interface®, accessed October 17, 2013, http://www.interfaceglobal.com/.
37. Brigham Young University, Purchasing Department, Surplus Sales Information, accessed October 17, 2013, http://surplus.byu.edu/.
38. J. Womack and D. Jones, *Lean Thinking* (New York: Free Press, 2003).
39. T. Coats, "Celebrate the Waste," *Inside Supply Management*®, (20:12), December 2009: 10; and, T. Manos, "Value Stream Mapping: An Introduction," Quality Progress, (39:6), June 2006: 64–9.

Chapter 9

1. J.L. Smith, "The Journey to Better Quality," *Quality* (February 2013), 16.
2. Blanchard, Supply Chain Management Best Practices.
3. "Reducing the Cost of Purchased Services," *Research on Demand*, Institute for Supply Management® Resource Center, 2004.
4. P.L. Carter, J.R. Carter, R.M. Monczka, J.D. Blascovich, T.H. Slaight and W.J. Markham, *Succeeding in a Dynamic World: Supply Management in the Decade Ahead*, (Institute for Supply Management® and W.P. Carey School of Business at Arizona State University, 2007).
5. Robert M. Monczka and Kenneth J. Peterson, *Supply Strategy Implementation: Current and Future Opportunities 2011*, (CAPS Research, 2011).
6. J. Gibbons and M.F. Chzanowski, "Creating an Alternative for Performance Concrete," *Structure*, February 2011, accessed October 24, 2013, http://www.structuremag.org/article.aspx?articleID=1212.
7. Six Sigma is the abbreviated form of six standard deviations from the mean and mathematically translates to about two defects per billion, which, strictly speaking, would be a pure Six Sigma process. Because no organization is nearly perfect enough to achieve such level of quality, the term *Six Sigma* has taken on the equivalent defect rate of 3.4 part per million, which takes into account + or − standard deviations of a specified average (www.siliconfareast.com, accessed October 24, 2013).
8. R. Aguayo, *Dr. Deming: The American Who Taught the Japanese About Quality*, Simon & Schuster, New York, 1991.
9. D. Shand, "Six Sigma," *Computerworld* (March 5, 2001): 38.
10. Lisa Ellram and Wendy Tate, "Bank of America: Services Purchasing and Outsourcing," *PRACTIX*, CAPS Research, May 2006.

11. Henk deKoning, John P.S. Verver, Jaap van den Heuvel, Soren Bisgaard and Ronald J.M.M. Does, "Lean Six Sigma in Health Care," *Journal for Healthcare Quality* (2006): 28: 2, 4-11.
12. P. Penfield, "Debating Parts Standardization," *eSide Supply Management*, (3:4) July/August 2010, www.ism.ws/pubs/eSide/eSideArticle.cfm?ItemNumber=20534, accessed October 24, 2013.
13. "Update 1 — Toyota to Sell Vehicles Using Common Parts in 2015," *Reuters*, March 27, 2013, accessed October 24, 2013, http://www.reuters.com/article/2013/03/27/toyota-parts-idUSL3N0CJAN920130327.
14. N. Kokemuller, "The Disadvantages of a Standardization Business," *AZCentral.com*, accessed October 24, 2013, http://yourbusiness.azcentral.com/disadvantages-standardization-business-11864.html.
15. State of Wisconsin, *State Procurement Manual: Standards Committees*, accessed October 24, 2013, http://vendornet.state.wi.us/vendornet/procman/prob8.asp.
16. Slovenia Institute for Standardization, "Standardization System in Slovenia," accessed October 24, 2013, http://www.sist.si/index.php?option=com_content&view=article&id=74&Itemid=106&lang=en.
17. Lisa Ellram and Thomas Choi, *Supply Management for Value Enhancement*.
18. R.David Nelson, "John Deere Optimizes Operations With Supply Management Efforts," *Journal of Organizational Excellence* (now *Global Business and Organizational Excellence*), (21:2), (February 2002).
19. 3M, "Flexible Secure Right Balance," 2007, accessed October 24, 2013, http://multimedia.3m.com/mws/mediawebserver?66666UuZjcFSLXTtmxfcnXfEEVuQEcuZgVs6EVs6E666666--.
20. International Organization for Standardization, accessed October 24, 2013, www.iso.org/iso/about.htm.
21. The British Assessment Bureau, "ISO Publish Latest Survey on ISO 9001," December 12, 2012, accessed October 24, 2013, http://www.british-assessment.co.uk/news/iso-publish-latest-survey-on-iso-9001.
22. The British Assessment Bureau, "ISO 14000 Continues to Grow," August 7, 2012, accessed October 24, 2013, http://www.british-assessment.co.uk/news/iso-14001-continues-to-grow.
23. "Benefits of International Standards," ISO, accessed December 4, 2013, http://www.iso.org/iso/home/standards/benefitsofstandards.htm.
24. United Nations Standard Products and Services Code® (UNSPSC®), accessed December 19, 2013, http://www.unspsc.org/.
25. American National Standards Institute (ANSI), accessed October 24, 2013, http://www.ansi.org/about_ansi/introduction/introduction.aspx?menuid=1.
26. ANSI Accredited Programs, accessed October 24, 2013, http://www.ansi.org/about_ansi/accredited_programs/overview.aspx?menuid=1.

27. IEEE, accessed October 24, 2013, http://www.ieee.org/about/today/at_a_glance.html.
28. Ibid.
29. W. Edwards Deming, *Out of the Crisis* (Cambridge, MA: Massachusetts Institute of Technology Center for Advanced Engineering, 1986).
30. K. Ishikawa (D.J. Lu, trans.), *What Is Total Quality Control?*, (Englewood, CA: Prentice Hall, 1985).
31. Juran®, The Source for Breakthrough, accessed October 24, 2013, http://www.juran.com/about-us/our-legacy/.
32. W. Edwards Deming, *Out of the Crisis*, (Cambridge, MA: Massachusetts Institute of Technology Center for Advanced Engineering, 1986).
33. N. Tague, *The Quality Toolbox*, 2nd ed. (Milwaukee, WI: ASQ Quality Press, 2005).
34. Zontec-The Power of SPC, "The Carlyle & Finch Co. Uses Synergy to Reduce Its Customer Defects to Zero," accessed October 24, 2013, http://www.zontec-spc.com/success-stories/case-studies/the-carlisle-finch-co-uses-synergy-to-reduce-its-defects-to-customers-to-zero/.
35. Kathryn M. Dodson, Hubert F. Hofman, Gowri S. Ramani and Deborah K. Yedlin, "Adapting CMMI for Acquisition Organizations: A Preliminary Report," *Special Report CMU/SEI-2006-SR-005* (Pittsburgh PA: Carnegie Mellon and Software Engineering Institute, 2006).
36. "Leveraging CMMI-ACQ and CMMI-DEV to Improve Supplier Performance," 2011 presentation, accessed October 24, 2013, http://cmmiinstitute.com/results/success-stories/.
37. G.A. Garrett and R.G. Rendon, *Contract Management: Organizational Assessment Tools* (Asburn, VA: National Contract Management Association, 2005).
38. Ibid.
39. Lisa Ellram, "Strategic Cost Management in the Supply Chain: A Purchasing and Supply Management Perspective," CAPS Research, Tempe, AZ, 2002.
40. R.J.J. Blakeman, *Benchmarking: Definitions and Overview* (Milwaukee, WI: Center for Urban Transportation Studies, University of Wisconsin-Milwaukee, June 2002), accessed October 24, 2013, http://www4.uwm.edu/cuts/bench/bm-desc.htm.
41. "Supply Chain Council Announces Award Winners," April 7, 2013, accessed December 5, 2013, https://supply-chain.org/supply-chain-council-announces-awards-winners.
42. Hines, *Supply Chain Strategies: Demand-Driven and Customer-Focused*, Routledge, London, 2013.
43. National Institute of Standards and Technology, accessed October 24, 2009, http://www.nist.gov/baldrige/award_recipients/lockheed-martin.cfm.
44. *Survey of Current Business*, "GDP and the Economy," February 2013, accessed October 24, 2013, https://www.bea.gov/scb/pdf/2013/02%20February/0213_gdpecon.pdf.

45. L. Marin and J. Miller, *Contracting for Public Sector Services*, (Herndon, VA: National Institute of Governmental Purchasing, 2006).
46. Van Weele, *Purchasing & Supply Chain Management*.
47. K.S. Nash, "How to Evaluate Vendor Performance," *Computer World*, June 3, 2008, accessed October 24, 2013, http://www.computerworld.com/s/article/9092738/How_to_evaluate_vendor_performance.
48. Modern Ghana, "Toyota Ghana Battles Counterfeit Spare Parts," *Ghanaian Chronicle*, March 19, 2012, accessed October 24, 2013, http://www.modernghana.com/news/384277/1/toyota-ghana-battles-counterfeit-spare-parts.html.
49. BMW Group, Press Club Middle East, June 12, 2013, "BMW Group Middle East Accelerates the Fight Against Counterfeit Automotive Parts," accessed October 24, 2013, https://www.press.bmwgroup.com/pressclub/p/me/pressDetail.html;jsessionid=plL5S0xM2nGth51zrTW1tvMK326fFTmnV2whLF6n5z74BL31SQpy!-43670277?title=bmw-group-middle-east-accelerates-the-fight-against-counterfeit-automotive-parts&outputChannelId=31&id=T0142762EN&left_menu_item=node__2367.

Chapter 10

1. RobertM. Monczka et. al. 2011; N. Kingsbury, Performance Measurement and Evaluation, Definitions and Relationships (Washington, DC); and U.S. Government Accountability Office, "Performance Measurement and Evaluation," 2011, accessed December 19, 2013, http://www.gao.gov/products/GAO-11-646SP.
2. Ibid.
3. Ann Oka, "Recognition: Why Metrics Matter," *Inside Supply Management*®, (21:9), September 2010, 12; and Sodexo, "About Us," accessed October 27, 2013, http://www.sodexousa.com/usen/about-us/About_us/sodexo-in-USA.aspx.
4. Hines, *Supply Chain Strategies: Demand-Driven and Customer Focused*.
5. Gore, *Serving the American Public: Best Practices in Performance Measurement, National Performance Review Benchmarking Study Report* (June 1997), accessed October 27, 2013, http://govinfo.library.unt.edu/npr/library/papers/benchmrk/nprbook.html.
6. Ibid.
7. "Measure Performance and Set Targets," *Info Entrepreneurs*, accessed October 27, 2013, http://www.infoentrepreneurs.org/en/guides/measure-performance-and-set-targets/.
8. K. Schwartz, "ABC: An Introduction to Balanced Scorecard," *CIO*, July 13, 2007, accessed October 27, 2013, http://www.karendschwartz.com/images/CIO_ABCs_of_Balanced_Scorecard.pdf.

9. Balanced Scorecard Institute, "Veolia Water Uses Balanced Scorecard to Drive North American Strategy," accessed October 27, 2013, https://www.balancedscorecard.org/Portals/0/PDF/BSCI_Veolia.pdf.
10. C. Freeland and A. Ward, "FedEx Founder Credits Supply Chain Flexibility," *Financial Times*, November 17, 2006.
11. NICE, accessed October 27, 2013, http://www.nice.com/quality-management/iso-9001%3A2008.
12. J.T. Shapiro and J.J. Mayer, "Outsourced and Under Your Control," *Inside Supply Management*®, (21:10), October 2010.
13. T. Neeley, "Accounting Changes Ahead," *Inside Supply Management*® (supplemental article), March 2010.
14. J.F. Kros and S.S. Nadler, "SOX in Today's Financial Climate," *Inside Supply Management*® (supplemental article), February 2012.
15. Ibid.
16. OpenAir®, accessed October 27, 2013, http://www.openair.com/home/OpenAirCaseStudy_Selectica.pdf.
17. Insurance Services Network, accessed October 27, 1013, http://www.isn-inc.com/news/news.aspx?nid=2342&cid=4.
18. Financial Services Agency, Financial Instruments and Exchange Act, accessed October 27, 2013, http://www.fsa.go.jp/en/policy/fiel/index.html.
19. Monczka et al., *Purchasing and Supply Chain Management*.
20. "Ford's Award-Winning Supplier Diversity Development Program Exceeds Minority-Owned Business Spending Goals," *Wall Street Journal*, March 14, 2013, accessed October 27, 2013, http://online.wsj.com/article/PR-CO-20130314-910585.html.
21. DiversityBusiness.com®, "Spend Analysis," 2009, accessed November 22, 2013, http://www.diversitybusiness.com/news/diversity.magazine/99200849.asp.
22. CAPS Research, "Measuring Supplier Diversity Program Performance," March 2012, accessed November 22, 2013, https://knowledge.capsresearch.org/publications/pdfs-protected/SupplierDiversity2012Metric.pdf.
23. Supplier Diversity Europe, accessed October 27, 2013, http://www.supplierdiversityeurope.eu/index.asp.
24. Port of Portland, Small Business Development Program, accessed October 27, 2013, http://www.portofportland.com/sros_sb_home.aspx.
25. Hilton Worldwide, accessed October 27, 2013, http://www.hiltonworldwide.com/development/performance-advantage/supply-management/supplier/diversity/.
26. Institute for Supply Management®, ISM *Principles of Sustainability and Social Responsibility with a Guide to Adoption and Implementation*, 2012, accessed October 27, 2013, http://www.ism.ws/SR/?navItemNumber=22324.

27. HP, "Design for Environment," accessed October 27, 2013, www.hp.com/hpinfo/globalcitizenship/environment/productdesign/index.html.
28. D. Javitch, "Establishing an Employee Review System," *Entrepreneur* (April 5, 2004), accessed October 27, 2013, www.entrepreneur.com/humanresources/employeemanagementcolumnistjavitch/article70172.html.
29. B. Nelson, *1501 Ways to Reward Employees*, Workman Publishing, 2012.
30. "Guidelines for Writing a Competency-Based Job Description," Northwestern University, accessed October 27, 2013, http://www.northwestern.edu/hr/compensation/Guidelines%20Competency%20based%20JD.pdf.
31. Robert Monczka and Phil Carter, "Supply Management Strategies for Success in the New Economy," 2011, CAPS Research, Tempe, AZ.
32. Ibid.

Chapter 11

1. Mary Siegfried, "Banks of Information," *Inside Supply Management*®, (22:3), May 2011, 32.
2. BrainyQuote®, accessed October 28, 2013, http://www.brainyquote.com/quotes/quotes/w/williampol125776.html.
3. *American Heritage Dictionary*, 5th ed., (Boston: Houghton Mifflin Company 2012), accessed October 28, 2013, http://ahdictionary.com/word/search.html?q=knowledge.
4. R. Andreu and S. Sieber, "Knowledge Integration Across Organizations," *Knowledge and Process Management*, (12:3), 2005, 153-160.
5. T. Frost and C. Zhou, "R&D Co-Practice and Reverse Knowledge Integration in Multinational Firms," *Journal of International Business Studies*, (36:6), November 2005, 676-87.
6. T. Andreeva and A. Kianto, "Knowledge Processes, Knowledge-Intensity and Innovation," *Journal of Knowledge Management*, (15:6), 2011, 1016-34; and T. Frost and C. Zhou, "R&D Co-Practice and Reverse Knowledge Integration in Multinational Firms," *Journal of International Business Studies*, (36:6), November 2005, 676-87.
7. Intuit QuickBooks®, accessed October 28, 2013, http://quickbooks.intuit.com/.
8. SAP, "ACH Food Companies: Transforming from a Commercial to a Consumer Branded Business," accessed October 28, 2013, www54.sap.com/bin/sapcom/downloadasset.ach-food-co-pdf.html.
9. Ariba®, accessed October 28, 2013, http://www.ariba.com/solutions/buy/supplier-management?campid=CRM-XI13-WEB-BING_NA&sd_source=bing&sd_medium=cpc&sd_campaign=supplier-management&sd_adgroup=supplier-management&sd_keyword=supplier%20relationship%20management%20software&sd_creative={creative}.

10. Ariba®, "Grupo Postadas," accessed October 28, 2013, http://www.ariba.com/assets/uploads/documents/Case%20Studies/Grupo+Posadas+Case+Study.081712.pdf.
11. M. Hoffman, "6 Ways WMS Can Improve Operations," *Food Logistics*, February 26, 2013, accessed October 28, 2013, http://www.foodlogistics.com/article/10879689/software-technology-sector-report-6-ways-wms-can-improve-operations.
12. "CRM Definitions and Solutions," *CIO*, accessed December 14, 2013, http://www.cio.com/article/40295/CRM_Definition_and_Solutions#2.
13. Mint Jutras, "The Pros and Cons of SAAS ERP," January 2012, accessed October 28, 2013, http://www.epicor.com/pandcofsaaserp/Documents/Pros%20and%20Cons%20of%20SaaS%20ERP%20Final.pdf.
14. Infosys, Interview with Gavin Solsky, accessed October 28, 2013, http://www.infosysbpo.com/offerings/functions/sourcing-procurement-outsourcing/Pages/impact-technology-trends-procurement.aspx.
15. Ibid.
16. Sciencewarehouse, "Where is Procurement and Technology Heading in 2013?," accessed December 19, 2013, http://www.sci-ware.com/where-is-procurement-and-technology-heading-in-2013.cfm.
17. Intel, "What is Big Data and Why Should You Care?," accessed October 28, 2013, www.intel.com/content/www/us/en/big-data/big-data-analytics-turning-big-data-into-intelligence-cmpg.html?cid=sem116p30981.
18. M.B. Whitfield, "Balance Risks in the Cloud," *Inside Supply Management*®, (24:2), March 2013, 12.

References

Chapter 1

Cavinato, J.L., A.E. Flynn, M.L. Harding, C.S. Lallatin, M.L. Peck, H.M. Pohlig, S.R. Sturzl and V. Tucker (Eds.). ISM *Glossary of Key Supply Management Terms*, 6th edition, Institute for Supply Management®, Tempe, AZ, 2014.

DeFeo, J.A. and W.W. Barnard. *Juran Institute's Six Sigma: Breakthrough and Beyond*, McGraw-Hill, New York, 2004.

George, M.L. *Lean Six Sigma*, McGraw-Hill, 2002.

Johnson, P.F., M.R. Leenders and A.E. Flynn. *Purchasing and Supply Management*, 14th ed., McGraw-Hill, New York, 2010.

Monczka, R., R. Trent, R. Handfield, L.C. Giuinipero and J.L. Patterson. *Purchasing and Supply Chain Management*, 5th ed., Brooks/Cole, a part of Cengage Learning, Inc., Mason, OH, 2012.

Womack, J.P. and D.T. Jones. *Lean Thinking*, 2nd ed., The Free Press, New York, 2010.

Chapter 2

Cavinato, J.L., A.E. Flynn, M.L. Harding, C.S. Lallatin, M.L. Peck, H.M. Pohlig, S.R. Sturzl and V. Tucker (Eds.). ISM *Glossary of Key Supply Management Terms*, 6th edition, Institute for Supply Management®, Tempe, AZ, 2014.

Kepner, C.H. and B.B. Tregoe. *The New Rational Manager*, Princeton Research Press, Princeton, NJ, 1981.

Lewis, J.P. *Project Planning, Scheduling and Control*, McGraw-Hill, 2011.

Mantel, Jr., S.J., J.R. Meredith, S.M. Shafer and M.M. Sutton. *Project Management in Practice*, McGraw Hill Companies, New York, NY, 2010.

Project Management Institute. *A Guide to the Project Management Body of Knowledge (PMBOK® Guide)*, 5th ed., Project Management Institute Inc., Newtown Square, PA, 2013.

Verma, V.K. *Organizing Projects for Success*, Project Management Institute, Newtown Square, PA, 1995.

Westland, J. *Project Management Life Cycle*, Kogan Page, London, 2006.

Chapter 3

Cavinato, J.L., A.E. Flynn, M.L. Harding, C.S. Lallatin, M.L. Peck, H.M. Pohlig, S.R. Sturzl and V. Tucker (Eds.). ISM *Glossary of Key Supply Management Terms*, 6th edition, Institute for Supply Management®, Tempe, AZ, 2014.

Dimancescu, D. and K. Dwenger. *World-Class New Product Development*, AMACOM, New York, 1996.

Krajewski, L.J., Ritzman, L.P. and M.K. Majoltra. *Operations Management: Processes and Supply Chains*, 12th ed., Prentice Hall, Upper Saddle River, NJ, 2012.

Johnson, P.F., M. Leenders and A.Flynn. *Purchasing and Supply Management*, 14th ed., McGraw-Hill, New York, 2010.

Maropoulos, P.G. and D. Ceglarek. "Design Verification and Validation in Product Life Cycle," ICIRP Annals - Manufacturing Technology, 2010, (59:2), pp. 740-759.

Porter, M. *Competitive Strategy*, The Free Press, New York, 1980.

Wheelwright, S. and K. Clark. *Leading Product Development: The Senior Manager's Guide to Creating and Shaping the Enterprise*, The Free Press, New York, 1994.

Chapter 4

Baumohl, B. *The Secrets of Economic Indicators*, Wharton School Publishing, Upper Saddle River, NY, 2005.

Cavinato, J.L., A.E. Flynn, M.L. Harding, C.S. Lallatin, M.L. Peck, H.M. Pohlig, S.R. Sturzl and V. Tucker (Eds.). ISM *Glossary of Key Supply Management Terms*, 6th edition, Institute for Supply Management®, Tempe, AZ, 2014.

Johnson, P.F., M.R. Leenders and A.E. Flynn. *Purchasing and Supply Management*, 14th ed., McGraw-Hill, New York, 2010.

Chapter 5

Cavinato, J.L., A.E. Flynn, M.L. Harding, C.S. Lallatin, M.L. Peck, H.M. Pohlig, S.R. Sturzl and V. Tucker (Eds.). ISM *Glossary of Key Supply Management Terms*, 6th edition, Institute for Supply Management®, Tempe, AZ, 2014.

Chase, R.B., F.R. Jacobs and N.J. Aquilano. *Operations Management for Competitive Advantage*, 10th ed., McGraw Hill-Irwin, Boston, MA, 2004.

Heizer, J. and B. Render. *Principles of Operations Management*, 11th ed., Prentice Hall, Upper Saddle River, NJ, 2014.

Krajewski, L.J., L.P. Ritzman and M.K. Majoltra. *Operations Management: Processes and Supply Chains*, 10th ed., Prentice Hall, 2012.

Makridakis, S.G., S.C. Wheelwright and R.J. Hyndman. *Forecasting: Methods & Applications*, 3rd ed., John Wiley & Sons, New York, NY, 1997.

Wilson, J.H. and B. Keating. *Business Forecasting*, 5th ed., McGraw-Hill Publishing Company, 2011.

Chapter 6

Ballou, R.H. *Business Logistics/Supply Chain Management*, 5th ed., Pearson Education, Upper Saddle River, NJ, 2004.

Bauhof, N. "Logistics Distribution and Warehousing 2006: Network Optimization." *Area Development Online*, August/September, http://www.areadevelopment.com/specialPub/ldw06/supplyChainOptimization.shtml.

Blanchard, D. *Supply Chain Management Best Practices*, 2nd ed., John Wiley & Sons, Hoboken, NJ, 2010.

Cavinato, J.L., A.E. Flynn, M.L. Harding, C.S. Lallatin, M.L. Peck, H.M. Pohlig, S.R. Sturzl and V. Tucker (Eds.). ISM *Glossary of Key Supply Management Terms*, 6th edition, Institute for Supply Management®, Tempe, AZ, 2014.

Christopher, M. *Logistics and Supply Chain Management: Creating Value-Adding Networks*, 4th ed., FT Press, Upper Saddle River, NJ, 2011.

Ellram, L.M. and T.Y. Choi. *Supply Management for Value Enhancement*, National Association of Purchasing Management, Tempe, AZ, 2000.

Foster, T.A. "Logistics Inside China: The Next Big Supply Chain Challenge," *Global Logistics and Supply Chain Strategies*, September, 2005, www.supplychainbrain.com/.

Foster, T.A. "Developers of DCs Have Become Key Strategic Partners," *Global Logistics and Supply Chain Strategies*, June, 2004, www.supplychainbrain.com/.

Gianakis, G. and D. Matthews. *Warehousing and Inventory Control*, National Institute of Governmental Purchasing, Herndon, VA, 2008.

Gilmore, D. "Welcome to the Intelligent Warehouse," *Supply Chain Manufacturing and Logistics*, 1999.

Hines, T. *Supply Chain Strategies: Customer-Driven and Customer-Focused*, Butterworth-Heinemann, London, 2004.

Hines, T. *Supply Chain Strategies: Demand-Driven and Customer-Focused*, Routledge, London, 2013.

Kempfer, L. "European Retailer Expands DC, Adds AS/RS," *Materials Handling Management*, March 2005, pp. 30–31.

Keyan, T. "Improving Warehouse Picking Operations: Voice Recognition Systems Offer Advantages That Scanning Technology Can't Touch," *Frontline Solutions*, May, 2004, http://findarticles.com.

Kuglin, F.A. *Customer-Centered Supply Chain Management*, AMACOM, New York, 1998.

Lysons, K. *Purchasing and Supply Chain Management*, 8th ed., FT Prentice Hall, London, 2012.

Nagel, J. (Ed.). *Supply Chain Management: A Procurement Perspective*, Hargreen Publishing, Melbourne, 2003.

Verzuh, E. *The Fast Forward MBA in Project Management*, 4th ed., John Wiley & Sons Inc., Hoboken, 2012.

Chapter 7

Blanchard, K. *Supply Chain Management Best Practices*, 2nd ed., John Wiley & Sons, Hoboken, NJ, 2010.

Cavinato, J.L., A.E. Flynn, M.L. Harding, C.S. Lallatin, M.L. Peck, H.M. Pohlig, S.R. Sturzl and V. Tucker (Eds.). ISM *Glossary of Key Supply Management Terms*, 6th edition, Institute for Supply Management®, Tempe, AZ, 2014.

Hines, T. *Supply Chain Strategies: Customer-Driven and Customer-Focused*, Butterworth-Heinemann, London, 2004.

Hines, T. *Supply Chain Strategies: Demand-Driven and Customer-Focused*, Routledge, London, 2013.

Hinkelman, E.G. *Dictionary of International Trade*, 9th ed., World Trade Press, Novato, CA, 2010.

Johnson, P.F., M.R. Leenders and A.E. Flynn. *Purchasing and Supply Management*, 14th ed., McGraw-Hill/Irwin, New York, 2010.

Lewicki, R.J, D.M. Saunders and B. Barry. *Essentials of Negotiation*, 5th ed., McGraw-Hill/Irwin, New York, 2011.

Monczka, R.M., R.B. Handfield, L.C. Giunipero and J.L. Patterson. *Purchasing and Supply Chain Management*, 5th ed., South-Western/CENGAGE Learning, 2011.

Prater, E. and K. Whitehead. *An Introduction to Supply Chain Management: A Global Supply Chain Management Support Perspective*, Harvard Business Review Press, 2013.

Stanley, L. and D. Matthews. *Logistics and Transportation*, National Institute of Governmental Purchasing, Herndon, VA, 2007.

Stanley, L. and D. Matthews. "Logistics, Transportation." In *Encyclopedia of Public Administration and Public Policy*, Jack Rabin (Ed.), Marcel Dekker, New York, 2003.

Tzu, S. and G. Gagliardi. *The Art of War: In Sun Tzu's Own Words*, Clearbridge Publishing, Seattle, WA, 1999.

Van Weele, A.J. *Purchasing & Supply Chain Management*, 4th ed., Thomson Learning, London, 2005.

Chapter 8

Blanchard, K. *Supply Chain Management Best Practices*, 2nd ed., John Wiley & Sons, Hoboken, NJ, 2010.

Brady, W. *Managing Fixed Assets in the Public Sector: Managing for Service Excellence*, Universal Publishers, Boca Raton, FL, 2001.

Broecklemann, R. *Inventory Classification Innovation: Paving the Way for Electronic Commerce and Vendor Managed Inventory*, CRC Press, Boca Raton, FL, 1998.

Buddress, L. "Getting the Most From Your Indirect Purchasing Dollar," ISM Annual Conference Proceedings, Institute for Supply Management®, Tempe, AZ, 2006.

Carter, P., J. Carter, R. Monczka, J. Blascovich, T. Slaight and W. Markham. *Succeeding in a Dynamic World: Supply Management in the Decade Ahead*, CAPS Research, Institute for Supply Management® and A.T. Kearney, Tempe, AZ, 2007.

Cavinato, J.L., A.E. Flynn, M.L. Harding, C.S. Lallatin, M.L. Peck, H.M. Pohlig, S.R. Sturzl and V. Tucker (Eds.). ISM *Glossary of Key Supply Management Terms*, 6th edition, Institute for Supply Management®, Tempe, AZ, 2014.

Cavinato, J., A. Flynn and R. Kauffman. *Supply Management Handbook*, 7th ed., Institute for Supply Management®, Tempe, AZ, 2006.

Christopher, M. *Logistics and Supply Chain Management: Creating Value-Adding Networks*, 4th ed., FT Press, Upper Saddle River, NJ, 2011.

Evers, P.T. and F.J. Beier. "Operational Aspects of Inventory Consolidation Decision Making," *Journal of Business Logistics*, (19:1), 1998, pp. 173-189.

Gianakis, G. and D. Matthews. *Warehousing and Inventory Control,* National Institute of Governmental Purchasing, Herndon, VA, 2008.

Hines, T. *Supply Chain Strategies: Demand-Driven and Customer-Focused*, Routledge, London, 20013

Hurlbut, T. "Cycle Counting," *Inc.com*, www.inc.com/resources/retail/articles/200506/counting.html.

Kieso, D., J. Weygandt and T. Warfield. *Fundamentals of Intermediate Accounting*, John Wiley & Sons, Hoboken, NJ, 2003.

Muller, M. *Essentials of Inventory Management*, 2nd ed., AMACOM, 2011.

National Institute of Governmental Purchasing. *Dictionary of Purchasing Terms*, 5th ed., Herndon, VA, 2004.

Rudski, R., D. Smock, M. Katzorke and S. Stewart. *Straight to the Bottom Line: An Executive's Roadmap to World Class Supply Management*, J. Ross Publishing, Fort Lauderdale, FL, 2006.

Stanley, L. and D. Matthews. *Logistics and Transportation,* National Institute of Governmental Purchasing, Herndon, VA, 2007.

Womack, J. and D. Jones. *Lean Thinking*, The Free Press, New York, 2003.

Chapter 9

Aguayo, R. *Dr. Deming: The American Who Taught the Japanese About Quality*, Fireside, New York, 1991.

Blakeman, J. "Benchmarking: Definitions and Overview," Center for Urban Transportation Studies, University of Wisconsin-Milwaukee, June, 2002, www.uwm.edu/Dept/cuts/bench/bm-desc.htm.

Blanchard, K. *Supply Chain Management Best Practices*, 2nd edition, John Wiley & Sons, Hoboken, NJ, 2010.

Deming, W.E. *Out of the Crisis*, Massachusetts Institute of Technology Center for Advanced Engineering, Cambridge, MA, 1986.

Dodson, K.M., H.F. Hofman, G.S. Ramani and D.K. Yedlin. "Adapting CMMI for Acquisition Organizations: A Preliminary Report." In *Special Report CMU/SEI-2006-SR-005*, D. Fisher and K. Kost (Eds.), Carnegie Mellon and Software Engineering Institute, Pittsburgh PA, 2006.

Ellram, L.M. and T.Y. Choi. *Supply Management for Value Enhancement*, National Association of Purchasing Management, Tempe, AZ, 2000.

Ellram, L. and W. Tate. "Bank of America: Services Purchasing and Outsourcing," *PRACTIX*, CAPS Research (9), May, 2006.

Cavinato, J.L., A.E. Flynn, M.L. Harding, C.S. Lallatin, M.L. Peck, H.M. Pohlig, S.R. Sturzl and V. Tucker (Eds.). ISM *Glossary of Key Supply Management Terms*, 6th edition, Institute for Supply Management®, Tempe, AZ, 2014.

Garrett, G.A. and R.G. Rendon. *Contract Management: Organizational Assessment Tools*, National Contract Management Association, Asburn, VA, 2005.

Hines, T. *Supply Chain Strategies: Customer-Driven and Customer-Focused*, Butterworth-Heinemann, London, 2004.

Hines, T. *Supply Chain Strategies: Demand-Driven and Customer-Focused*, Routledge, London, 2013.

Ishikawa, K. (D.J. Lu., Trans.). *What Is Total Quality Control?*, Prentice Hall, Englewood, CA, 1985.

Karten, N. "Key Steps in Establishing a Service Level Agreement," www.nkarten.com/slaservices.html, 2003.

Tague, N. *The Quality Toolbox*, 2nd ed., ASQ Quality Press, Milwaukee, WI, 2005.

Van Weele, A.J. *Purchasing and Supply Chain Management*, 5th ed., CENGAGE Learning EMEA, London, 2010.

REFERENCES

Chapter 10

Cavinato, J.L., A.E. Flynn, M.L. Harding, C.S. Lallatin, M.L. Peck, H.M. Pohlig, S.R. Sturzl and V. Tucker (Eds.). ISM *Glossary of Key Supply Management Terms*, 6th edition, Institute for Supply Management®, Tempe, AZ, 2014.

Hines, T. *Supply Chain Strategies: Demand-Driven and Customer-Focused*, Routledge, London, 2013.

ISM Committee on Sustainability and Social Responsibility. ISM *Principles of Sustainability and Social Responsibility with a Guide to Adoption and Implementation*, Institute for Supply Management®, 2012.

Monczka, R.M., R.B. Handfield, L.C. Giunipero and J.L. Patterson. *Purchasing and Supply Chain Management*, South-Western CENGAGE Learning, 2011.

Rudski, R., D. Smock, M. Katzorke and S. Stewart. *Straight to the Bottom Line: An Executive's Roadmap to World Class Supply Management*, J. Ross Publishing, Fort Lauderdale, FL, 2005.

Chapter 11

American Heritage Dictionary, 5th ed., Houghton Mifflin Company, Boston, 2012.

Blanchard, K. *Supply Chain Management Best Practices*, 2nd ed., John Wiley & Sons, Hoboken, NJ, 2010.

Cavinato, J.L., A.E. Flynn, M.L. Harding, C.S. Lallatin, M.L. Peck, H.M. Pohlig, S.R. Sturzl and V. Tucker (Eds.). ISM *Glossary of Key Supply Management Terms*, 6th edition, Institute for Supply Management®, Tempe, AZ, 2014.

Christopher, M. *Logistics and Supply Chain Management: Creating Value-Adding Networks*, 4th ed., FT Press, Upper Saddle River, NJ, 2011.

Monczka, R.M., R.B. Handfield, L.C. Giunipero and J.L. Patterson, *Purchasing and Supply Chain Management*, South-Western CENGAGE Learning, 2011.

Radack, S. (ed.). *The System Development Life Cycle (SDLC)*, NIST, http://csrc.nist.gov/publications/nistbul/april2009_system-development-life-cycle.pdf.

80/20 rule 220, 254

A

ABC Classification 220-1
ABC inventory classification 254
Absolute value 156-7
Accurate forecasts 101, 117, 120, 151
Ace Electrical 269-70
ACH Food Companies Inc 311
Activities
    management-related 53
    organization's 288
    project-related 46
Actual cost of work performed (ACWP) 61-2
Actual costs, scheduled 61
Adidas 75, 322
Administrative budget 125
Agency
    national 102, 104
    regional planning 115
Aggregate demand 267
Agilent Technologies 267
Agreement
    basic 275
    incorporating confidentiality 162
    long-term volume purchase 293
    master 219
    new trade 134
    nondisclosure 47
Air freight 191-2
Alpha values 139, 142

American Institute for Economic Research 116
American National Standards Institute (ANSI) 250, 252, 279, 338
Analysis
    cause-and-effect 36
    cost/benefit 249
    decision 35
    decision tree 10, 22
    insourcing/outsourcing 52
    macroeconomic 114
    scenario 50
    stakeholder 42
Application service provider (asp) 309
Ariba 312, 342-3
ARIMA 151
Arizona State University 115, 223, 300
Arnseth, L. 319, 321, 327
Asset
    classification 219
    management 213-18, 226, 242, 268
    recovery 3, 214-15, 218, 240
Asset and inventory management 213
Assets
    disposition of 217, 236, 238
    existing 218
    fixed 215-17, 242, 312
    intangible 214
    long-term 213, 216
    long-term tangible 214
    noninventory 237
    organization's 219, 236
    physical 17, 38

short-term 214, 222
tangible 214
total 7
unneeded 236
Association for Operations Management 115
Association of American Railroads (AAR) 190, 332
Audit
  committees 293
  reports 294
  requirements 202
Audits
  external 251, 291-2
  financial 287, 292
  freight bill 205-6
  post-project 64-5
Automated storage and retrieval systems (AS/RS) 175
Average aggregate inventory 206
Average costing 226
Average demand 132, 142-3
Average inventory value 226

B

Balance, insourcing/outsourcing 5
Balance sheet 214-15, 223, 226
Balanced scorecards 269, 288-9
Bar codes 177-8, 214, 216, 236
Benchmarking 75-7, 85, 266
Bid process 57, 239
Bidding, two-step 53
Big data 315, 317, 343

Blanchard, D. 330, 337, 347-51
BloombergBusinessWeek 322
BMW Group Middle East 340
BorgWarner Morse 68
Bottom line 335-6, 349, 351
Box-Jenkins Method 150-1, 163
Bronson Methodist Hospital 14, 319
Budget
  cycle 30
  development 162
  materials/operations 125
  planned 27
  traditional 49
Budget at completion of the project task (BAC) 62
Budgeted cost of work performed (BCWP) 61
Budgeted cost of work scheduled (BCWS) 61
Buffer stock 230
Building and Urban Development 171, 329
Bulk carriers 194-5
Bulk storage 171, 173, 184
Bulk storage warehouse 166
Bullwhip effect 160, 219-20
Bureau of Economic Analysis (BEA) 101, 112, 325
Business
  case 32, 43, 71
  continuity 168, 182, 228
  cycles 94, 101-2, 118
  intelligence 121

plan 77
planning 288, 310
strategy 5, 71, 234, 314
Business Forecasting 150, 346
Business processes 121, 241, 306, 310, 317
   internal 269, 289
   standard 261
Business units 4, 289, 316
   multiple 312
   strategic 20

C

C-TPAT 179, 200-1
Capabilities
   organization's supply management 260
   supplier's 82, 271
Capacity, absorptive 304
Capacity analysis 81
Capacity cushion 78
Capacity forecast 121
Capital budget 125
CAPS Research 5, 85-6, 300
Carriage Insurance Paid (CIP) 197, 199
Carriage Paid (CPT) 197, 199
Carrying costs 191, 227, 229-30, 248
Carter, P. 287, 335, 337, 349
Case study 319, 325, 328-30, 334
Cash flows 40-1, 218, 224, 286
Cash inflows 40
Cash outflows 40
Caterpillar's supply chain 207

Causal modeling 153-4
Cavinato, J. 245, 335, 345-51
Ceiling price 58-9
Census Bureau 115
Centers
   supply chain analytics 21
   trans-shipment 306
Certified Professional in Supply Management® (CPSM®) 300
C&G Supplies 158
Change control process 60
Change management 58
Change orders 19, 54, 59-60
Chartered Institute of Purchasing and Supply (CIPS) 115
Chartered Institute of Transport and Logistics 171
Chicago Board Options Exchange 116
Christopher, M. 215-16, 307, 331, 335-6, 347, 349, 351
CIP (Carriage Insurance Paid) 197, 199
Cisco Systems 85
CISG (Contracts for the International Sale of Goods) 100
Classifying inventory 220
Closed contract 26
Cloud computing 306, 309, 314-15
CMM (capability maturity model) 260-2, 279
CMM software 262
CMMI (capability maturity model integrated) 261-2, 279
CMMM (contract management maturity model) 263

Co-location 262

Coca Cola PlantBottle 80

Coincident indicator 102

Collaborative Planning, Forecasting and Replenishment (CPFR) 45, 161

Competitive market conditions 87

Compliance audits 271

Computer-aided manufacturing (CAM) 72

ConAgra 117

Consumer Price Index (CPI) 102, 104

Container Security Initiative (CSI) 201, 333

Container shipping 190

Continuous quality improvement 292

Contract administration 2, 4, 27, 57, 59, 263

Contract closeout 263

Contract closure process 64

Contract law 54

Contract management 13, 261, 264, 339, 350

    system 294

Contract terms 56, 59

Contracts

    cost-plus-fixed-fee 58

    cost-plus-incentive fee 58

    cost-plus-percentage-of-cost 58

    fixed-price-with-incentive fee 58

    forward exchange 99

    public sector 295

Contracts for the International Sale of Goods (CISG) 100

Control

    corporate governance 294

    federal 95

    project manager's 30

    statistical 18, 258

Core processes 14-15, 261

Corner warehouse flow 172-3

Corporate social responsibility (CSR) 296

Corrective action 26, 205, 225, 290

Cost analysis 62, 71, 90, 106, 216

Cost/benefit analysis 249

Cost management 27-8, 242, 267, 273, 275, 319

Cost performance index (CPI) 61-2, 102, 104-6, 117

Cost-plus-fixed-fee contracts 58

Cost-plus-incentive fee contracts 58

Cost-plus-percentage-of-cost contracts 58

Cost variance 61-2

Costs

    acquisition 179, 229, 232

    activity 208

    administrative 12

    benefit 169

    competitive 193

    expected 10-11, 55, 62

    fixed 229, 268

    fulfillment 20

    holding 83, 227-9, 242

    in-house 270

    inspection 100

internal 88
landed 236
life-cycle 86
material 208
nonvalue-added 16
opportunity 227
overhead 227
receiving 228
supplier's 58, 271
switching 76
training 38
transaction 239
unit 88, 152-3
variable 202

Counterfeit components 278

Countries
    developing 96, 113, 170, 306
    emerging 194
    exporting 196

Cox Global Manufacturing 124

Cp 258

CPFR 45

CPI (cost performance index) 61-2, 102, 104-6, 117

Cpk 258

CPT (Carriage Paid) 197, 199

Critical Path Method (CPM) 48

Cross-docking 167, 174, 177

Cross-flow warehouse flow 172

Currency 99, 108
    home country's 108

Currency exchange rates 112, 117

Currency exchanges 99

Current Business 112, 339

Customer relationship management (CRM) 133, 311, 313, 317

Customer service measurements 207

Customer surveys 70

Customs and Border Protection (CBP) 200, 333

Customs-Trade Partnership Against Terrorism (C-TPAT) 179, 200-1

Cycle counting 176, 223, 335, 349

Cycle time 234

Cycles
    changing economic 32
    economic 118
    plan-do-check-act 253, 290

D

Dairy Fresh Farms 321

Damaged stock 235, 237

Damping factor 139, 141

Dangerous Goods Transportation Act 333

Dannon 235, 336

DAP (Delivered at Place) 197, 199

DAT (Delivered at Terminal) 197, 199

Data integrity 314

Data management 121, 216, 304-5

DDP (Delivered Duty Paid) 197-9

DDU (Delivered Duty Unpaid) 197, 199

Dealers 232, 238

Decision analysis 35

Decision forks 10

Decision tree analysis 10, 22

Decomposition approach 130

Defects 17, 37, 50, 203, 236, 246

Defense Procurement and Acquisition Policy)(DPAP) 330

Define

   measure, analyze, improve, control (DMAIC) 246-7

   mesure, analyze, design, verify (DMADV) 246-7

Deflator, implicit price 106

Deliverables 25-6, 44, 46, 55, 60

Delivered at Place (DAP) 197, 199

Delivered at Terminal (DAT) 197, 199

Delivered Duty Paid (DDP) 197-9

Delivered Duty Unpaid (DDU) 197, 199

Delivery

   dock 216

   management 180-1

   performance 255, 268, 270

   problems 34, 127, 189, 203

   reliability 267, 269-70

   requirements 46

   terms 198

Deloitte 54, 127, 320, 327

Delphi Method 131, 134-5, 138, 163

Demand-based manufacturing strategy 233

Demand data 131-2, 136-8, 142, 144, 150-1, 219

Demand forecasting process 128

Demand forecasts 78, 94, 100, 119-23, 125, 128-30, 134, 214

   independent 123-4

   long-term 129

   next period's 131

Demand planning 119, 131, 187

Deming, W.E. 255-6, 258, 279, 337, 350

Department of Defense (DoD) 178, 238, 263

Department of Economic and Social Affairs 326

Department of Labor 102, 104, 325

Department of Transportation 201, 332, 334

Dependent demand 122

Derivative ideas 69

Design SOW (statement of work) 54

Destination country 197, 199

Destination port 199-200

Developing supplier measures 269

Deviations, standard 157, 337

Diagrams

   cause-and-effect 36-7, 256

   fishbone 36, 256

Dictionary of International Trade 333, 348

Dictionary of Purchasing Terms 349

Differencing 151

Diffusion index 110

Disadvantaged Business Enterprise Program 295

Disposal 170, 201, 218, 235

Disposal marketplace 238

Disposition
    methods 237, 239
    process 219
Distribution centers 167
    high-velocity 180
    high-volume 176
    regional 161, 207
Distribution channels 79, 90, 168
Distribution requirements planning (DRP) 304, 313
Distribution resource planning (DRP II) 314
Distribution systems 97, 167, 175, 177, 183
Diversity 9, 295-6
Dock configuration 176
Documents, solicitation 53, 86
Dot Foods 183

E

Early purchasing involvement (EPI) 85
Early supplier involvement (ESI) 82, 91
Earned value (EV) 60-1, 288
Earned value management system (EVMS) 60, 288
Economic activity, measure of 102
Economic conditions 82, 114-15, 125
    current 118
    harsh 264
    healthy global 108
Economic data 101
Economic indicators 94, 101-2, 111, 113-14, 117-18, 136

Economic order quantity (EOQ) 229
Economic Research Service 326
Economic survey 113
Economic trends 101, 108
Economies
    developing 6
    general 102
    sluggish 194
    weakening 33
Economy
    closed 95
    market 95
    mixed 95
Electronic data interchange (EDI) 310
Ellram, L. 87, 329, 337-9, 347, 350
Employee development plans 284
Employee evaluations 281, 296, 299, 301
Employee performance 282, 296-9
    evaluating 298
    improved 298
Energy Information Administration 115-16
Enterprise resource system 6
EOQ (economic order quantity) 229, 231
ERP (enterprise resource planning) 6, 303, 310-12
ERP systems 156, 306, 310-11, 314
Error detection 314
Errors
    squared 154, 159
    standard 157

Estimated (remaining cost) to completion (ETC) 62
European Union (EU) 179
Evaluation
    360-degree performance 284
    formative 296, 301
    qualitative 298
    summative 296
Evaluation process 266, 299
Excess inventory 130, 233, 237
    carrying 219
Exchange rate fluctuation 99
Exchange rates 303
Executive opinion 128, 131
Expected values 10, 154
Exponential smoothing
    seasonal 150
    trend-adjusted 132
    triple 150
Exponential smoothing method 138-9, 144, 156
Export documentation 196
Export packer 196
Extended resource planning 309

F

FAS (Free Alongside Ship) 197-9, 324
FCA (Free Carrier At) 197-8
Feasibility study 39-40
Federal Energy Regulatory Commission (FERC) 191
Federal Motor Carrier Safety Administration 334
FedEx Supply Chain 192
Feedback 77, 265, 279, 281-2, 286, 298
FIFO (first in, first out) 226, 242
Financial Accounting Standards Board (FASB) 292
Financial Instruments and Exchange Law 294
Financial Services Agency 341
Fishbone diagrams 36, 256
Five Forces Analysis 75
Fixed assets 215-17, 242, 312
Fixed costs 229, 268
Fixed location system 174
Fixed order quantity 228
Fixed-price-with-incentive fee contracts 58
Fluctuations in warehouse space required 174
Flynn, A. 245, 335, 345-51
FOB (Free On Board) 197-9
Food and Drug Administration (FDA) 274
Forbes 322, 324
Forecast
    aggregate 130
    annual 130
    current 138
    economic 115
    financial 68
    higher-level 130
    industry capacity 121
    material 122, 234-5

medium-term 129

order 161

period 139

qualitative 132, 135

quantitative 132, 135

rolling six-month 130

short-term 129

ten-year 114

volume 129

Forecast accuracy 129, 133, 139, 155-6, 158, 161, 163, 221

Forecast errors

absolute 157

minimizing 120

tracking 163

Forecast methods 131-2, 156, 163

Forecast models 117, 128, 155, 163

Foreign exchange rates 151, 325

Forex Economic Calendar 325

Formative evaluation 296, 301

Forward exchange contracts 99

Fourth-party (4PL) logistics 188

Fourth-party logistics provider (4PL) 193

Fraser Johnson, P. 67, 194, 321, 331, 333, 335, 345-6, 348

Free Carrier At (FCA) 197-8

Freight claims 188, 204-5

Freight classifications and rates 202

Functional matrix 28-9

G

GAAP (Generally Accepted Accounting Principles) 281, 292-3

GAAP and SOX audits 301

Gantt charts 47, 50

GDP (Gross Domestic Product) 95, 101, 111-13, 274

GDP growth 112, 114, 117

General Agreement on Tariffs and Trade (GATT) 96

Geopolitical conditions 97, 126

Giunipero, Larry C. 18, 334, 348, 351

Global logistics 193-4, 201, 210

Global sourcing 99, 228, 303, 306

Global supply chains 193

Globalization 94, 96, 193-4, 209

GmP (Good Manufacturing Practices) 273-4

GNP (gross national product) 101

Grocery Manufacturers of America 329

Gross domestic product (GDP) 111, 113, 274

Gross National Product (GNP) 101

Guidebook on Transport and Handling Dangerous Goods 334

H

Haier 98, 324

Handbook of Logistics and Distribution Management 335

Handfield, Robert B. 18, 323, 334, 345, 348, 351

Harding, M.L. 245, 345-51

Hazardous materials 170, 201-2

Hedging interest rates 325

Hedging strategies 99

Hilton Worldwide 341

Hines, T. 174, 329-30, 332-4, 336, 339-40, 347-51

Histogram 254

Hitachi Ltd 127

Horizontal demand 135-6

HP (Hewlett-Packard) 80, 237, 296

I

IBM 69, 79, 217, 335

IMF (International Monetary Fund) 113-14, 326

Implicit price deflator 106

Import clearance 197-9

Importers 179, 198-200

Incoterms®, applying 200

Incoterms® Rules 196-200, 209, 333

Independent demand 123

Indexes
    composite 109-10
    cost performance 61-2
    diffusion 110
    economic 111
    industry price 102

India's Indian Institute of Materials Management 115

Insource/outsource decision 10, 82-3

Inspections 60, 63, 180, 275

Institute for Electric and Electronic Engineers (IEEE) 250

Institute of Business Forecasting and Planning 116

Insurance 104, 199, 227, 277

International Chamber of Commerce (ICC) 196, 198, 200, 333

International Cotton Advisory Council (ICAC) 115

International Financial Reporting Standards (IFRS) 292-3

International Journal of Purchasing and Materials Management 240, 323, 328

International Monetary Fund (IMF) 113-14, 326

International Standardization Organization (ISO) 250-2, 260, 279, 281, 292, 301, 338

Inventory
    actual 225, 231, 287
    adjustment 225
    carrying 228
    classification 188
    classification techniques 220
    consolidating 232
    continuous 223
    cost of 227, 248
    dollar value of 226, 298
    holding 166, 229
    in-process 187, 233
    leaner 232
    managing 183
    moving 166, 184
    on-hand 160
    out-of-date 170

physical 223, 225

supplier-managed 213, 293

transporting 168

turnover 206, 208, 223-4

valuation 226, 242

Inventory management 213, 215, 219-20

Inventory management

Just-in-Time 233

software 229, 231

Inventory models 216

Inverted T warehouse flow 171, 173

Investment recovery 217, 236

Invitation for bid (IFB) 53

Ishikawa, K. 253, 256, 339, 350

ISM *Report On Business*® 108, 111, 117-18

ISM® *Principles of Sustainability and Social Responsibility* 9

ISO (International Standardization Organization) 250-2, 260, 279, 281, 292, 301, 338

J

JIT 166, 168-9, 174, 233, 248-9, 306

JJ International 138-9

Journal of Business Forecasting 114, 327-9

Journal of Supply Chain Management 84, 323

K

Kanban 233

Kepner, C. 34-5, 345

Kepner-Tregoe Rational Process Analysis 34

Key performance indicators (KPIs) 269, 286, 301

Knowledge

collective 304

experiential 132

Knowledge exchanges 305

Knowledge management 304-5, 310, 317, 342

Knowledge Management Model 305

Knowledge workers 21, 304, 317

KPIs (Key performance indicators) 281, 286-7, 301, 311, 315

Krajewski, L. 346

Kraljic, Peter 12, 319

L

Labor costs 102, 169-70, 176, 185

Labor management 180

Labor markets 126

Lagging indicator 102

Lallatin, C. 245, 345-51

Latent damages 203

Lead time 287

Leading indicator 102

Lean supply chain approach 19, 22

Lean thinking 17, 247, 279, 337, 345, 349

Least squares method 132

Leenders, M. 345-6, 348

Less than carload (LCL) 192

Less than truckload (LTL) 192

Letters of credit 196
Leverage Items 12
Life cycle
    project's 24
    system development 304, 307-9, 317, 351
Life-cycle costs 287
LIFO (last in, first out) 226, 242
Litigation 205
Local buying preferences 96-7, 117
Locations
    distant geographic 305
    less-than-ideal manufacturing 36
    multiple 168, 232
    physical 174
    seller's 198
Logistics
    audits 208
    complex 5
    inbound 79-80, 333-4
    reverse 188, 236, 334
    service providers 237, 306-7
    third-party 176, 192
Logistics cost
    estimating 188
    managing 189
    total 208
Logistics Distribution and Warehousing 330, 347
Logistics providers
    fourth-party 193, 210
    third-party 79, 187, 210

Loss, risk of 199-200
Loss transfers, risk of 197-8

M

Macrodata 108
MAD (mean absolute deviation) 157-9, 164
Maintenance repairs and operating (MRO) budget 125
Make-or-buy 10
Management
    category 4, 161, 220
    fleet 187
    human resources 14, 27, 301
Manual order picking 175
Manufacturing ISM *Report On Business*® 109
Manufacturing resource planning (MRP II) 122
MAPE (mean absolute percentage error) 157-9, 164
Maritime law 190
Market analysis 75
Market economy 95
Market index 285
Market research 69, 128, 131-4, 163
Master production scheduling 310
Material Handling & Logistics 330
Material reject rating (MRR) 270
Material shortages 126-7, 163
Materials handling 171
Materials resource plan (MRP) 122
Matrix organization 30

Matthews, D. 192, 330, 337, 347-9

Mean absolute deviation (MAD) 157-9, 164

Mean absolute percentage error (MAPE) 164

Mean squared error, see MSE

Mean squared error (MSE) 157, 159-60, 164

Mechanized system 242

Microforecast 108

Milestones, project's 63

Millard Refrigerated Services 177

Miniwarehouses 167

Minority, women and emerging small business (MWESB) 295

Mixed economies 95

Models

    economic 95

    least squares regression 154

    single-period 132, 151

    supply chain mapping 209

Monczka, R. 18, 287, 294, 323, 334, 337, 340-1, 345, 348-9, 351

Money markets 125-6

Motor carriage 189, 192

Motorola 16

Moving average 131, 136, 142, 159, 163

    weighted 131, 137-8, 163

MRP (materials resource plan) 122, 309-10, 317

MRP II (manufacturing resource planning) 122, 304, 310, 317, 327

MSE (mean squared error) 157, 159-60, 164

Multichannel disposition plan 225, 237, 242

Multimodal shipment 197-8

Multiple regression 154

N

Naive forecast 131

National Association of Manufacturers 115

National Association of Purchasing Management 2

National Contract Management Association 264, 339, 350

National Defense Industrial Association (NDIA) 331

National Environmental Agency (NEA) 202

National Institute of Governmental Purchasing (NIGP) 192, 230, 349

National Motor Freight Classification™ (NMFC) 202, 334

Needs analysis 71

Negotiation process 57, 86, 107, 117

Nelson, R. D. 338

Net present value, see NPV

Nike 75

Non-Manufacturing ISM *Report On Business*® 110

North American Industry Classification System (NAICS) 103

NPV (net present value) 40-2, 72

O

Objectives
- organizational 1, 296
- project's 31
- strategic 2, 8, 21-2, 70, 90, 184, 189, 244

Obsolescence 83, 166, 222, 224, 227

Occupational Safety and Health Administration (OSHA) 179

Ocean freight forwarders 193

Ocean Spray's Experience 328

Office for National Statistics (ONS) 102

Office of Data and Economic Analysis 332

Online indexes 115

Operating costs 175, 208
- lower 166, 185

Operations budget 125

Option assessment 37

Order fulfillment process 15, 242

Order quantities
- economic 229
- fixed 228-9

Ordering costs 229-30

Organisation for Economic Co-Operation and Development (OECD) 96, 113, 326

Organizational structures 24, 28, 65, 271
- functional 29

Outcome forks 10

Outcome probability 10

Outsourcing 52, 183, 261, 263

decision 183
- strategic 183, 279

Over-the-wall approach 67

Over/under shipments 269-70

Ownership, total cost of 270

P

Packaging 80, 196
- budget 81
- design 208
- materials 80-1

Parameter estimation 151

Pareto analysis 36-7, 220, 254-5

Pareto chart 37, 255

Partnerships 184, 200, 218, 234-5

Parts per million (PPM) 274

Patterson, J. 334

Peer review 299

Performance
- benchmarking 206
- contractor's 54
- employee's 298-9, 301
- financial 236, 269
- managing 272
- measuring 279, 284
- measuring quality 244
- reporting 27
- supplier's 264, 270
- supply management department's 8

Performance dashboard 218

Performance measurement process 284, 286

INDEX

Performance metrics 53, 264

Performance SOW 54

Periodic inventory systems 231

Perpetual inventory control system 231

PERT (Program Evaluation and Review Technique) 48

Petersen, K. 323

Peugeot-Citroen 127

Physical stock-checking system 223

Picking systems 216

Plan-do-check-act (PDCA) 253

Plan value (PV) 288

Planning

    capacity requirements 310

    distribution requirements (DRP) 313

    distribution resource (DRP II) 314

    enterprise resource (ERP) 303, 310, 317, 327

    financial 310

    manufacturing resource (MRP II) 122, 310, 317

    materials requirement/material resource (MRP) 309

    operational 310

    risk management 28

    strategic 5, 114

PMBOK® 27-9, 53, 345

Pohlig, H. 245, 345-51

Political climate, changing 96, 117

Porter, M. 75-6, 346

Porter's Five Forces Analysis 75

Portfolio matrix 10, 12

Post-project audit 64-5

PPI (Producer Price Index) 102-7, 117, 325

PPI to CPI Comparison 105-6

Price escalation clauses 103

Price forecasting 122

Price indexes 104

Primary stakeholders 42

Principles of Sustainability and Social Responsibility 8

Prioritization matrix 34

Priority tools 214, 227

Problem analysis 35

Problem-solving 162

Process audit 271

Process flow costing 16

Process groups 26

Process improvement

    initiatives 90, 207

    methods 16

    metrics 19

Process mapping 13, 15, 241

Processes, bid 57, 239

Product development life cycle 262, 279

Product development team 68, 72, 77, 88

Product life cycle 120-1, 174, 346

Product portfolio management 70

Production capabilities 69

Production capacity 78

Profit center 207-8

Profit margin 7, 38, 71, 76, 86, 202

Profitability ratio 7

Program Evaluation and Review Technique (PERT) 48

Project

    budgets 46, 48-9

    business case 32, 43, 65

    capital improvement 40

    charter template 44

    closeout 65

    complex 43, 48, 51, 63, 65, 288

    continuous improvement process 156

    contracts 65

    costs 30, 38-9

    deliverables 46, 247

    execution 25-6, 54, 57

    expenses 49

    goals 34

    initiation 31

    leader 29

    life cycle 25, 42, 64-5

    long-term 112

    midsize 42

    milestones 44

    monitoring and control 59

    objectives 45

    organizational structures 28-9

    parameters 34

    phase 26, 52

    plan 45-6, 48, 52

    schedule 39, 45-6, 48, 53, 60, 63

    scope 26, 43, 63

    selection of 71, 247

    sponsor 42-3, 45

    status reports 63

    tasks 46, 48-9, 59, 62-3

    technology improvement 58

Project management

    discipline of 24, 29

    process 57, 247

    team 25, 51, 63

    tool 288

Project Management Institute (PMI) 24, 27-9, 109, 111, 320, 345

Project Management Life Cycle 38, 43, 320, 345

Property, plant and equipment 216

Protectionism 95-6, 100, 117

Prototype 72

Purchasing & Supply Chain Management 287, 332, 340, 348

Purchasing Magazine 323

PV (plan value) 288

Q

QFD (Quality Function Deployment) 245

QMS (quality management system) 85, 251

Qualified products list (QPL) 85, 249

Qualified suppliers 53, 273

Qualitative factors 298, 301

Qualitative forecasting techniques 131

Quality assurance 244-5, 252, 272, 274, 316

Quality constraints 57

Quality control 27, 244-5, 279

Quality Control Handbook 255

Quality Function Deployment (QFD) 245

Quality improvement 16, 244-5, 253, 290

Quality management principles 16, 254

Quantitative factors 298

R

Radio frequency identification (RFID) 178, 231

Rail transportation 190

Random errors 156

Random location systems 174

Real-time forecasts 127

Recession 101, 118, 136

Reconciliation, of inventory 224-5

Recovery, disposition/investment 2, 189

Recycling 215, 226, 237, 336-7

Regression 154
    analysis 132, 155-6
    linear 147-8, 154
    multiple 154

Remedial training 272

Reorder point 229

Request for Information (RFI) 53-4, 86

Request for Proposal (RFP) 52-4, 56, 70

Request for Quotation (RFQ) 53

Resolution process 204-5

Resource loading 45

Resource requirements plan 51

Responsibility matrix 51

Return on assets (ROA) 6-7, 22

Return on investment (ROI) 311

Reverse logistics (RL) 188, 236-7, 334, 336

RFID (Radio frequency identification) 178, 231

Risk
    analysis 1, 10, 22, 39, 43, 46, 50-1
    costs 227
    geopolitical 97
    management 24, 28, 46, 50, 53
    matrix 50-1
    possible project 50
    quantitative risk analysis 28

Ritzman, L. 346

Rivalry 75

Rudski, R. 335-6, 349, 351

Run chart 256

S

Safety 9, 113, 265, 296

Safety stock 219, 230-2

Sales forecast 115, 129, 134, 285

Sarbanes-Oxley Act (SOX) 281, 293

Scenario analysis 50

Schedule performance index (SPI) 61-2

Scope
    project management plan 26
    project's 25, 30, 43, 45, 60

Scope creep 58

SCOR (Supply Chain Operations Reference) 209, 266-8, 279

Scorecards 71, 209, 266

SDLC (system development life cycle) 307-9

Seasonal exponential smoothing 150

Seasonality 150-1

Secondary stakeholders 42

Securities and Exchange Commission (SEC) 116

Security
- border 98, 179
- plan 308
- risks 173

Self-assessment 299, 301

Service development
- process 68-9, 73-4
- schedule 82
- team 83

Service level agreement (SLA) 84, 274-6, 279, 313, 350

Service level agreement template 277-8

Set-aside programs 295

Ship agents 195

Ship brokers 195

Shrinkage 213, 224, 227

Sigma processes 246, 337

Simple moving average 136

Simple regression 154

Simplification 250

Singapore Chemical Industry Council (SCIS) 334

Single dock 176

Site visit 13

Six Sigma 16-18, 36, 246-7

SKUs (stock-keeping unit) 129-30, 174, 214, 220-1, 225

Slope 148-9, 155

Smith, M. 336-7

Smock, D. 349, 351

Social responsibility 9, 89, 296

Social responsibility principles 8, 89

Sodexo 284, 340

Solicitation process 263

Sourcing process 247, 261
- strategic 312

SOW (Statement of Work) 54, 84
- functional 54
- level-of-effort 54

SPC (Statistical Process Control) 258

Specifications 248-9, 255, 258-9

Spoiled items 238

Sport Obermeyer 133

Staff development 299

Stakeholder analysis 42

Stakeholders
- external 121
- internal 42, 57-8, 74, 220, 269
- primary 42
- secondary 42

Standard CMMI Appraisal Method for Process Improvement (SCAMPI) 262

Standardization 94, 226, 248-50, 252, 279, 338

Standards committee 248-9, 338

Stanley, L. 192, 330, 332, 335, 348-9

Staples 137, 184

Statement of Work, see SOW
Statistical process control, see SPC
Stewart, S. 349, 351
Stock-keeping unit, see SKUs
Storage
    advanced design 176
    chemical 177, 179
    locations 81
    refrigerated 177
Strategic business units (SBUs) 20
Strategic cost management 323, 339
Strategic plans, developing 130
Structures
    functional 29
    organizational 24, 28, 65, 271
    projectized 29-31
    work breakdown 45-8
Sturzl, S. 245, 345-51
Substitute products 12, 75-6, 83
Summative evaluation 296
Supplier
    assessment 261
    audits 271
    capabilities 69, 74, 78, 90, 262
    deliveries 38, 109-10
    development 39, 47, 273
    development program 42
    diversity 282, 294-5
    involvement 323
    market research 2
    partners 273
    quality 38, 279
    rating system 269-70
    research 86, 91
    scorecards 276
    selection 13, 57, 65, 271-3
    training 272
Supplier Capability and Capacity Analysis 81
Supplier Diversity Development (SDD) 294
Supplier-managed inventory (SMI) 234-5, 242
Supplier performance 21, 206, 243-4, 264-5, 272
    gauge 267
    levels 120
    managing 264, 275
    measurement 264
Supplier relationship management 24, 242-3, 247, 312, 317
Suppliers
    international 4, 100, 108, 230, 272, 293
    minority-owned 294-5
    preferred 11, 310
    role of 68
    strategic 5
    supplier's 267
Supply Chain Council 209
Supply Chain Council's SCOR 267
Supply Chain Management Review 320
Supply management
    components of 2, 189
    defined 2, 332

lean 19
responsibility of 65, 192, 272
strategic 304
terms 21
Supply management budget 125
Supply Management Handbook 221, 335, 349
Surplus
assets 218
inventory 239
materials 214, 235, 237, 240-2
obsolete equipment/material 236
plant 218
property 226, 237-8
Survey of Current Business 112, 339
SWOT analysis (Strengths, Weaknesses, Opportunities and Threats) 31-2, 75
System development life cycle (SDLC) 307-9
Systems audit 271

T

Target cost 19, 58-9, 87-9
Tariffs 96, 100, 108, 117, 194, 211
Team
appraisal 262
cross-company 45
organizational 71
technical 4, 52
Team-building exercises, appropriate 57
Teaming, cross-functional 84
Technology
cloud 180
forecast 127
mobile 182
roadmaps 81, 85, 90
Technology trends, predicting 132
Temperature-controlled warehouses 167
Tesco PLC 32-3
Third-party logistics (3PL) 176, 192
Through-flow warehouse flow 172
Throughput requirements 175
Time management 27
Time series forecasting models 135, 163
Top-down forecasting 130
Toyota Production System (TPS) 17, 336
Tracking signal 158-9, 164
Trade
maritime 199
world market 95
Trade barriers 95-6, 117
Trade deficit 107-8, 115
Transfer price 208
Transformation 6, 288
Transportation
domestic 195
global 188
highway 189
international air 190
modes 10, 81, 169-70, 189, 191, 199, 209
multimodal 190
outbound 79, 187-8
providers 169-70, 190, 192

truck 103

waterway 197-200

Tregoe, B. 34-5, 345

Trend-adjusted exponential smoothing 132

Trend-adjusted forecast 144-6

Triple exponential smoothing 150

Trucking 167, 189-91

Truckload 192

Tucker, V. 245, 345-51

Two-by-two matrix 12

Two-dock system 176

U

Uniform Commercial Code (UCC) 100, 198

Unique identification devices (UID) 178, 185

United Nations (UN) 100, 113, 326

United Parcel Service (UPS) 203

UPS (United Parcel Service) 203

UPS Supply Chain Solutions and Menlo Worldwide Logistics 192

V

Valuation, of inventory 226, 242

Value stream mapping (VSM) 17, 19, 241-2, 288, 301, 337

Variable costs 202

Variable order systems 230-1

Virtual warehouse 183, 242, 331

W

Walmart 67, 76, 79, 177, 231, 324, 329

Warehouse
  capacity 185
  flow 171, 173
  function 183
  inventories 225
  layouts 171, 185
  location 168, 174
  operations 175, 226
  security 177
  space requirements 174

Warehouse management system (WMS) 180-1, 313

Warehouses
  cross-flow 173
  through-flow 173
  virtual 183

Warehousing trends 182

Waste
  hazardous 89
  materials 89
  reducing 234

Weighted average method 273

Weighted moving average method 137-8

Westland, J. 38, 43, 320

Wheel Weight System 250

Wheelwright 346

Whirlpool Corp 97

Winter's Model 132, 150, 163

Work breakdown structure (WBS) 45-8

World Economic and Social Survey 113

World Economic Outlook 114

World Economic Situation and Prospects 113

World Gross Domestic Product 95

World Health Organization 225, 273, 335

World Trade Organization 96, 323-4, 333